BYRON

By ANDRÉ MAUROIS

BYRON

ATMOSPHERE OF LOVE

ASPECTS OF BIOGRAPHY

A VOYAGE TO THE ISLAND OF THE ARTICOLES

DISRAELI: A PICTURE OF THE VICTORIAN AGE

BERNARD QUESNAY

ARIEL: THE LIFE OF SHELLEY

CAPTAINS AND KINGS

MAPE. THE WORLD OF ILLUSION

BYRON

From the Leigh Hunt Miniature

Courtesy of the Pierpont Morgan Library

BYRON

BY

ANDRE MAUROIS

Translated from the French
by Hamish Miles

NEW YORK
D. APPLETON AND COMPANY
MCMXXX

PRINTED IN THE UNITED STATES OF AMERICA

PREFACE

THE original sources of any life of Byron are his letters and journals (as edited by Lord Ernle and the late John Murray), his poems, the biography by Thomas Moore, Lord Lovelace's *Astarte*, and a certain number of contemporary memoirs. In an appendix at the end of the present work will be found the sources of each chapter as well as references for the quotations.

Lady Lovelace was good enough to give me permission to consult her family papers; and the abundance of material therein made my sole difficulty one of selection. I made a particular study of the papers which threw light on Byron's religious perplexities, and of Lady Byron's unpublished journal. To Mr. Harold Nicolson, a most erudite and generous colleague in Byronic study, I am indebted for the communication of a remarkable document—the copy of Moore's *Life* which belonged to J. C. Hobhouse and was marginally annotated by him. These notes by the poet's most intimate friend provide several new anecdotes and some curious hints on Byron's moral development. I must also thank Lord Lansdowne, who entrusted me with the unpublished correspondence of Byron with Miss Elphinstone; Colonel Murray, who did me the great favour of placing his records at my disposal; the Comtesse Le Marois, who sent me a letter of the Abbé de Brême concerning Byron at Milan; Lady Airlie and Lady Jersey; Mr. Clement Du Pontet, librarian of

Harrow; Mr. Brecknock, the librarian of Hucknall Torkard; Mr. Charles Ian Fraser, the present proprietor of Newstead Abbey; Mr. Gordon George, who made some researches for me amongst the Austrian secret-police reports; M. de Vivie de Régie, to whom we owe the publication of the documents regarding Medora Leigh's life in France; and finally, in Greece, M. Camborouglou, M. Andreades, and the Mayor of Missolonghi. I need hardly add that, like all students of Byron's life and works, I am deeply indebted to Lord Ernle.

On the publication of *Ariel* I was reproached by several critics for the absence of a definite chronology, and for insufficient attention to the poems in that study of a poet's life. These criticisms are, I think, just; and I have accordingly tried here to mention dates as often as possible, and have also added as an appendix a chronological table. Also, as will be seen, I have made frequent use of Byron's poetry in recounting the story of his career.

Having already written a life of Shelley, I could hardly re-tell once more a certain number of facts which are, nevertheless, necessary for an understanding of the life of Byron. I have only briefly recalled them. The reader unacquainted with the details, and desirous of knowing them, will find them either in Dowden's *Life of P. B. Shelley* or in the more recent biography by Mr. W. E. Peck (1927).

There remains one difficult subject—or one that has been made so by certain distortions. Willingly or unwillingly, every biographer of Byron must take sides on the incest question. The word itself I use simply in following the Byronic tradition, although in my own opinion this incest is something of an imaginary crime. Not only was Augusta no more than a half-sister to Lord Byron, but she had hardly ever been seen by him until that moment when, in 1813, he met her and fell in love with her. I cannot understand any doubt of the reality of this love being possible after the publication of *Astarte,* of the letters to Lady Melbourne, or of the biography of Lady Byron herself.

My conviction is decided by (*a*) the correspondence with Lady Melbourne, the authenticity of which is denied by nobody, and which, if incest be ruled out, is robbed of all intelligible sense; (*b*) the innumerable letters exchanged between Lady Byron, Augusta Leigh, Mrs. Villiers, Medora Leigh and Ada Byron, in which Byron's love for Mrs. Leigh is treated as a known and indisputable fact; (*c*) by M. de Vivie de Régie's book, which, in proving that Medora was Byron's daughter, definitely fixes the beginning of the liaison in the summer of 1813.

I hope that, while treating this subject without hypocrisy, I have made the reader share those feelings of admiration, affection and pity which, as I think, Byron's character is bound to arouse. Above all, I have made it my concern to keep things in their true perspective, and not to make this secondary theme the central subject of a life of Byron. The conflict which is the essence of the Byronic spirit existed before the incest; the separation was not brought about by the incest; and after 1818 Augusta was no more in Byron's life than a ghost that had been laid. Lord Byron and Lady Byron have often been confronted by writers as if it were necessary that in an unhappy marriage one party should be deemed guilty. Lord and Lady Byron both had irritating faults, and both had great virtues. They were not made for a life in common, but it will be seen from the words I quote, that in the end they did justice to each other more lucidly and calmly than did certain of their posthumous champions. To the reader anxious to form his own opinion on this question, I can only offer the advice that he consult: (*against my view*) Mr. Richard Edgcumbe's *Byron: the Last Phase*, and the same writer's articles; (*for a not-proven* verdict) the first part of Mr. John Drinkwater's study, and Lord Ernle's article in the *Quarterly Review;* and (*sympathetic to my own view*), *Astarte,* Sir John Fox's *The Byron Mystery*, my friend Charles Du Bos's *Byron*, and Miss Ethel Colburn Mayne's *Life of Lady Byron.* I cannot mention Miss Mayne without thanking her for having made such kind mention of our common task in the preface to her book; for I too have kept the pleasantest memory of her courtesy in these circumstances.

I should be happy if this book were fortunate enough to send back to Byron's works some readers, both English and French, who pass stern judgment on them without knowing them.

Byron's poetry was that of a restless age. The French Revolution had given birth to great hopes, and it had disappointed them. The Napoleonic wars had been the occasion of acts of unavailing heroism. Millions of men had experienced, as Byron did, the feeling of the injustice and madness of the universe. For them as for himself, his poems were "the volcano, the eruption of which prevents an earthquake."

After 1830 the life of Europe changed. The middle classes came into power; and science was placing in men's hands forces of which they could not yet see the limits. It was an age of middle-class hopes. Destiny was yielding. A poem on Don Juan shocked pious aristocrats and triumphant shopkeepers alike. The subjects of Queen Victoria, engaged in Empire-building, had no wish to learn that Empires rise and fall, one after the other, like the waves of the sea. Carlyle, who had been fond of his Byron, moved away from him. A volcano? Yes, he reflected, Byron had had the useless, dangerous strength of a volcano. And he wrote that now they were gazing sadly on the ashes of a crater which ere long would be filled with snow.

Thus the prophet joined hands with the merchant in condemning Childe Harold. Here and there a bolder spirit, a Ruskin or a Browning, recognised his strength and his greatness. In France, Flaubert drew sustenance from Byron, and in the course of a pilgrimage to Chillon, in 1845, he found a sacred joy in the sight of that name carved in the stone. "All the time," he wrote, "I thought of the pale man who once came there, paced to and fro, wrote his name on the stone, and went away again. . . . Byron's name is written slantwise, and it is already black, as if they had been putting ink on it to make it stand out; indeed, it shines out on the grey pillar, and leaps to the eye as soon as one comes in. Beneath the name the stone is slightly eaten away, as if the mighty hand that leant there had worn it with its weight." But paltry spirits rejoiced in the failure of a genius. When Leconte de Lisle, as a young man, went to see Béranger, the song-writer told him that he did not admire Byron. "Pooh! Verses like Byron's! I can make them in my sleep, dreaming, any night!"—*"Ah, mon cher maître!"* answered Leconte de Lisle, "if only you would always sleep!"

Then the anti-Byronic reaction reached the better spirits. In France as in England, the realism of prose and the vulgarity of life inspired poets with the desire to seek refuge in purity of form. Keats and Shelley and Swinburne were set above Byron. In 1881 Matthew Arnold defended Byron in a celebrated preface, placing him above either Keats, who died too young, or Shelley, "beautiful and ineffectual angel, beating in the void his luminous wings in vain." Swinburne and his friends protested, and triumphed. Arnold had prophesied that when the year 1900 arrived, and England came to count "her poetic glories in the century which has then just ended," Byron's would stand with Wordsworth's as the first of these. He was mistaken. In 1900 Byron's poetry met with nothing but the chilly indifference of the æsthetes. He was judged by *The Corsair* or *The Giaour*, by poems which he had himself condemned. There were very few (there still are) who had read the last cantos of *Don Juan*, the third Canto of *Childe Harold*, the short lyrics, the *Prometheus*, and the admirable prose journals.

A life of Byron is not a critical study of Byron's poetic worth or his literary influence. I have pointed to the theme, but I have not treated it. Those who would wish for further and fuller ideas I should advise to read the preface by Ernest Hartley Coleridge to his unrivalled edition of the poems; the excellent lectures of Professor H. J. C. Grierson of Edinburgh; and (when they appear) the Clark Lectures given by Mr. Desmond MacCarthy at Cambridge in 1929.

A. M.

TRANSLATOR'S NOTE

THE translation of M. Maurois' book has of course involved reference to the numerous original sources from which its material is drawn. In all direct quotations, whether from poems, journals, letters, the accounts of contemporaries, or the comments of later writers, I have given the original text. The English reader of this biography, therefore, has the advantage of following Byron's story illustrated by the recorded words, written or spoken, of Byron and his circle.

Further, with M. Maurois' permission, I have been able in many instances to give more complete quotations, both in prose and verse, than the author found practicable in the French.

H. M.

CONTENTS

CONTENTS

PART III

ILLUSTRATIONS

PART I

Seigneur, j'étais dans le néant, infiniment nul et tranquille. J'ai été dérangé de cet état pour être jeté dans le carnaval étrange. . . .

PAUL VALÉRY.

Even if Calvinism had been carved on tables of stone and handed down from Heaven by the Almighty Hand, it would not have lived if it had not been found to agree more or less with the facts.

MARK RUTHERFORD

I

THE BYRONS OF NEWSTEAD

1500–1784

THROUGH the enchanted Sherwood Forest, close to Nottingham, a little band of black-habited monks, canons regular of the Augustinian Order, came wandering among the oaks. King Henry the Second of England, threatened with excommunication for the murder of Thomas à Becket, had promised the Pope to do penance and to endow monasteries. A site was chosen in a valley, close to a spring and a lake; the trees were felled, to the glory of God and for the salvation of the king's soul; a wide tract of land was cleared. The Gothic windows, ogive and rose, took shape in the grey stone, and a cloister, small but exquisite. Monastic severity was tempered by the charm of a landscape of streams and woods. The Abbey had been dedicated to the Blessed Virgin, and was given the name of Newstead, "the new place," *Sancta Maria Novi Loci*.

The rule of the Order was simple. The monks were forbidden to have any private possessions; they were to love God and their neighbours, conquer the flesh by fasting, give no man cause of offence, and avert their eyes from women. In addition, they distributed yearly alms to the poor in memory of their founder.

For three centuries the Abbots of Newstead reigned in steady succession on the borders of the lake. Then times grew harder, the piety of the faithful more grudging. The taste for learning was spreading; the gifts of monarchs passed to colleges, to universities, to hospitals. This community born of a king's remorse was threatened by a king's caprice. "Mistress Anne Boleyn is not one of the handsomest women in the world. She is of middling stature, swarthy complexion, long neck, wide mouth, bosom not much raised, and in fact has nothing but the king's great appetite and her eyes which are black and beautiful." But she was nevertheless the cause of a great schism. King Henry the Eighth requested the Pope to annul the bull authorising his marriage with Catherine of Aragon. The Pope refused. The peers of the Boleyn faction assured the king that by repudiating the pontifical authority and proclaiming himself head of the English Church, he could satisfy at once his love of Anne and his love of gold.

All religious houses with an income of less than two hundred pounds were declared confiscate to the Crown, and a visitation of the monasteries was begun by ecclesiastical and fiscal commissioners. The law, always venerated in England, required that a "voluntary surrender" should be obtained from the monks; and a certain Dr. John London became famous for his skill in methods of swift persuasion. With the signing of the deed, the king took possession of the monastic house, sold whatever it might contain, and gave the estates to some great landlord, of whose fidelity to the new Church he thus made certain. The sale of goods ruined the monks, but brought little wealth to the king. Manuscripts were bought by hucksters for wrapping up their goods; the inventory of a library would become simply—"Old books in the choir: 6 pence." Of the clerks thus despoiled, a certain number received authorisation to exercise a secular ministry, whilst others were given a few shillings' pension; almost all left the country, making for Ireland, Scotland, or Flanders. "Thus was the Church made a prey, every bad bird daring to beautify himself with her fair feathers."

At Newstead, Dr. London had the deed of surrender signed by the prior, John Blake, and seven canons, on July 21, 1539. The prior received a pension of £26, and each of the others £3 6s. 8d. Before leaving, the monks cast into the lake their founder's charter, and a lectern surmounted by a brass eagle which they had managed to abstract from Dr. London's soldiery. Then they departed. Henceforth there was none to pray beneath the yews of Newstead for the souls of the kings. Already the head of Mistress Anne Boleyn, crowned with its black tresses, had been slashed off by the executioner's sword. The country-folk mourned the passing of the monks, believing that they would still haunt their empty cells, and that the Abbey would bring ill luck to any man bold enough to buy it. A year later, in 1540, King Henry sold the monastery for £800 to his faithful subject Sir John Byron, known as "Little Sir John with the Great Beard."

The Byron who thus succeeded the canons of Newstead was the head of one of the oldest families in the county. The Byrons, or Buruns, had come over from Normandy with the Conqueror, and distinguished themselves in the Crusades, as later at the siege of Calais; they were the owners of great landed estates, not only in the neighbourhood of Nottingham, but also at Rochdale and Clayton in Lancashire. Their motto was *Crede Biron,* "Trust in Biron"—for they wrote the name thus in French fashion, being kinsmen of the Marquis de Biron. "Little Sir John with the Great Beard" transformed the Gothic Abbey into an embattled castle; and to that seat his descendants remained faithful. One of them, a staunch friend of King Charles the First in the Civil War a hundred years later, commanded a cavalry regiment with equal measure of bravery and rashness; he charged too soon at Edgehill, and again at Marston Moor, and for this double blunder was made a peer of the realm as Baron Byron of Rochdale, while Prince Rupert made an entry in his journal: "by the improper charge of Lord Byron, much harm was done." But the new lord's constancy was of more worth than his strategy. He never abandoned the royal cause. Newstead was besieged by the Parliamentarians; sulphur and molten lead spattered the ancient walls; those glassy waters which once had borne so clearly the sound of hymn and psalm, now cast back into the woods the cries of the stricken, the clashing of muskets, the blare of trumpets. After the triumph of Cromwell, Lord Byron was among Charles the Second's entourage in France; nor did his loyalty waver there, for Lady Byron, his wife (Mr. Pepys informs us), was the exiled monarch's seventeenth mistress.

Round the Abbey, however, the forest was slowly retreating before the advance of tilled fields, farms, and villages. Great herds of deer roved among the oaks. The Byrons' demesne was no longer isolated, since other rich families had come and raised their houses in this countryside. Of these the finest, and the nearest, was Annesley, the seat of the Chaworths, which was joined to Newstead by a long avenue of oaks, known as the "Bridal Path": for the two families had been united by the marriage of the third Lord Byron with Elizabeth, daughter of Viscount Chaworth. This third baron, who lived on until the end of the seventeenth century, was almost totally ruined. Time had made good the prophecies foretold when the Abbey was put up for sale; the phantom of a black-hooded monk wandered by night through the vaulted corridors, and the family fortune was ill-starred. The dark legend of the Byrons was finally and for ever confirmed by the two sons of the fourth baron; for the elder, the fifth Lord Byron, was tried by his peers for murder, and the younger, a sailor, became the most luckless admiral of the realm.

The story of the fifth Lord Byron's murder of his cousin, Mr. Chaworth, the proprietor of Annesley, is tragically puerile. The county gentlemen coming up to London from Notts were in the habit of forgathering, once a month, at the Star and Garter tavern in Pall Mall. On January 26, 1765, the usual meeting had gone off very cheerfully, when talk turned upon the best methods of preserving game. Mr. Chaworth was strong for dealing sternly with poachers; Lord Byron declared that the best way to preserve game was to pay no heed to it. Mr. Chaworth then remarked, rather acrimoniously, that he himself and Sir Charles Sedley, a common neighbour of theirs, had more game on five acres than Lord Byron had on all his manors, and were it not for their precautions, Lord Byron would no longer have a single hare on his land. Lord Byron asked where Sir Charles Sedley's manors lay. And Mr. Chaworth replied: "If you want information with respect to Sir Charles Sedley, he lives in Dean Street, and, as to myself, your lordship knows very well where to find me."

These drily uttered words had closed the conversation; but on leaving the room, Lord Byron found Mr. Chaworth on the staircase. The two men exchanged a few words, and then asked a waiter to show them to an empty room. The waiter placed a candlestick on the table; the two gentlemen closed the door behind them; and a few minutes later a bell rang. The innkeeper found Mr. Chaworth and Lord Byron at grips, and the former severely wounded. He was carried to his lodgings and there died.

A peer accused of murder could be tried only by the House of Lords, and a few months later Lord Byron was invited to place himself in custody in the Tower of London. Thence, in a coach escorted by mounted guards, he was conveyed to Westminster Hall. The executioner's axe was placed beside his lordship, the blade turned toward him. The county gentry who had been present on the day of the altercation were examined; the first witness gave the cautious reply: "My ears are not the best at any time." A surgeon explained how the sword had penetrated the navel and made a wide gash in the stomach; asked whether this wound had been the cause of Mr. Chaworth's death, he said he had no doubt of it. Lord Byron then tendered a plea of Not Guilty, and the vote was taken, starting with the peers of the most recent creation and ending with the princes of the blood. The accused was found Not Guilty of murder, but Guilty of homicide; and this, by virtue of a special statute affecting peers, was tantamount to acquittal. The usher called out his "Oyez! Oyez!" and judgment was read out. The Lord High Steward snapped his white wand, and William, fifth Lord Byron, was set at liberty to return to his seat at Newstead.

As a matter of fact, none of the friends of either combatant could really regard the murderer as a grave offender, for Mr. Chaworth had notoriously been a fire-eating bully. The victor, to his dying day, kept the sword with which he had killed his cousin hung on his bedroom wall. But locally, where he had long been known as "Wicked Lord," the crime transmuted him into a creature of legend and terror. Appalling tales were told, some of them quite false. It was untrue, for instance, that in a burst of fury he had shot his coachman dead with a pistol, placed the corpse beside his wife inside the carriage, and himself driven the grisly couple home. Nor was it true that he had flung his wife into one of the Abbey ponds to drown her. But it was true that his temper was vile, that he always carried pistols in his belt, and that he drove the unhappy Lady Byron to flight from Newstead. He immediately replaced her with a servant-girl known to the villagers as "Lady Betty."

Under the sordid rule of Lady Betty the Abbey became a pigsty. The servant-mistress made a cowshed of the Gothic chapel, and turned some of the splendid vaulted halls into stables. As for the Wicked Lord, his severance from mankind was completed by the marriage of his only son with a cousin-german, a match decided upon against the father's judgment. Thenceforward Lord Byron did all that he could to ruin his heirs. He paid his gambling debts with the oaks of the park, felling five thousand pounds' worth and stripping his marvellous forest nearly bare of timber. Horace Walpole passed that way about this time and noted: "Newstead delighted me. There is grace and Gothic indeed,—good chambers and a comfortable house." But the present lord, he added, was a madman, who had cut down all his trees, "and planted a handful of Scotch firs, that look like ploughboys dressed in old family liveries for a public day." As a finishing touch in the spoliation of his son, Lord Byron killed two thousand seven hundred head of deer in the park, and granted a twenty-one years lease of the Rochdale estate, where coal-seams had just been discovered, at the ridiculous rental of sixty pounds a year.

His pleasures were those of a mischievous child. He would go down in the dark and open sluice-gates on the streams in order to damage the cotton-mills; he emptied his neighbours' ponds; and on the edge of his own lake he had two small stone forts constructed, with a fleet of toy ships which he used sometimes to launch. He would spend whole days directing naval battles between the vessels and the forts; they fired on each other with miniature cannon. Lord Byron crouched in one of the forts, whilst his manservant, Joe Murray, lay stretched in a boat commanding the fleet. Sometimes, again, his lordship would lie on the stone flags of the Abbey kitchen and amuse himself by staging races of crickets up and down his own body, flipping the insects with straws when they were sluggish. The servants used to say that these crickets knew their own master and obeyed him.

His young brother's life had been no less rich in drama. John Byron, grandfather of our hero, was a sailor, gallant but unlucky, and known to his shipmates as Foulweather Jack because he could never set sail without a storm brewing. He had been appointed midshipman in the storeship *Wager,* which was to take part in an expedition against the Spanish Colonies but foundered on a reef off the Chili coast. It was a terrible scene: enormous waves came dashing over the wreck; one sailor went raving mad; the crew mutinied; the captain had to fire point-blank on his men. Young Byron, however, composed an account of the shipwreck, which he published later as the *Narrative, containing an account of the great distresses suffered by himself and his companions on the coast of Patagonia.* The *Narrative* had some success and became, in its way, a classic of the sea.

In 1764 Captain Byron was ordered to make a voyage of discovery round the globe aboard his ship *Dolphin.* He passed through the straits of Magellan, saw once more the coast of Patagonia, and completed his trip round the world so rapidly that he discovered no land at all, except the Disappointment Islands. Yet, as his biographer remarked, there were so many unknown lands to be discovered on his course, that he must have had great difficulty in steering clear of them. On his return this discreet explorer was appointed Governor of Newfoundland, and later advanced to be vice-admiral; in which capacity, during the American war, he commanded a fleet despatched to intercept the French fleet under the Comte d'Estaing. The first time that Admiral Byron put to sea, he met with a terrific storm which sank one of his vessels and disabled several others. The second time, he fell in with Estaing, but, loyal to family traditions, he attacked too soon and was beaten. After this he was entrusted with no further commands, and died, still a vice-admiral, in 1786.

Admiral Byron had two sons. The elder John (father of our hero), was a soldier, whilst the second, George Anson, was in the navy. John had been trained in a French military academy, and entered the Guards, serving in the American war while he was still hardly more than a boy. His violent character, wild behaviour and soaring debts, gave him the well-earned nickname of "Mad Jack"; and on his return to London at the age of twenty he made a total conquest of the Marchioness of

Carmarthen, a young woman of great beauty whose husband, Lord Carmarthen, Duke of Leeds, was the Lord Chamberlain. He was a kindly and cultivated man, but his wife doubtless preferred young Captain Byron's wildness; for no sooner did her father's death leave her with the title of Baroness Conyers and an inheritance of £4,000 a year, than she fled with her lover, deserting the Lord Chamberlain and her three children. Lord Carmarthen obtained the divorce for which he petitioned.

For some time the young couple lived at Aston Hall, a house belonging to Lady Conyers; then, seeking refuge from scandalmongers and creditors alike, they crossed over to France. There Lady Conyers gave birth to a daughter, the Hon. Augusta Byron, and died in 1784. Her death was due, said fashionable London, to her husband's ill-treatment; to rashness, said the Byrons, in having gone out hunting when hardly risen from her confinement. Her income was a life-interest only, and vanished with her.

II

THE GORDONS OF GIGHT

1784–1790

BATH was at that time the fashionable spa; and thither the young widower proceeded, to air his grief as he walked its curving terraces. There he made the acquaintance of a young Scottish lady, an orphan and an heiress, Miss Catherine Gordon of Gight. Small and plump, with a long nose and too high a colour, she was far from being a beauty. But her father's death had left her the mistress of her own property, and she owned some £23,000; £3,000 of this was in ready cash, which was useful for settling pressing debts, and the balance was represented by the Gight estates, salmon fishings, and shares in an Aberdeen bank.

Catherine Gordon might not be beautiful, but she was of good birth, and "proud as Lucifer" of her name, which was one of the most honourable in Scotland. The first laird of Gight, Sir William Gordon, had been the son of the Earl of Huntly and Annabella Stuart, sister of King James the Second. But although the family history opened thus royally, a more tragic sequence of events could hardly be imagined. William Gordon was drowned, Alexander Gordon murdered, John Gordon hanged for the killing of Lord Moray in 1592, another John Gordon hanged in 1634 for the assassination of Wallenstein—it seemed as if a Gordon of Gight had been strung up on every branch of their family tree. In Scotland longer than elsewhere, manners had remained feudal, almost indeed barbaric. A Gordon did not hesitate to waylay in a lonely place an Aberdeen lawyer who had actually dared to seize the horse of a friend of his; and if the Crown authorities thereupon called the citizens of Aberdeen to arms to arrest the offender, the townsfolk cannily sat tight. A dangerous breed of well-born brigands thus came into being, and even in childhood their temper was clearly shown. In 1610 three young Gordons barricaded themselves in the Aberdeen Grammar School, and there, with sword and pistol, resisted an all-night attack. It was something beyond their control, something inborn. The sixth laird, a conscious evildoer, used to say: "I can tak' no rest. I know I will die upon a scaffold. There is an evil turn in my hand."

For a whole century these lairds of Gight kept the north country in terror. The Scottish ballads told plenty of their exploits of these cruel, fascinating, cynical men, There is one that tells of a Gordon who was adored by his wife whilst he himself loved the lady of Bignet. He was sentenced to death for the murder of five orphans whose fortune he coveted, and on the day of his execution his wife came to beg the king's pardon:

> O Geordie, Geordie, I lo'e ye weel,
> Nae jealousie could move me;
> The birds in air that fly in pairs
> Can witness how I lo'e ye.

The king was touched and granted a pardon; but when he was set free Gordon turned on his wife, crying fiercely:

> A finger o' Bignet's lady's hand
> Is worth a' your fair body!

Such were the lairds of Gight, men marked with the brand of Cain; and even although the Crown became stronger during the eighteenth century and was able to compel a respect for law, the string of violent deaths went on as before. Alexander Gordon was drowned; his son George Gordon was drowned (doubtless suicidally) in the Bath Canal. And this last-named was the father of the Catherine Gordon who, a few years later, was inflamed by the gallant eyes of Captain Byron with a love as fierce and reckless as that of her ancestress in the ballad.

She had been brought up by her grandmother, a Duff, likewise of course a Scotswoman, by whom she was instilled with the rigid thriftiness of their people; and Mrs. Duff had also seen to it that Catherine received a pretty fair education and was imbued with the traditionally Whig politics of the Duffs. Catherine Gordon was fond of reading, and wrote letters which were confused in appearance but swift and lively in style. She had all the violent temper of the Gordons, and no less of their impulsiveness in action. But she also had their courage, as was made very plain when she married this most formidable of husbands on, of all days, May 13, 1784, and at Bath, the very place where her father had drowned himself.

The young couple went north to settle at Gight, which was a fine estate. But they received none too warm a welcome from the relatives and friends of the Gordons. Into these puritan fastnesses Captain Byron had imported his habits of dissipation, and every night there was dancing and drinking at Gight. Some cousins of Mrs. Byron who came one Saturday evening were terror-stricken as they wondered whether even the Sabbath would be respected: "the reels left off just before the clock struck midnight." The Scots looked scornfully on this stranger, this Southron, this Englishman, who was flinging a Scottish fortune to the winds, and they blamed the light-headed heiress who fancied herself a beauty, decked herself with feathers and silks, hid the squatness of her neck under strings of jewellery, and had found a husband just with her money. "O whaur are ye ga'en?" sang the nameless rhymesters:

O whaur are ye ga'en, bonny Miss Gordon?
  O whaur are ye ga'en, sae bonny and braw?
Ye've married, ye've married wi' Johnny Byron,
  To squander the lands of Gight awa'.

This youth is a rake, frae England he's come;
  The Scots dinna ken his extraction ava;
He keeps up his misses, his landlord he duns,
  That's fast drawen the lands o' Gight awa'.

And the rhymesters spoke truth. The young Sassenach was quickly scattering the Gordon fortune. The first thing to go was the £3,000 of ready money; after which, the captain made his wife sell the shares in the Aberdeen Banking Company, and then the salmon fishings. Next, the woods of the estate were stripped, and £8,000 was borrowed on mortgage. On the banks of a loch near Gight there were herons which had nestled there for centuries, and to which an old family saying attached a prophetic value:

When the herons leave the tree
The Laird o' Gight will landless be.

And in the year 1786 the Gight herons took flight across the water on to Lord Haddo's ground. "Let the birds come," said he, "and do them no harm, for the land will soon follow." And in the following year he purchased the estate for £17,850, a sum which the Scots lawyers wisely resolved to keep in their own hands, as creditors were making trouble.

A year before this the Byrons had left Gight; it had become too heavy for their poverty to bear. They wandered about England for a while and then, when the bailiffs became too familiar, they crossed the Channel. Mrs. Byron's relatives in Scotland bewailed the lot of "the poor unhappy creature," and they were right: her life was a sorry one. In France her husband, a crony of the Marshal de Biron, who treated him as a kinsman, became the friend of several great noblemen, and entered on a life of gambling and amours, extravagance and debt. Yet Catherine Gordon kept up her courage, good Scotswoman that she was, lived thriftily, and struggled hard to bring up little Augusta. At Chantilly, where the couple spent a long time, Augusta was very ill, and was nursed by her step-mother. "I still recollect with a degree of horror the many sleepless nights and days of agony I have passed by your bedside drowned in tears, while you lay insensible and at the gates of death. Your recovery certainly was wonderful, and thank God I did my duty." And indeed she had no cause for self-reproach. She adored her "Byr-r-ron," whose name she pronounced with her native rolling of the "r"; she loved his beauty, his brutal sincerity, and his recklessness—but she dreaded the future. In 1787 she became pregnant. When the time of her confinement drew near, she longed to return to England. Augusta's maternal grandmother, Lady Holderness, thereupon offered to take over the little girl, who was thenceforth brought up by her mother's family.

In London this strange descendant of the Stuarts found

herself a lodging in a genteel enough quarter. Her condition was that in which women feel the greatest need of protection, but she found herself forsaken; the captain was living at Dover or in Paris, only visited her to ask for money, and in a week had spent the sums which he squeezed from her indulgence. The only person in the world who concerned himself with her was a lawyer, to whom she had been recommended by friends in Aberdeen, Mr. John Hanson, whose wife put Mrs. Byron in touch with a nurse, Mrs. Mills, and a man-midwife, Mr. Combe. And on January 22, 1788, the child was born. He was named George Gordon Byron, for there was a testamentary condition that the heir of the Gordons of Gight should bear their name. That name was his sole heritage.

On her return to England Mrs. Byron had learned that she was ruined, reduced even to penury. The sale of Gight had been in vain, for the captain's appetite was such that he could swallow up one estate a month. No sooner had one promissory note been paid off than others kept surging up. The lawyers in Scotland wrote stern letters to their client. A bill of exchange for £400 signed "Jack Byron," was presented by a broker in Paris; during the same week £50 had to be sent to Mrs. Byron in London, and £30 to Mr. Byron at Dover. Things could not go on like that. Already only £4,222 was left over from the monies obtained for the Gight estate, and of that £1,222 were earmarked as burdens on the property; the remaining £3,000 was invested at five per cent., settled on Mrs. Byron and her son inalienably, and the Scots lawyer entrusted a colleague in London with the payment to Mrs. Byron of £150 per annum in small sums. The very first Sunday she sent her servant-girl to his house with a receipt for £100. He refused. A few hours later the girl returned with a receipt for £25, and a beseeching letter.

Catherine Byron herself was perfectly capable of living on £150 a year, but she could not resist her husband. When she heard that in a few weeks he had piled up fresh debts to the tune of £1,300, the Gordon fury blazed up; she tore her cloak and caps, and flung plates at the servant's head; but no sooner did she see Jack Byron's eyes again, than she was left speechless. "Mrs. Byron is afraid that she has not the resolution to refuse any request Mr. Byron may make to her personally," wrote the London attorney to his Scottish colleague. "He has not a farthing left and she informs me that she is in a similar situation."

She was twenty-three. As a girl she had seen herself heiress of a great name and a great fortune; in her weakness she thought herself worthy of being loved, and had imagined that she was; she on her side had loved to distraction, and was loving still. (*"Je ne change qu'en mourant,"* was her pathetic motto.) She had to face the fact that she had been tricked and fleeced, that she was now in poverty, with a husband, an infant, a nurse and a house, all on her hands. Many a woman would have lost her head; and occasionally Catherine did lose hers. In her distress she felt a wild desire to bolt for Scotland, for Aberdeen. She no longer owned one square foot of land up there, but at least she would be at home again in the land of her own forbears. Here in London, with the pestering of the duns, her misery was more than she could bear. And off she went.

Captain Byron did not follow immediately. Life was not treating him very kindly either. He had lost the ravishing Lady Conyers and the £4,000-a-year which enabled him to live gaily with his brilliant French friends, and now found himself tied to a ruined wife, who had never been beautiful and was now becoming ludicrously stout, and, for all the royal blood in her veins, looked rather like the wife of a village grocer. She wanted to drag him into a remote and stern countryside, with a cruel climate, where a sober and steady clan looked askance at the English prodigal. He was in no hurry.

Mrs. Byron had found furnished rooms in Aberdeen at a reasonable price; and there she settled with her two Scotch maids, Agnes and May Gray, sisters who took turn about in nursing little George—or "Geordie" as they called him in the North. The child was as handsome in face as his father, but when he was old enough to walk his mother was alarmed to notice that he was lame. His feet were normal in shape, and the legs of equal length; but if the boy put his heel on the ground, his ankle twisted over. He could only stand erect on his toes. The doctors who were consulted advised specially constructed boots, and the blame was attributed to awkward handling at birth due to the excessive modesty of Mrs. Byron. The tendons of the ankle seemed to be paralysed. The Aberdeen physician corresponded with the celebrated anatomist, Dr. John Hunter, who had special boots made, which he sent to Scotland; but the little Byron continued to limp alongside May Gray through the streets of Aberdeen.

An affectionate and very intelligent child, but with a violent temper. Like his mother, he was capable when angry of passionate sulks. Before even he was breeched, being reprimanded one day for soiling a new dress, he snatched it with both hands and ripped it from top to bottom, glaring defiance at his nurse. A child's notions of life are shaped in its earliest years. What did this little boy see around him? His parents had tried to live together, and had to give up the attempt. Embittered by adversity, Mrs. Byron had grown extremely irritable. "She is very amiable at a distance," wrote her husband, "but I defy you and all the Apostles to live with her two months; if anybody could live with her, it was me." For a time they had occupied separate lodgings in Aberdeen, one in Queen Street, the other in Broad Street, paying calls on each other and drinking tea with each other. She still remained powerless to resist the melting glances of her husband, and once again Jack Byron succeeded in coaxing her to borrow £300; she gave him this capital and paid the interest on it herself, which reduced her own income to £135. On this she lived without incurring one penny of debt, still proud as Lucifer, but giving way at times to terrific bursts of temper. And then the china flew hither and thither across the rooms.

The child observed his parents with earnest curiosity. Other little boys had fathers and mothers who lived together and loved each other. But his mind was awakening to life amid a hubbub of quarrels, reproaches and complaints. He could see that the servants regarded his parents as creatures mad, dangerous, and on occasion comical. He was marked off from other boys by his family, but still more so by his infirmity. Why should his wretched ankle give way beneath him? So ashamed was he that he never raised the question. One day in the street a woman stopped to talk to May Gray. "What a pretty boy Byron is!" she said. "But what a pity he has such a leg!" The child's eyes blazed with anger, and striking her with a toy whip, he cried: "Dinna speak of it!" Every night he had to go through a tiresome treatment, because it was hoped that a cure might be effected by bandaging the foot.

Towards the end of the year 1790, John Byron obtained from his wife and his sister, Mrs. Leigh, a little money with which to flee to France. Mrs. Leigh was the owner of a house at Valenciennes; and there the derelict captain settled, involved in the French Revolution without understanding it, fooling with the chamber-maids at the inn, and for ever short of a louis. Some letters addressed to Mrs. Leigh give glimpses of the last tossings of this piece of flotsam: "Valenciennes, December 1, 1790. . . . As for me, here I am, and in love with whom? A new actress who is come from Paris, she is beautiful and played last night in *L'Épreuve Villageoise*. . . . As for Madame Schoner—she fairly told me, when drunk, that she liked me, and I really do not know what to do. . . . No duns appear, as Fanny bites them all, and I am never at home. We are all well here, and Joséphine in the best order—as she gets no money and plenty of abuse, it is the only way to treat her." He went to the Valenciennes theatre, in the box annually rented by his sister. "There is a new piece called *Raoul de Créqui* and one expression is: 'J'ai sauvé mon Roi, mais je meurs content.' Everybody cried 'Bis' and 'Vive le Roi!' and 'Vive la Nation!', for me, what with the Juice of the Grape, and remembering our Ancestors were French, I cried as much as anybody, and now they say 'que cet Anglais est aristocrate en diable.' For my Amours, these are all finished and everybody says 'je suis très amoureux but très inconstant. Un clou chasse l'autre' and I believe I have had one third of Valenciennes, particularly a Girl at l'Aigle Rouge, an Inn here I happened to there one day when it rained so hard. . . . She is very handsome and very tall, and I am not yet tired." Towards the summer of 1791 the letters became tragic: "I am really without a shirt. . . . I have not a sou. . . ." The grocer and butcher refuse to go on feeding him. "I have but one coat to my back, and that in rags. . . . I would rather be a Galley Slave. . . ." "I have not a shirt to my back nor a coat, as the one I had here is totally used. . . ." A few days later he died. It was said to be suicide.

His death was a sore blow to his wife, who had never lost her love for him. "My dear Madam," she wrote to her sister-in-law, "you wrong me very much when you suppose I would not lament Mr. Byron's death. It has made me very miserable, and the more so that I had not the melancholy satisfaction of seeing him before his death. If I had known of his illness I would have come to him. . . . Notwithstanding all his foibles, for they deserve no worse name, I ever sincerely loved him. . . . You say he was sensible to the last. Did he ever mention me? Was he long ill, and where was he buried? Be so good as to write all these particulars, and also send me some of his hair."

Little George never forgot his father; he had always admired him. He was left alone now in life, with a woman whose fickleness of humour brought showers of kisses straightway on a storm of blows. He knew her to be unhappy. He both feared and pitied her. And when he went and picked fruit in the garden of John Stuart, the professor of Greek at Aberdeen, he would always ask if he might take some apples home "for poor dear Mother."

III

PREDESTINATION

1792–1798

AND the Lord had respect unto Abel and his offering: but unto Cain and his offering he had not respect. And Cain was very wroth, and his countenance fell. And the Lord said unto Cain, Why art thou wroth and why is thy countenance fallen?"—May Gray was reading the Bible aloud, and the little Byron was listening with passionate eagerness. He did not understand all the words, but he felt the strange and terrible poetry of the Book. Why did the Lord refuse poor Cain's sacrifice? "Because of his sin," said May Gray. Sin? What was sin? Cain had not yet slain Abel. No, but Cain was damned, said May Gray. Damned? What did damned mean? It meant that Satan would take him, and have him burnt in the fires of hell, for ever and ever. May Gray often spoke of Satan. She liked to frighten you. She used to tell terrifying ghost-stories, and said the house was haunted. At night when she was rolling those vexatiously tight bandages round his ailing little heels, she made him repeat Psalms. He liked that strong, singing rhythm, and two of them, in the Scottish metrical version, were special favourites of his. The First:

> That man hath perfect blessedness
>   Who walketh not astray
> In counsels of ungodly men,
>   Nor stands in sinners' way. . . .

—and the Twenty-third:

PREDESTINATION

The Lord's my shepherd, I'll not want,
He makes me down to lie
In pastures green; he leadeth me
The quiet waters by. . . .

And May Gray snuffed the candle. She had orders to stay near the child in the next room, but he knew that she went out. When she had gone he was frightened. All Scotland seemed full of ghosts, the house was close to a graveyard, and then there was that awful Satan, and the Lord. In the darkness the child could feel evil things prowling about him. He crept along the corridor to a window from which he could see a light, and there he remained until the cold forced him back to bed.

May Gray was strict. Mrs. Byron was mad. One day she said to him: "You little dog, you're a thorough Byron; you are just as bad as your father." And another time she clasped him exceedingly tight, saying that his eyes were as glorious as the captain's. She told him how through her he was descended from the Gordons, and how they had been powerful chiefs of royal blood; but May Gray and her friends would tell how the Gordons had murdered and been hanged and drowned—damned no doubt, like Cain, and whisked off, no doubt, by the Devil. Of the Byrons, his mother did not speak so often. Nevertheless he knew from her, and through his nurse, that somewhere in the middle of England, in an old castle, there was a Wicked Lord who was the head of his family, that his family was an old one and had produced great warriors and sailormen. To be a Byron was to have a mysterious advantage over all these little boys he envied with their strong legs and peaceful parents. One day he threw a stone at a bird and accidentally hit a little girl. She cried. They tried to force him to beg her pardon, but he fell into one of his silent rages. "Do you know that I am Byron's son?" he asked her. An hour later he came back of his own accord, bringing sweets for the victim.

At the age of four years and ten months he was sent to school, a short walk from his home. It was kept by Mr. Bowers, who was known as "Bodsy," and the fees were five shillings a quarter. "I have sent George to you that he may be kept in abeyance," wrote Mrs. Byron to Bodsy. The school was a low, dirty room, its floor riddled with decaying holes. There the children learnt to read in a book of one-syllabled words. "God made man—let us love Him. . . ." The Byron boy had a good memory, and soon had learned the first page by heart. He then announced that he could read. And actually recited to his mother his little couplet—with great success, until she turned to the next page and he started off again with "God made man. . . ." The text, alas, was different, and the impatient Mrs. Byron slapped her son. Returning to Bodsy's he learnt that "God made Satan—and Satan made sin. . . ." Satan and sin were regular subjects in these Scottish schools.

When Bodsy's learning seemed inadequate, Mrs. Byron saw to it that her son had private lessons from two professors of the college. One was named Ross, a pious little minister with gentle manners, who brought the boy quickly forward and inspired him with a passion for history. In particular, George Byron was extremely fond of Roman history, and read the story of the battle of Lake Regillus scores of times. His other master was a melancholy young man named Paterson, the son of a shoemaker and a good Latinist. With him Byron began his Latin, and continued his religious education, for Paterson, like May Gray, was a stern Presbyterian. No doubt he did his best to bring his own Calvinist doctrine within the grasp of a child's comprehension. "We are corrupt from our birth up, in that we have participated in Original Sin. Certain men, united to Jesus Christ by the Holy Ghost, can be raised to a life of holiness; those who are not thus saved are condemned to everlasting punishment. As for the operation of the Holy Ghost, that depends on the choice of God, who has predestined some to life everlasting, and others to damnation." This plunged the seven-year-old boy into deep reflections. Was he himself among the elect or among the reprobates? Surely these violent Gordons and Byrons had been almost all of them damned? He himself felt the inward surge of sudden involuntary furies; the blood rose to his face, and for an instant he knew not what he did. Could this be diabolic possession? And yet there were other moments when he felt himself so tender and good. It was all very frightening. But was it true?

His alert mind followed the events of the French Revolution with passionate eagerness. Its dramatic history left the people of the small Scottish town divided. The articles of the Aberdeen newspaper were headed: "The Flight to Varennes," or "Danton"; the local intelligence was relegated to the foot of the column. Mrs. Byron, a ruined aristocrat, and, besides, a woman reared in Whig views by her Duff grandmother, professed advanced political opinions. To her sister-in-law, at Valenciennes, Mrs. Leigh, she wrote, "I am very much interested about the French, but I fancy you and I are on different sides, for I am quite a Democrat and I do not think the King, after his treachery and perjury, deserves to be restored. To be sure, there has been horrid things done by the People, but if the other party had been successful, there would have been as great cruelty committed by them." And like his mother, the young Byron was on the side of the People. Moreover, he was now reading much for himself. Brown the bookseller, at the sign of Homer's Head, used to lend out the latest novelties, and despite her poverty Mrs. Byron subscribed to this circulating library.

Her son begged her to bring home all the histories of Rome and Greece and Turkey. He also read, with delicious terror, his grandfather's narrative of the shipwreck. Around him all the talk was of war. Volunteers were drilling on the square. His earliest dreams were of military glory. "I will some day or other," he said, "raise a troop, the men of which shall be dressed in black and ride on black horses. They shall be called 'Byron's Blacks,' and you will hear of their performing prodigies of valour."

One day in 1794, when Mrs. Byron was drinking tea with the neighbours, someone asked her whether she knew that Lord Byron's son had died. She started in her seat. It was surprising that so young a man should be dead, but what was more incredible was that her own son should have become heir to the title, to Newstead, and to all the family property, without anyone thinking of informing her. But it was none the less true. Lord Byron's son had died in Corsica at the siege of Calvi; and between this little auburn-haired boy and the peerage, there stood only the old dotard waging his naval battles against his manservant on the lake at Newstead, or lying on the kitchen floor racing his crickets.

The mother of the heir wrote Mrs. Leigh a stern letter of protest against the treatment inflicted on her by the family. It was humiliating to learn news of that kind through strangers, and certainly Lord Byron could not now do less than help the mother of the future head of the family to give her son an education befitting his rank. But Lord Byron was just the man to savour a cruel joy in thinking of "this little boy at Aberdeen" who, pinched and a cripple, was awaiting the day of his lordship's death. He ignored Mrs. Leigh's letters and continued, fiercely and methodically, to lay waste the domains and heritage of the Byrons.

And so, for all her anger, Mrs. Byron had to drop the idea of sending her boy to an aristocratic school, and had to let him continue his studies at the Aberdeen Grammar School. Nevertheless, this was a seminary of venerable tradition, founded in 1256, and doubtless one of the oldest in the three kingdoms. Its ancient buildings were thatched with heather. Latin was the main subject, five hours a day of it. The pupils were nearly all poor, their pocket-money a penny a week. There George Gordon Byron gained a reputation of being a superb player of marbles, and was well liked by his companions, although he had startled them at first by his affectionate and violent temperament. The porter of the college used often to give chase to this lad with the red hair and waistcoat who limped up to tease him. The townsfolk called him "Mrs. Byron's crookit de'il"; "a verra takin' lad, but ill to guide," said one of his teachers. Despite his infirmity he had great courage, "always more ready to give a blow than to take one." Although his legs were easily tired he had learned to fight for quite a long time on end, standing on his toes, and one day when a boy had insulted him and an immediate encounter was impossible, the young Byron promised the offender to deal with him some other time. In the following week he stopped the boy in the street, and conscientiously thrashed him. On his return home, May Gray asked him why he was out of breath; and he replied that he had to keep a promise, because he was a Byron, and the family motto was *"Crede Biron."* He knew that he would one day be lord of Newstead. His mother was once reading out before him a parliamentary report when a friend in the room remarked: "We shall have the pleasure, some time or other, of reading your speeches in the House of Commons." "I hope not," answered the boy. "If you read anv speeches of mine, it will be in the House of Lords."

He was an intelligent pupil, but not a good worker. It was the custom at the Grammar School to seat the top boys on the front bench, and the tail of the class at the back of the room. Sometimes, to stir the spirit of ambition, the master would reverse this order, and on these occasions, with Byron on the front bench, the master would greet him laughingly with "Now, George, man, let me see how soon you'll be at the foot again." Outside school he had private lessons in handwriting and French, with no great success. But he read much more than his companions. "I was never seen reading, but always idle and in mischief, or at play. The truth is that I read eating, read in bed, read when no one else read, and had read all sorts of reading since I was five years old." The Bible had given him a taste for the East, and he was particularly fond of the *Thousand and One Nights,* the books of Baron de Tott, the letters of Lady Mary Wortley Montagu, and Dr. Moore's *Zeluco.*

Zeluco was a fashionable novel, with a hero who had tormented George Byron through many a sleepless night. Like himself, this Zeluco had lost his father in childhood, and showed violence of character from his early years. As an orphan he became inflammable as powder, bursting into flashes of rage at the least provocation. Zeluco reared a tame sparrow, which he loved, but one day killed. Near the end, when Zeluco had become a man, he strangled his own child. This story filled Byron with delight and disquiet. Fearful of becoming a Zeluco, he enjoyed the fear. Some of the Gordons had been monsters no less terrifying than Zeluco.

When his German teacher wanted to make him read Gessner's *Death of Abel,* he was pleased at the rediscovery of that troubling story of Cain which had haunted him. But the tragedy was too tedious, and while he translated it, Byron reflected that it could be no crime to rid the world of so wearisome a creature as Gessner's Abel. But the problem of Cain continued to trouble him. In his childish thirsting after justice, he felt pity for the Reprobate. Why had God allowed Cain to slay his brother? Why did God sometimes allow George Byron his desire for cruelty and impiety? He thought of red hell-fire. His imagination was keen. His school companions enjoyed listening to him when he improvised the stories he drew from his reading, and when they were snowed up in a chance shelter by a winter blizzard, Byron told them stories from the *Arabian Nights,* and they forgot the cold.

After a bout of scarlet-fever in 1796, his mother took him to spend a few days at a farm. He was enthusiastic over the Highland landscapes, and loved the mountains veiled in their blue mists, and the wild beauty of Deeside and of the peak of Lochnagar, whose summit came sometimes into view above snow-white clouds. He enjoyed wandering amongst the strangely shaped rocks at the foot of the waterfalls, leaping from one to another as well as his lameness allowed him, and regaling himself with terrific tales of his forebears, the cateran chiefs who had plundered these glens. He himself then wore the Highlander's plaid and bonnet, and felt himself a Scot through and through. A childish love, pure but deep, for a farmer's daughter bound his heart to this valley. Mary was the name of his beloved, and she had long golden ringlets. In her presence he felt a keen and tender thrill.

At the age of nine he had discovered that one can find an infinite happiness merely in a presence. Returning to Aberdeen, he fell in love with his cousin, Mary Duff, a little girl with hazel eyes and dark brown hair. He admired her features; he could conceive of nothing more beautiful. He liked to walk with her, to sit beside her, to caress her gently. All his thoughts now were of his cousin's face, his cousin's gowns; he could not sleep; he talked of nothing but Mary Duff. When parted from her, he pestered his mother to write to Mary Duff, and love made this child so compelling that, willy-nilly, Catherine Byron had to shrug her shoulders and become her son's amanuensis.

How passionate he was, and how shy! At the thought of his game leg and his hobbling gait, he felt ridiculous and ashamed. He would have liked to hide away—to vanish. Sentimental, tender and dreamy, he would suddenly, for no visible reason, turn fierce. Sometimes after a long silence he made a gesture of brutality that seemed quite inexplicable. One day at table he snatched up a knife and pressed it so hard against his chest that his mother was terrified. The origins of these extravagances were the harder to guess at because of his spiteful memory, tenacious of grievances for a very long time. The cause of one of these outbursts was often an incident of several weeks back.

One day in 1798, when he was ten, the news came that the lord of Newstead was dead. The Wicked Lord had left this life—for what infernal habitation?—and little George Gordon Byron became the sixth baron. When he was told, he ran to the mirror and asked his mother if she could see any difference in him, for he could see none. At school next morning, under the thatched roof, the roll of pupils was called, and the master, looking at him, called him, not now plain "Byron" but *"Dominus de Byron."* He could not bring the usual *"Adsum"* to his lips, and burst into tears.

He had now to leave Aberdeen to go and take possession of his inheritance, and in the autumn of 1798 Mrs. Byron, her son, and May Gray set off for Newstead. Before leaving, she sold her furniture; the whole effects of the young baron's mother produced the sum of £74 17s. 7d.

IV

LITTLE LORD BYRON

1798–1801

OF the three travellers, it was no doubt the youngest who found the liveliest pleasure in this romantic journey. Intelligent and reflective, he let no detail escape him as he gazed on the lochs and great heather moorlands of Scotland, and then on all the greenery of England's woods and meadows. As they skirted Loch Leven, Mrs. Byron told George the story of Queen Mary's escape and reminded him of his own Stuart blood. So he was Lord Byron? And on his way to take over his domains? Palaces, gardens, servants were his? Perhaps the villagers would curtsey to him? The adventure seemed to him no less amazing than one from the *Arabian Nights*.

A few miles from Nottingham the carriage entered Sherwood Forest. The Newstead toll-bar brought the travellers to a halt. In front of them stood an immense oak, saved by ingenious neighbours from the axe of the Wicked Lord, and on their right were the iron gates leading into the park. Mrs. Byron affected to be ignorant of her whereabouts, and, inwardly exultant, addressed the toll-keeper, asking her whose mansion this might be. The woman replied that its owner, Lord Byron, had but lately died.

"And who is the next heir?"

"They say it is a little boy who lives at Aberdeen."

"And this is he—bless him!" exclaimed May Gray,

as she turned to the young lord leaning on her knee, and kissed him.

The carriage passed through a coppice or two, a pinewood, and then suddenly, at the bend of the avenue, Newstead came into the travellers' view. On the edge of a wide lake, half-covered with reeds, there rose the gracious Gothic shape of the Abbey, grey beneath a grey sky, peaceful and perfect. Like all children endowed with great imagination, Byron had built a dream background against which he would have longed to live and reign. Newstead was more lovely than all his dreams.

The women stepped out, and the old servant, Joe Murray, approached. The inspection of the house began. May Gray's face lengthened, and Mrs. Byron began to storm. Everything was in ruins. Roofs, walls, floors—nothing had been repaired for years and years. The dirt and disorder were beyond belief. The servants excused themselves by describing the follies of the old Lord Byron, and the boy listened intently. The story of this old misanthrope's way of life set unknown chords vibrating within him. "He always went armed, a pistol in each pocket." How well the child understood that! In his schoolboy battles the weakness of his legs made him always apprehensive of being betrayed by his physique; but the pistol was his weapon, the very thing to redress the balance between himself and the strong. From the age of seven he himself had been just the same, and carried toy pistols in his pockets. The story of the Chaworth duel. . . . "Shortening his sword, he ran him through. . . ." There, that was just right. The old man pointed out the great avenue, the Bridal Path, which led over to Annesley, the Chaworths' home. Then he told them about the crickets: "After his lordship died, they left Newstead in such quantities that the hall was black with them, and we trod on them by the hundred. . . ." Yes, the crickets had lost their master, the strange satanic wizard who drilled them with flicks of straw; and doubtless they had departed to seek some other evil genius. How sinister, how beautiful this family was! And it was his! As he listened to the old servant and walked through the rooms ("This is a haunted room; a black-hooded monk is seen sometimes. . . . And here was their refectory, here the kitchen. . . . This Saracen's head carved on the wall is a relic of Robert Byron, who died on the Crusade. . . .") he took possession of that heritage more real than fields and houses, more important than grey eyes and coppery hair—the picture that a man fashions of his ancestors.

This first contact attached Byron to Newstead as firmly as to Mary Duff. In old Murray's company, he explored the vaulted passages and lacework cloisters, the avenues, brooks and springs. He planted an acorn in the soil, saying that the tree would be "his" oak. He would gladly have stayed for ever in this enchanted inheritance, but Mrs. Byron had seen the impossibility of living in a ruin. To restore the Abbey was no easy matter. The fortune of Byron, a peer of England and a minor, would be administered by the Court of Chancery; his mother would not be able to undertake any great expenditure; and in any case, the fortune was in land, not in ready money. Until the accounts were audited, Mrs. Byron, although the young lord's mother, had only her £150 to live on. She selected as her son's representative the London attorney, Hanson, who had formerly befriended her at the time of her confinement, and after a few days left Newstead to settle at Nottingham.

MRS. BYRON

AFTER A PAINTING BY THOMAS STEWARDSON

In the possession of Lieut. Col. John Murray

She lodged in a dark narrow street in the upper part of the town, near the Castle. The small apartments were no better than those she had left in Aberdeen. To the child this was a sad blow: the fairy-tale palace was shrinking to a pumpkin; and in this unfamiliar town he was more unhappy than in Scotland. Mrs. Byron had to make several journeys to London in an attempt to procure the grant of a royal pension during her son's minority, and she left him behind at Nottingham in May Gray's care. But May Gray was unworthy of the trust. Hanson came down from London to see his young lordship, his client, and took an immediate fancy to the child. He questioned the neighbours, and what he heard left him indignant.

"I assure you, Madam," he wrote to Mrs. Byron, "I should not have taken the liberty to have interfered in your domestic arrangements, had I not thought it absolutely necessary to apprize you of the proceedings of your Servant, Mrs. Gray; her conduct towards your son while at Nottingham was shocking, and I was persuaded you needed but a hint of it to dismiss her. . . . My honourable little companion, tho' disposed to retain his feelings, could not refrain, from the harsh usage he had received at her hands, from complaining to me, and such is his dread of the Woman that I really believe he would forego the satisfaction of seeing you if he thought he was to meet her again. He told me that she was perpetually beating him, and that his bones sometimes ached from it; that she brought all sorts of Company of the very lowest Description into his apartments; that she was out late at nights, and she would take the Chaise-boys into the Chaise with her, and stopped at every little Ale-house to drink with them. But, Madam, this is not all; she has even—traduced yourself. I entertain a very great affection for Lord Byron, and I trust I shall not be considered solely in my professional character, but as his Friend. I, introduced him to my Friends, Lord Grantley and his Brother, General Norton, who were vastly taken with him, as indeed are every one. And I should be mortified in the highest degree to see the honourable feelings of my little fellow exposed to insult by the inordinate Indiscretions of any Servant. He has Ability and a quickness of Conception, and a correct Discrimination that is seldom seen in a youth, and he is a fit associate of men, and choice indeed must be the Company that is selected for him."

Hanson was right. Little Lord Byron had mental powers very rare in a child of his age. A difficult life will often hasten the growth of intelligence. A happy child simply lives, and accepts the truth from its parents; but a child brought up in the din of quarrelling passes judgment on its parents, and builds up its own image of the world, often a harsh one. May Gray had told him that the wicked are delivered into everlasting fires; if she had really believed it would she herself have dared to live the life she did? No doubt the whole thing was a lie—a lie for grown-ups. Or was May Gray perhaps like Cain, damned from all eternity? If so, chaise-boys and ale-houses could make no difference. But then God was surely unjust? What could one believe? Why did he, in his innocence, suffer? Since he had become Lord Byron, his mother was less patient than ever at the sight of his lameness. She had been recommended to try a Nottingham quack named Lavender, and had entrusted the ailing lad to his care. Lavender was a brute. His treatment consisted solely of forcibly twisting the child's hapless foot, and screwing it tightly in some wooden contrivance. Byron was then taking Latin lessons from an American, Mr. Dummer Rogers; and this worthy man was pained by the sight of the agonised expression on his pupil's little face as they read their Virgil and Cicero together. It was caused by Lavender's instruments of torture. "It makes me uncomfortable, my lord, to see you sitting there in such pain as I *know* you must be suffering."—"Never mind, Mr. Rogers," said the boy, "you shall not see any signs of it in *me*."

Like Hanson, Rogers had instantly become very fond of this plucky child. It was no common thing to find a ten-year-old pupil asking for the number of his lessons to be increased. "Mr. Rogers," wrote Byron to his mother, "could attend me every night at a separate hour from the Miss Parkynses. . . . I recommend this to you because, if some plan of this kind is not adopted, I shall be called, or rather branded with the name of dunce, which you know I could never bear. I beg you will consider this plan seriously and I will lend it all the assistance in my power." The neighbours too were pained to see this glowing young creature handed over to the mercies of a May Gray or a Lavender. The latter, during the visits for treatment, enjoyed the joke of sending the young lord to fetch him his beer, and Nottingham was scandalised at the sight of the master of Newstead limping through the streets, carrying with all possible caution (for he dreaded a beating) the quack-doctor's pint of beer.

Yet he retained his gaiety; even as regards his tormentor his revenge took a humorous form. Lavender was a pompous ignoramus, but pretended a knowledge of all languages. The boy scribbled all the letters of the alphabet on a scrap of paper, arranging them haphazard in the semblance of sentences, and then laid this script before the conceited bully. What language was this, he asked. "Italian," answered the charlatan. And Byron burst into triumphant laughter. Impostors! That was what Lavender and May Gray were! Hatred of hypocrisy was becoming one of his strongest sentiments.

In the end Mrs. Byron obtained a Civil List pension of £300 a year, which would enable her to live in London. John Hanson looked round for a school for Byron, and fixed on Dr. Glennie's Academy at Dulwich; he also succeeded in persuading Byron's cousin, Lord Carlisle (whose mother was a sister of the vice-admiral), to become the boy's guardian. In his youth the Earl of Carlisle had been a prodigious dandy, who made the journey to Lyons just to buy embroidered silk waistcoats; he had published some verse, odes and tragedies; and then, having married, he had embarked on a serious political career and become Lord-Lieutenant of Ireland. Had Mrs. Byron been other than she was, he might have been a devoted guardian of the child. But the very first encounter of this great gentleman of elegance and refinement with that noisy, irritable, slightly ridiculous woman, sufficed to set the tone of their future relations. Mrs. Byron found Lord Carlisle haughty and affected, and labelled him as one of her "enemies," while the noble earl regretted his kindly step and resolved to see as little as possible of this woman who smelt of whiskey, dressed badly, and spoke with a crude accent.

Dr. Glennie, Byron's new instructor, was likewise quick to feel the consequences of Mrs. Byron's humour. Like all who were brought into contact with Lord Byron, he too had instantly felt for him a blend of affection and respect. He admired this crippled boy who tried so bravely to rival the sturdiest boys of the school in athletic pursuits. He enjoyed talking with him, for few children of his age were so well-read. He found originality in him. The boy recited verses, and was familiar with almost all the poets; and on Sundays he would speak of the Bible with such lively zest that the book was manifestly a friend to him. The other boys at school liked him well enough, but they sometimes called him "the Old English baron," because he spoke rather too frequently of his title, and laughed when they saw that stout woman with her brawny arms arriving for a bawling argument with Dr. Glennie. "Byron," said the most venturesome among them, "your mother is a fool." And gloomily he answered, "I know it."

Not but what she loved her son in her own way; and possibly Lord Carlisle and Dr. Glennie would have realised this extenuating circumstance had they observed her with a more indulgent eye. Perhaps they would have noted her courage in penury, and her generosity when generosity was possible; but she irritated them so much that they had no wish to probe her more deeply. They judged her vulgar—but she was only extravagant. On one Saturday, without warning, she bore her son home and kept him indoors, in defiance of all proper usage. Dr. Glennie complained to Lord Carlisle, who made one attempt at intervention but only got his first taste of the Gordon furies, and wrote to the schoolmaster: "I can have nothing more to do with Mrs. Byron. You must now manage her as you can."

The opinions of his masters and companions strengthened a sentiment in Byron which had long ago been born of his own observations—namely, a fierce and silent scorn for his mother. Yes, he reflected, she was a fool.

He felt responsible for her, and bore her a grudge for not being a possible recipient for a tenderness which he knew would be in vain. In his younger days he had feared her. Now he stood up to her. When a passion seized her she would chase him through the whole house; and the tragic and comic were strangely blended in the spectacle of this squat gnome pursuing that lovely limping angel.

Colour was given to the holidays by a fresh love, childish and heartfelt, for Margaret Parker, a cousin, "one of the most beautiful of evanescent beings." She was a slip of a girl, thirteen years old, whose dark eyes, long eyelashes, and Grecian cast of feature Byron was never to forget. "I do not recollect scarcely anything equal to the *transparent* beauty of my cousin, or to the sweetness of her temper, during the short period of our intimacy. She looked as if she had been made out of a rainbow—all beauty and peace. My passion had its usual effects upon me—I could not sleep—I could not eat—I could not rest. . . ." He tried to write verses for her. In his eyes she seemed the incarnation of a gentleness and innocence for which, impelled by deep and sure instinct, he had searched the world from childhood to find refreshment for his too ardent soul. He had found it in two children, and nowhere else.

During the holidays that year, in 1801, Mrs. Byron, whilst staying at Cheltenham, consulted a fortune-teller of some notoriety at that time, a certain Mrs. Williams. This person told her that she was the mother of a lame son, who would be twice married, his second wife being a foreigner; and the two dangerous periods of his life, she said, would be his twenty-seventh year and his thirty-seventh. Mention was made of this prophecy in the child's hearing, and he was deeply impressed.

V

HARROW-ON-THE-HILL

1801–1802

IN 1801 it was decided that Byron, as befitted his rank, should enter one of the great public schools, and Harrow was chosen. Hanson took him there. The school was not far out of London; from the hill on which its brick buildings stood clustered amid the great trees, it overlooked a wide panorama of wood and stream beyond which, invisible yet present, lay the city. To Byron, at the age of thirteen and a half, the ascent to these unfamiliar scenes was impressive. Alarming legends went the rounds regarding life at the public schools, the rigour of their rules, the cruelty of the older boys. What would be the welcome of this cruel, derisive society to a lame and callow boy? No doubt he was Lord Byron, but he had been told that nobody would care a straw about that; indeed, the American ambassador had lately sent his son to Harrow "because it was the only school in which no special favour was attached to rank."

For more than fifteen years the head-master of Harrow had been Dr. Joseph Drury, a man of about fifty, good-hearted, just and firm, who had endowed the school with such prestige that under his rule the number of pupils was amazingly increased. Eloquent, intelligent and even-tempered, he devoted a great part of his time to conversation, and even walks, with the boys. "It was a positive pleasure," noted one of them, "to be reprimanded by Dr. Drury."

Hanson introduced Byron to him, telling him that the boy's education had been neglected, but that there was a "cleverness" about him. The doctor thanked the attorney, saw him to the door, and after his departure took Byron into his study, trying to make him talk of his studies and enjoyments. "I soon found that a wild mountain colt had been submitted to my management. But there was mind in his eye." Drury was no superficial observer; he saw at once that the dominant trait in his new colt was pride, and that his fear was lest, on account of his faulty preparation, he might be placed in a form below his age. The master gave him his word that for a time Byron would be entrusted to a teacher for private tuition, and would not be placed in a form until he could join the boys of his own age. And apparently this reassured the newcomer slightly.

His first days at school were unhappy. With three hundred and fifty pupils, it would have been a miracle if there had been none to tease a cripple who was naturally both truculent and proud. His leg had not improved, and he was now obliged to wear special boots which his mother had made for him by Sheldrake, the well-known London bootmaker. Sometimes he would wake up in the morning to realise that his companions were putting his heels in a basin of water—in cruel allusion to the precautions he had to take. He might perhaps have been able to placate his tormentors just by submission, but submissiveness was no part of his nature. A fatherless child, he had early learnt to despise all authority. His mind recognised no duty of obedience to beings whose weakness he had discerned; and his pride forbade him to bow from prudence where he could not bow from respect. Brought up by his mother in admiration for the French Revolution, he thus retained an adoration of Bonaparte, the soldier of the Republic; he had brought to school a small bust of the First Consul, and defended it with all the violence of his fists against the schoolboy patriots. His infirmity inspired him with a dread of being looked down upon, so he showed himself haughty, combative, and quick to take offence. Physically he was rather stout, but his features were handsome, the eyes and the lines of his eyebrows admirable, his hair wavy and of a ruddy fairness. The passion he infused into everything was fascinating. He worked only by fits and starts, but at the right moment the boy was capable of writing thirty or forty Latin hexameters straight off. He did not learn his lessons, but his wide reading had given him a rich measure of general knowledge. He was erudite and lazy.

Byron's first conquest at school was that of the delightful Dr. Drury. A few experiments had shown the Head that this young thoroughbred could be led by a silken string more easily than by a rope. He held him by the thinnest of cords, and was rewarded. Byron attached himself to his master; Dr. Drury was the first person holding authority over him whom he found to be both stern and just. And justice was something of which he stood in great need. He felt—because children, like men, always do feel these things—that Drury admired him. Lord Carlisle invited the head-master to come and tell him of his ward. "He has talents, my lord, which will add lustre to his rank," declared the doctor. "Indeed?" said my lord, with surprise but with no visible satisfaction.

After the master, the boys succumbed gradually to Byron's charm. It was a very complex charm, compounded first of unlimited courage in speech as in deed.

There was nothing mean in this boy; he could not tell a lie. Nobody in the whole school rejoiced in a fight more than he. There was something chivalrous in his bearing. He had taken a fancy to a younger boy named William Harness, who was lame like himself; and seeing Harness being ill-treated by a bigger and stronger boy, he said to him: "Harness, if anyone bullies you, tell me, and I'll thrash him if I can!" Robert Peel was at Harrow at this time, proud in bearing but unhappy underneath. What could be done with a child who recited Pitt's speeches and lived in a world of his own? The solemn gravity of young Peel was a temptation to teasing schoolboys, and they played practical jokes on him. One of his tyrants inflicted the bastinado on him, and as Peel was writhing beneath the raining blows, Byron came up. He was not strong enough to fight the torturer, but, with red cheeks and wet eyes, he asked in a voice quivering with fright and indignation: "How many stripes do you mean to inflict?"—"Why, you little rascal, what's that to you?" answered the other.—"Because, if you please," said Byron, "I would take half!"

The Harrow boys were good judges of character, and after a year recognised that this companion of theirs was of metal unalloyed. He liked games, and longed to excel in them in spite of his physical inferiority. He particularly enjoyed swimming and diving; in the water his infirmity ceased to be a handicap. Naturally brave and rebellious, he was soon the inspiring force of all perilous adventures. The mountain colt strained his silken thread almost to breaking-point. When, after one of these freaks, he saw Dr. Drury looking sadly toward him, he was pained, for he was fond of his head-master, but it was something stronger than himself. His hand, like that of his Scottish ancestor long ago, had "an evil turn in it." Sometimes he was himself amazed by actions he had just committed. A rush of blood surged up, he hit out, he smashed. How could he help it? He was Byron.

That first year of school had not been very happy; at the beginning Byron had pained, and been pained. But his infirmity itself helped to make him a personage of note, one whom the masters did not confound with the rank and file of the boys. He tired quickly, and was of dreamy character, both traits which made him frequently seek out solitude. And they saw him climbing, with a book under his arm, towards the church in its narrow surrounding graveyard on the top of Harrow Hill. There was a grave there beneath a great tree, the tomb of an unknown man, John Peachey by name; and on that stone, sheltered by the branches of an elm, Byron used to sit. From her window, Dr. Drury's wife used to watch him limping painfully as he climbed the stony path of the graveyard. "There goes Byron," she would say, "struggling up the hill like a ship in a storm without rudder or compass."

The sentiment that drove Byron thus perpetually toward the graveyard was somewhat complex. He was troubled by the idea of death; terrified in childhood by so many accounts of Hell, he preferred to picture the dead as entering on a dreamless sleep in just such tranquil corners as this one, under pale leafage stirring softly in the breeze. He had lately learned of the death of his fair cousin, Margaret Parker, who had died at fifteen—she whom he had called "most beautiful of evanescent beings." He thought of her dark eyes, her long lashes. Had they really laid that frail body in a coffin, and buried it in the earth—that body he had gazed on so happily? The bitter-sweetness of these despairing thoughts astonished him. His reverie took form in rhyming phrases:

> Within this narrow cell reclines her clay,
> That clay where once such animation beam'd;
> The King of Terrors seized her as his prey,
> Not worth nor beauty have her life redeem'd.

The boys passing that way used to point to Byron in the distance, sitting there on "his" tomb. He knew the astonishment he aroused, and knew that astonishment always borders on admiration. There was a touch of blandishment in that melancholy of his.

VI

THE MORNING STAR

1803–1804

> Newstead! fast-falling, once-resplendent dome!
> Religion's shrine! repentant Henry's pride!
> Of warriors, monks, and dames the cloister'd tomb,
> Whose pensive shades around thy ruins glide. . . .

IN April 1803 Newstead had been let for five years to Lord Grey de Ruthyn, a young nobleman of twenty-three. Byron would thus resume possession of his inheritance at the time of his majority. Mrs. Byron had retained a lodging at Nottingham, at her son's request: he was anxious to remain domiciled not far from his beloved Abbey. But when the summer holidays came round, Lord Grey sent Byron a cordial invitation to spend them at Newstead itself, and Byron accepted with enthusiasm, to his mother's great indignation: "A fine reward! I came to Nottingham to please him, and then he hates the town."

It was not so much Nottingham he hated as the company of Mrs. Byron—and besides, how could he withstand the joys of living at Newstead? It was with ecstasy that he saw again the lake, the noble house, the dark line of yew trees. Lord Grey, knowing he was only to be there for a short time, let everything go to pieces, but in the very fact of this desolation of something beautiful, there was a melancholy that delighted Byron's heart. The wind soughed in the vaulted courts; in the garden the roses were throttled by tall hemlock and thistles; and at dusk the bats fluttered through the unglazed windows beneath which, three hundred years earlier, the choir of monks had chanted their orisons to Our Lady. In the park he looked for the oak he had planted six years before, when he came thither for the first time. He found it. The little tree was growing, and the discovery gladdened him. He loved omens of mystery. And half in earnest, he declared that his destiny would thenceforth be linked with that of this oak: "as it prospers, so shall I prosper."

Seated near those ruins, he liked to conjure up the pictures of his ancestors: John Byron who rode out on the Crusades, Paul and Robert who fell in the valley of Cressy, Rupert who fought on Marston Moor—all once young and pensive like himself, turbulent and tender, but skeletons now, dust and clay, gliding phantoms.

But to him the greatest charm of these parts was their proximity to Annesley, the great sister-house of Newstead, under whose roof dwelt Miss Mary Ann Chaworth, a great-niece of the Mr. Chaworth who was killed in the famous duel. Byron had made the acquaintance of his Annesley neighbours in London. The Chaworths had of course been embroiled with the Wicked Lord so long as his life lasted, but they had no reason for keeping up the grudge against a boy of fifteen for an episode in which he had had no part. Besides, Mr. Chaworth was dead, Mrs. Chaworth had married again, and Mary Ann Chaworth, her daughter, could not feel any rancour against a youthful cousin who gazed on her with manifest admiration and apparently thought her a great beauty. She was seventeen, with lovely eyes and straight, calm eyebrows, her hair parted straight down the middle. She, of course, never supposed that a crippled schoolboy, even if he were Lord Byron of Newstead, could possibly make a husband for Miss Chaworth of Annesley. Soon, she knew, her hand would be given to one of those sturdy, hard-riding country gentlemen who asked for her dances at the assemblies. But the schoolboy had fire and vision; he had read widely; he never bored her. She was an untamed creature, as well she might be, an only girl brought up alone in a vast park, artless and ignorant of life. How was she to know that, by encouraging this boyish folly, she was doing more harm than by curing it at the start by a feigned coldness? Besides, was she really acting harmfully? Is it not a good thing that young men should know strong passions? Mary Chaworth accepted this ardent boy-admirer of hers with a good grace, and he on his side began shaping the most absurd dreams. To one who devoured novels and tragedies, was not this adventure the most splendid in the world? The Byrons and Chaworths, reft apart by a murder, had been the Montagues and Capulets of this countryside; could there be any doubt that he and Mary were not destined to become the Romeo and Juliet of a most affecting drama in real life? True, she was a little older than he—but how little! Two years or so. Were there not plenty of couples to be found where the wives were a year or two older than their husbands? Surely it would be tempting for her to reunite by a marriage those two jewels of the shire, Newstead and Annesley? Was not the long avenue between the houses called the Bridal Path? Byron yielded to such dreams with all the optimism of a sweet illusion.

At the beginning of the holidays he began to make a habit of galloping over to Annesley every morning. The country between the two places was delightful: hilly prospects, wide meadows with browsing sheep, dotted with noble isolated trees. At the back of the house one stepped straight out from Mary's room on to a long terrace bounded by a wall with a festooned top, fashioned, as it seemed, of garlands suspended end to end from the stone balls of the pillars. The ivy that covered the whole of this wall was like some beautiful, yielding drapery, green and alive. From the terrace a flight of steps, branching majestically, and adorned at its head by the Chaworth arms, led one down to the park. Underneath, the two branches of the steps framed a wooden door, and Byron, who always carried pistols in his pocket, used to amuse himself when passing that way by firing at this door. The Chaworths smilingly displayed the marks of his bullets. "All these Byrons are dangerous," they used to say. The old vendetta, far from being an embarrassment, was a subject for joking that linked these two young people. When Byron was offered a bedroom at Annesley, so that he need not return to Lord Grey's at Newstead in the evening, he declined at first with the blend of irony and seriousness that was peculiarly his own, declaring that he did not dare, that the old Chaworths would step down from their frames to turn out a Byron. One evening he gravely remarked to Mary: "In going home last night I saw a *bogle*." They smiled and offered to give him shelter; and from that night he spent every night at Annesley.

How delicious these holidays were! To be madly in love, and to live under the same roof as one's beloved—to see her in the morning come out upon the terrace, still bathed in sleep—to saddle a couple of horses, and set off across the meadows at a gallop! Often they would go and sit together on the hill at the end of the Bridal Path, crowned with its "peculiar diadem" of trees. It was the last spur of those ridges. Over the gentle slope

THE TERRACE OF ANNESLEY HALL

From a photograph by Walter North

at their feet stretched a sea of ferns, stirring faintly in the wind, and then a pool, fields and woods, with here and there across the vast horizon a few dwelling-places, the smoke curling upward from the rustic roofs. Mary Chaworth gazed at this fair plain, caressed by the early sun. Byron gazed at Mary Chaworth. In all the universe he saw nothing but her. That face had become the sole spectacle worthy of contemplation. He had looked at it until he could never forget it. He breathed no more; he no longer existed save through her. She was his very eyesight, for he followed her gaze and saw only through her eyes. She was the Ocean wherein every stream of his thought found its goal. He called her the Morning Star—the Morning Star of Annesley. When out of her company, he gave himself over to long, idle dreaming filled solely and entirely by this image, as once by images of Mary Duff or poor little Margaret Parker.

Sometimes during these excursions their bodies touched, or hand brushed hand. The contact made the boy's blood leap. He accompanied Miss Chaworth to see some underground grottos which were visited in a boat: "I had to cross in a boat (in which two people only could lie down) a stream which flows under a rock, with the rock so close upon the water as to admit the boat only to be pushed on by a ferryman (a sort of Charon), who wades at the stern, stooping all the time. The companion of my transit was M.A.C., with whom I had been long in love, and never told it, though *she* had discovered it without. I recollect my sensations but cannot describe them, and it is as well." An ardent child can live for years on a memory like that. But there was a painful evening at Matlock, a small spa where there was dancing. For dancing the lame youth had a scorn bordering on hatred. He had to remain seated while Miss Chaworth danced; and when she came back to sit down beside him, escorted by an unknown partner, he said bitterly: "I hope you like your friend?" But next day he had his revenge, for Matlock lay near his property of Rochdale, and he enjoyed pointing out to his beloved the thirty-two thousand acres that would belong to him when he had won his law-suit, with manorial privileges in every parish of the district.

Did not Miss Chaworth perceive that beneath this naïve parading of wealth were hidden a deep love, and the desire to vanquish her? She guessed it, and did not think it serious. She affected to regard Byron as a brother. The man she herself loved was a certain Mr. John Musters, a country gentleman, a great horseman. Seated beside Byron on the Diadem Hill, casting her vague, pure gaze over the waving bracken, she was scanning the distance for Mr. Musters' horse. But a woman can never resist the pleasure of leading a lover on. However young, however badly off the man may be, it is always a joy for her to feel that over one soul she holds sway. Mary Chaworth gave Byron a portrait and a ring. The poor boy was frenzied enough without such favours as these. In any case, even if she had wished to keep him away, she certainly could not have done it; he had no wish to be cured. He was not even cured by an incident which he noted as "one of the most painful of those humiliations to which the defect in his foot had exposed him." One evening at Annesley, when Mary Chaworth had preceded him up the first flight of stairs, Byron, who was still in the hall, overheard a conversation at the top of the stairs between her and her maid. "Do you think I could care anything for that lame boy?" Mary was saying, and the words were like a stab in his heart. He plunged out of doors into the dark night, and without knowing what he was doing ran without stopping all the way to Newstead. Sadness and rage, a longing to die and a longing to kill—the most violent feelings laid siege to him all through the night.

Next morning he returned, and never mentioned what he had overheard. At fifteen years old, he was already experiencing that agonising yearning for someone which leads one to endure anything rather than forswear the sight of a face, the sound of a voice, the touch of a hand. So madly in love was he that, when September brought the end of the holidays, he refused point-blank to go back to Harrow. Mrs. Byron ordered him to go; she did not like to see him going about with these Chaworths. "I know," he wrote to her, "it is time to go to Harrow. It will make me *unhappy;* but I will *obey*. I only desire, entreat, this one day, and on my *honour* I will be over tomorrow in the evening or afternoon. I am sorry you disapprove my companions, who, however, are the first this County affords, and my equals in most respects; but I will be permitted to chuse for myself. I shall never interfere in your's and I desire you will not molest me in mine." Strangely determined, this letter for a boy of fifteen. Mrs. Byron granted the single day. But Byron did not leave the next day, nor the next week, nor even in the next fortnight. On October 4 Dr. Drury wrote a surprised letter to Hanson to ask what had become of his pupil. Hanson made enquiries of Mrs. Byron, and received the following letter: "You may well be surprised, and so may Dr. Drury, that Byron is not returned to Harrow. But the Truth is, I cannot get him to return to school, though I have done all in my power for six weeks past. He has no indisposition that I know of, but love, desperate love, the *worst* of all *maladies* in my opinion. In short, the Boy is distractedly in love with Miss Chaworth, and he has not been with me three weeks all the time he has been in this county, but spent all his time at Annesley. If my son was of a proper age and the lady *disengaged,* it is the last of all connexions that I would wish to take place; it has given me much uneasiness."

Byron missed school for a whole term, only returning in January, 1804. But his three months' remission was none too happy. He had quarrelled with his host and tenant, Lord Grey, for grave and mysterious reasons which, with a stubborn bashfulness, he refused to reveal either to his mother or to Hanson. The rift made it impossible for him ever to return to Newstead; he could not now remain in the same room as Lord Grey, and when the latter entered a house, Byron went out of it. As for his dalliance with Mary Chaworth, that was of course unhappy. A rejected lover is always mistaken if he insists on having at least the company of his loved one. The hours one hopes to save drag their painful length through undercurrents of resentment, and silences heavy with suspicion. So this was love, the sentiment he had thought so beautiful? By the time he left in January, he was almost glad to return to Harrow. His only regret was at leaving his beloved Newstead; he turned to view the Abbey once more from afar, and wrote an elegy on his departure:

Shades of heroes, farewell! your descendant, departing
From the seat of his ancestors, bids you adieu!
Abroad, or at home, your remembrance imparting
New courage, he'll think upon glory and you.

VII

ROMANTIC FRIENDSHIPS—THE DOWAGER

1804–1805

And friendships were form'd, too romantic to last.

NEWSTEAD and Annesley had lost their charms; Harrow seemed less detestable. The hardships of fagging were over for Byron. Dr. Drury, who bore no resentment for this three months' truancy, had selected him as one of the small band of pupils whom he personally instructed in Greek and Latin. His friends and old comrades in torture, Tom Wildman and Long, had likewise become powers in the land. It was his turn now to claim the services of fags, but he was far from treating them as his elders had treated him. He gathered round him younger boys of great beauty; he liked nothing better than to protect the young and helpless—it flattered his pride, satisfied his instinct for tenderness. His favourite was Lord Clare, but he was also fond of the Duke of Dorset, Lord Delawarr, and young Wingfield. He defended them against the other monitors. Once when Wildman had put Delawarr's name on a punishment list, Byron said to him: "Wildman, I find you've got Delawarr on your list. Pray don't lick him."—"Why not?"—"Why? I don't know, except that he's a brother peer. But pray don't do it."

His prestige in the school was increasing. He was chosen to declaim in public on the Harrow Speech Day: "Lord Byron: *Latinus, ex Virgilio,*" announced the speech-bill. When he took the narrow path into the graveyard, boys and masters would watch him with affectionate indulgence as he went up to "his" tomb. As Dr. Drury had divined his genius, ruder spirits had become kinder to his whims. A court of handsome striplings followed him about with their respectful admiration.

> Here first remember'd be the joyous band,
> Who hail'd me chief, obedient to command;
> Who join'd with me in every boyish sport—
> Their first adviser, and their last resort. . . .

Why was he liked? Simply perhaps because he was a difficult friend. His clear and piercing sincerity, and his changeable humour, made him disquieting, like certain women. His friendships had something of torment in them. Love had betrayed him, and seeking refuge in another sentiment, he brought to that the same violence. *"L'amitié qui, dans le monde, est à peine un sentiment est une passion dans les cloîtres"*—he underlined the words in his Marmontel. Even for his favourite, Lord Clare, Byron's friendship was far from being a calm, unbroken affection. In this case he showed himself jealous, ardent and exigent. From one study to the other several letters daily passed from "Big" Byron to "Little" Clare. Byron reproached Clare with a dreadful offence in having called him "dear Byron" instead of the usual "my dear Byron." Another time he made a scene with his friend because the latter had appeared sad over the departure of Lord John Russell for Spain. Sometimes it was he who inflamed Clare's jealousy by his welcome of new companions, and then Clare in his turn would take offence: "Since you have been so unusually unkind to me, in calling me names whenever you met me, of late, I must beg an explanation, wishing to know whether you choose to be as good friends with me as ever. I must own that, for this last month, you have entirely cut me—for, I suppose, your new cronies. But think not that I will (because you choose to take into your head some whim or other) be always giving up to you, nor do, as I observe other fellows doing, to regain your friendship; nor think that I am your friend either through interest, or because you are bigger and older than I am. No,—it never was so, nor ever shall be so. I was only your friend, and am so still—unless you go on in this way, calling me names whenever you see me."

These stirrings of jealousy reminded Byron of his other passion—stronger than ever, alas!—for the Morning Star of Annesley. Those wide eyes, the Bridal Path, Mary's spinet, were still mingled with all his daydreams. A bitter blend of regrets and desire! How he longed to stifle this painful feeling, to wrench it from his heart! He hunted out all the authors who spoke of love ironically, with detachment and sarcasm, and he enjoyed sharing with his friends the libertine verses, fashionable at that moment, of Thomas Little—the pseudonym of Thomas Moore. Yes, this was the right way of love, seeking its enjoyments, not its passion. But powerful images still sprang from that memory of the outstretched bodies in the boat, under the low arch of rock, or of the warm August days on the Diadem Hill.

Easter came, but he viewed the approach of the holidays joylessly. After the quarrel with Lord Grey he could not spend them at Newstead; there was nothing for it but to go and join, as he said, "the Dowager." Mrs. Byron had left Nottingham and settled a few miles from Newstead, in the small town of Southwell. There she had found a very simple house dignified by the stately name of Burgage Manor. She was not taken up by the county families, who had needed only one meeting to set her down as vulgar, tiresome, impossible. The townspeople were more indulgent; and the Dowager was on good terms with the Pigot family, who occupied the other large house in Southwell, opposite to hers.

Byron was deeply vulnerable, and had very keen intuitions whenever a point of pride was at stake; he instantly realised the impression his mother had made on the local gentry. And this filled him with a feeling of hostility not only against these supercilious manor houses, but also against the person who had earned their disdain. He might be at his ease nowadays at school, but in new surroundings he still remained shy. His infirmity left him with a surpassing dread of having to walk in the presence of people unknown to him. He had a horror of the gesture of surprised pity which the disclosure always provoked. And to this sense of shame, which had been his from childhood, there had now been added the consciousness of his mother's inferiority, and, since the episode of Mary Chaworth, a terror of women. When presented to a woman, he was so deeply troubled that he could do nothing but count under his breath: "One, two, three, four, five, six, seven. . . . One, two, three, four, five, six, seven. . . ." He adored them, and hated them. He hated them because he adored them. If only he could conquer these creatures of mystery, humble them, give them their turn of suffering, wreak his vengeance on them! But how could he? He was a cripple, he was poor, he felt ridiculous. Nevertheless, a young Southwell girl, Elizabeth Pigot, succeeded in taming him. "The first time I was introduced to him," she said, "was at a party at his mother's, when he was so shy that she was forced to send for him three times before she could persuade him to come into the drawing-room, to play with the young people at a round game. He was then a plump, bashful boy with his hair combed straight over his forehead. . . . The next morning Mrs. Byron brought him to call at our house, when he still continued shy and formal in his manner. The conversation turned upon Cheltenham, where we had been staying, the plays, etcetera; and I mentioned that I had seen the character of Gabriel Lackbrain very well performed. His mother getting up to go, he accompanied her, making a formal bow, and I, in allusion to the play, said, 'Good-bye, Gaby.' His countenance lighted up, his handsome mouth displayed a broad grin, all his shyness vanished, never to return, and upon his mother's saying, 'Come, Byron, are you ready?'—no, she might go by herself, he would stay and talk a little longer; and from that moment he used to come in and go out at all hours, as it pleased him, and in our house considered himself perfectly at home."

For some months he had had another confidante. This was his half-sister Augusta. Sixteen years before, at the time of Mrs. Byron's confinement, Augusta had been handed over to her maternal grandmother; and Lady Holderness, who held her son-in-law's second wife in horror, had stopped all communication between Mrs. Byron and the little girl. So Augusta had never really seen her brother, the "Baby Byron" of whom she had often heard them talking. In 1801 Lady Holderness died, and the girl, adopted by her noble family, had lived either with her half-brothers and sister, or with her cousin Lord Carlisle, Byron's guardian.

After her ladyship's death, Mrs. Byron had tried to renew her connection with Augusta, whose social status dazzled her and for whom she retained the affection natural in a woman toward the child she has tended. In 1801 she wrote Augusta one of those letters of anticipatory pointedness which people write when they expect to be treated superciliously. "As I wish to bury what is past in *oblivion,* I shall avoid all reflections on a person now no more; my opinion of yourself I have suspended for some years; the time is now arrived when I shall form a very *decided* one. I take up my pen now, however, to condole with you on the melancholy event that has happened, to offer you every consolation in my power, to assure you of the inalterable regard and friendship of myself and my son. We will be extremely happy if ever we can be of any service to you, now or at any future period."

Augusta did not live up to the safeguarding pessimism of Mrs. Byron; she took an immediate and lively interest in her brother; and he, alone in the world except for his dangerous mother, was thrilled to find that he had a sister, a friend, who, although a little older than himself (for she was twenty to his sixteen), was graceful, distinguished, and in every way appropriate to the family he would like to have had and had not. Hitherto he had rarely written to her, but at the beginning of the Easter holidays he made his excuses, and added: "I will now endeavour as amply as lies in my power to repay your kindness, and for the Future I hope you will consider me not only as *a Brother* but as your warmest and most affectionate *Friend,* and if ever Circumstances should require it your *protector.* Recollect, My Dearest Sister, that you are *the nearest relation* I have in *the world both by the ties of Blood* and *affection*. If there is anything in which I can serve you, you have only to mention it; Trust to your Brother, and be assured he will never betray your confidence. When You see my Cousin and future Brother George Leigh, tell him that I already consider him as my Friend, for whoever is beloved by you, my amiable Sister, will always be equally Dear to me." For Augusta was betrothed to her cousin-german, Colonel George Leigh of the Tenth Dragoons, a grandson of the admiral.

The girl was highly pleased by her brother's letters. He was the most delightful of correspondents all the time he was at Southwell. And charming letters they certainly were: "My beloved sister . . . My ever-dear sister . . . My amusement is writing to my Augusta, which wherever I am will always constitute my greatest pleasure. . . ." They were packed with delicate sentiments and childlike confidences: "Also remember me to poor old Murray"—the Wicked Lord's old man-servant, who had been pensioned off with the Duke of Leeds pending Byron's recovery of Newstead—"and tell him we shall see that something is to be done for him, for while I live he shall never be abandoned in his old age." Again, "you tell me you don't know my friend Lord Delawarr; he is considerably younger than me, but the most good tempered, amiable, clever fellow in the universe. To which he adds the quality (a good one in the eyes of women) of being remarkably handsome, almost too much so for a boy. . . ." "When I leave Harrow I know not; . . . I like it very well. The master, Dr. Drury, is the most amiable *clergyman* I ever knew; he unites the Gentleman with the Scholar, without affectation or pedantry; what little I have learnt I owe to him alone, nor is it his fault that it was not more." And then, growing bolder, he told her his ideas of love. Thomas Little and Mary Chaworth had moulded a sceptic. He told Augusta how he was going to a ball at Southwell, with the intention of there falling wildly in love with some lady or other: "it will serve as an amusement *pour passer le temps* and it will at least have the charm of novelty to recommend it, then you know in the course of a few weeks I shall be quite *au désespoir,* shoot myself and Go out of the world with éclat, and my History will furnish materials for a pretty little Romance which shall be entitled and denominated the loves of Lord B. and the cruel and Inconstant Sigismunda Cunegunda Bridgetina, etc., etc., Princess of Terra Incognita."

If Augusta replied that love is a very serious emotion, and that she for her part loved her colonel of dragoons to the pitch even of suffering, he answered her: "That you are unhappy, my dear Sister, makes me so also; were it in my power to relieve your sorrows you would soon recover your spirits; as it is, I sympathise better than you yourself expect. But really, after all (pardon me, my dear Sister) I feel a little inclined to laugh at you, for love, in my humble opinion, is utter nonsense, a mere jargon of compliments, romance, and deceit; now, for my part, had I fifty mistresses, I should in the course of a fortnight, forget them all, and, if by any chance I ever recollected one, should laugh at it as a dream, and bless my stars, for delivering me from the hands of the little mischievous Blind God. Can't you drive this Cousin of ours out of your pretty little head (for as to *hearts* I think they are out of the question)?" Thus was cynicism following on the heels of disappointment in love. The malady was taking its normal course.

MRS. MUSTERS [MARY CHAWORTH]

After a Painting by Thomas Phillips

In the possession of Lieut. Col. John Murray

But Augusta was first and foremost the confidante of her young brother's chief distress in life—the conduct of "my amiable mother, whose *diabolical* disposition . . . seems to increase with age, and to acquire new force with Time." He had long despised her, but living with her during the holidays, he had now come to loathe her. With the fierce directness of his race, he could not conceal his feelings; and this did not help to mollify the Furies. Hardly a day passed but a quarrel rose and broke like a thunderclap, heavy objects were hurled across the rooms, cries rang through the house. She declared her son to be a monster, and in league with her worst foes—Lord Carlisle and Mr. Hanson. She taunted him with his quarrel with Lord Grey; whereupon, with a youthful taste for the dramatic, he conjectured that the Dowager was in love with that young man. "She has an excellent opinion of her personal attractions, sinks her age a good six years, avers that I was born when she was only eighteen, when you, my dear Sister, know as well as I know that she was of age when she married my father, and that I was not born for three years afterwards." He might have overlooked these failings of a woman at the turning of her age, but that she heaped insults on him, cursed the ashes of his father, and told him he would become "a r-real Byr-r-on." "Am I to call this woman mother? Because by nature's law she has authority over me, am I to be trampled upon in this manner? Am I to be goaded with insult, loaded with obloquy, and suffer my feelings to be outraged on the most trivial occasions? I owe her respect as a Son, But I renounce her as a Friend. What an example does she shew me! I hope in God I shall never follow it. I have not told you all, nor can I; I respect you as a female. . . ."

The truth of the matter was that Mrs. Byron was profoundly unhappy. She had been widowed at twenty-seven; her life was spoilt; she lived the life of an exile in this unfriendly English shire. And why? To watch over the interests of a son who did not appreciate the sacrifice, who hated Southwell to which she had come only for his sake, and who said so—for he was brutal, like his father, like his uncle the homicide, like all the Byrons. And yet this hard Scotswoman felt capable of all this devotion! In her day she had given all to her husband; she would gladly have given all to her son. But was he still her son, this haughty and exigent young stranger who stood aloof from her and passed judgment on her? Gradually she was losing her child as she had lost her husband. She would have longed to keep tender hold of him, but with this hopeless life before her she lost her head and could merely scream.

After these scenes came regrets, on both sides. Byron sought to find excuses for his mother: "I am sorry to say the old lady and myself don't agree like lambs in a meadow, but I believe it is all my own fault. . . . I do not however wish to be separated from *her* entirely, but not to be so much with her as I hitherto have been, for I do believe she likes me; she manifests that in many instances, particularly with regard to money which I never want, and have as much as I desire. But her conduct is so strange, her caprices so impossible to be complied with, her passions so outrageous, that the evil quite overbalances her *agreeable qualities*." This alternating rhythm of generosity and rage was a dangerous thing to bring into the life of a young creature. He blamed his mother, but got into the habit of irritating her. The violent quarrel in which everything is blurted out was at first a torture to him, but it became a habit. He realised it, and judged himself with open eyes, with implacable clearheadedness. He would gladly have separated from this woman. "Such, Augusta, is my mother; *my mother!* I disclaim her from this time."

Augusta did her best. She wrote several understanding and considered letters to Hanson explaining what was going on, informing him of her fear that Mrs. Byron had taken to drink, and telling him that she thought it desirable that Byron should be sent elsewhere for his next holidays—to Hanson himself if he were agreeable to having him. She was going to discuss this with her friendly cousin, Lord Carlisle. And the latter declared his readiness to authorise anything, provided it did not oblige him to any direct contact with Mrs. Byron, who still filled him with the utmost terror.

The end of the holidays was depressing. Mrs. Byron had a letter from Scotland informing her of the marriage of Mary Duff, the pretty cousin whom her son had loved and caressed so tenderly when he was nine years old. Rather maliciously, she told him the news. She felt a secret pleasure in wounding this overweening son of hers—but how could she know that a childish affection had really been a passion with a force that was not yet exhausted? Byron's reaction terrified her. "I really cannot explain or account for my feelings at that moment; but they nearly threw me into convulsions, and alarmed my mother so much that, after I grew better, she generally avoided the subject—to me—and contented herself with telling all her acquaintance."

That same year he said farewell to Mary Chaworth. Sometimes during the holidays he had been asked over from Southwell to Annesley; but the spell was broken; it was clear that for her that lovely romance had been merely a plaything. Everybody knew of her engagement to Jack Musters. Byron went for a walk with her to the Diadem Hill, and spoke to her with the utmost calm. He had learnt now to be disdainful instead of ebullient.

"The next time I see you, I suppose you will be Mrs. Chaworth?" *

"I hope so," she answered.

Rather a cruel reply; but why, she wondered, was he so ironical? She had been kind to a schoolboy's folly—and this was her reward. He paid her one last visit. She came to him where he awaited her in the oratory. He was pale. Sitting down, he traced a few lines on paper, trembled, and shook his head in despair. Serene and confident, Mary Chaworth entered. She knew he loved her, she knew he was unhappy. He rose and took her hand coldly; they exchanged one last smile; then he rushed from the room, leapt on his horse, and passed forth for the last time from the great sculptured gateway. Early in the following year she was married. A true cynic would have become a friend of the couple, and waited for the future to produce its revenge; but Byron had loved Mary Chaworth too well to be capable of any sentimental machiavelism toward her. Apart from Augusta, and perhaps Mrs. Byron (who knows?—she understood more than she seemed to, did the poor Dowager, and wanted to console though she could only wound), nobody detected the profound changes which

* Mr. Musters for a time assumed the name of Chaworth.

this marriage had worked in Byron's soul. In 1804 Augusta had in her brother a tender and enthusiastic youth; when she saw him again, in 1805, his character was so completely altered that she could hardly recognise him.

VIII

GODS ON MOUNT IDA

1805

THE Byron who returned to Harrow for his last school-year was a troubled adolescent, divided against himself. He was glad to go back. Like all shy people, he liked the monotony of an existence wherein the human beings are familiar and activities are well ordered. There nobody took the least notice of his limping leg, and his authority was increasing. The holy of holies at Harrow was an old class-room, the Fourth Form Room, its walls lined with dark oak panelling a full three centuries old. As a monitor, Byron had become one of the guardians of this sanctuary, and three times he had carved a bold vigorous BYRON in the wood, amid many illustrious names. There is always a small band of demigods who rule in an English public school, and of this sanctified band Lord Byron was now part. The slopes of Harrow Hill, overlooking the plains where the ploughmen toiled and the rival teams waged their cricketing battles, made him think of Homer's Mount Ida, from whose summit the Gods looked down upon the works and wars of mortals.

But the Gods themselves have their passions; and Byron was continually tormented by fierce and jealous friendships. The favoured friend now was young Delawarr, "almost too beautiful for a boy"; but Clare was jealous, others likewise, and even on Mount Ida the Immortals were embroiled. Be it at Southwell or at

Harrow, it was difficult to dream one's dreams in peace. Delawarr himself did not have so exalted a notion of friendship as Byron. The latter was ready to give his life, to sacrifice everything for his friends, and it amazed him to find that other people's sentiments were so weakly and so lukewarm. Almost every day a poem of blame, or complaint, or scorn would hurl like a blazing thunderbolt on one of these too-well-beloved subjects of the youthful God:

> In thee I fondly hoped to clasp
> A friend whom death alone could sever;
> Till envy with malignant grasp,
> Detach'd thee from my heart for ever.

Or, another day:

> You knew that my soul, that my heart, my existence
> If danger demanded, were wholly your own;
> You knew me unalter'd by years or by distance,
> Devoted to love and to friendship alone.

The "joyous band" who were the recipients of these letters were amazed—then smiled—and then forgot. But a graver event was threatening the happiness of Harrow and of Byron: the wise Drury was to retire at Easter. During these last few months he had not always been satisfied with his favoured pupil. Byron was working better, and was now third boy in the school, but his mind was the prey to a spirit of turmoil. His animal spirits were too vigorous, said the worthy doctor. He was struck by Byron's deficiency of judgment; this lad was the most intelligent he had ever known, but he acted at times like a madman. The doctor, who felt himself responsible for the moral health of the school, did not like the intellectual and sentimental hold which Byron had taken over his young disciples. In December, 1804, he had gone so far as to ask him, regretfully, to leave Harrow. Mr. Hanson and Lord Carlisle then intervened, and the doctor had allowed himself to be dissuaded. The pupil bore his master no grudge. He was fond of him. The man who first succeeds in impressing the spirit of an adolescent with respect for a higher moral force will always retain a degree of authority in his sight which not even pride can lessen. For Byron the last lesson of the last day was a scene of regrets. Nothing was said. That would have run counter to the school's most intimate tradition. But the young lads of the doctor's circle felt unmistakably that a happy chapter in their lives was closed.

Who would succeed him? Amongst several aspirants was the doctor's brother, Mark Drury; and his most dangerous rival was a young man, an able mathematician, the Rev. George Butler. The boys had no knowledge of the real worth of either, but the name of Drury was enough to fire them with an impassioned partisanship; a Drury faction took shape, headed by Byron's friend, Tom Wildman. One boy remarked to Wildman: "Byron, I know, won't join, because he doesn't choose to act second to anyone; but by giving up the leadership to him, you may at once secure him." Wildman accepted this counsel and Byron became the head of the cabal.

The head-mastership was decided by a vote of the Governors, and Drury and Butler received exactly the same number of suffrages. The constitution of the school provided that in such a case the final choice should be made by the Archbishop of Canterbury. The tide of excitement rose higher and higher. And one morning the news went round that the Archbishop had chosen

Dr. Butler. The change of régime marked the opening of a period of revolt. Byron and Wildman, the life and soul of this sedition, never walked abroad without loaded pistols. What did they want with them? To kill Dr. Butler? There was some talk of that. Certain of the more headstrong conspirators proposed to sprinkle gunpowder along the route which Dr. Butler had to take to reach the Fourth Form Room, and to blow him up. But a boy named James Richardson stopped them by begging his comrades not to destroy the walls on which the names of their fathers had been carved.

Byron, for no particular reason, in one of his Gordonian rages, tore down the iron gratings from the windows of the master's house. Asked for an explanation of his conduct, he loftily replied, "Because they darkened the hall." Dr. Butler very sensibly tried to treat his young foes with good humour, but he could not win them over. Byron poured out satirical verses on him, in which he dubbed him "Pomposus," and took as his motto: "Liberty or Rebellion!"—

> Pomposus fills his magisterial chair;
> Pomposus governs—but, my muse, forbear:
> Contempt, in silence, be the pedant's lot;
> His name and precepts be alike forgot. . . .

Word of these disputes reached Dr. Drury in his retirement, and he sought to smooth matters down by a personal visit to Harrow. The boys were waiting for him on the London road at the foot of the hill; they unyoked the horses from his carriage, and dragged it in triumph to the top. He decided not to return again.

Byron's last term at Harrow was wholly taken up with this crisis in domestic politics. He worked little, and was regarded as a brilliant but idle pupil. Nevertheless, he had learnt plenty of Latin, and a little Greek. On Speech Day in 1805 he made two public appearances, reciting this time in English, and was especially remarkable in *King Lear*. He had invited his sister Augusta to come and hear him: "I *beg, Madam,* you may make your appearance in one of his Lordship's most *dashing* carriages, as our Harrow *etiquette* admits of nothing but the most *superb* vehicles on our Grand Festivals." The tone was humorous, but it masked a real desire to dazzle his friends with the elegance of his sister, for it was something really fresh and delightful for him at last to count one member of his family of whom he was not ashamed. And doubtless he was satisfied that day, both with her and with himself, for he scored a great success, and saw himself as a second Garrick. He was more proud of his talents as actor and orator than of the countless verses he had written these three years back. His qualities, he afterwards said, were far more oratorical and martial than poetical; and Dr. Drury, his great patron, believed that he would become an orator. He shone most brilliantly in passages expressive of vehement passion. He also remained the great swimmer of the school, and, what was remarkable in one so lame, he played cricket well enough to take part in the Eton-Harrow match of 1805.

That was the last episode of his schooldays. What did he bring away from Harrow? A keen zest for friendship, and a certain familiarity with the poets. Had he begun to grasp the many-sided enigma of life? No. One thing seemed unhappily all too certain—that other human beings felt far less than he did the need of sentiments unalloyed. Men or women, youths or girls, they all came prudently to terms with love, or with truth, or with God. Could he ever do likewise? He had no wish to—but what place was there in the universe for George Gordon, Lord Byron? Toward the end of his Harrow days, he jotted this note on the fly-leaf of his *Scriptores Græci:* "George Gordon Byron, Wednesday, June 26th, A.D. 1805, 3 quarters of an hour past 3 o'clock in the afternoon, 3d school,—Calvert, monitor; Tom Wildman on my left hand and Long on my right. Harrow-on-the-Hill." A strange craving, this that a youth has, to remind himself of his own identity, to take and note his bearings. What could Byron be dreaming of, on his slashed oak bench, that 26th day of June in the year 1805? Of the school he was soon to be leaving? Of Cambridge, where Lord Carlisle wanted to send him? It was sad to see the change looming so close. He had been more happy there than elsewhere—Pomposus and a few childish squabbles notwithstanding. In that small, close community he was accepted as a prince of the youth. Wildman here on his left, and Long there on his right, were friends, and sure friends. Gay young voices in the paved court, faces that smiled as he met them on his way, animated groups which he could join as he passed—how different was the Sacred Mount from that hostile and disquieting Outer World! Outside, what could he hope for? Mary Chaworth? But she was to be married during the holidays. Women? But would not they all be something like her? His mother? A Fury. His home? A hell. The Carlisles? But did that elegant guardian really want to see him?

This mettlesome yearling needed a light hand on the rein. The natural gaiety of childhood concealed a deepening vein of luxuriating melancholy. He was haunted by the idea of Death, whose blows he had already seen dealt on those near to him. He had composed mourning verses on his fair cousin, on several of his youthful friends. For the last time he went up to the graveyard to brood beneath the branches of the elm.

"JOHN PEACHEY . . ."

Who had he been, this John Peachey whose bones were whitening beneath this stone? And now they were over, those bitter-sweet daydreamings where he looked out over the fair plains, and beyond them to a dormant London. The young hero of Mount Ida was about to go forth from the abode of the Gods, to mingle with the agonies of mortal men. Would he one day return to sleep beneath this grass which had been the playground of his youth? His tomb. . . . Like this John Peachey, he desired only a single name for the stone that would mark it; but the name must be one of glory:

> My epitaph shall be my name alone:
> If *that* with honour fail to crown my clay,
> Oh! may no other fame my deeds repay!
> *That,* only *that,* shall single out the spot
> By that remember'd, or with that forgot.

The first lap was hardly begun, and already he was looking forward to repose after the race.

IX

TRINITY COLLEGE, CAMBRIDGE

1805–1806

Youth is a time during which the conventions are, and should be, ill-comprehended—either blindly fought or blindly obeyed.

PAUL VALÉRY

HE went into residence at Trinity College, Cambridge, in October, 1805. For the first time in his life he found himself rich, for the Court of Chancery had allowed him an annual sum of £500 from his revenues, one of the handsomest incomes in college. He would have a horse, and a manservant, and he felt as independent "as a German Prince who coins his own cash, or a Cherokee Chief who coins no cash at all, but enjoys what is more precious, Liberty. I speak in raptures of that Goddess because my amiable Mama was so despotic. . . ."—"I shall be perfectly independent of her, and, as she has long since trampled upon, and harrowed up every affectionate tie, it is my serious determination never again to visit, or be upon any friendly terms with her. This I owe to myself and to my own comfort, as well as justice to the memory of my nearest relations, who have been most shamefully libelled by this female Tisiphone." Harsh words, but Byron's childhood had been simply one prolonged "scene," in which a temperamental mother had screamed her most violent emotions from the house-tops. In a sense of shame, or in subtlety, he had had no lessons.

Trinity College. A castellated gateway, flanked by twin towers, opening on to an immense rectangular court surrounded by Gothic buildings. A flowered fountain in the centre quickened the still background into life with its leaping jet of water. On the right of the court was the chapel, and further on the Master's house, covered with Virginia creeper. A vaulted corridor brought one to the second courtyard, Nevile's Court, more solemn and more sombre, but nobly proportioned and with a cloister running right round it. Here were Byron's rooms, handsome apartments after his own heart, which he at once set about furnishing in a style befitting their splendour.

At the University no less than at school, it was his secret longing to become a centre, a leader of men. He had the troubled ambition of the weak, tempered by a dreamy laziness. At Trinity all the undergraduates were of about the same age as himself, and there was no scope for that cherished taste of his for showing a protective tenderness towards his juniors. In the first few days he realised that, except for a few studious souls who strained their eyes in scanning Greek verses by candlelight, the correct thing was to do nothing. Those were the days when it was the fashion in England to drink deep and play high. "No one can study the personal or public history of the eighteenth century without being impressed by the truly immense space which drinking occupied in the mental history of the young, and the consequences of drinking in that of the old." A guest who could not put down more than two bottles of port during dinner was a poor companion. A man was described as a "four-bottle man" or a "five-bottle man." My lords Panmure and Dufferin were renowned as being six-bottle men. Gambling was held in equal repute. Lord Holland gave large sums of money to his son, Charles James Fox, at the age of fifteen, in order, as he said, to let him serve a proper apprenticeship to gambling. High play in all its forms was a profession rather than a pastime in London society.

Cambridge mimicked London. Reading and culture, for which Byron had a sincere though haphazard taste, bored these undergraduates. He dined in hall at first. At the High Table on its daïs, the Fellows—and on occasion the Master—ate under the gaze of King Henry the Eighth. Byron soon looked on them with scorn. What savour did they draw from life, these pedants with neither poetry nor greatness of soul? They enjoyed feeble puns, erudite quips, college tittle-tattle, and good fat livings in the Church. After hall, people met in each other's rooms, and there was drinking, with card-playing, far into the night. Byron hated drinking, but he was eager to make a good impression. He sent an order through Hanson for four dozen of port, sherry, burgundy and madeira. Cards he liked no better than he did wine. "I had no coolness, nor judgment, nor calculation," he said. But he went the way of the others. It would be ludicrous—would it not?—for a young nobleman with ancestors damned to the devil, to live the life of an ascetic.

He awoke with his head muzzy with fumes of claret. The chapel bell was ringing in the morning air. He had to attend, and with a white surplice over his shoulders on a saints' day. The sweet, celestial strains of the organ enveloped the drowsy undergraduates. The day was beginning. Byron's tutor had soon realised that he had a pupil of whom he would see little, and who had resolved to do no work. Byron had bought a fine grey horse with the name of Oateater, which he rode every morning in a white hat and a silver-grey cloak—an extravagant get-up, but it was the day of the dandies. Could he not be the Brummell of Cambridge? And then, if the weather were fine, he went off to bathe.

He had picked upon a bend of the river some way out from Cambridge, a deep place sheltered beneath spreading branches. The companion of his sport, and his only friend, was his school- and class-mate of Harrow days, Edward Noel Long ("Tom Wildman on my left hand, Long on my right"), an honest and generous youth, very straightforward, and like Byron a great swimmer and a great reader. It was a real joy to go with Long and bring up a plate, an egg, or a shilling, from fourteen feet of water. In the depths of the stream there was an old tree-stump to which Byron loved to cling, wondering to himself how the devil he had come into this strange waterscape. In the evening Long would come to Byron's room and play the flute or the 'cello to him, while Byron listened as he drank his favourite beverage—soda-water. The rhythms of the music suggested rhythms of verse to his mind, and threw him into that sensuous, melancholy reverie that he loved, through which swam the cloisters of Newstead, the bats fluttering in the ruined chapel, the terrace at Annesley, Mary Chaworth and her songs, the elm leaves whispering in the breeze above John Peachey's tomb, and Margaret's eyes, closed now for ever. Sometimes they would read aloud to each other. "*His* friendship, and a violent, though *pure,* love and passion—which held me at the same period—were the then romance of the most romantic period of my life."

Who was the object of this passion, as violent as it was pure? The Cambridge colleges maintained choirs for their chapels, and a chance meeting made Byron acquainted with one of the Trinity choristers, a lad of fifteen named Edleston, whom he saved from drowning. Later, at the services, he noted the beauty of this lad's voice, and became friendly with him. The friendship was typical of those which he bestowed on someone not only younger than himself, but inferior in rank and fortune. Over Edleston he secured a spiritual domination far more easily than over Clare or Delawarr, and in exchange he granted a powerful and unlimited protection. The young chorister, although slightly intimidated at first, nevertheless returned his affection. He made Byron the gift of a cornelian heart, and a poem was composed:

No specious splendour of this stone
  Endears it to my memory ever;
With lustre only once it shone,
  And blushes modest as the giver.

Some who can sneer at friendship's ties,
  Have, for my weakness, oft reproved me;
Yet still the simple gift I prize,
  For I am sure the giver loved me.

He offer'd it with downcast look,
  As fearful that I might refuse it;
I told him, when the gift I took,
  My only fear should be to lose it.

The writing of verses was becoming his greatest pleasure. He did not read nearly so much as he used to; nowadays he preferred to dream, to swim, and, above all else, to let himself sink benumbed into a seeming inertness, in the depths of which rhymes, rhythms and strophes would rise into being.

This life would have been agreeable enough, and Byron, a creature of habit, would have grown used to it as to any other if it had not been exceedingly costly. From November onwards it became clear that the allowance of £500 a year, which had seemed so princely before his first attempts at independent living, was slender for an undergraduate who wanted to cut a fine figure. The end of every month brought its bill from the college kitchens, always a stiff one, because Byron entertained his friends in his own rooms instead of dining in hall. He had left debts behind him at Harrow which had to be paid. At Cambridge he had had to furnish his rooms. He wrote to Hanson to demand an additional sum from the Court of Chancery. His relations with the lawyer had altered. He was no longer the small boy asking for help; he was the noble lord treating his agent—"that fool Hanson"—with haughty scorn. The attorney replied sternly that if Lord Byron led a simpler life his income should suffice him. Byron brutally retorted that if he were not given the wherewithal to pay his debts, he would negotiate a loan with the moneylenders. A young man who was the owner of Newstead and Rochdale, and not far from his majority, need have no difficulty in finding cash—at a hundred per cent. interest!

The sole objection of the moneylenders was that if Byron, a minor, should die too soon, their risk could be covered only by the signature of a relative of full age. He thought of Augusta. He assured her that she was risking nothing, because if he did die, she would inherit from him, and, if he lived, he would pay. "If you have the least doubt of my integrity, or that you run too great a risk, do not hesitate in your refusal." Augusta gave him her signature, and he was thus enabled to borrow several hundred pounds. It was not long before Mrs. Byron had word of this, and she was terrified: "that boy will be the death of me, and drive me mad!—where can he get hundreds? Has he got into the hands of moneylenders?" And, a little later: "Lord Byron has given £31 10s. to Pitt's statue. He has also bought a carriage, which he says was intended for me, which I *refused* to accept of, being in hopes it would stop his having one. . . . I much fear he has fallen into bad hands, not only in regard to money matters, but in other respects. My idea is that he has inveigled himself with some woman."

It was true that having money in his pocket he had not only ceased to do anything, but had even gone down from the University. He had taken up his abode at No. 16, Piccadilly, in rooms rented by Mrs. Byron for her visits to London. He kept a mistress, a girl of humble station, living at Brompton, whom he dressed in man's clothing and passed off as his brother. He took her down to Brighton on Sundays, where he had rented a small house facing the Pavilion. The strollers on the beach admired the agile grace with which this lame young man jumped into his boat. In town he spent a great part of his time with Jackson and Angelo, the Bond Street instructors in the various noble arts of self-defence. Jackson was a pugilist, Angelo a fencer, and their establishment was fashionable and elegant. "Gentleman" Jackson, as he was called, was the champion of England, although he had only made three appearances in the ring, and was a magnificent fellow, who could sign his name with an eighty-pound weight placed on his fingers. His word was law in the sporting world. And

Byron, who called him "my old friend and corporal pastor and master, John Jackson, Esq., Professor of Pugilism," admired his scarlet jacket, lace cuffs, breeches and silk stockings, and treated him with deference. The violent exercise to which Jackson and Angelo submitted him made him lose flesh, and to grow slimmer was his keenest desire. Besides, where could he have gone if he had not Jackson and Angelo? He knew literally nobody. He heard much tantalising talk of the dandies, of George, Prince of Wales, of Charles James Fox; and he saw the women as they passed down St. James's smiling to Brummell in his regular seat in the famous window of White's. But Lord Byron was alone, a poor, provincial squire, with neither family nor friend. And in this way he spent a whole term in London.

When he came back to Cambridge in the spring he brought his new circle with him. The young woman from Brompton was in his train, the boxer Jackson, and the fencing-master Angelo. His lordship welcomed Angelo to Cambridge with full honours, invited him to dinner, sent out to St. John's for some of the capital beer for which that college was famed, and even came to the stage-coach to offer his guest one last tankard of ale at the moment of his departure—to the amazement of the other passengers. His tutor reproached him with the company he kept. He retorted that Jackson's manners were infinitely superior to those of the Fellows of Trinity. His scorn of University life remained unaltered: "Nobody here seems to look into an Author, ancient or modern, if they can avoid it. The Muses, poor devils, are totally neglected, except by a few Musty old *Sophs* and *Fellows,* who, however agreeable they may be to Minerva, are perfect Antidotes to the *Graces.*

Even I (great as is my inclination for Knowledge) am carried away by the Tide having only supped at Home twice. . . ." The life he was living was crazy. It bored his spirit and drained his pocket; but he felt in honour bound to lead no other.

X

HOURS OF IDLENESS

1806–1807

> For a man to become a poet (witness Petrarch and Dante), he must be in love, or miserable. I was both when I wrote the *Hours of Idleness.*

AT the end of the summer term in 1806 he returned to Southwell, where his arrival was marked by a violent scene. Before the eyes of the stupefied Pigot children, Mrs. Byron hurled the shovel and tongs at her son's head; he left the house, took shelter with his friends, and left for London without seeing her again. From London he wrote to Pigot: "Many thanks for your amusing narrative of the last proceedings of my amiable Alecto, who now begins to feel the effects of her folly. I have just received a penitential epistle, to which, apprehensive of pursuit, I have despatched a moderate answer. . . . Her soft warblings must have delighted her auditors, her higher notes being particularly musical, and on a calm moonlight evening would be heard to particular advantage. . . . Seriously, your mother has laid me under great obligations, and you, with the rest of your family, merit my warmest thanks for your kind connivance at my escape from 'Mrs. Byron *furiosa*'. . . . Oh! for the pen of Ariosto to rehearse, in epic, the scolding of that momentous eye—or rather, let me invoke the shade of Dante, for none but the author of the *Inferno* could properly preside over such an attempt."

A brave gaiety, but bitter. The Dowager pursued him

to London, and after an engagement of several hours she "at length retired in confusion, leaving behind the artillery; field equipage, and some prisoners." She returned to Southwell, and Byron, with the honours of war on his side, went off to spend a few weeks on the Sussex coast, and then took a short trip to Harrogate along with John Pigot. This young man, the brother of Elizabeth, a medical student, was both pleasant and cultivated. He was amused by his companion's equipage. The doors of his chaise bore the Byron arms, with the motto *"Crede Biron"*; a pair of saddle-horses followed, in charge of a groom; inside the vehicle travelled Byron and Pigot, and with them Frank, the valet, and two dogs—Boatswain, a Newfoundland, and Nelson, a bull-dog. Byron was not rich—why did he persist in carting round such a staff and such a menagerie? He showed a curious inability to eliminate from his life anything that had accidentally entered it. In a moment of caprice, he had attached this valet, these horses and dogs, to his person; and he kept them. At heart, he was loyal. His lingering sentimentality forced him into attachment to all that he came in direct contact with. John Pigot, an astute observer, witnessed many instances of this Byronic shyness during their stay at Harrogate. His companion forced him to a life of curious retirement: when they took their meals in the public dining-room, Byron always insisted on their going up to their rooms again at the earliest possible moment. Pigot was surprised to note the degree of horror which his friend felt for drinking (for all his notoriety as a fast liver), and how strict was the régime he followed. His pleasures consisted, apparently, of writing verses, horse exercise, and watching women at a distance. Notwithstanding the Mary Chaworth episode, he remained dangerously susceptible to their charm; but before Pigot he posed as the man who has realised the perils of love, has tried women in the balance, and scorns them. The way to conquer them, my dear Pigot, was not to love them, but to despise them:

> Why, Pigot, complain of this damsel's disdain,
> Why thus in despair do you fret?
> For months you may try, yet, believe me, a sigh
> Will never obtain a coquette.
>
> Would you teach her to love? for a time seem to rove;
> At first she may frown in a pet;
> But leave her awhile, she shortly will smile,
> And then you may kiss your coquette.

Would that he himself had followed this prudent and ingenuous prescription in the days of his "M.A.C."!

The two friends returned at last to Southwell, and Byron took up his quarters with the Dowager, who for the moment was checkmated. The poor lady was horrified when she saw her son coming home with two servants, a stable, and a kennel; but she dared not say a word for fear of seeing his back again, and only wondered how all this caravan was to be provided for. Byron did not seek to deceive her as to the motives of this family reconciliation. He had spent all the moneylenders' loan, and had no funds either for travelling or for going back to Cambridge next term. The sole charm he saw in Southwell was that he could live there free of charge. Besides, with his astonishing passivity, a few days were enough to drop him into the Southwell groove; he began to follow a daily routine; and thereafter he was hardly less contented than in his rooms at Trinity. He had now a new goal in life—to become a poet. It was Elizabeth

Pigot who had given him the idea. One day she had read him some verses, and he had told her, "I write some, too"; and then he read her his poem to Delawarr:

> "In thee I fondly hoped to grasp . . ."

The charming Elizabeth expressed her wholehearted admiration; and another day he was reading some verses of Burns' to her, when he said, "I like that metre," and straightway on the same model composed the fragment:

> Hills of Annesley, bleak and barren,
> Where my thoughtless childhood stray'd,
> How the northern tempests, warring,
> Howl above thy tufted shade!
>
> Now no more, the hours beguiling,
> Former favourite haunts I see;
> Now no more my Mary smiling
> Makes ye seem a heaven to me.

Elizabeth was charmed by the poem, and touched by this recollection of a hapless love. She was a perfect friend for Byron, one of those delightful and tenderly devoted girls without a trace of coquetry, whom men in their folly do not love. She twitted him with his shyness. In his bad moments, this Cambridge dandy still found himself obliged to repeat under his breath: "One, two, three, four, five, six, seven. . . ." But Elizabeth's admiration gave him assurance. She offered to copy his verses, and prepare a manuscript version for a publisher.

And from now on Byron had what he liked—a routine. He spent the night working, went to bed very late, rose later still, and, when it was almost afternoon, went across the road to hand Elizabeth Pigot his work of the previous night. If other visitors arrived the shy poet escaped through the window. He then went on to another friend, the Rev. John Becher, the young Southwell clergyman, a man of sound judgment with whom Byron had long conversations on destiny and the universe. Becher strove to convince Byron that the Providence against which he grumbled had dowered him with a rich diversity of boons —with rank, wit, a fortune (very shortly), and above all with "a mind which placed him above the rest of mankind."—"Ah! my dear friend," said Byron mournfully, placing a finger on his brow, "if *this* places me above the rest of mankind, *that*"—and he pointed to his foot— "places me far, far below them." Frequently he would arrive at Mr. Becher's with an epistle replying to the advice proffered him the evening before:

> Dear Becher, you tell me to mix with mankind:
>   I cannot deny such a precept is wise;
> But retirement accords with the tone of my mind:
>   I will not descend to a world I despise. . . .
>
> I have tasted the sweets and the bitters of love;
>   In friendship I early was taught to believe;
> My passion the matrons of prudence reprove;
>   I have found that a friend may profess, yet deceive.

In this Southwell retreat he pictured himself as an aged hermit, made misanthropic by wisdom and misfortune. He breakfasted face to face with the Dowager, but to reduce her to silence he read throughout the meal. The afternoon was given over to out-of-door pursuits. He bathed and dived in the river, borrowing objects from his friends to throw into the water for the amusement of recovering them; he startled all Southwell with pistol-shooting in the garden; and he rode on horseback, none too well—his knowledge of horseflesh was so slight that once he expressed eagerness to buy some horses which he saw passing in the street, without recognising them as his own. But the real aim of all these exercises was to keep slim. Violent activity and light diet were his rule. A game of cricket wearing seven vests and an overcoat, not an ounce of meat in the twenty-four hours, one single meal a day, no beer—at such a price his ribs were kept visible and his pale features took on a peculiar charm. The evenings he spent with friends, at the Pigots' or the Leacrofts'. Of young ladies Southwell had no lack, and these creatures he had by now come to know well enough to lose his fear of them. Faithful to the precepts he had laid down for his friend John Pigot, he paid his attentions to them all, sending them verses, trying to embrace them, and taking part in their private theatricals. With one girl, of very modest condition, he had an intimacy of a more sensual kind, a new Mary with golden tresses, and he was proud to show to the more reserved Julia Leacroft and Ann Houson a lock of hair she had given him. He preened himself on his inconstancy. There was a lady in Southwell who owned a large agate, found in a tumulus, which she kept in her work-basket. She once told Byron that this amulet had the power of preventing its owner from ever falling in love. "Give it to me!" he exclaimed with sudden violence. "It is just what I want!"

Day followed day, and their monotony was helpful to steady work. The mild stimulus of his flirtations provided at once an antidote to ennui and material for his poems. An artist has need both of regularity in his life, for he is fond of his work, and also of some waywardness in it, as that enlivens his spirit. Byron was working well. He collected and revised his verses to Delawarr, Clare and Dorset, his translations from Catullus and

Virgil, the poem of Edleston's cornelian, his elegies on Newstead, and his love poems to various young ladies. The collection was shaping nicely. It could have been entitled: "George Gordon Byron—*Amatoria Omnia.*" The author re-read his verses with charmed surprise. Was this little book going to bring him fame? Elizabeth Pigot thought so.

Byron had his volume printed by Ridge, a Newark printer, under the title of *Fugitive Pieces;* and when the first two copies were ready, he took them to Pigot and Becher. But the effect was far from being what Byron had expected and hoped. The young clergyman read his friend's verses, but so shocked was he by a poem addressed *To Mary,* that he judged it impossible for Byron to issue the volume. Poor Byron, expectant of eulogies, received from Becher an epistle in embarrassed rhyme imploring him to suppress the book. It was a painful blow, but the response was instantaneous. Byron promised to destroy the whole edition, and fulfilled the promise that very evening. Every copy was burnt, except the one which had already gone to John Pigot, then at Edinburgh University, and (rather amusingly) Becher's own copy. It is hard for a young author to have to renounce his first book. Byron was courageous in his sacrifice.

And then, without losing a day, he set to work again with the printer, suppressed "the unlucky poem to my poor Mary," and within a few weeks produced *Poems on Various Occasions,* which appeared in January, 1807. "This volume," he said, "is *vastly* correct, and miraculously chaste."

The author distributed copies to his old Cambridge friends, and to his new friends at Southwell. From Cambridge he received eulogies; in Southwell, the book raised a storm. The Leacroft family was up in arms. There was mention in one poem of a Juliet. Was not this their Julia? Another, entitled *To Lesbia,* an ironic poem in Byron's pet vein of lofty scorn of love, looked also as if it might be addressed to her. In any case, the whole of Southwell was saying so. It was intolerable. Julia's brother, Captain Leacroft, demanded an explanation from Byron. The latter consulted Mr. Becher; Mentor and Telemachus united in the composition of a circumspect reply; but this mean trick of interpretation, this hypocritical shamefacedness, and the consequent imbroglio, finally sickened Byron with Southwell. Of the small town he had all the horror appropriate to those who have not yet known the city, and that scorn of the provinces which can only be dispelled by sojourn in a metropolis. He had been bored at Southwell inasmuch as his life there had been uneventful, but bored in a pleasingly gentle way; the incidents attending the publication of his book were an interruption at once of his ennui and his happiness. It was a trait of his character that he should long for the excitements of a life of turmoil, yet hate the life when he found it. Miss Pigot, the maternal Elizabeth—"dear Queen Bess" as he called her—became the confidante of this growing disdain: he hated Southwell, "your *cursed, detestable,* and *abhorred* abode of *scandal,* where excepting yourself and John Becher, I care not if the whole race were consigned to the *Pit* of *Acheron,* which I would visit in person rather than contaminate my sandals with the polluted dust of Southwell." He was eager to quit the place. His mother did not hold him back. "Lord Byron has now been with me seven months, with two menservants, for which I have never received a farthing, as he requires the five hundred a year for himself. Therefore it is impossible I can keep him and them out of my small income. . . ."

He stayed a few months longer, to finish off a new and enlarged version of his poems, destined this time for the larger public. The title was changed, and the book was now called *Hours of Idleness,* by George Gordon, Lord Byron, a minor. "A minor"—this was a comical touch; but he had written a preface which he thought would be sure to gain him indulgence: "These productions are the fruit of the lighter hours of a young man who has lately completed his nineteenth year. As they bear the internal evidence of a boyish mind, this is, perhaps, unnecessary information. . . . To a few of my own age the contents may afford amusement; I trust they will, at least, be found harmless. It is highly improbable, from my situation and pursuits hereafter, that I should ever obtrude myself a second time upon the public. . . . The opinion of Dr. Johnson on the poems of a noble relative of mine, 'That when a man of rank appeared in the character of an author, he deserved to have his merit handsomely allowed,' can have little weight with verbal, and still less with periodical censors; but were it otherwise, I should be loth to avail myself of the privilege, and would rather incur the bitterest censure of anonymous criticism than triumph in honours granted solely to a title." As soon as publication took place, in June, 1807, he left for London to supervise in person the distribution to the booksellers.

It is agreeable, at the age of twenty, to find oneself in London on a fine June day, with a little money, a great name, and a book hot from the press. Henceforth the "*worthy* and *lamblike* Dame" was to be left solitary in her provincial midlands; the "cursed" Southwell was far away; and up there "Queen Bess" received frank, straightforward letters: "Southwell is a damned place—I have done with it—at least in all probability; excepting yourself I esteem no one within its precincts. You were my only *rational* companion; and in plain truth, I had more respect for you than the whole bevy, with whose foibles I amused myself in compliance with their prevailing propensities. You gave yourself more trouble with me and my manuscripts than a thousand *dolls* would have done. Believe me, I have not forgotten your good nature in this *circle* of *sin,* and one day I trust I shall be able to evince my gratitude." He was sincere; for all these Julias and Marys who had allowed his caresses he had nothing but contempt; his "animal spirits" and his pride drove him into their pursuit, but deep in the inmost hidden shrine, there lurked a calvinistic little Scot clinging to his respect for virtue.

His main concern now was to know whether *Hours of Idleness* would make his name known as a poet. He was pleased enough with its success. One London bookseller, who had agreed to take a few copies into stock, had disposed of them and was asking for more. Ridge, the Newark printer, had sold fifty in a fortnight. Fifty—that was splendid! Doubtless the readers were mainly Southwell people; but for all his scorn the young author was curious to learn their opinion. "What ladies have bought?" he asked Elizabeth. "Are they liked or not in Southwell?" Regarding the judgments of these alarming and unknown creatures, the London readers, it was harder to obtain information. Byron had sent a copy to Lord Carlisle, who replied with the polite letter which one writes before opening a book one has decided not to read. One of his cousins, Lord Alexander Gordon, told him that his mother, the Duchess of Gordon, had "bought the volume, admired it exceedingly, in common with the rest of the fashionable world, and wished to claim her relationship with the author." But her Grace did not fulfil this desire, and left her young kinsman uninvited. "In every bookseller's window I see my *own name,* and say nothing, but enjoy my fame in secret." There was one bookseller who had sold seven. Seven—that was magnificent! So said the bookseller, and Byron gladly believed him. He was an active author, and busied himself directly with the despatch of copies to the principal watering-places: "Carpenter (Moore's publisher) told me a few days ago they sold all theirs immediately, and had several enquiries made since, which, the books being gone, they could not supply. The Duke of York, the Marchioness of Headfort, the Duchess of Gordon, etc., etc., were among the purchasers; and Crosby tells me the circulation will be still more extensive in the winter, the summer season being very bad for a sale, as most people are absent from London." A few critics had taken notice of *Hours of Idleness:* "I have been praised to the skies in the *Critical Review,* and abused greatly in another publication. So much the better, they tell me, for the sale of the book: it keeps up controversy, and prevents it being forgotten. Besides, the first men of all ages have had their share, nor do the humblest escape;—so I bear it like a philosopher."

He was still very much alone. Few visitors called at Dorant's, the hotel where he stayed in Albemarle Street. One of his old Harrow schoolmasters, Henry Drury, tried to find him, but in vain. There also turned up a man who claimed to be his distant kinsman, Robert

Charles Dallas, whose sister had married George Anson, Byron's uncle. Dallas was a novelist and a translator of works from the French. He was a solemn fellow, who believed the aim of an author was to be "the auxiliary of the Divine and the Moralist," and having heard of *Hours of Idleness* from a relative, had bought the slender volume. After reading it he wrote to Byron: "My Lord —Your poems were sent to me a few days ago. I have read them with more pleasure than I can express, and I feel myself irresistibly impelled to pay you a tribute on the effusions of a noble mind in strains so truly poetic. . . . Your poems, my Lord, are not only beautiful as compositions;—they bespeak a heart glowing with honour, and attuned to virtue, which is infinitely the higher praise. . . . I have no doubt that you will reflect more honour on the Peerage than the Peerage on you."

Rather a ludicrous letter, the young cynic must have thought. But Dallas was the first writer who had noticed his work, and he received a courteous reply: "Though our periodical censors have been uncommonly lenient, I confess a tribute from a man of acknowledged genius is still more flattering. But I am afraid I should forfeit all claim to candour, if I did not decline such praise as I do not deserve. . . . But my pretensions to virtue are unluckily so few, that though I should be happy to merit, I cannot accept, your applause in that respect. . . . The events of my short life have been of so singular a nature, that, though the pride commonly called honour has, and I trust ever will, prevented me from disgracing my name by a mean or cowardly action, I have been already held up as the votary of licentiousness, and the disciple of infidelity. . . . In morality, I prefer Confucius to the Ten Commandments, and Socrates to St. Paul (though the two latter agree in their opinion of marriage). In religion, I favour the Catholic emancipation, but do not acknowledge the Pope. . . . I hold virtue, in general, or the virtues severally, to be only in the disposition, each a *feeling,* not a principle. I believe truth the prime attribute of the Deity, and death an eternal sleep, at least of the body. You have here a brief compendium of the sentiments of the *wicked* George, Lord Byron; and, till I get a new suit, you will perceive that I am badly cloathed." —The document filled the solemn Dallas with admiration and perplexity.

Nothing could be more diverting than to turn author; and already Byron was shaping plans of work for the future. He thought of collecting the old Gaelic traditions of the Scottish Highlands, and translating the ancient poems, which he could publish "under the denomination of *The Highland Harp,* or some title equally *picturesque.*" He also conceived the idea of an epic poem on the subject of Bosworth Field; but that would be a work of three or four years. Some stanzas on Mount Hekla perhaps? But pending the laurels of poetic fame, he cultivated those of the swimmer. Under Jackson's watchful eye, he swam through London, down the Thames from Lambeth for a distance of three miles. Leigh Hunt had been bathing that day, and was dressing again when he noticed a head bobbing up and down in the water like a buoy, whilst at a distance a man of respectable appearance watched the swimmer from the bank. The man on dry land was Mr. Jackson, the fashionable pugilist; the buoy was George Gordon, Lord Byron, a minor.

XI

THE TRINITY MUSKETEERS

1807–1808

WHAT was he to do with life? It could not be spent in swimming and rhyming. Towards the end of June he went up to Cambridge in order, as he thought, to bid the University farewell; and once again he saw the glorious court of Trinity, the smooth lawns of the Backs. So slim and ethereal had he become that neither the dons, nor his fellow-undergraduates, nor the porter recognised the puffy youth they had known a year before. A strict and athletic régime had given him the face of a young ascetic. His look was that "of a beautiful alabaster vase lit from within." Against this transparent complexion, his chestnut hair with its coppery sheen (he was becoming a little less red-headed as he grew older) stood sharply out, as likewise his blue-grey eyes, looking anxiously out beneath the long, dark, drooping eyelashes. Undergraduates unknown to him watched him admiringly as he wandered through the cloisters of Nevile's Court. Amongst the number, he chanced upon one whom he fancied he recognised, and who likewise looked at him hesitatingly; it was his chorister, Edleston. He was on the point of leaving Cambridge—he was poor—and was taking a place in a mercantile house in London. Byron was touched at this meeting, and offered to invest money in the firm so that Edleston could become a partner; or else Edleston could leave London when Byron attained his majority and come to live with him at Newstead. "Queen Bess" of Southwell was duly informed of the revival of this passion: "I certainly love him more than any human being, and neither time nor distance have had the least effect on my (in general) changeable disposition. In short, we shall put *Lady E. Butler* and *Miss Ponsonby* to the blush, Pylades and Orestes out of countenance, and want nothing but a catastrophe like *Nisus* and *Euryalus,* to give *Jonathan* and *David* the 'go-by.' He certainly is perhaps more attached to me than even I am in return. During the whole of my residence at Cambridge we met every day, summer and winter, without passing *one* tiresome moment, and separated each time with increasing reluctance. I hope you will one day see us together. He is the only being I esteem, though I *like* many." (Lady Eleanor Butler and Miss Ponsonby, the "Ladies of Llangollen," were two inseparables, who had become famous for their having lived together for thirty years on end, dressed in very masculine style, wearing powdered wigs, and looking "exactly like two respectable superannuated clergymen.")

As Byron had deserted Cambridge for a whole year, the splendid rooms he had furnished had been given to another member of the college, Charles Skinner Matthews. Byron made his acquaintance, and found him most agreeable. Matthews was a young man of wit and erudition, and a good writer both in Latin and English. He had the reputation of being proud and rather difficult to know; but he gave Byron a pleasant welcome, and was very favourably disposed towards him. When he had been given these rooms, he had been told by his tutor: "Mr. Matthews, I recommend to your attention not to damage any of the movables, for Lord Byron, sir, is a man of tumultuous passions." The phrase had delighted Matthews. When friends came to see him, he would advise them to be very careful in touching the door-handle "because Lord Byron, sir, is a man of tumultuous passions." He greeted his "landlord" with a mention of his "tumultuous passions" in an amusingly sardonic tone. In Matthews' rooms Byron met a few other undergraduates of the same intellectual type, and glimpsed the possibility of living at Cambridge in a circle much more congenial than that of his freshman year. His tastes inclined him to intellectualism, his pride to dissipation. But in these new acquaintances he found a titillating blend of high living and high thinking, which allowed one to be intelligent without repining. How was it that he had not known them sooner? It was easy enough to understand. During his first year at Cambridge, they had looked down upon him. For what was he at that time? An over-stout youth, shy and arrogant, without any merits to excuse his loftiness. He had been left severely alone. But now he was the author of a volume of verse, which Cambridge had read because it dealt in part with the University, and he was looked upon in quite a different light. He realised this, was pleased, and decided to come up again in October for another year.

Next term he took back his rooms, and thenceforth was part of a faithful band of friends. First of all there was Matthews, whom Byron greatly admired. Out of his hours of study, Matthews had a pretty taste for frivolity. He took Byron with him on nocturnal expeditions through Cambridge, shouting under the tradesmen's windows. He was a scholar, but fond of fencing and boxing and swimming—though Byron, the expert, criticised Matthews for his laborious style of swimming, with his body too high out of the water, and told him he would be drowned if he persisted in swimming in that way. Matthews, on his side, was a vigorous and penetrating critic of Byron's ideas, and completed the destruction of the lingering relics of his Aberdonianism. Matthews believed in nothing, and laughed at God and Devil alike. A course of reading in Voltaire had already robbed Byron of his childhood faith, and Matthews's forthright opinions confirmed him in his scepticism.

His other intimate friend of that last year at Cambridge was very different. John Cam Hobhouse, the son of an eminent merchant in Bristol, was of Nonconformist stock and advanced Whig ideas and, like Matthews, a scholar and a great lover of the classics. He was busy with an essay upon the origin and aim of sacrifices—"your Essay upon Entrails," Byron called it,—and was a ready participant in the amusements of the group, but with a touch of cautious reserve not to be found in Matthews. He rode to hounds whilst the others went swimming, a fact which indicated certain distances. The cast of Matthews's temper was not exactly to Hobhouse's taste; the latter was an unbeliever, but in a very serious vein. As a convinced liberal, he had founded an undergraduates' Whig Club, and also the "Amicable Society," which latter broke up after a few months because of its perpetual dissensions. He held the Bourbons in horror, and took to Byron immediately because of the deep admiration they shared for Napoleon. The inner truth was that Hobhouse had a deep-rooted natural preference for the serious side of life, and cherished the small political influence he had already acquired in the University. He was an impartial friend, who told you of your own faults but did not tell them to others. Matthews and Hobhouse exchanged amusingly acid letters—"Your atrabilarious disposition, Hobhouse. . . ." During Byron's first year of residence, Hobhouse had looked askance at this limping lordling who sat his horse so badly and made himself foolishly conspicuous with his white hat and light grey clothes; but Hobhouse had a taste for poetry, and recognised the signs of a budding talent in *Hours of Idleness*. For Byron's feminine capriciousness he now felt merely a masculine and tender indulgence. In the little group of Byron's friends Hobhouse was the personification of Common Sense—Matthews, of Fantasy.

The last of the four musketeers who held sway at Trinity in 1808 was Scrope Berdmore Davies. In bearing as in dress, he recalled George Brummell, the Beau. There was no hint of showiness in his attire, and he was calm and reserved, but overflowing with wit, speaking in a dry caustic tone that only heightened the charm of an irresistible stammer. In aquatic sports Davies was Byron's chief rival. He spent most of his time at the gaming-table, and won largely, being a steady, calculating player. Byron had no instinctive taste for gambling, but took to it to please Davies, and drew Hobhouse's sermons on his head in consequence: ". . . to be sure you must give it up; for you are to be seen every night in the very vilest company in town—could anything be more shocking, anything more unfit? I speak feelingly on this occasion, *non ignara mali miseris*, etc. I know of nothing that should bribe me to be present once more at such horrible scenes. Perhaps 'tis as well that we are both acquainted with the extent of the evil, that we may be more earnest in abstaining from it. . . ." But Hobhouse was in a minority in the set, and life at Trinity that year moved pretty fast. Byron had introduced a new friend, in the shape of a tame bear. When the college authorities asked what he wanted it for, he told them, "to sit for a fellowship"—a reply which was not greatly relished. And there arrived from London a stream of jockeys, prize-fighters, gamesters, and women, all to sup with my Lord Byron. Yet the worthy Hobhouse retained his affectionate esteem for him—and indeed there was nothing really mean in this adolescent bereft of a proper upbringing. His courage knew no limits, and he always showed a keen desire to take risks for others, as also much kindness towards his inferiors. Out of his quarterly allowance of £125 he always earmarked £5 for old Murray, his Newstead retainer. He was a good giver and never had a penny-piece of his own. He went on borrowing, and the total of his debts was soaring dizzily. "I may, if possible," he wrote to Hanson, "convert my Title into cash, though I am afraid twenty pounds will be too much to ask as Times go, if I were an Earl . . . but a Barony must fetch ten, perhaps fifteen, and that is something when we have not as many pence." In January 1808, he owed over £3000, including £300 to the Jews, £800 to Mrs. Byron, and a £1000 elsewhere; and by March he was writing: *"Entre nous,* I am cursedly dipped; my debts, *every* thing inclusive, will be nine or ten thousand before I am twenty-one."

He mingled hard work with fast living. The edition of *Hours of Idleness* was exhausted, and he was preparing another; but he made the poet a slave to the whims and humours of the man, and suppressed or added texts in accordance with the ups and downs of his loves and hates. For some time he had known by hearsay that a violently hostile article was being prepared against him by the *Edinburgh Review,* the great Scottish Whig organ; passages had been read from it at Lady Holland's. Nothing could have been more painful to Byron; but he awaited the onslaught with good spirits. He wrote to Becher: "Tell Mrs. Byron not to be out of humour with them and to prepare her mind for the greatest hostility on their part." The number did not appear until the end of February 1808. Byron opened it feverishly, and read: "The poesy of this young lord belongs to the class which neither gods nor men are said to permit. Indeed, we do not recollect to have seen a quantity of verse with so few deviations in either direction from that exact standard. His effusions are spread over a dead flat, and can no more get above or below the level, than if they were so much stagnant water. As an extenuation of this offence, the noble author is peculiarly forward in pleading minority. We have it in the title-page, and on the very back of the volume; it follows his name like a favourite part of his *style*. . . . He possibly means to say, 'See how a minor can write! This poem was actually composed by a young man of eighteen, and this by one of sixteen!' But, alas, we all remember the poetry of Cowley at ten, and Pope at twelve, and so far from hearing with any degree of surprise that very poor verses were written by a youth from his leaving school to his leaving college, inclusive, we really believe this to be the most common of all occurrences; that it happens in the life of nine men in ten who are educated in England; and that the tenth man writes better verse than Lord Byron."

The anonymous critic proceeded to accuse him of flaunting his lordly title, and informed him that the fact of rhyming and counting a certain number of feet does not constitute the whole art of poetry, concluding with some railing at the tone of Byron's preface: "Whatever judgment may be passed on the poems of this noble minor, it seems we must take them, and be content; for they are the last we shall ever have from him. He is at best, he says, but an intruder into the groves of Parnassus; he never lived in a garret, like thorough-bred poets; and 'though he once roved a careless mountaineer in the Highlands of Scotland,' he has not of late enjoyed this advantage. Moreover, he expects no profit from his publication; and whether it succeeds or not, 'it is highly improbable, from his situations and pursuits hereafter,' that he should again condescend to become an author. Therefore, let us take what we get and be thankful. What right have we poor devils to be nice? We are well off to have got so much from a man of this Lord's station, who does not live in a garret, but 'has the sway' of Newstead Abbey."

It was an abominable article. The insistent way in which the young man's rank was flung in his face was simply an inverted snobbery, more stupid even than the ordinary kind. Its tone lacked dignity and proportion. Byron was bowled over when he read it; a visitor who happened to come in when he had just finished it found him in such a state of collapse that he asked Byron whether he had just been challenged to a duel. He dined that evening with Scrope Davies, and drank three bottles of claret in the attempt to drown his wrath; but nothing relieved him until he began to express his indignation in verse. After the first twenty lines he felt better.

Who was the author of this grotesque attack? For a long time Byron believed it to be Jeffrey, the editor of the *Edinburgh;* but it was actually Henry Brougham, a man with a wide range of malice; he criticised a physicist no less unfairly than a poet, and his article on Thomas Young's wave theory of light was a fair match in harshness and incompetence for his essay on *Hours of Idleness*.

Byron's first reaction had been to complete, and to publish at the earliest possible moment, a satire against his enemies; but happily he realised that he would do better to wait, and that the best retort would be to compose a poem of real excellence. "I regret that Mrs. Byron is so much annoyed. For my own part, these 'paper bullets of the brain' have only taught me to stand fire." They had also gained a new friend for him in Francis Hodgson, a young don at King's College.

On July 4, 1808, Byron received the degree of Master of Arts, and left Cambridge. That last year had wrought a great change in him. Harrow had been the period of sentimental, almost amorous, attachments; Cambridge had opened his eyes to intellectual friendships. In that dry, bracing air of sceptical cynicism he breathed freely. With Hobhouse, Davies, and Matthews he could show himself lighthearted in love and at long last free. But with such a boyhood behind him, can a man ever be free?

XII

THE POLISHED SKULL

1808–1809

One enjoys whatever is uncommon, even when it is something painful. CHATEAUBRIAND

FOR some months, in the hurly-burly of her retreat at Southwell, Mrs. Byron had felt anxiety regarding the next return, and the imminent majority, of her son. Her feelings for him were very much those which she had felt for her redoubtable husband. She feared him, worshipped him, and execrated him. What would he do, when once he was master of his own fortune, this new "Bryr-r-on" crossed with the Gordon stock? What blend of a Wicked Lord with a Mad Jack would reign at Newstead? And she, the thrifty Scottish widow who could live without a penny of debt on her £135 a year—why must *she* always be responsible for the males of this prodigal blood? During these last months of Byron's minority Hanson was bombarded with anxious letters. The Rochdale question must be settled at any cost, and a revenue thus secured for Byron; otherwise he would perpetrate some folly: "Although I have as high an opinion of my son's abilities as anyone may have, yet I am sensible that clever people are not always the most prudent in regard to money matters." The lawyers who had the Rochdale case in hand received letters of the most insulting vigour: "I will speak the truth. Why is my son permitted to be plundered by you and Mr. Hanson?" True enough, maybe; but the brutal tone ruffled the lawyers exactly as it had permanently estranged Lord Carlisle. They grew tired of the Byron business. Hanson made a marginal note: "What impudence!" Yes, impudent she was, poor Dowager; but what could she do? She was neither pliant nor dexterous; she was a Gordon, all violence, and she had a sore load of troubles. For instance, it was essential that Lord Grey de Ruthyn should leave the Abbey before Byron's return, "as I would not have them meet on any account, as they hate each other and I am sure they would quarrel, which might end very seriously." And Heaven alone knew what state Lord Grey would leave Newstead in: "I have not seen Newstead myself, but all the country talks of it and says it is quite disgusting for any person in the character of a gentleman to keep a place in such a beastly state."

The question that chiefly occupied her was whether, now that Byron had gone down from Cambridge, he would invite her to stay at Newstead and keep house for him. On his return she was informed: "Dear Madam, I have no beds for the Hansons or anybody else at present. . . . I shall live in my own manner, and as much alone as possible. When my rooms are ready I shall be glad to see you: at present it would be improper and uncomfortable to both parties. You can hardly object to my rendering my mansion habitable, notwithstanding my departure for Persia in March (or May at farthest), since *you* will be *tenant* till my return."

He certainly had found Newstead in an incredible state of dirt and dilapidation. In the park "his" oak—the tree with which he believed his fortunes to be linked—was moribund, almost throttled by rank grass. He disentangled it, tended it, and saved it. To repair the whole of the Abbey would have been a ruinous undertaking, and useless as well. He furnished a bedroom for himself, in the centre of which was a huge canopied four-poster curtained with Chinese stuffs; and he hung a few engravings on the walls—Jackson the boxer in his handsome blue coat; a portrait of the old retainer Murray, the only being besides his dogs whom he loved (as he declared); and then some views of Harrow and the Cambridge colleges. King's, Trinity, and Jesus—it was curious, this need of his for being hemmed in by his household gods. Was it because in childhood he had felt so lonely, so abandoned? He began by hating new persons and new places; but once he had made personal contacts with them, they became part and parcel of his own egoism, and thus sacred. From his window he could see the reedy banks of the lake, the swans, the battlements of the Wicked Lord's forts, and the fair hills stripped of their woods. One door opened into the haunted chamber, an unfurnished stone apartment, wherein from time to time, at night, a quaking servant-girl would encounter a black-hooded monk. A built-in staircase led down to another room which served him as study and drawing-room. A few rooms had been furnished for friends. But the rest of the place, the vast vaulted corridors, the numerous cells opening out of the cloister, remained bare and abandoned.

How he loved Newstead! He never tired of his dreaming there: now stretched nearly all day long on a sofa, trying rhymes or sketching a poem; now in the garden, where he liked to work leaning on the trunk of an oak felled by the Wicked Lord, which formed a natural, ivy-clad desk.

He had no desire to know the neighbouring squires;

THE COURTYARD OF NEWSTEAD ABBEY

From a photograph by Walter North

a few of them paid calls, which he left unreturned. An invitation to dine at Annesley, however, he accepted, being anxious to face the ordeal of seeing his Mary again, married, now Mrs. Chaworth-Musters: "I was seated near a woman to whom, when a boy, I was as much attached as boys generally are, and more than a man should be. I knew this before I went, and was determined to be valiant, and converse with *sang froid;* but instead I forgot my valour and my nonchalance, and never opened my lips even to laugh, far less to speak; the lady was almost as absurd as myself, which made the object of more observation than if we had conducted ourselves with easy indifference. You will think all this great nonsense. . . . What fools we are! We cry for a plaything, which, like children, we are never satisfied with till we break open, though like them we cannot get rid of it by putting it in the fire." A nurse brought in a little girl of two years old. Byron was pained when he detected in that still half-moulded face the firm, attractive features of the father, and those eyes into which he had so often gazed on the Diadem Hill. He looked at the husband, this vigorous man who boasted that he had never opened but one book—*Robinson Crusoe.* The dogs were barking in the kennel near by. Mary said not a word. She was stealthily observing that Byron had become slim and handsome. When he got back to Newstead, he threw himself on his sofa and wrote a poem:

> Well, thou art happy, and I feel
> That I should thus be happy too;
> For still my heart regards thy weal
> Warmly, as it was wont to do.
>
> . . . .
>
> When late I saw thy favourite child,
> I thought my jealous heart would break;

But when the unconscious infant smiled,
  I kissed it for its mother's sake.

I kissed it,—and repress'd my sighs
  Its father in its face to see;
But then it had its mother's eyes,
  And they were all to love and me.

Mary, adieu! I must away;
  While thou are blest I'll not repine;
But near thee I can never stay;
  My heart would soon again be thine.
. . . .

Away! Away! my early dream
  Remembrance never must awake:
Oh! where is Lethe's fabled stream?
  My foolish heart, be still, or break.

The only people he desired to see were his Cambridge friends. He took pride in showing them his Abbey, and Hobhouse was the first to come. Byron enjoyed living with Hobhouse; they had a grumbling, affectionately gruff friendship for each other; and when together, they worked like an old and faithful couple, each on his own account, Byron on his satire, which he daily stiffened and sharpened, and Hobhouse, contagiously affected, at certain philosophic poems. When they grew tired of writing, they stripped and plunged into the lake, or, if the weather were too cold, into a curious underground pool which Byron had fashioned by a reconstruction of the monks' cellars. They amused themselves with the training of Boatswain, the Newfoundland, Byron jumping into the water fully clothed and pretending to drown so as to be rescued by his dog. Old Murray waited on them at table; and more than once, after dinner, Hobhouse saw Byron fill a glass of madeira and hand it over his shoulder to Joe Murray as he stood behind his chair, saying with a cordiality that lit up his whole face: "Here, my old fellow!"

A pleasant life. But the vicinity of Annesley was still painful. It is almost intolerable to live close to a woman one has loved. In her astonishment at the coldness of the man she has known impassioned, she shows more tenderness; and Hope, most stubborn of sentiments, faintly renews its flush. But the victim knows it to be vain. The best remedy is flight—and Byron planned to go in the spring. He spoke of travel during his visits to Annesley, and when Mary in all innocence asked him why he wanted to go away she received some verses in reply:

When Man, expell'd from Eden's bowers,
  A moment linger'd near the gate,
Each scene recall'd the vanish'd hours,
  And bade him curse his future fate.

. . . .

Thus, lady! will it be with me,
  And I must view thy charms no more:
For, while I linger near to thee,
  I sigh for all I knew before.

In flight I shall be surely wise,
  Escaping from temptation's snare;
I cannot view my paradise,
  Without the wish of dwelling there.

But he took good care not to show these verses to Hobhouse, who had a horror of sentimentalism, and whose favourite poet was Pope, the classic, the witty, the temperate.

Poor Boatswain caught rabies. Byron nursed him like a friend, and sponged with his own bare hands the froth that ran from his gaping jaws. The Newfoundland remained affectionate to the last, and bit nobody but himself.

When he was dead, Byron said: "I have now lost everything except old Murray." He had long kept saying that he wished to be buried with his dog, and he turned his attention to the construction of a vault. With a strange and characteristic gesture of defiance, he had this monument raised on the site of the altar in the ruined chapel of the monks. A foundation of large circular steps led to a finely chiselled pedestal with an engraved inscription, supporting an antique urn, the beautiful outline of which stood out against the bare ogive windows. On one side of the pedestal he had inscribed:

NEAR THIS SPOT
ARE DEPOSITED THE REMAINS OF ONE
WHO POSSESSED BEAUTY WITHOUT VANITY
STRENGTH WITHOUT INSOLENCE
COURAGE WITHOUT FEROCITY
AND ALL THE VIRTUES OF MAN WITHOUT HIS VICES.
THIS PRAISE WHICH WOULD BE UNMEANING FLATTERY
IF INSCRIBED OVER HUMAN ASHES
IS BUT A JUST TRIBUTE TO THE MEMORY OF
BOATSWAIN, A DOG
WHO WAS BORN AT NEWFOUNDLAND, MAY 1803,
AND DIED AT NEWSTEAD ABBEY, NOVEMBER 18, 1808.

Byron told Joe Murray that he would have him buried in the same vault. But Murray showed scant enthusiasm. "If I was sure his lordship would come here too," he said, "I should like it well enough; but I should not like to lie alone with the dog."

On January 22, 1809, Lord Byron of Newstead celebrated his majority. In the Abbey courtyard an ox was roasted whole for the vassals, and at night a ball took place at which the grave Hanson danced, having come down from London to represent his noble client. An indignant letter from Mrs. Byron denounced these sumptuary expenses. As for the young lord himself, he dined in London on egg and bacon, and a bottle of ale—a frugal meal, yet even that was an infraction of Byron's strict regimen. On the eve of his coming-of-age, he had had news of the death of his friend Edward Long, drowned in a shipwreck on his way to Lisbon. Byron opened his old school-book again, his *Scriptores Græci* of Harrow days, on the cover of which he had written, only four years ago: "Wildman on my left hand, Long on my right . . ." and added:

> *Eheu Lugaces, Posthume! Posthume!*
> *Labuntur anni. . . .*

B. January 9th, 1809.—Of the four persons whose names are here mentioned, one is dead, another in a distant climate, *all* separated, and not five years have elapsed since they sat together in school, and none are yet twenty-one years of age.

The grave was already playing a strangely premature part in this adolescence. No longer was it on the tomb of the unknown Peachey that he would dream, but on that of the dog Boatswain—that is, on his own—and over the resting-places of his vanished friends, and over that wherein lay buried the loves of his childhood. Life was like this, and the Byrons were marked down for woe. So be it. Destiny must just be defied. Dallas, the dutiful Dallas, called at his hotel that evening of his coming-of-age, and found him very brilliant—and more flippant than ever regarding matters of religion.

Nothing remained now but to leave England, and Hobhouse had promised to go with him. But whither bound? Byron had no idea. To the East—to Persia—

to India—to the Tropics perhaps. It mattered little, so long as he could leave Annesley, memories, creditors, all far behind. There was nothing to hold him. The Dowager had become a figure in the distance; and in any case, she would have Newstead during his absence. He only needed to settle up a few urgent affairs.

The first of these was the publication of the satire. At last it had been completed, brilliant, filled to overflowing with venom, and so malicious that Dallas, who was entrusted with finding a publisher, had to try several before he could find one to print it. Not only were the Scottish critics harshly dealt with, but most of the English poets as well: even Thomas Moore, so much admired by the Harrovian youth; and even his own guardian, Lord Carlisle, against whom Byron now harboured fresh grievances. Not only had Carlisle made no acknowledgment of the dedication of *Hours of Idleness,* beyond a letter of cold commonplaces, but he had also wriggled out of complying with his ward's requests for the simplest services. Being now of full age, Byron had formally to take his seat in the House of Lords, and on such occasions it was customary for a young peer to be attended by a relative or friend. He wrote to Carlisle; he received only advice in reply. So Byron went down alone, on March 13, to take his seat in the Upper House.

The obliging Dallas was his only companion, shocked to see a young man of such birth and talents so completely ignored and neglected by his family that not a soul was with him on such a day. Byron himself was cruelly aware of how solitary he was in the world. The privileges of rank and title which would be his were very great. England at that time was entirely ruled by the descendants of a few noble families; and both of the great parties in the State drew their chiefs from that aristocracy of which Byron ought to have been part. The conduct of this aristocracy was still marked by all the freedom of the eighteenth century, and the most immoral actions were instantly forgiven to such of its members as could perpetrate them with sure-handed detachment. It was not surprising that the young Byron should rate his being a lord very highly indeed. But unfortunately his circumstances left him on the outermost fringe of this delightful society. He had the title, but neither the privileges, the friendships, nor the necessary competence.

He was received in the ante-chamber by an official who went to advise the Lord Chancellor of his arrival. There were only a few peers present in the splendid chamber with its gilded woodwork when Byron entered. He passed in front of the Woolsack, where Lord Eldon, the Lord Chancellor, presided over the House, and went forward to the table at which he had to take the oath. At the end of the brief ceremony the Lord Chancellor left his seat, and walked up to him with outstretched hand. Byron gave a stiff salutation, hardly touching Lord Eldon's hand with his fingertips. The Lord Chancellor was hurt, and resumed his place. Byron threw himself carelessly on one of the vacant Opposition benches, and, after a few minutes, rose to join Dallas again outside, remarking to him: "If I had shaken hands heartily he would have set me down for one of his party—but I will have nothing to do with any of them, on either side. I have taken my seat, and now I will go abroad."

A fortnight later *English Bards and Scotch Reviewers*

made its appearance. The satire was highly successful. The steely sureness of the lines pointed to an unmistakable talent. The volume was unsigned, but the name of Lord Byron was attached to it by all the men of letters, by some with rancour, by others admiringly, but by all with astonishment. It was a Roland for an Oliver, and a round had been won; he had nothing left to do in this country. All that he lacked to be off was money. With £12,000 of debts to his name, to whom could Byron turn to borrow the necessary £4,000? Hanson was instructed to find the sum. If need be, he must sell one of his properties; but it must be Rochdale, not Newstead: ". . . come what may, Newstead and I stand or fall together. I have now lived on the spot, I have fixed my heart upon it, and no pressure, present or future, shall induce me to barter the last vestige of our inheritance. I have that pride within me which will enable me to support difficulties. I can endure privations; but could I obtain in exchange for Newstead Abbey the first fortune in the country, I would reject the proposition. . . . Mr. Hanson talks like a man of business on the subject—I feel like a man of honour, and I will not sell Newstead."

One means of salvation would have been to marry a rich heiress. This had been Mrs. Byron's view when she saw her son on the road to ruin "unless, indeed, coal mines turn to gold mines, or that he mends his fortune in the old and usual way by marrying a woman with two or three hundred thousand pounds. . . . He must marry a woman of *fortune* this spring; love matches is all nonsense." And Byron himself wrote: "I suppose it will end in my marrying a *Golden Dolly* or blowing my brains out; it does not much matter which, the remedies are nearly alike." The solution was actually found in the quite unexpected way of a loan from Scrope Davies. The witty and stammering Davies had continued to lead in London the gambling life he had led at Cambridge, losing and winning on a very large scale. His friends would leave him in the small hours, drunk, in some gaming-house, and find him again next day, miraculously returned home, still asleep in the late afternoon, with a chamber-pot beside his bed crammed with several thousands of pounds. Heaven alone knew how they'd been won, and Scrope knew not where. On some such auspicious morning, Davies was able to advance Byron the sum necessary for his travels.

Before setting off, Byron was anxious to arrange a gathering at Newstead of that little Cambridge group whose keen-edged intelligence had been so potent in modelling his own. In May, 1809, the lighthearted Matthews, and Hobhouse the methodical, came to stay at the Abbey. A few days were passed in amusing foolery. The seeming solemnity of the place and its haunting shades gave the spice of contrast to the revelling of the young men. At the entrance, to the right of the steps leading into the hall, was chained a bear; to the left, a wolfhound. If you came in without a call to announce your arrival, you only escaped the bear and the hound to find yourself under the fire of a group of young marksmen practising with their pistols beneath the vaulting. They numbered five, including the young lord of the house. They rose late in the mornings, and breakfast remained on the table until everyone had come down. Then they read, fenced, continued their pistol-practice, went for a ride, rowed on the lake, or played with the bear. Dinner was between seven and eight. And after dinner, they passed round a human skull brimming with burgundy. It was the skull of some monk, whose skeleton had been struck by the gardener's spade. Byron had had it mounted as a cup by a Nottingham jeweller, who had sent it back "with a very high polish, and of a mottled colour like tortoiseshell." On this goblet he had composed the lines:

I lived, I loved, I quaff'd, like thee:
I died: let earth my bones resign;
Fill up—thou canst not injure me;
The worm hath fouler lips than thine.

Better to hold the sparkling grape
Than nurse the earth-worm's slimy hood;
And circle in the goblet's shape
The drink of gods, than reptile's food.

As a final touch to this macabre setting, the guests attired themselves in monkish habits, and Byron, as Abbot of Newstead, or Abbot of the Skull, as his friends called him, presided over the chapter, crosier in hand. The cellar was good, and the servant-maids provided the other pleasures of the company. Byron was quite proud of this little troupe of pretty girls recruited for his household in the neighbouring villages. These lax morals seemed to him feudal and idyllic, not to say flattering as well. In local legend the Abbey was becoming the seat of a new Wicked Lord, and the Newstead horses were coming to forget the Bridal Path of Annesley.

Thus passed the month of May. It was decided that in June Hobhouse and Byron would start together for Gibraltar, and thence go on to Malta and the East. He did not see his sister Augusta before leaving. In 1807 she had married the famous cousin, Colonel Leigh, a gentleman-in-waiting to the Prince Regent, and lived at Six Mile Bottom, near Newmarket. She had given birth to a little daughter during the previous year, and Byron wrote to her: "I return you my best thanks for making me an uncle, and forgive the sex this time; but the next *must* be a nephew. . . . Mrs. Byron I have shaken off for two years, and I shall not resume her yoke in future. . . . I never can forgive that woman, or breathe in comfort under the same roof. I am a very unlucky fellow, for I think I had naturally not a bad heart; but it has been so bent, twisted, trampled upon, that it has now become as hard as a Highlander's heel-piece." Thereafter, letters became few. When the satire was published, Augusta had sided with Lord Carlisle, and for this Byron bore her a grudge. Still another bond was loosening.

Nevertheless, this heart as hard as a Highlander's heelpiece was still very sensitive. Byron made a collection of portraits of his friends to take with him on his travels. Enslaved to that need for clustering his domestic gods around him, he commissioned one of the leading miniaturists of the day to paint portraits of his friends. Yet they were a heartless crew, he found. To make his departure the dramatic climax he would have liked, he wished his friends could themselves have entered into his mood of melancholy. But they were cheerful fellows; they had ridden his horses, drunk his wine, and kissed his wenches; but hypocritical tears they refused. Just as in Harrow days he had been pained by Clare's lukewarmness, so now he complained of men in general. Dallas, during these last days, found him misanthropic, disgusted with life because he was grossly attacked in vile prints, more terrified than ever in feminine society, and talking of friendship in the surly tones of a Timon of Athens execrating humanity on the threshold of his cave.

Before he left he suffered one last disappointment, in the aloofness of Lord Delawarr. True, they had exchanged portraits surmounted by their family crests. But Delawarr was a being without a soul. "Will you believe it?" said Byron to Dallas, "I have just met Delawarr, and asked him to come and sit for an hour with me; he excused himself; and what do you think was his excuse? He was engaged with his mother and some ladies to go shopping! And he knows I set out tomorrow, to be absent for years, perhaps never to return! Friendship! I do not believe I shall leave behind me, yourself and family excepted, and perhaps my mother, a single being who will care what becomes of me." The incident left its mark on him. All his life he was to speak of the way Lord Delawarr had wounded him by deserting him, the eve of his departure, to go to a milliner's with some women. Yes, Timon of Athens was in the right. So long as you had a pottage to give the curs to lap, you could have men's mouths, men's eyes, even men's hearts. But only let them guess that death, or a journey, or ruin, was about to stop you from sharing in their pleasures, and instantly they would leave you bare, exposed to every wind that blows. Delawarr, in going to the milliner's, can never have even faintly imagined that this trifling act would make him the target of such shattering invective.

Matthews behaved better. On the eve of the departure he entertained Hobhouse and Byron to a magnificent dinner. Already the pair had jointly dropped into the tone proper to travellers, one of pleasantry, detachment, and slight artificiality. Before embarking, Byron wrote some stanzas for Mary Musters:

> 'Tis done—and shivering in the gale
> The bark unfurls her snowy sail;
> And whistling o'er the bending mast,
> Loud rings on high the fresh'ning blast;
> And I must from this land begone,
> Because I cannot love but one.

Were these feelings genuine? Was he going away because he loved her still, and could not bear to live near to her? A man is not so simple as that. When he supped with Matthews and Hobhouse, when he laughed as he listened to the irresistible stutter of Scrope Davies, he had scarce a thought for Mrs. Musters. But a first love brands a boy deeply; and of all those fair, sad memories round which Byron loved to weave his sensuous reveries, the Annesley days remained the sharpest.

XIII

CHILDE HAROLD'S FIRST PILGRIMAGE

1809–1811

Lord Byron was the unique object of his own attention.
STENDHAL

ON June 26, 1809, the two friends embarked on Captain Kidd's packet at Falmouth, bound for Lisbon. Hobhouse already revolving archæological notes in his brain, took with him one hundred pens, two gallons of ink, and several volumes of blank paper. And once again Byron had become the lodestone for a whole troop of attendants. The aged Murray was to come as far as Gibraltar, the sea-air being beneficial to his health. The actual duties of bodyservant were entrusted to William Fletcher, the valet from Newstead, who had lately married, and grumbled at being parted from his wife Sally. The train was completed by Robert Rushton, a young page known as Bob, a farmer's son to whom Byron took a fancy "because, like myself, he seems a friendless animal," and by a German valet recommended by Dr. Butler of Harrow.

Hodgson received a description in heroi-comic verse of the departure, and of Hobhouse vomiting forth now his breakfast and now his first travel impressions. "It has pleased Providence to interfere in behalf of a suffering public by giving him a sprained wrist, so that he cannot write, and there is a cessation of ink-shed. . . . I leave England without regret—I shall return to it without pleasure. I am like Adam, the first convict sentenced to transportation, but I have no Eve, and have eaten no apple but what was sour as a crab."

And Mrs. Byron too had her farewell letter: "The world is all before me, and I leave England without regret, and without a wish to revisit anything it contains, except yourself, and your present residence. Believe me, yours ever sincerely. . . ." He had left her the bear, the wolfhound, and the Paphian girls.

The voyage was trying. At Lisbon the travellers came into touch with the Continent at war. The French under Junot had just given place to the English troops of General Crawford. Hobhouse, the president of a radical club, was shocked by the morals of a country where a clerical tyranny ruled supreme. The dead lay exposed in the churches with saucers on their breasts, and their burials waited until enough money had been put in to pay the priest. The Inquisition had not been abolished. Men were impressed for the army in the open street. Byron, more fiery than Hobhouse, and impatient of all constraint for others as for himself, was eager to preach rebellion, but he relished the contrast of the wretchedness of mankind with the beauty of the Portuguese scene. He enjoyed the orange trees gilding the deep green of the valleys, the monasteries perched on the tops of their crags. "I am very happy here, because I loves oranges, and talks bad Latin to the monks, who understand it, as it is like their own—and I goes into society (with my pocket-pistols), and I swims in the Tagus all across at once, and I rides on an ass or a mule, and swears Portuguese, and have got a diarrhœa and bites from the mosquitoes. But what of that? Comfort must not be expected by folks that go a pleasuring."

From Lisbon to Seville they travelled on horseback. The highway was dotted with crosses, each commemorating a murder, and they met a prisoner and some spies who were being taken to Seville to be hanged. In the spectacle of this world where death and love had always something direct, something animal, there was an appeal that went straight to Byron's heart. From Seville he wrote to his mother that he was lodged in the house of two fair Spaniards, and remarked that the women "are, in general, very handsome, with large black eyes, and very fine forms. The eldest honoured your *unworthy* son with very particular attention, embracing him with great tenderness at parting (I was there but three days), after cutting off a lock of his hair, and presenting him with one of her own, about three feet in length, which I send, and beg you will retain till my return. Her last words were, *Adios, tu hermoso! me gusto mucho*—'Adieu, you pretty fellow! you please me much.' She offered me a share of her apartment, which my *virtue* induced me to decline; she laughed, and said I had some English *amante* (lover), and added that she was going to be married to an officer in the Spanish army." And then by way of Cadiz—"sweet Cadiz, full of the finest women in Spain"—the two friends went on to Gibraltar. There they had to part with old Murray and young Rushton, both of whom were worn out with travelling. Byron sent them back to Newstead, and kept only Fletcher with him. To Mrs. Byron he wrote: "Pray take some notice of Robert, who will miss his master; poor boy, he was very unwilling to return."

On board the Malta packet from Gibraltar, Hobhouse was much liked by the passengers. He had mixed with them from the first, and in the evenings, after dinner, told anecdotes over the wine—they nearly all came from Scrope Davies, reflected Byron, listening from afar. Byron was less sociable, and was viewed with less favour. A sparing eater, he left the table before the others, and kept himself aloof, gazing at the sea and seeming to breathe the sombre poetry of the cliffs. With nightfall and the lighting of lamps, he went forward and sat on a roll of sailcloth, where he stayed for hours watching the play of moonbeams on the waves. Wrapped in their pale gleam, he seemed vaguely to recall the figure of Coleridge's Mariner after he had slain the albatross. "He was a mystery in a winding-sheet, crowned in a halo." His fellow-passengers mistook his craving for solitude for mere scornfulness, and judging him harshly, noted the downward glance of his eyes, the perturbed defiance of his mien. He never seemed natural; he handled Fletcher roughly; he seemed restless, ill at ease. Could they have guessed the painful anxiety of spirit masked by this conduct, they would have pitied him. Byron sought refuge in the mute companionship of waves and stars because he was afraid of men. Only, having once assumed an attitude because it was natural to him, he had to keep to it because he thought it noble. As he watched the slow-swinging prow of the vessel cleaving the waters, he reflected that each wave was taking him one step the farther from his shames. Over the failures of his youth he still brooded, but with more of a melancholy pleasure, and as if they were those of a stranger. Why should he not write a poem on this pilgrimage? From childhood there had been violent emotions piling up within him, which now, fermenting in his burning spirit, were forming a sort of molten lava. . . . He conjured up a hero whom he would call by his old family name, Childe Burun, and this would be Byron, the mournful, voluptuous Byron of whom Hobhouse knew nothing, and would understand nothing even if he did. . . . The vessel was dancing in the moonlight.

On the third day out some of the passengers were amusing themselves on deck with pistol-shooting at bottles. Byron joined in, and proved the best shot. This restored his spirits. Hobhouse, whom he had been treating in an offhand way on account of a harmless joke, informed his new friends with kindly but condescending indulgence, that he had to be treated just like a child.

At Malta Byron took lessons in Arabic from a monk, and in platonic love from Mrs. Spencer Smith. This lady had undergone the most romantic adventures, been arrested by Napoleon's soldiery, and rescued by an Italian nobleman who had chivalrously respected her. "Her delicate elegance of bearing," wrote the Duchesse d'Abrantès, "her white, diaphanous skin, her fair hair and willowy movements—a whole bearing impossible to describe except by saying that she was the most graceful of living creatures—all gave her the semblance of an apparition in a happy dream. . . . There was something of the sylph in her." Her charming, short-sighted eyes looked at men with an uncertainty at once troubled and troubling. Byron was fascinated. But his brand-new philosophy of love forbade him to yield, and a naïve grudge against sentiment gave him the will to be unsusceptible.

Fair Florence found, in sooth with some amaze,
One who, 'twas said, still sighed to all he saw,
Withstand, unmoved, the lustre of her gaze.

A "seeming marble heart"—that was how he liked now to see himself, an adept if he chose in that art of seduction which merely consists of a scorn for women and confidence in oneself, but disdainful of conquests too easily made. Was this true? The fair Florence received from Byron the great yellow diamond from the ring he wore, and her lovely, peering eyes were not so soon to vanish from his dreams. But he had no great difficulty in cutting free from this new Calypso.

Albania at this time was an almost unknown country. Its wild mountains reminded Byron of the Scotland he had known in his childhood. The men wore skirts to the knee, not unlike the kilt, and goatskin cloaks. Ali, the Pacha of Yanina, a man renowned for his courage and his cruelty, was informed by the English Minister of the arrival of a young gentleman of noble birth, and invited the travellers to pay him a visit. The background enchanted Byron, the Albanians in their broidered tunics, the Tartars with their high caps, the black slaves, the horses, the drums, the muezzin chanting from the minarets of the mosques, "There is none other God than Allah." The terrible Ali Pacha was a small man, seventy years of age, five-foot-six in height, with a white beard and manners of dignified courtesy. But he notoriously had no hesitation about roasting a foe on a gridiron, or flinging fifteen women into a lake for having annoyed his daughter-in-law. He asked why Byron had left his native country so young, and added that he would instantly have recognised his noble birth by the smallness of his ears, his curling hair, and the whiteness of his hands. These words delighted Byron so much that for several months they appeared in all his letters. Ali Pacha, a

Zeluco in real life, was long to remain one of Byron's heroes. Love of power, scorn of moral and social laws, a taste for enwrapping mystery—the whole personality of Ali moved Byron profoundly. Bandits, corsairs, robber-chiefs—all such beings of the outlawed class appealed to him, through reaction against hypocrisy, and through his appreciation of courage. His sympathy was returned, and the Pacha provided the two Englishmen with guides and an armed escort for their return.

To traverse a wild country under the protection of a half-barbarian soldiery was a bold but intoxicating adventure. Byron discovered, as he imagined, that he was at heart a man of action. He feared nothing. He liked his Albanian warriors, finding them both simple and loyal, and having always a taste for primitive beings who divert the mind without burdening it. It was in their midst, at Yanina, that he began the writing of his *Childe Burun*, which, after the first Canto, became *Childe Harold*. He wrote it in the Spenserian stanza, the nine lines of which, he thought, gave scope for variety of tone. Hobhouse, for his part, was taking notes for a narrative.

From Albania they wanted to go to Greece by sea, but were prevented by a storm and the incompetence of the sailors. "I was nearly lost in a Turkish ship of war, owing to the ignorance of the captain and crew, though the storm was not violent. Fletcher yelled after his wife, the Greeks called on all the saints, the Mussulmans on Allah; the captain burst into tears and ran below deck, telling us to call on God." The sails were torn to shreds, the crew were incapable of handling the vessel, and Fletcher kept repeating, not unplausibly, that they would all find "a watery grave." Byron, whose leg prevented him from helping matters, was worn out by his vain efforts at consoling Fletcher and, wrapping himself in his Albanian cloak, lay down on deck and calmly went to sleep. When he woke the storm had spent itself and the vessel had been stranded on a beach where they were welcomed by Suliotes. This mountain clan of fierce and noble men had managed to remain a free people, serving the Pacha, but always as mercenaries, and paid before entering battle. They had an ugly reputation, but gave the shipwrecked travellers a kindly welcome, dried their clothes for them, fed them, and offered them the spectacle of a dance round the night-fires, and a magnificent song, the refrain of which boasted that they were "robbers all at Parga!" Later, when Byron begged them to accept a few coins, the chief answered him: "I wish you to love me, not to pay me."

The saying pleased Byron. He admired these men of violent passions, adepts in murder and in friendship. His scorn for religions waxed greater. In the space of a few weeks he had seen Catholics and Protestants, the Mussulman and the Orthodox, and found in them all the same human animal. "I like the Albanians much; they are not all Turks; some tribes are Christians. But their religion makes little difference in their manner or conduct." A favourite theme in his letters was the contrast between poor William Fletcher of Newstead who plodded along beneath the rains of the Albanian mountains under an umbrella, and his new native attendants, all indifferent and all splendid. "Fletcher, like all Englishmen, is very much dissatisfied, though a little reconciled to the Turks by a present of eighty piastres from the Vizier. . . . He has suffered nothing but from cold, heat, and vermin, but he is not valiant, and is afraid of robbers and tempests."

Rebuffed by the sea, they decided to reach Greece overland. It was a magnificent ride through the mountains. In the evenings the Suliote escort sang stanzas which Byron, helped by the interpreter, transposed. And at last they reached the plains and halted in a small town called Missolonghi, on the edge of a vast lagoon. They were in Greece.

Byron was stirred. From childhood he had loved this land, through the poets and the writers of history. Nor was he disappointed. To eyes accustomed to the stern northern climes, landscapes wreathed in mist, shifting veils of cloud, this indigo sky and light air, those rocky mountains picked out with touches of ochre and saffron, made up a picture of light and joy. He crossed the Gulf of Lepanto, first as far as the white fortified town of Patras, and then again in the other direction to land at the foot of Parnassus. Every word of the guide kindled a memory. Here was the country of Meleager and Atalanta, the land of the boat of Erymanthus. That snowy ridge seen in the distance was Helicon, and there was a thrill in lying down beside the cave of Pythia. At Delphi Hobhouse and Byron carved their names on the columns of a temple. Huge birds were wheeling overhead. Eagles, said Byron; buzzards, said Hobhouse. But even Hobhouse warmed as they approached Athens. To the natural beauties of the scene were added potent associations: courage, the love of freedom, the taste for beauty, eloquence—the grandest human virtues had sprung from this parched and pure soil.

At last, on December 24, 1809, after riding the

whole morning through the pines and olives, one of the guides called out: "My lord! My lord! The village!" It was Athens. Down there in the plain, some way off, they saw a town clustering round a high rock, and beyond the town, the sea.

The guide's word was exact. Athens at that time was a large village. The Turks were in occupation of the town, and, being more conquerors than administrators, were abandoning it to its fate. In the official café near the bazaar the Agas could be seen squatting and smoking their narghilis. A Turkish garrison was encamped on the Acropolis, to which Byron and Hobhouse climbed, bearing the Ottoman governor a gift of sugar and tea. They were cordially welcomed by this famished functionary, who had to pay his men out of his own allowance of 150 piastres. He walked them round the white fragments of the temples. "Ah, my lord," said Fletcher, "what fine chimneypieces could be made with all this marble!" Byron seemed more interested in the memories of Pericles than in the beauty of the Parthenon. "Well, this is really very grand," said Hobhouse.—"Very like the Mansion House," answered Byron coldly.—Yet he was moved by the contrast between the past splendour of the spot and its present meanness. Was it from Newstead that he had derived this taste for ruined buildings and ruined empires? Did he find there some shadowy symbol of his own destiny? It was more complex. His courage, his need for escape, marked him out as one of those men who are born for a life of action. And he knew it. With admiring envy he followed the meteoric rise of a Bonaparte. But his infirmity doomed him to a lacklustre life, and he savoured at once the grandeur and the hollowness of other men's actions. Just as he used to enjoy sitting amongst the graves on Harrow Hill, so now he took his pleasure brooding over the shattered columns of that vast graveyard of empires that stretches bordered by pines and cypresses, from Gibraltar to the Hellespont.

If the slavery of the populace had shocked him in Portugal, it outraged him still more in the land of Miltiades and Themistocles; and the manuscript of *Childe Harold* was filled with calls to rebellion:

> Fair Greece! sad relic of departed worth!
> Immortal, though no more; though fallen, great!
> Who now shall lead thy scatter'd children forth,
> And long accustom'd bondage uncreate?
> Not such thy sons who whilome did await,
> The hopeless warriors of a willing doom,
> In bleak Thermopylæ's sepulchral strait—
> Oh! who that gallant spirit shall resume,
> Leap from Eurota's banks, and call thee from the tomb?

"What can I do?" said a young Athenian to him one day, when Byron had been reproaching him with submissiveness.

"Slave!" cried Byron. "You are not worthy to bear the name of Greek! What can you do? Avenge yourself!"

Hobhouse and he had rented rooms in two neighbouring houses, Byron with the widow of a British vice-consul, Mme. Theodora Macri. An open balcony looked down on an inner courtyard, where a lemon tree grew and three young girls came and played. Byron could not miss this opportunity of falling in love, with Greece rather than a Greek. "I almost forgot to tell you that I am dying for love of three Greek girls at Athens, sisters. I lived in the same house. Teresa, Mariana and Katinka are the names of these divinities—all of them under fifteen." For Teresa, the eldest, he wrote a poem:

Maid of Athens, ere we part,
Give, oh, give me back my heart!
Or, since that has left my breast,
Keep it now, and take the rest!
Hear my vow before I go,
Ζώη μοῦ οχς ἀγαπῶ

"My life, I love you"—a fine refrain, though in point of fact it was Childe Harold rather than Byron who loved Teresa. Nevertheless, it was for her that, following an Eastern love-usage he had been told of, he one day tore his breast with the point of his dagger. She accepted the gesture with the utmost calm, as a homage due to her beauty.

The French consul, Fauriel, accompanied them through Attica. Through groves of olive and meadows of asphodel they proceeded as far as Cape Sunium. The white columns of a temple enframed the "purple sea," and on one of them Byron, the eternal schoolboy, wrote his name. Then, seated on the marble steps, he drank in the calm of the promontory where he was alone with the waves. He felt very happy. This perpetual springtime, this cloudless sky, were heavenly. He grew attached to the Greeks. "They are ungrateful," he said, "but who has ever done the Greek people a service?" What gratitude need they owe to their Turkish oppressors—to the English who robbed the Acropolis of its masterpieces—to the French who gave them advice and no help? Byron was furious to see Lord Elgin's agents negligently spoiling the metopes of the Parthenon. Even the Turkish governor wept when he saw one of the pediments being smashed. All the same, for all his love of the Greeks, Byron got along well with the Turks. The town prefect was so attentive as to beat a man who had insulted the two Englishmen, with fifty blows of a rod in the presence of Fletcher. Hobhouse was gratified, and made a note: "Whatever I may think of it at home, abroad autocracy has its advantages."

A pilgrim can make no halt. An English vessel, the *Pylades,* was setting out for Smyrna; they took passage on board. Amid the Isles they were rocked by the waves of the sea of Ulysses, waves the colour of wine-lees, with crests of opal. And at Smyrna Byron completed the second Canto of his poem. Hobhouse had no great opinion of it. Exaggerated sentiments, he kept saying, and rhetorical declamation; he preferred Pope. Byron himself, very fond of eighteenth-century poetry, was almost astounded by what had been the spontaneous expression of his emotions; but he stuffed the manuscript away at the bottom of his portmanteau. He would find some other path to fame.

The frigate which brought them from Smyrna to Constantinople put in at the Isle of Tenedos. From there he saw the entrance to the Dardanelles, the narrow cleft that separates two continents. A swift tide flowed like a river between two high banks, bare and dull-hued. And that was the Hellespont, where Leander had swum across to join his lover. Byron was eager to imitate him. He made two attempts. The first failed, but on May 3 he succeeded, swimming from Europe to Asia and remaining an hour and a half in the water. His companion, Mr. Ekenhead, beat him by five minutes. Neither of them was tired, only rather chilled, and Byron was prodigiously proud of himself. He wrote to his mother, to Hodgson, to the whole world, that he had swum from Sestos to Abydos, and the exploit, together with complaints about Fletcher, and the praise bestowed by Ali Pacha on the smallness of his ears, became one of the main themes of his letters. "I shall begin by telling you, having only told it you twice before, that I swam from Sestos to Abydos. I do this that you may be impressed with proper respect for me, the performer; for I plume myself over this achievement more than I could possibly do on any kind of glory, political, poetical, or rhetorical."

During this stay on Tenedos he saw the Troad. Mount Ida, calling up memories of Harrow, overlooked the Trojan plain; of the city there remained nothing but the tombs of its destroyers, large mounds that recalled the Danish barrows in parts of the English countryside. Faithful to his taste for the final void and the sleep of heroes, Byron lingered in meditation before the tomb of Achilles. And then the frigate set sail for Constantinople, dropping anchor between the Seraglio and the Seven Towers on May 13, 1810.

It was the situation of Stamboul that Byron chiefly enjoyed—the European and Asian slopes all dotted with palaces, the gilded cupola of St. Sophia, the island of Prinkipo faintly sketched in the distance. St. Sophia itself struck him as decidedly inferior to St. Paul's in London. "I speak like a cockney," he said. It was true. Hobhouse's judgment was that the oriental bazaars are "not very striking buildings to one acquainted with the shops and wealth of London." Still, it was interesting to stroll among the tombs of the Sultans, in a scarlet uniform broidered with gold, and a plumed hat, and followed up by the janissaries whom Byron had of course engaged. The Ambassador, Sir Robert Adair, and his secretary, Stratford Canning, treated the pair of pilgrims as persons of importance, and they were presented to the Chief Pacha. Regarding the visit to the Government palace, a dispute of etiquette arose between Lord Byron and Mr. Canning, and as the latter refused to take second place in the procession, Byron left it. He sulked for three days, and then wrote a dignified letter acknowledging that he had been wrong. He went down the Bosphorus again, and went to sit on the blue rocks of the Symplegades which stand sentinel at its entrance and, as the ancients declared, closed in to crush passing vessels. He did nothing all day long but smoke, ride on horseback, and row across to Sweet Waters on the Asiatic side; but he was satisfied. Fletcher was the sole thorn in his flesh: "the perpetual lamentations after beef and beer, the stupid, bigoted contempt for everything foreign, and the insurmountable incapacity of acquiring even a few words of any language, rendered him, like all other English servants, an incumbrance. I do assure you, the plague of speaking for him, the comforts he required (more than myself by far), the pilaws which he could not eat, the wines which he could not drink, the beds where he could not sleep, and the long list of calamities, such as stumbling horses, want of tea, etc., which assailed him, would have made a lasting source of laughter to a spectator and inconvenience to a master."

At last, on July 24, 1810, Byron and Hobhouse left Constantinople. Hobhouse returned to England; Byron wished to make another stay at Athens. There was no grief in their parting. For a year they had made good-humoured fun of each other, but a long voyage is a stern test of a friendship and a change was welcome. To his mother Byron wrote: "I am very glad to be once more alone, for I was sick of my companion,—not that he was a bad one, but because my nature leads me to solitude, and that every day adds to this disposition." The parting was agreeably pathetic; Hobhouse described it in his journal: "Took leave, *non sine lacrymis,* of this singular young person, on a little stone terrace at the end of the bay, dividing with him a little nosegay of flowers; the last thing perhaps that I shall ever divide with him." Hobhouse's letter to Byron after their parting ended with the following postscript: "I kept the half of your little nosegay till it withered entirely, and even then I could not bear to throw it away. I can't account for this, nor can you either, I dare say." He was fond of Byron, fonder than he would say. As for Childe Harold, the sentimentalist in verse was by no means so in prose. "Your last letter," he said, "closes pathetically with a postscript about a nosegay; I advise you to introduce that into your next sentimental novel. I am sure I did not suspect you of any fine feelings, and I believe you were laughing, but you are welcome."

During his second sojourn in Athens Byron lodged at the monastery of the Capucins. It was a beautiful place, Hymettus in front, the Acropolis behind, with the Temple of Zeus on the right and the town to the left. "Eh, Sir, there's a situation, there's your picturesque! Nothing like that, Sir, in Lunnon, no not even the Mansion House." The monument of Lysicrates was enclosed within the monastery buildings, a charming little circular temple out of which the monks had made a library, opening on a grove of orange trees. The life led in this monastery was none too sanctified. Besides the *Padre Abbate* there was a *scuola* consisting of six adolescent *ragazzi,* three of whom were Catholics, and three Orthodox. Byron organised boxing contests between Catholics and Orthodox, and the abbot rejoiced to see the Catholics win. The life was like that of a school, gay, noisy and licentious, and Byron, who had never ceased to regret his Harrow friends, joined in it with boyish delight. He had conceived one of his protective passions for young Nicolo Giraud, a new Edleston, a French protégé, a Greek subject, who spoke Italian and taught Byron that language. "I am his 'Padrone' and his 'amico' and the Lord knows what besides. It is about two hours since, that, after informing me that he was most desirous to follow me over the world, he concluded by telling me it was proper for us not only to live, but *morire insieme.*"

The days were long peals of laughter. Byron was roused in the morning by these young Italian sprites crying, *"Venite abasso!"*—to which the voice of the brother gravely replied, *"Bisogno bastonare."* Intrigues were past counting. The mother of Teresa Macri had reappeared on the scene. "She was mad enough to imagine I was going to marry the girl: but I have better amusement." Fletcher, the married man who had so loudly bewailed the separation from his Sally, had taken a Greek mistress; and the two Albanian servants and the interpreter had followed his example. "Vive l'amour!" wrote Byron to Hobhouse. "I chatter with everybody, good or bad, and tradute prayers out of the mass ritual: but my lessons are sadly interrupted by scamperings, and eating fruit, and peltings and playings: and I am, in fact, at school again, and make as little improvement now as I did there, my time being wasted in the same way." In the evenings there were amazing receptions of Turkish dignitaries at the Reverend Abbot's. The Mufti of Thebes and the Governor of Athens got drunk, despite Mohammed, and the Attic feast shone brilliantly.

Naturally he had to swim across the Piræus. The boy Nicolo was a poor swimmer. As Byron was diving from the breakwater an English voice hailed him from a vessel near by. It was the Marquis of Sligo, a Harrow friend, who was on board a brig that belonged to him, in company with Lady Hester Stanhope. Byron was quite well pleased to meet them, and made several excursions with them; but he was far from being so natural with these English people as he was with his young Italians. Lady Hester was rather severe: "he had a great deal of vice in his looks—his eyes set close together, and a contracted brow. . . . Strange character: his generosity was for a motive; one time he was mopish, and nobody was to speak to him; another, he was for being jocular with everybody." One contact with English company, and the frail structure of his happiness quivered. Their presence alone sufficed to conjure up a society for which Byron had both a conscious horror and an unconscious respect. Once away from boys or from foreigners, he was haunted by the preoccupation of what people might think of him. He knew that he was a crazy, outlandish fellow. He had childish superstitions, and strange habits, such as that of always having loaded pistols at his bedside. He did not like being observed. Hobhouse himself had been cramping, and if Fletcher frequently irritated his master, it was largely because, even in this wild Athenian life, amid the orange trees, the boy monks and the Turks, the Sancho of Newstead still persisted, a slightly comical but none the less formidable guardian of the Conventions.

During this second stay Byron made several expeditions into the Morea, going as far as Tripolitza, and always making a halt at Patras, where the British consul, Mr. Strané, acted as his banker. He liked this port where the vessels with their painted hulls, recalling the fleet of Agamemnon, unfurled their sails beneath the steep white town. But it was an unhealthy spot; when the wind blew across from Missolonghi, and in the mosquito season, malaria reigned supreme. Byron, badly looked after, very nearly died of it. What could a poor devil with fever do against a murderous doctor? He wrote a little epitaph for himself:

> Youth, Nature, and relenting Jove,
> To keep my lamp *in* strongly strove;
> But Romanelli was so stout,
> He beat all three—and *blew* it *out*.

Fletcher had lost his head; but fortunately his Albanian attendants nursed him, and told the doctor that they would kill him if their master died. Was it this threat, or Jove, or youth? At last Byron picked up again. This illness had enabled him to judge how little he clung to life. There he lay, alone, his teeth chattering with fever, two months by sea from his native land. "I looked to death as a relief from pain, without a wish for an after life, but a confidence that the God who punishes in this existence had left that last asylum for the weary." And he added, in Greek: "He whom the gods love dies young."

He returned to Athens worn out and very pale, and the régime that he followed to preserve his slimness and beauty was certainly not one to build up his strength—a Turkish bath three times a week, his drink a compound of water and vinegar, and rice as his sole nourishment. His life throughout that winter was much the same as before his illness. He worked a little, and wrote a couple of satires, one in the manner of Pope, *Hints from Horace,* and the other a piece of slashing invective against Lord Elgin, *The Curse of Minerva.* One day he asked one of the Capucins, Father Paul d'Yvrée, if he could be allowed to inhabit one of the cells. Perhaps a monastic life would save him from his boredom and melancholy. He said that he was no atheist, and asked the father for a crucifix, which he kissed with tears. Religion, like everything, had to be a strong sensation for Byron.

Hanson was sending no further remittances and was demanding the presence of his client to defend Newstead and Rochdale, which were threatened by creditors and lawyers. Alas, he must go home! And Fletcher was sent off as advance guard, laden with baggage and a letter for Mrs. Byron: "Pray take care of my books and several boxes of papers, and pray leave me a few bottles of champagne to drink, for I am very thirsty. . . . I suppose you have your house full of silly women, prating scandalous things."

Travel had improved Fletcher, and he was less insular. "Fletcher, after having been toasted and roasted, and baked, and grilled, and eaten by all sorts of creeping things, begins to philosophise, is grown a refined as well as a resigned character, and promises at his return to become an ornament to his own parish, and a very prominent person in the future family pedigree of the Fletchers."

A few weeks after the valet, the master himself embarked on the *Volage* frigate, Nicolo Giraud accompanying him as far as Malta. He brought home two Greek servants; one of the Albanian servitors, whom he had to dismiss, rushed from his room in tears. "For my own part, when I remembered that, a short time before my departure from England, a noble and most intimate associate had excused himself from taking leave of me because he had to attend a female relation to a milliner's, I felt no less surprised than humiliated by the present occurrence and the past recollection."

From Malta the voyage took thirty-four days. He was alone, without interesting companions, but he liked his solitude. All in all he had not been unhappy on these travels of his. He had been nearly wrecked in a Turkish boat, enjoyed a passion for a married lady at Malta, visited a Pacha, loved three young Greeks in Athens, crossed the Dardanelles, written some verses, and learnt Italian in the monastery. He had viewed splendid scenery, evoked heroic memories, recaptured six months of youth. He had talked with Frenchmen, Italians, Greeks, Turks, and Americans, and had been able to estimate the ideas and manners of other countries. A century of smoking in the London clubs, or yawning in a country-house, could not have given him a tithe of the useful and amusing knowledge he now possessed.

It is always interesting to observe, in the course of a life, the gradual formation of the stony strata which, hardened by time, will shape and limit a man's character. On the ancestral basis of Gordon violence and Byron sensuality, there had been laid a physical deposit, in an infirmity inspiring hatred of the world and a beauty giving the means of avenging himself. On the gloomy and narrow religion taught by his first Scottish masters, there had been superimposed, but without destroying the first, the Voltairean deism of the Cambridge undergraduates, and on the ingenuous sentimentalism of adolescence, a strongly ironical humour. The view of the universe which now graced this inner landscape was simple. This world had been created, for no object known to ourselves, by a God who seemed indifferent to our ills. Moved by their passions, men pursued either agreeable sensations, which was wise, or fame, which was foolish. Empires rose and sank like the waves of the sea. All was vanity, save pleasure.

This teaching had been strongly confirmed by his journeying in the Orient. Go where he might, Byron found life a stern business, vice omnipresent, and death both easy and close at hand. The fatalism of Islam had reinforced his own. Its treatment of women had satisfied him. The multiplicity of religions was proof of their weakness. He brought back doubts, as solid as acts of faith. His long solitude had taught him some truths regarding himself. He knew now that he was happy only as an outlaw, and had loved those lands where he cared not about anybody and where none had cared about him. Distance had taught him contempt. How could you grow excited over a pedant's hostile essay when the Atlantic and the Mediterranean rolled between you and him, when the thunder of hyperborean reviews was dulled by the moaning of the Hellespont? Henceforth he would know that, if things went askew with him in England, a fortnight of sea would bring him to white islands beneath a sky for ever blue.

Alone on the deck of the frigate he watched the waves rise and fall. To what was this long passage bringing him? To his mother? He had no intention of seeing her for a long time. "You will be good enough to get my apartments ready at Newstead; but don't consider me in any other light than as a visiter. I must only inform you that for a long time I have been restricted to an entire vegetable diet, neither fish nor flesh; so I expect a powerful stock of potatoes, greens, and biscuit; I drink no wine. I have two servants, middle-aged men, and both Greeks. . . . I don't suppose I shall be much pestered with visiters; but if I am, you must receive them, for I am determined to have nobody breaking in on my retirement: you know that I never was fond of society, and I am less so than before. I have brought you a shawl, and a quantity of attar of roses." As a landlord, his sole desire was to split up the farm of a certain B——— in order to provide Fletcher with a small property. "I shall not interfere further than (like Buonaparte) by dismembering Mr. B———'s kingdom, and erecting part of it into a principality for field-marshal Fletcher! I hope you govern my little empire and its sad load of national debt with a wary hand."

Apart from her, whom would he find? Hobhouse? But of Hobhouse he had no news; it was said that he had adopted the "monstrous disguise" of a soldier. Hodgson? Yes, certainly; but Hodgson had become pious. Augusta? He had all but forgotten Augusta. What the deuce was he going to do in this country? Extract his farmers' rents at Newstead, sell coal at Rochdale, pay debts in London—mean tasks all. Whom would he see? Ah, there was Dallas, the solemn and serviceable Dallas. A few days before arrival he wrote to Dallas: "After two years' absence, I am retracing my way to England. . . . I have seen everything most remarkable in Turkey, particularly the Troad, Greece, Constantinople and Albania. . . . I don't know that I have done anything to distinguish myself from other voyagers, unless you will reckon my swimming from Sestos to Abydos, on May 3d, 1810, a tolerable feat for a modern."

PART II

He was born with too tender, too loving a heart; but his over-expansive sensibility had attracted the mockery of his comrades. He was proud and ambitious, clinging to others' opinion as children do, and so he studied particularly to hide every outward sign of what he regarded as a dishonouring weakness. He achieved his aim, but his victory cost him dear. He was able to screen from others the emotions of his over-tender soul, but in shutting them within himself, he made them a hundred times more cruel.

PROSPER MÉRIMÉE

The great object of life is sensation—to feel that we exist, even though in pain. It is this "craving void" which drives us to gaming—to battle—to travel—to intemperate, but keenly felt, pursuits of any description, whose principal attraction is the agitation inseparable from their accomplishment.

BYRON

XIV

TIMON OF NEWSTEAD

1811–1812

"You're getting damned romantic."
"No, bored."

ERNEST HEMINGWAY

HE stopped at Reddish's Hotel in St. James's Street. He had brought back the shawl and the attar of roses for his mother, some marbles for Hobhouse, and for himself a phial of Attic hemlock, four Athenian skulls, and some live tortoises. Dallas had been looking out for his arrival for several days, and immediately turned up. Byron seemed to be in good spirits and talked of his travels with animation; Dallas asked whether he had brought back a narrative. No, "he had never had the least idea of writing about them; he believed satire to be his *forte,* and to that he had adhered, having written . . . a Paraphrase of Horace's *Art of Poetry*." He seemed to be satisfied with that, and entrusting Dallas with the manuscript, asked him to come back next morning.

Dallas spent the day in reading these *Hints from Horace*. . . . He was fond of young Byron, and was heartily eager to find good in the poem, but—what a disappointment! Was this all that had come out of two years of travel and adventure? A chilly pastiche, some labored jesting, no freshening of form or of thought? He returned to Reddish's Hotel next morning in some embarrassment, with a few mumbled compliments, and asked whether he had not written anything else. . . . Yes, Byron had also brought home a few short poems, and a large number of stanzas on the voyage. They did not deserve to be read, but if Dallas liked, he would make him a present of them—and he pulled a bundle of papers from a trunk. Dallas had to promise to have the paraphrase of Horace published at the earliest possible date, and went off carrying *Childe Harold's Pilgrimage* under his arm.

> Whilome in Albion's isle there dwelt a youth,
> Who he in virtue's way did take delight;
> But spent his days in riot most uncouth,
> And vex'd with mirth the drowsy ear of Night. . . .
>
> Childe Harold was he hight:—but whence his name
> And lineage long, it suits me not to say;
> Suffice it, that perchance they were of fame,
> And had been glorious in anotner day. . . .
>
> Childe Harold bask'd him in the noontide sun,
> Disporting there like any other fly;
> Nor deem'd before his little day was done
> One blast might chill him into misery.
> But long ere scarce a third of his pass'd by,
> Worse than adversity the Childe befell;
> He felt the fulness of satiety:
> Then loathed he in his native land to dwell,
> Which seem'd to him more lone than Eremite's sad cell.
>
> For he through Sin's long labyrinth had run,
> Nor made atonement when he did amiss,
> Had sigh'd to many though he lov'd but one,
> And that lo'd one, alas! could ne'er be his. . . .

Byron! Here at last was the real Byron, whom Dallas found in these disdained verses. It was all there: his mother, his sister—

Childe Harold had a mother, not forgot,
Though parting from that mother he did shun;
A sister whom he loved, but saw her not
Before his weary pilgrimage begun. . . .

his Abbey—

Monastic dome! condemn'd to uses vile!
Where Superstition once had made her den,
Now Paphian girls were known to sing and smile. . . .

No doubt the poem was lacking in plan and order; no doubt the Paphian girls had been the girls from the farm, and the labyrinth of Sin a booth at a village fair. But the sentiment inspiring their slightly factitious eloquence was sincere. Dallas found here Byron's misanthropy, his luxurious ennui, the gloomy pleasure that he found in declaring the emptiness of all human affairs.

Ancient of days! August Athene! where,
Where are thy men of might? thy grand in soul?
Gone—glimmering through the dream of things that were;
First in the race that led to Glory's goal,
They won, and pass'd away—is this the whole?
A schoolboy's tale, the wonder of an hour!
The warrior's weapon and the sophist's stole
Are sought in vain, and o'er each mouldering tower,
Dim with the mist of years, gray flits the shade of power.

Dallas could not contain his enthusiasm, and on the evening of the 16th he wrote to Byron, who had gone on a pilgrimage to Harrow: "You have written one of the most delightful poems I ever read. . . . I have been so fascinated by *Childe Harold* that I have not been able to lay it down." But on seeing Byron again he was amazed to hear him speak of this work with a quite unfeigned contempt. "It was anything but poetry." He had shown the poem to a good critic, who had damned it—hadn't Dallas noticed the marignal comments on the manuscript? The important thing was to find a prompt publisher for *Horace*. Dallas had the good sense to hold his ground: "I am so convinced of the merit of *Childe Harold* that as you have given it to me, I shall certainly publish it."

Byron had written to his mother that he was detained in London by Hanson for the signing of some papers, and that he would visit her as soon as he could. It was rather a cold letter for a son coming back after two years' absence; it began with "My dear Madam," but the closing paragraph had a cordial air to it—"You will consider Newstead as your house, not mine; and me only as a visiter." Was the solitary matron pleased at this homecoming? During those two years she had gone through many agonies. During her stay at Newstead she had made it her pride to lay no penny of expense on her son, with her own pension she could support herself and one servant, but not the gardener. She had suggested to Hanson getting rid of the gardener: "it can be no advantage to Lord Byron's property to have the gardens kept in order, as they produce nothing that can sell." And she sent Hanson the accounts:

For labourers in the garden	£156
— a game keeper	39
— Joe Murray	50
— a female servant	30
— a wolf-dog	20
— a bear	20
— taxes	70
Total	£385

Well, she had not got £385 a year—what was to be done? "I have reduced my expense here as much as possible. The female servant I sent off nearly a year ago. Two of the dogs I have sent to the farmers to keep them for nothing; the bear, poor animal, died suddenly about a fortnight ago." A true Catherine Gordon letter—she got rid of a servant to save expense and kept a bear to its dying day.

Ever since Byron's departure she had been haunted by the idea that she would not see him again. When she got his letter from London she said to her maid, "If I should die before Byron comes down, what a strange thing it would be!" That same week she fell ill—a trifling indisposition, but one which was made serious by her stoutness and a fortuitous incident. An upholsterer's bill provoked a burst of passion, in the course of which she had a stroke, and she died without recovering consciousness.

Byron was still in London, arguing with Dallas and busy with an action against a pamphleteer for defamation of character. He was just making ready to leave for Newstead and Rochdale when he was told of his mother's illness, and next day, August 1, he had news of her death. He had always believed in coincidence; the Fate of the Byrons had contrived the cruellest and most shocking of catastrophes for this homecoming. On the way he wrote to Pigot: "My poor mother died yesterday! and I am on my way to attend her to the family vault. . . . Thank God her last moments were most tranquil. I am told she was in little pain and not aware of her situation. I now feel the truth of Mr. Gray's observation, 'That we can only have one mother.' Peace be with her!" On his arrival at the Abbey the domestics told him about the apoplectic seizure. During the night Mrs. By, one of the house servants, heard deep sighs, entered, and found him seated beside the corpse. "Ah, Mrs. By!" he said, bursting into tears, "I had but one friend in the world and she is gone!" An artifice of sentiment? Certainly not. Beneath all their bitter quarrels there had subsisted the sense of a profound link, forged of their kindred natures. She was dead; and death, which makes human beings the subject of sorrowful and poetic musing, attached Byron to the memories of their link. That evening he wrote to Hobhouse: "There is to me something so incomprehensible in death, that I can neither speak nor think on the subject. Indeed, when I looked on the mass of corruption which was the being from whence I sprung, I doubted within myself whether I was, or whether she was not. I have lost her who gave me being, and some of those who made that being a blessing. I have neither hopes nor fears beyond the grave." On the day of the burial he refused to follow the funeral procession. Standing in the Abbey door, he watched the body of his mother, followed by the tenant farmers, move off towards the little church of Hucknall Torkard. Then he summoned the lad Robert Rushton, with whom he used to box—and told him to fetch the gloves. His silence, and the unwonted violence of the blows, were the only betrayal of his feelings.

Two days later he heard that the charming and cynical Matthews had been drowned in the Cam. Caught in the water-weeds, he had vainly struggled to free himself in the course of a long and terrible agony. How often had Byron said to him, "You swim badly, Matthews; if you persist in keeping your head so high, you will drown yourself!" What a homecoming! His mother . . . and one of his best friends. . . . The invisible Foe was striking swift and hard. "Indeed the blows followed each other so rapidly that I am yet stupid from the shock. . . . Some curse hangs over me and mine. My mother lies a corpse in this house; one of my best friends is drowned in a ditch. What can I say, or think, or do? . . . Peace be with the dead! Regret cannot wake them. With a sigh to the departed, let us resume the dull business of life, in the certainty that wc also shall have our repose."

Alone in his vast Abbey, surrounded by his strange talismans—the monk's skull, the skulls of the Athenians, Boatswain's empty collar—he called to mind the merry evenings he had spent in this same room, with Hobhouse and Matthews. He wrote inviting Hobhouse to come; and they both drank to the memory of Matthews. "We will drink to his memory, which though it cannot reach the dead, will soothe the survivors, and to them only death can be an evil." Pending this visit, or one from Hodgson, he was alone, alone with his dogs, his hedgehogs, his tortoises, "and other Greeks." He yawned. "At twenty-three I am left alone, and what more can we be at seventy? It is true I am young enough to begin again, but with whom can I retrace the laughing part of life?" He had once more begun his reveries on the sofa, chewing tobacco the while, a new habit he had acquired in order to stave off his hunger. He might have seen something of the local gentry; but "I am not a social animal, and should feel sadly at a loss amongst Countesses and Maids of Honour, particularly being just come from a far country, where ladies are neither craved for, or fought for, or danced after, or mixed at all (publicly) with the men-folks, so that you must make allowance for my natural diffidence after two years' travel."

No, no—he would not go courting a second Mary Chaworth. He busied himself with his "sensual comfort." The squad of Paphian girls had been dispersed. He brought back the prettiest, and restocked the estate: "the partridges are plentiful, hares fairish, pheasants not quite so good, and the girls on the manor. . . . As I am a great disciplinarian, I have just issued an edict for the abolition of caps; no hair to be cut, on any pretext; stays permitted, but not too low before. . . . Lucinda to be commander of all the makers and unmakers of beds in the household." Thus, in the life of Newstead, just as in the mediæval sculptor's Dance of Death, the bare, youthful bodies would alternate with skeletons and skulls.

He worked little. No new poems. His sole amusement was in loading *Childe Harold,* the proofs of which he was beginning to receive, with prose notes. Dallas, a devout believer, had protested against such stanzas of *Childe Harold* as recorded the multiplicity of mankind's religious beliefs only to deduce their common weakness. "Although among feeble and corrupt men religions may take their turn; although Jupiter and Mahomet, and error after error, may enter the brain of misguided mortals, it does not follow that there is not a true religion. . . . Although a skull well affords a subject for moralizing, although in its worm-eaten state, no saint, sage, or sophist can refit it,—it does not follow that God's power is limited, or that what is sown in corruption may not be raised in incorruption." Whereupon the immortality of the soul had been restored by Byron to the rank of an amiable hypothesis, and the eighth stanza of the second Canto became:

> Yet if, as holiest men have deem'd, there be
> A land of souls beyond that sable shore,
> To shame the doctrine of the Sadducee
> And sophists, madly vain of dubious lore;
> How sweet it were in concert to adore
> With those who made our mortal labours light! . . .

Here and there he added a stanza to celebrate a dead friend, and Mrs. Byron, Wingfield and Matthews had each their funerary stele. And to his dead Byron added Edleston, the Cambridge chorister, donor of the cornelian. Like the rest, he had his stanza—and also a poem on a broken heart, and the verses *To Thyrza.*

In happier times Byron would have long mourned for Edleston, but he had now, as he said, almost lost the sense of grief, and was sated with horrors. After so many proofs, how could he doubt Fate's hostility? He was now certain that any person to whom he might become attached would, by that very affection, be doomed.

Since returning, Byron had once again exchanged a few letters with his sister Augusta. He had not seen her again, but he knew she was unhappy. The Colonel Leigh whom she had so warmly desired to marry was a libertine and gambler, who left his home for ten months in the year, and only came back to attend the Newmarket races and give his wife a child. "I am losing my relatives and you are adding to the number of yours; but which is best, God knows. . . ." The tone of their correspondence had altered. Byron was no longer the young brother seeking protection; although Augusta was already twenty-seven, he felt much older than his sister, somewhat tender too, and paternal. "Good even, child," he ended his letters. She was slightly intimidated by this brother, now a stranger to her, girt with the glamour of distant travels. "I began a letter to you, but destroyed it, from the fear of appearing troublesome." Nevertheless, she used to write. They were the long, obscure letters of a woman always being upset by a crying child or the grumblings of an ill-paid servant, the sentences cluttered up with dashes, exclamation marks, and words and phrases underlined. She was insistent that he should marry: "I am so very glad to hear you have sufficiently overcome your prejudices against the fair sex to have determined upon marrying; but I shall be most anxious that my future Belle-Sœur should have more attractions than merely money, though to be sure *that* is somewhat necessary."

On marriage as on so many other matters, Byron was a slave to Convention. A ruined young nobleman marries to regild his scutcheon. He does not love his wife—that would be laughable—but he makes her respected by others, and he is attached to the children who will carry on his race and name. Such was Newstead law. And Byron answered Augusta: "As to Lady Byron, when I discover one rich enough to suit me and foolish enough to have me, I will give her leave to make me miserable if she can. Money is the magnet; as to women, one is as well as another, the older the better, we have then a chance of getting her to Heaven. . . . You ask after my health; I am in tolerable leanness, which I promote by exercise and abstinence. I don't know that I have acquired anything by my travels but a smattering of two languages and a habit of chewing tobacco."

The pose was agreeable; the price of his contempt for men and women was a rather irksome solitude, but the contempt had its charms. He was Lord Byron, Baron Byron of Rochdale, Timon of Newstead, misanthrope. Since Boatswain's death he loved nobody but the Newfoundland's memory, a famished roebuck, and three Greek tortoises. He would marry an aged heiress, and as for his property. . . . He drew up a curious testament, whereby Newstead would pass to George Anson Byron; Rochdale was to be sold, the proceeds of the sale being devoted to a payment of the enormous sum of £7,000 to Nicolo Giraud, of Athens and Malta, on his majority, while Fletcher, Joe Murray and the Greek servant, Demetrius Zograffo, would each receive £50 a year, and Robert Rushton the same sum as well as £1,000 on his majority. The mill of Newstead he bequeathed to Fletcher, and his library to Hobhouse and Scrope Davies. And he added: "The body of Lord Byron to be buried in the vault of the garden of Newstead, without any ceremony or burial-service whatever, or any inscription, save his name and age. His dog not to be removed from the said vault." The lawyers protested against this clause, but Byron was insistent and had it retained.

He made several journeys to London during October and November, and then returned to spend Christmas at Newstead. Winter came; the lawns were covered with snow, and the almost empty Abbey was pleasantly melancholy. He had visits from two friends. One of these, William Harness, was the slightly crippled boy whom he had befriended at Harrow, and the other was his Cambridge friend, Hodgson, who was preparing for Holy Orders. Harness was twenty-one, Byron twenty-three, Hodgson twenty-eight. Those three weeks passed pleasantly. Byron was adding finishing touches to *Childe*

Harold, the others worked on their own concerns, and in the evenings they discussed poetry or religion. Since his travels Byron had very definite ideas on this latter theme: "Christ came to save men; but a good pagan will go to heaven, and a bad Nazarene to hell. . . . If mankind may be saved who never heard or dreamt, at Timbuctoo, Otaheite, Terra Incognita, of Galilee and its prophet, Christianity is of no avail: if they cannot be saved without, why are not all orthodox? It is a little hard to send a man preaching to Judæa, and leave the rest of the world—negers and what not—dark as their complexions, without a ray of light to lead them on high; and who will believe that God will damn men for not knowing what they were never taught?"

Hodgson, budding clergyman though he was, found difficulty in driving Byron from his metaphysical stronghold because he held no definite position: "I am no Platonist, I am nothing at all; but I would sooner be anything than one of the seventy-two sects who are tearing each other to pieces for the love of the Lord. . . . As to your immortality, if people are to live, why die? And our carcasses, which are to rise again, are they worth raising? I hope, if mine is, that I shall have a better pair of legs than I have moved on these two-and-twenty years, or I shall be sadly behind in the squeeze into Paradise."

After the vacation the visitors left him and he was alone, bereft even of his servant-mistresses, for he had just discovered that one of them, of whom he was rather fond, was deceiving him with a yokel. A trifling episode, if it had not affected him in an extraordinary way. When he narrated the story to Hodgson, he asked him as a favour, never to speak of a woman in any of his letters, nor even to make the slightest allusion to the existence of that sex. Really, there was nothing in the wide world one could lean upon. He thought with regrets of the cries of the Italian boys beneath the orange trees, beside the monument of Lysicrates. "I am growing nervous. . . . Your climate kills me; I can neither read, write, nor amuse myself, nor anyone else. My days are listless and my night restless, I have very seldom any society and when I have, I run out of it." What was to be done in wintry, funereal Newstead? Go on with *Childe Harold?* He would have needed sunshine and blue skies: "I cannot describe scenes so dear to me by the coal fire."

In a very confidential and heartfelt letter to Harness he said: "The latter part of my life has been a perpetual struggle against affections which embittered the earliest portion; and though I flatter myself I have in a great measure conquered them, yet there are moments when I am as foolish as formerly. I never said so much before, nor had I said this now, if I did not suspect myself of having been rather savage, and wish to inform you this much of the cause. You know I am not one of your dolorous gentlemen: so now let us laugh again." And it was true: he never had said so much before, but that was precisely the clue to so many apparent contradictions. For years he had been striving to slay a Sentimentalist within himself who had pained him to excess. He was far too courageous to settle down to the rôle of dolorous gentleman, but imagining that he had lost all trust in womankind as in mankind, he was trying to live like a Corsair of pleasure, without love and without friendship. The disaster was, that with these stifled passions, he grew bored to breaking-point.

Those who have suffered, and whose sufferings are healed by habit or forgetfulness, have a prodigious aptitude for ennui, because pain, while making our life intolerable, fills it at the same time with sentiments of such strength that they conceal its real emptiness. Byron had begun his life with a great love. That love had been rebuffed, but it had given the youth a craving for a sentimental excitement that had become essential to him. Like a traveller whose palate is jaded by spices and who finds all healthy food flavourless, Byron could no longer taste the relish of life in a calmness of heart. He believed himself ready to pursue any violent passion, even a lawless one, provided that it gave him that ever-fleeting sense of his own existence. To the same friend Hodgson, whom he had once exhorted to a greater gaiety, he addressed an epistle in which Mary Chaworth was once again evoked:

But let this pass—I'll whine no more,
Nor seek again an eastern shore;
The world befits a busy brain—
I'll hie me to its haunts again.
But if, in some succeeding year,
When Britain's May is in the sere,
Thou hear'st of one whose deepening crimes
Suit with the sablest of the times,
Of one, whom love nor pity sways,
Nor hope of fame, nor good men's praise,
One, who in stern ambition's pride,
Perchance not blood shall turn aside;
One rank'd in some recording page
With the worst anarchs of the age
Him wilt thou *know*—and *knowing* pause,
Nor with the *effect* forget the cause.

Hodgson, ever the indulgent optimist, noted in the margin that the poor fellow did not believe a word of this.

But Byron was a more unhappy and a more complex being than his friends at the time believed.

He determined to go and settle in London. There he would at least find Parliament, and proofs to correct—"anything to cure me of conjugating the accursed verb *ennuyer*. . . ."

XV

ANNUS MIRABILIS

1812

Who does not write to please the women?

BYRON

IN London he was no longer reduced, as in the old days, to the society of Hanson and Dallas. The latter had entrusted *Childe Harold's Pilgrimage* to John Murray, an energetic and clever publisher, who was already talking to his friends of the poem he would shortly be publishing. When Byron was returning from the fencing-room he liked to drop in on Murray. He made rather a fuss, complained of the printers' delays, and then, picking out one of the books on the shelves as a mark, he thrust at it with the tip of his cane, repeating "Quart, sixte . . . quart, sixte . . ." while Murray was reading out the new stanza that Byron had brought him. "A good idea, Murray, eh? A good idea?" asked Byron, without ceasing his attack or his murmured "Quart, sixte . . . quart, sixte. . . ." Murray, who cherished his bindings, was relieved to see his visitor's back. And from there Byron would go on to dine with his friend Tom Moore at Stevens's in Bond Street.

Tom Moore was that same "Thomas Little" whose poems of blameless eroticism, a few years earlier, had thrilled the Harrow schoolboys. At the time of Byron's publishing his *English Bards,* a passage in that satire had offended Moore, who wrote a letter of challenge to him at Hodgson's address. Byron had already set off for the East, and the letter remained at Hodgson's unopened. On Byron's return Moore made inquiries about his letter. Byron replied that he had never received it, had a search made, and sent back the letter with its seal intact in token of his good faith. Moore had lately married a charming young woman and had no desire for any fighting; he suggested substituting a luncheon for the duel.

If Moore had to give a luncheon, his immediate impulse was to give it at the famous Samuel Rogers's, who owed his eminent place in the literary world as much to the perfection of his table as to the rarity of his poems. The son of a rich radical banker, he had already entered his father's bank when, at the age of twenty-seven, he had amazed the town by publishing quite a good poem, entitled *The Pleasures of Memory*. A banker-poet—here was something new! Lord Eldon, whose banker was Mr. Gosling, commented: "If old Gozzy even so much as says a good thing, let alone writing, I will close my account with him the next morning." But Rogers had made a good impression, and the most exclusive houses had opened their doors to this witty, malicious, precious little man, thin as a skeleton and white as a corpse.

A corpse does little. Rogers had kept his activities prudent and refined. He had arranged his house like a poem, with meticulous care, in an ideal position overlooking the Green Park. Everything in it was perfect: beautiful furniture in a cold classical tone, beautiful paintings, a library of the best editions of the best authors, and alabaster vases on the tables. Nothing was lacking save a wife, but Rogers had remained a bachelor. An æsthete lives his life in slow-motion, and marriage means too abrupt a decision. Sometimes he would tell his dear friend Lady Jersey: "If I had a wife, I should have somebody to care about." But she answered him: "How could you be sure that your wife would not care about somebody else?" So he entertained alone in his exquisite home, giving delicate dinners seasoned with the keen, acid wit of the master of the house, whose malice was as natural as his egotism, and who was generous with his money, in the way that rich men sometimes are when they can thus find an easy way of being sparing with their hearts.

A dinner at Rogers's was a work of art—exquisite in cooking, in the choice of guests, in everything. For this luncheon of reconciliation he invited only one poet besides Byron and Moore—Thomas Campbell; and he begged Moore and Campbell to let him be alone when he received his unknown guest, for he knew that Byron was lame and he was afraid that the young man might feel some embarrassment on entering. They were all struck by Byron's beauty, and by the nobility of his manner. He was in mourning for his mother, and his black clothes brought out to the full the spiritual quality in his pallor. Rogers asked him if he would take soup.

"No, I never take soup."

"Some fish?"

"No, I never take fish."

The mutton was served. The same question, the same reply.

"A glass of wine?" suggested Rogers.

"No, I never taste wine."

In despair Rogers asked what Byron did eat and drink.

"Nothing but hard biscuits and soda-water."

Unfortunately there was neither one nor the other in the house, and Byron lunched on potatoes crushed on his plate and sprinkled with vinegar. They found him interesting, but shy. A few days later Rogers happened to meet Hobhouse, home at last from his soldiering, and learning that he was a friend of Byron's, asked him: "How long will Lord Byron persevere in his present diet?"

"Just as long as you continue to notice it," answered Hobhouse.

From that day onwards Byron and Moore were inseparables. Byron, the "friendless animal," only asked for someone to attach himself to. He admired Moore, who struck him as being marvellously at home in a world where Byron himself knew not a soul. Byron was the lord of Newstead, Moore the son of a Dublin grocer. But from childhood Moore had given proof of a graceful facility in poetry and music alike. At fifteen he was paraphrasing Anacreon, or sitting at the pianoforte, improvising, to his own accompaniment, songs to Irish airs. The Dublin drawing-rooms were rivals for the favours of a man with such gifts of entertainment, and from this "boudoir education" Moore had retained a gay confidence in life and an ingenuous enjoyment in being something of a libertine. Murray did not care for him, and said he was a snob and a tale-bearer, but Byron found him a cheerful friend, delighted to go about with a lord, and always ready to leave his charming wife for an evening of song and wine and laughter. Moore, indeed, struck him as "the epitome of all that is most exquisite in poetical or personal accomplishments." Hardly a night but they dined together at the St. Albans or at Stevens's: or rather, Moore dined while Byron munched his biscuits, asking Moore whether he did not find that eating beef made him ferocious. When alone, Byron frequented the Alfred Club, a somewhat sober and literary place, but a decent enough resource for a rainy day. Thanks to Moore and Rogers he was beginning to find his way about the shady taverns, and to know the dandies of Fop's Alley, and the gambling hells. He masked his invincible distaste, and thrust down the puritan part of himself, but he was not completely at his ease.

He often spoke of selling Newstead and going to settle on the Isle of Naxos; he would adopt the costume and the customs of the Orient, and spend his life in studying Eastern poetry. The chill of the English winter depressed him, and the spiritual atmosphere of the country did likewise. It was a time of authoritarian politics. The Continental war scarcely affected the ruling classes. Their mode of life was easy, their gilded leisure occupied with foxhunting, lovemaking, and Parliament. The external struggle provided a good excuse for stifling liberty of thought, and Cobbett had had two years of gaol for denouncing a military scandal. Uncomprehendingly the people were suffering from the industrial revolution, but against all their complaints a stock objection was set up—patriotism and reasons of State.

In the House of Lords at this time, a Bill was under discussion designed to punish with severity those workers in the industrial centres who were smashing machinery; they had been doing so because they blamed the machines for robbing them of their livelihood. During his stay at Newstead Byron had seen some of these things for himself. The manufacturers round Nottingham had been installing new stocking-frames which enabled one man to take the place of seven. The workless had come into contact with the cavalry, and the Government had had to send down two additional regiments to Nottingham. They wanted to apply the death penalty to the "frame-breakers."

Byron had seen these poor creatures with his own eyes, and realised their honesty of purpose. He decided to speak. He enjoyed rising amid these great gentlemen and telling them some stern home-truths about their cruelty. He had never forgotten the little boy in Aberdeen, brought up in the common school, and asking for apples to take home to his poor mamma. It also happened that the captain of militia at Nottingham who had manhandled the workers so brutally was Jack Musters, the man who had taken Mary Ann from him. Musters could be very kindly disposed towards a rustic with a pretty wife, but against the hosiery workers he harboured an old hatred, and had always taken a malicious joy in prosecuting them for poaching. Byron's private memories thus joined hands with the tradition of his mother's family to make him, as regards this question, a very advanced Whig. He got into touch with Lord Holland, who was to speak on the same subject.

Dallas was bidden to meet him at St. James's Street, and Byron declaimed his speech, in his most unnatural voice. It was not at all bad. He portrayed the sufferings of the work-people, "men liable to conviction on the clearest evidence of the capital crime of poverty. . . . And what are your remedies? . . . These convulsions must terminate in death. . . . Are there not capital punishments enough in your statutes? . . . Will the famished wretch who has braved your bayonets be appalled by your gibbets?" As an orator he seemed brilliant enough, if a trifle theatrical. It was not exactly prudent, in this assembly, to affirm that never "in the most oppressed provinces of Turkey did I behold such squalid wretchedness as I have in the very heart of a Christian country." On coming out he was met by Mr. Dallas, who was so sadly cumbered with an umbrella that he could only proffer his left hand to congratulate Byron. The latter, satisfied with himself and with the praises of Lord Holland and Lord Grenville, insisted on the right. This speech attracted the attention of Whig circles to the young peer, and the doors of Holland House, which the redoubtable Lady Holland had made into one of the social and intellectual strongholds of London, were opened to him. A few days later Murray published the first two Cantos of *Childe Harold's Pilgrimage.* Up to the last moment Byron had been doubtful of his poem's worth. He was always shy in mentioning it, and Dallas too, alarmed by his responsibility, was no less anxious. But success was certain.

Murray was a clever and active publisher, and had been talking of *Childe Harold* to his friends for some time past. He had distributed certain choice pages of the poem to writers and to fashionable people who could give the book a good send-off. Samuel Rogers had had the proofs since January. He read the poem aloud to his sister, and remarked that this was something which, for all its beauty, would never catch the public favor; they would like neither its whining, discontented tone, nor the hero's loose mode of life. Convinced of a certain failure, he spoke in high praise of the new poet and quoted certain stanzas which excited curiosity. Rogers was then the ruling power in certain literary salons, particularly in that of Lady Caroline Lamb, whom he praised "to the skies" for her wit and grace. He brought her the proofs of *Childe Harold,* begging her not to show them to anyone. The same day she went the round of the town, telling everybody that she had read the new poem, and that it was a marvel. To Rogers she said: "I must see him. I am dying to see him!"

"He has a club foot, and he bites his nails," said Rogers.

"If he is as ugly as Æsop, I must see him!" she answered.

And soon every woman was thinking likewise. Byron's life had been abruptly transformed, as that of the hero in some Eastern tale, touched by an enchanter's wand. "I awoke one morning and found myself famous," he wrote. One evening he had known London as a desert peopled by three or four acquaintances; the next, it was a city of the Arabian Nights, crowded with lighted palaces opening their portals to the most illustrious of young Englishmen. A great fashionable society (that is, as Byron said, the four thousand persons who are still up when others are in bed) is always subject to very swift tides of admiration and disgust; amongst these men and women who meet every day and every night, a new reputation makes its way with the force and speed of a thunderbolt. After all, they needed something to admire. The French Revolution, and then Bonaparte, had given birth in thousands of young Europeans to glorious hopes which Napoleon had betrayed. In England especially, the sentiment of the vanity of life was dominant in a society sickened of pleasures by laxity of morals, of martial ambition by long-drawn-out wars, of political ambition by the continuance of a Tory government made invincible by danger.

The poets, in their impotence or timidity, had not

voiced this secret revulsion. *Childe Harold* was the first to echo the tragic scepticism of a sickened generation. Art had at last fallen back into step with life. At last a young Englishman, akin to those who read him, had discovered the Europe of 1812 as revolution and wars had left it. For a people severed from all Continental life by ten years of blockade, the story of a journey in Albania amongst the Suliotes was more amazing than a voyage to the Indies or the South Sea Islands. They enjoyed the bold originality of the political notes which accompanied *Childe Harold.* It was a poem of the sea; and the Viking breed, so long held off from the Ocean by the blockade, could catch in it that salt tang of sea-spray which they were beginning to miss. Even the opposition of the Tory critics helped Byron. It was a good joke when the *Quarterly Review* trounced him for having spoken with scorn of "hired ruffians," and went on to ask with anxiety whether these were the opinions of a peer of the realm on His Majesty's Army. For twenty years past the poets had one after another been converted to official propriety; and there are always moments in the life of a people when even those who enjoy the advantages of an established order grow tired of it. At such a moment in the life of England, *Childe Harold* appeared.

But it sometimes happens that after a literary triumph, its author comes as a disappointment. Yet here the author was a match for his work. He was a nobleman of ancient lineage, and Society was grateful to him for bringing the prestige of genius to a class that was often attacked. He was young, and he was handsome, with his grey-blue eyes shining with emotion under the long eyelashes, his pale skin so delicate that it seemed almost transparent, and his mouth like that of a charming

GEORGE GORDON, LORD BYRON

woman, sensitive and capricious. . . . Even his infirmity heightened the interest that was felt in him. The gloomy story of his hero was his own story. Everyone knew that he, like Childe Harold, had returned from Greece and Turkey, and all the sustained melancholy, the solitude, and the woes of the Childe were attributed to Lord Byron. A work of art ought to suggest the reality of the sentiment which it expresses; but how much stronger and more natural is that suggestion if the public believe, rightly or wrongly, that these sentiments are the author's!

The whole of London talked of Byron, and only of Byron. Crowds of famous people begged for introductions or left their visiting-cards. The carriages in front of his door in St. James's Street impeded the traffic. In one bookshop there was a copy of *Childe Harold* exhibited which had been specially bound for the Princess Charlotte, daughter of the Regent. The Prince Regent himself had Byron presented to him, and spoke to him at length of poets and poetry. At Mayfair dinner conversation seemed to be nothing but one long, incessant murmur of "Byr'n . . . Byr'n . . . Byr'n. . . ." Every season in those days had its lion, political, military, or literary; and Byron was the unrivalled lion of the parties of 1812.

Women thrilled as they imagined the great Abbey, the heinous passions, and that "marble heart" of Childe Harold, withheld, yet coveted the more. They laid instant siege to him, a troop of charmers. They were afraid of him, and found the rarest delights in that fear. Lady Roseberry, talking with him in the doorway of a room, suddenly felt her heart beat so violently that she could scarcely answer him. And when he himself divined the effect he produced, he kept trying the fascinating power of his famous "underlook." Dallas heard him one day reading *Childe Harold* aloud. He was no doubt seeking to find in himself what others were admiring. "I trust all the gloom of his youth will be dissipated for the rest of his life," prophesied Dallas.

But Dallas was wrong. That melancholy was part and parcel of the character whom the readers of the poem had loved, and Byron was quite aware of it. Knowing that his hosts were expecting to receive Childe Harold, he entered their drawing-rooms with a mournful disdain, masking with icy reserve the inborn shyness of the Byrons. He no longer had to murmur, as in Elizabeth Pigot's time, "One, two, three, four, five, six, seven . . ." when presented to a lady. But beneath a few dry words he concealed a profound disquiet. In this world so full of life and colour, which was welcoming so suddenly and noisily after having so long ignored him, he had no relatives, no friends. These men and women all seemed to have known each other from childhood; they addressed each other by Christian names and nicknames. He knew not one thing about them. He was afraid of seeming ridiculous by showing Southwell manners, or by his infirmity, and this very fear gave him a fascination of which he was not yet conscious. Motionless while others danced, on account of his game leg, he stood there in the embrasure of some gilded doorway, looking exactly like his hero standing erect in the prow of a ship, his eyes far-fixed upon the waves.

Moore, in the course of their brief friendship, had always found Byron a gay companion, with an almost childlike gift for laughter, and he often tried to make fun of this sombre, triumphant gloom. But Byron declined to admit that it was a pose. No, his melancholy was something heartfelt, his gaiety was merely on the surface; in his heart reigned despair. He remained uncomfortable in this new world. He was assured that he had it at his feet. But he was sceptical; he could hardly bring himself to believe in the success of his poem. With blunt frankness, Hobhouse had declared that after Pope there was no more to be done, and this was also Byron's opinion. They both believed that *Childe Harold's* success was due to the expression of morbid sentiments, but that good taste would ere long carry the day, and the public would desert Byron to return to Pope.

Nevertheless, that spring season of 1812 was flushed higher and higher with the Byronic fever. "The subject of conversation, of curiosity, of enthusiasm of the moment," wrote the Duchess of Devonshire, "is not Spain or Portugal, warriors or patriots, but Lord Byron! . . . The poem is on every table and himself courted, flattered, and praised whenever he appears. He has a pale, sickly but handsome countenance, a bad figure, and, in short, he is really the only topic of every conversation—the men jealous of him, the women of each other." His few private acquaintances, Rogers, Tom Moore, Lord Holland, were besieged with requests for introductions. A little girl named Elizabeth Barrett had serious thoughts at this time of dressing as a boy and running away to become Lord Byron's page. At dinner parties the women tried to juggle with their places in order to be beside him. Rogers was amused by the manœuvres of certain noble ladies who wrote asking him to dine, and added in a postscript: "Pray, could you not contrive to bring Lord Byron with you?" It was an amazing destiny for the young cripple who, only a few years before, had been gingerly carrying the pint-pot of a charlatan through the streets of Nottingham.

Lady Caroline Lamb, who had wanted to see him "if he were as ugly as Æsop," met him at Lady Westmoreland's. Coming close to him, she now saw the wondrous features, those perfectly arched eyebrows, that curling hair in which a few faint ruddy gleams still shone, that mouth of a Greek statue, the lips turning slightly down at the corners. For a moment she listened to that soft, low voice, so musical that children said of him "the gentleman who speaks like music." She observed his studied courtesy, his proud and almost insolent humility. And she saw the women thronging round him, turned on her heel, and moved away. That evening she wrote in her journal: "Mad, bad, and dangerous to know."

Two days later she was at Holland House when Byron was announced. He was presented to her, and said: "This offer was made you the other day. May I ask why you declined it?"

She was tall and slender; her large hazel eyes looked questioning. Beautiful? No, but fragile and alluring. Byron asked whether he might come and see her; speaking with her, he observed with curiosity this animal so new to him—a well-born woman. She said pretty things, sometimes sentimental, sometimes brilliant, with a curious voice, agreeable in spite of the slightly nasal drawl peculiar to the Devonshire House coterie.

In her journal, beneath the first phrase about Lord Byron, she added: "That beautiful pale face is my fate."

XVI

LOVE

1812–1813

MAD? Bad? How quick to criticise this young woman was! What had she noticed to make her so stern? The bitter tang of his replies? The fierceness of his scorn? The disdain in the pout of his lips? Those eyes that seemed so vexed and impatient beneath the drooping eyelids? . . . Mad? Bad? He was neither one nor the other. But dangerous to know—yes; and above all mistrustful, a wounded spirit ever on his guard. Never again would a Mary Chaworth wound him; he believed he knew what women were, and how they must be treated. Gone for him were the days of tenderness and abandon; he had been taught hardness by this far from angelic sex—and the lesson would not be lost on him.

On his first visit to Melbourne House (for Lady Caroline lived with her mother-in-law, Lady Melbourne) he found Rogers and Moore visiting her. She had returned from a ride, and flung herself on a settee without changing her dress. When Lord Byron was announced she fled. "Lord Byron," said Rogers, "you are a lucky man. Here has Lady Caroline been sitting in all her dirt with us, but as soon as you were announced, she fled to make herself beautiful." He frowned when he saw the other two men. Could he not find her alone? She asked him to come back at dinner time. He came, and before long was the only one to be seen at Melbourne House.

The house was one of the most brilliant in London, the intellectual centre, together with Holland House, of the Whig party. The Lambs, who bore the Melbourne title in the peerage, belonged to a family of fairly recent fortune, whose rank had been reached by the stages of natural progression. Early in the eighteenth century a lawyer of that name had grown rich, and about 1750 his son had bought the property of Brocket Hall. He owned half a million sterling in landed property as well as half a million of money, and, in accordance with the unwritten laws of the realm, had been made a baronet. Marrying a lady of singular beauty, Elizabeth Milbanke by name, the baronet had entered Parliament, and the Prime Minister, who needed a majority and knew how to command one, had transformed him into Lord Melbourne. Thereafter Lady Melbourne, helped by a great skill in the saving of appearances and a wit that reminded one of *Les Liaisons Dangereuses,* had been enabled without scandal to live a life of much excitement, to attract the favour of the Prince of Wales, and achieve the conquest of London.

The Melbournes had two sons. The father's favourite was the elder, who resembled him; the mother's was the younger, William Lamb, who bore a resemblance to Lord Egremont. She spoiled him to the pitch of folly. He was fond of reading, dreaming, and versifying, and held sport in abhorrence. Freed from any discipline, reared in surroundings of the most prodigal extravagance and the most complete moralistic freedom, and ignored by a father who lived in the house like a silent and disapproving guest, he had grown to be an indolent, witty, and depraved young man. In 1805 he married Caroline Ponsonby, daughter of Lord Bessborough, and she it was who had lately met Lord Byron.

It was a love match, and a bold one. Caroline was adorable and dangerous. Her mother, Lady Bessborough, had had a slight stroke of apoplexy three years after her daughter's birth, and had been obliged to hand over the task of bringing up the child to her aunt, Georgiana, Duchess of Devonshire. The duchess gave her the care she gave her own children—that is, she left her to the servants. Brought up in luxury and confusion —"served on silver in the morning, she would carry the costly plates into the kitchen, among the ever-quarrelling servants,"—the little girl had no notion of there being anyone in the world but dukes, marquises, and beggars. "We had no idea that bread or butter was *made;* how it came, we didn't pause to think, but had no doubt that fine horses must be fed on beef. At ten years old, I couldn't write. . . . I spelt not, but made verses that all thought beautiful. For myself, I preferred washing a dog, or polishing a spur, or breaking in a horse if they would let me." The consequences of this upbringing struck the doctors as disquieting: Lady Caroline was capricious, and subject to violent rages and such vagaries of mood that sometimes her reason was feared for. She had no lessons before the age of fifteen; but then she suddenly discovered Greek and Latin, learned music, French and Italian, painted, acted plays, sketched, drew caricatures, and in a few years became one of the most original young women in London.

She had a horror of the "conventional." Her letters she dated "Heaven knows what day"; in sending her brother a book she declared that she did not know her address. Her sensibility was notorious; before a reading that Benjamin Constant was to give in London, her cousin, Harriet Cavendish, wrote: "I have begged that Caroline may be present, to cry and make sensation for us." And one of her greatest charms was her gift of slipping without any transition, like the fairies of Shakespeare, from gloom to gladness, from easy pleasantry to poetic gravity. Ariel, the Sylph, the Young Savage—so her admirers styled her, and marvelled at her graceful incoherencies; the more sensitive of them regretted that she was rather spoiled by preciosity and pedantry; women put her down as artificial, and forced by her craving for admiration into too deliberate a posing.

She had first met her future husband, William Lamb, when she was thirteen and he nineteen. She had already read verses of his, and "longed to meet him." She saw him, and loved this bright-eyed youth, something of a dandy, with an air of negligence that suited him to perfection. He was delighted with her. "Of all the Devonshire House girls," exclaimed William Lamb, "that is the one for me!" And from that day he was determined to make her his wife. For a long time she did not want him. "I adored him, I knew I was a fury, and I would not marry him." He was tenacious in his pursuit, and in 1805 he caught her.

On her wedding-day she was ravishing, but a prey to nerves. She broke into a fury with the officiating bishop, tore her gown, swooned, and had to be taken away in her carriage. It was a strange beginning, but her charming husband seemed to enjoy spoiling this fragile plant still more. William Lamb held morality in horror; it was tiresome, it was in bad taste. "Wrong as it is, I never can feel repentance or regret for the hours which I have passed in pursuits which really amused me at the time, although they were pursuits of folly or vice." Lady Melbourne, a woman of experience, shared her son's feelings regarding morality, but not regarding what should be actually said about it. Certainly, a woman could do anything with impunity, as she had proved—but there were ways and ways. She did not approve of her daughter-in-law's quite unveiled coquetry, or of the too manifest gladness with which she welcomed the attentions of, say, Sir Godfrey Webster. But William laughed at that, and Caroline was wilder than ever.

Lady Melbourne, during her long life, had been admirably successful in combining freedom with respectability, and she was anxious to instruct Titania in a less faery and more worldly wisdom. The clash was evident between "the stately woman, mature but still beautiful, with a clear brain and mind," so ironically precise, and this unreal daughter-in-law of hers who flattered her, caressed her, and explained to "my dear, my dearest Lady Melbourne" that her attitude simply followed from that of her husband. It was William who had called her a prude, who had told her she was affected and amused himself with teaching her things that she had never heard of—and the upshot of it all was that she thought everything permissible to her. But it was curious that even William, despite his mask, was beginning to seem unhappy. What did he want? In her light style, its gay frankness faintly clouded with sadness, she begged him to have a care for their *ménage:* "I think lately, my dearest William, we have been very troublesome to each other. . . . I will be silent of a morning, entertaining after dinner, docile, fearless as a heroine in the last volume of her troubles, strong as a mountain tiger. . . . *You* should say to me: *Raisonnez mieux et répliquez moins.*" He was content to note in his diary: "Before I was married, whenever I saw the children or the dogs allowed to be troublesome in any family, I used to lay it all to the fault of the master of it, who might at once put a stop to it if he pleased. Since I have married, I find this was a very rash and premature judgment." Such was the couple, already more than half-severed by a disappointed wife, into whose life Lord Byron suddenly entered.

It was a new rôle for him, that of *cicisbeo,* and pleased him more than he admitted. He enjoyed arriving about eleven in the morning, to share in the femininities of the boudoir, opening the letters, fondling the children, and choosing the dresses for the day. During its first weeks this Melbourne House friendship remained platonic. Byron talked at great length in his serious voice, dandling Caroline's little boy on his knee. He knew that she expected him to be Byronic rather than Byron, and talked to her of the curse that lay upon his family, of the Gordons, the Wicked Lord, the death that struck down everything he loved, of how his mother and his friends had died within a month, of his marble heart, too, and the lovely women of the East. She listened admiringly: so different from William, she thought, and so beautiful.

Did he love her? She was not his "type." For all its grace, her body seemed too thin to be really beautiful, and she had not those gazelle-like eyes, that "shyness of the antelope," that grace of a Peri for which Byron had been seeking from his childhood days. But what she did possess was an "infinite vivacity," and, if pride

LADY CAROLINE LAMB IN HER PAGE'S COAT

After a Miniature by an Unknown Artist

In the possession of Lieut. Col. John Murray

played its part, it was certainly flattering for a young man to become an intimate at Melbourne House, when a fortnight before he had only had a few friends here and there in London. Decidedly, he was tempted to yield to a sentiment which, in her, seemed so powerful. Dallas was at Byron's house one day, and saw a page absurdly tricked out in silk and laces, and Byron "so enraptured that his time and thoughts were almost entirely devoted to reading her letters and answering them." The worthy Dallas even deemed it necessary to put him on his guard against a world most parlous for virtue, and a woman whom everyone declared to be mad. But Byron was only too much on his guard.

This aristocratic society into which he was at last gladly finding his way, a society still deeply imbued with the morals and manners of the eighteenth century, was ruled by its senses, not its sentiments. It was nicely attuned, not perhaps to the deepest Byron, but to that sarcastic, disillusioned Byron who was the friend of Tom Moore or Samuel Rogers. As a matter of prose, it preferred the "Madame de Merteuil" tone of old Lady Melbourne to the fanciful style of her daughter-in-law. Lady Melbourne professed a systematic libertinism which Byron admired and strove to imitate; but he never entirely attained it; there was a streak of tenderness in him that remained vulnerable to the slightest touch. But just because this hard philosophy was secretly beyond his reach, he felt an almost cringing respect for the men, and even more for the women, who had made it their rule of life. Lady Caroline often bored him; Lady Melbourne intimidated him and charmed him with a freedom of spirit which he could enjoy only by fits and starts. In rounding off the process of his conversion to the new scepticism in love, she played the part that Matthews had done at Cambridge in bringing him to scepticism in religion. Here at Melbourne House, just as earlier at Trinity, the convention of unconventionality was the most exacting of all. "Lady Melbourne, who might have been my mother, excited an interest in my feelings that few young women have been able to awaken. She was a charming person—a sort of modern Aspasia, uniting the energy of a man's mind with the delicacy and tenderness of a woman's. . . . I have often thought that, with a little more youth, Lady Melbourne might have turned my head, at all events she often turned my heart, by bringing me back to mild feelings, when the demon passion was strong within me." After the mother, the person he chiefly preferred in the household was the husband, William Lamb, "as much above me as Hyperion above the Satyr." Must he then betray this loyal and intelligent man who had confidently offered him the hand of friendship? The force of female treachery appalled him.

To Lady Caroline he often showed astounding hardness of heart. One spring morning he brought her the first rose and the first carnation. "Your ladyship, I am told," he said to her ironically, "likes all that is new and rare—for a moment." She answered him in a letter, written on an amazing notepaper, the lace edging of which formed shell patterns at each corner of the sheet. It was a letter at once touching and irritating, in which the preciosity of the form spoiled the fond submissiveness of the tone, comparing herself to the sunflower, which, "having once beheld in its full lustre the bright and unclouded sun that for one moment condescended to shine upon it, never while it exists could think any lower object worthy of its worship and admiration."

The humility was ill-timed. Byron liked women to treat him "as a favourite and somewhat forward sister," not as an overlord. Pleasure and love are always closely linked in a man's mind with the first, unforgetable experiences which have revealed them to his spirit. In the adolescent Byron, pleasure, the gift of creatures both facile and gay, had been a break in the solitary ruminations of his melancholy Platonism. He admitted two extreme types of women: the *beau idéal,* shrinking and chaste, which he had formed out of an imagined Mary Chaworth or the childlike shade of a Margaret Parker; and the companion of pleasure. But the bold lover, the woman still exigent in love, seemed to Byron to fall short of the conventions. As Lady Hester Stanhope had formerly observed, he did not perceive the sentiments of others. He had no wish to perceive them. Lady Caroline's passionate remarks struck him merely as a tiresome and vulgar noise that drowned the inward music. He would have liked familiarity, lightness, a blend of gay frivolity and fleeting melancholy; he felt the constraint of adoration, and there was lassitude as he turned his heads towards it.

Lady Caroline, who could write such charming letters to a husband she no longer loved, descended in writing to Byron to an almost intolerable pathos. She imagined she would please him by displaying Society to his gaze, and she arranged morning parties for him to which the most beautiful and remarkable women in London were invited. But the drawing-room tittle-tattle wearied the Pilgrim who, six months earlier, had been smoking so peacefully under an azure sky, gazing at the mountains. Lying on his sofa at Newstead he had written: "Anything rather than conjugate from morning to night the accursed verb *ennuyer*." He was already thinking regretfully of his lost solitude.

He was being closely observed by an intelligent young girl who saw him there. She was a country niece of Lady Melbourne's, Anne Isabella Milbanke—Annabella she was called for short—of good education and a religious bent, who, during her visits to London, was watching its society, and her wild cousin Caroline with a somewhat scornful eye. On March 24 she had made a note in her diary: "Have finished Lord Byron's *Childe Harold,* which contains many passages in the best style of poetry." On the 25th she was invited to a "morning-party for waltzing" at Melbourne House. The delightful Lady Jersey was there, murmurous with words and necklaces, the graceful, red-haired Miss Elphinstone, and a score of other beauties. There was a woman singer. Annabella Milbanke thought that these men and women seemed to be listening to the music "as a duty." Caro Lamb pointed out Lord Byron to her. She found him haughty, "his mouth continually betraying the acrimony of his spirits"; and she thought he was right to despise these fribbles and follies. She would not be introduced that day because of "all the women absurdly courting him," but a few days later she saw him again, found him shy, and tried to make him talk. "He spoke his surprise at my not being disgusted with scenes in which there was scarcely one person who, on returning home, dared to look into themselves."

She admired the remark. It corresponded to her own feelings, and besides, it was sincerely spoken. Amidst this turmoil which he had not the courage to stand clear of, he regretted that other Byron, the dreamer of Athens and Newstead. But why was he telling this fair young stranger things that he had said to nobody? There was something provocative in her. Her complexion was fresh, her cheeks round and pink. She was not tall, but she was admirably formed. On entering the drawing-room, Byron asked Moore if she were some lady's companion.

"No," answered Moore in a whisper, "she is a great heiress; you should marry her and repair Newstead."

Byron spoke to Caroline Lamb in high praise of Miss Milbanke, even drawing an unflattering parallel between the two cousins. She was fascinated, and accepted his rebuffs. Byron had only to express his disapproval of this mode of life, or of these too frequent parties, and in particular his detestation of dancing (a dislike of very old standing) for waltzes and quadrilles to be seen no more in Melbourne House. He asked her never to waltz again. And she promised. Loving and vanquished, she was completely at his mercy. She wrote him bold, insensate letters in which she offered him not only her love, but all her jewels, too, if he were in need of money.

She did not become his mistress at once, and it may be that he would have spared her had he not still been tortured by the memory of a first unhappy love. But in Byron's self-made philosophy, a woman who did not give herself gave nothing of herself, and despised a lover too cowardly to force her. Caroline's mother, Lady Bessborough, thought herself clever in telling this compromising visitor that, whatever appearances might be, he was not loved and that Caroline would send him packing. He did not reply; but he determined not to pursue Lady Caroline—for pursuit would have been vain—but simply not to get out of her way. A week later she was his.

He had taken her with perfect coolness. He was a hateful and stern lover to her, judging his mistress without any illusions, with all the keen and pitiless realism which was the natural form of his mind when he was not himself in love. "I never knew a woman with greater or more pleasing talents. But these are unfortunately coupled with a total lack of common conduct. . . . Your heart, my poor Caro (what a little volcano!), pours lava through your veins. . . . I have always thought you the cleverest, most agreeable, absurd, amiable, perplexing, dangerous, fascinating little being that lives now. . . . I won't talk to you of beauty; I am no judge. But our beauties cease to be so when near you, and therefore you have either some, or something better." A compliment with reservations! And she sadly reflected that he had been ashamed to love her because she was not pretty enough. She displeased him with those very traits that for others were the charm of her spirit; her imagination was inflamed with books, and she wanted her love affair to be a love romance. She imagined she could keep this poet by quoting poets to him. He listened distantly to his mistress's Greek and Latin and her fashionable anecdotes, and his thoughts turned back to the silent languor of the Morning Star of Annesley, or the mute women of the East.

If he let one day pass without visiting her, she would send him one or other of the extraordinary little pages who surrounded her. Sometimes she even disguised herself as a page to take him a note. "A scene worthy of Faublas," commented Byron, who loathed these extravagances. She had become friendly with the valet, Fletcher, and wrote beseeching him to open the apartment to her. If she were not invited to a ball which Lord Byron was attending, she would shamelessly wait for him in the street. "Your little friend Caro William," wrote the Duchess of Devonshire, "is doing all sorts of imprudent things for him and with him. . . . Byron is going back to Naxos and then the husbands may sleep in peace. I should not be surprised if Caro William were to go with him, she is so wild and imprudent." This naïve adoration ought to have touched Byron, but it only annoyed him; he thought she would make him a laughing-stock, and—a more curious sentiment—he actually condemned the love of which he was the object. To the Bible-bred young Scot in Byron, Lady Caroline was the woman taken in adultery. "Like Napoleon, I have always had a great contempt for women; and formed this opinion of them not hastily, but from my own fatal experience. My writings, indeed, tend to exalt the sex; and my imagination has always delighted in giving them a *beau idéal* likeness, but I only drew them as a painter or statuary would do—as they should be. . . . They are in an unnatural state of society. The Turks and Eastern people manage these matters better than we do. They lock them up, and they are much happier. Give a woman a looking-glass and a few sugar-plums, and she will be satisfied." But the husband, William Lamb, was no Turk. His diary took on a melancholy tinge; in marriage, he reflected, "nothing is fixed. Their [women's] opinion rises and falls according to what they hear in the world, according to the lightest observations or the most casual remarks. . . . By marriage you place yourself on the defensive instead of the offensive, in society."

Lady Bessborough, now more clearly enlightened, was

even more perturbed than her son-in-law. She had known stirring times in her own youth, and in its day her liaison with Lord Granville had been notorious. But never had she gone so far as her daughter and dressed herself in carter's clothing to be able to break in upon her lover and keep watch on him, or stood waiting in the rain while people came out from a ball. In despair Lady Bessborough summoned Hobhouse to call on her, to discuss this wretched affair that was dishonouring the two families. Hobhouse was always ready to preach a sermon to his friend, but how did a rupture depend upon the latter? Byron was as weary as Lady Bessborough herself of Caroline Lamb's follies. He did not conceal this from Lady Melbourne, who was not only open-minded in her views, but adroit in her psychology, and gladly discussed the adventure with her daughter-in-law's lover. He infinitely preferred the society of Tom Moore or Hobhouse to that of a hussy.

He even enjoyed more serious distractions, for Annabella Milbanke saw him at a lecture on religion, writhing in an odd way at every mention of that word. She rounded off her stay in London by attending a course on the density of the Earth, at which she took learned notes. Byron was mildly amused by this love of science in a woman, and in his conversations with Lady Melbourne dubbed Miss Milbanke "the Princess of Parallelograms." Nevertheless, he could not repress a feeling of affectionate respect for her. Whatever else she might be, this well-built girl who discoursed of the density of the Earth, she was chaste.

At Miss Milbanke's request, Caroline had submitted to Byron a few of her cousin's poems, which he found fairly interesting: "she is certainly a very extraordinary girl; who could imagine so much strength and variety of thought under that placid countenance?" And he added: "I have no desire to be better acquainted with Miss Milbanke; she is too good for a fallen spirit to know, and I should like her more if she were less perfect." Too perfect—she read this verdict, for the letter was meant to be shown to her; and naturally she noted it with a modesty tinged with a trace of complacency, for her sole imperfection was that she knew her own perfection. She was an only child, worshipped by her parents, asked in marriage by five or six young men during her first season in society, and she believed herself infallible. Her soul was generous, even passionate, but she would sometimes seem cold and calculating, in that she was for ever seeking to rationalise her actions. Her mind was that of a good mathematician, believing in a precise knowledge of everything, and to her the poetic, superficial erudition of a Caroline Lamb seemed trumpery. Her cousin's pose of childishness annoyed her, and she commented that the charm of her usual stupidity was being spoilt by a new affectation of Byronic melancholy, and also that "though Caro Lamb would defy the world's censure, she dares not lose its notice and its wonder by descending from the conspicuous heights of folly to the humble paths of reason." She, of course, followed the paths of reason—but did she follow them humbly? "Your Annabella is a mystery," wrote the Duchess of Devonshire to her son, who had lost his heart to her; "liking, not liking; generous-minded, yet afraid of poverty; there is no making her out. I hope you don't make yourself unhappy about her; she is really an icicle." She was not an icicle. Like Byron, she had had romantic friendships in childhood.

In the girlish dreams which she very early began to confide to a diary (for she had a literary bent), she saw herself the heroine of all the historic acts of devotion. She had defended Thermopylæ, she had tended the plague-stricken. Then religious feeling had made her try to overcome her impetuosity, and she thought she had managed it. "Lord Byron makes up to her a little; but she don't seem to admire him except as a poet, nor he her, except as a wife."

Was it only as a poet that she admired him? We may doubt it. Listening to the story of her cousin's scandalous passion for Lord Byron, she satisfied herself that "he is sincerely repentant for the evil he has done, though he has no resolution (without aid) to adopt a new course of conduct and feeling." A fallen angel, he said of himself; and she gravely approved, thinking that perhaps it was she, the sincere believer, who would provide the help this very handsome angel needed for his redemption. He was quite simple with her, "and very good-natured." Yet she noticed a tendency to gallantry in him, and that he was quite different with women from what he was with men. Anne Isabella Milbanke was much more concerned with Lord Byron than was good for her salvation, in this world at least.

August 1812. The conduct of Caroline Lamb, always extravagant, was becoming insufferable. One morning Lady Bessborough called on her daughter and begged her to come to Ireland with her; William would join them there, and an end would be made of this sorry business. Lord Melbourne arrived while she was in the house, and spoke severely to Caroline. She lost her temper and replied so impudently that the terrified Lady Bessborough ran downstairs to summon Lady Melbourne. When they came up together Lady Caroline had fled without dressing. Old Lord Melbourne explained that she had threatened to go and live with her lover. "Go and be damned!" he retorted.

Together the two mothers rushed to Byron, whom they found alone, and no less startled than themselves. The step taken by these two great ladies amused him. A year before he had been unknown to them; and to-day they were both on their knees supplicating his intervention to send back their daughter and daughter-in-law to her husband's house. A curious revenge. A tip to the Lamb's coachman elicited the address to which Lady Caroline had been driven, and he found her at the house of a doctor in Kensington. Almost forcibly he brought her back to her mother, who, under the stress of her emotion, had just had another stroke.

The story went the rounds of London. The Prince-Regent himself summoned Lady Bessborough and told her that he thought them all mad, mothers and daughter alike, and that Lord Byron had bewitched the whole family. In particular he condemned this consultation of the mothers with the lover: "I never heard of such a thing in my life—taking the mothers for confidantes! What would you have thought of my going to talk to Lady Spencer in former times?" As Lady Spencer was Lady Bessborough's mother, this exclamation struck the latter as so ludicrous that, in spite of the subject, she could not help laughing.

Mother and mother-in-law, husband and lover, all were now begging Lady Caroline to leave London. Byron told her that her refusal to do so showed her weakness and egotism. But she remained, although he was no longer willing that she should visit him, staying on in the hope of a chance meeting in the street or a drawing-room, and of being able to write the next day, telling him how handsome she had found him. "How very pale you are! . . . *ma è la beltà della morte*, or a statue of white marble, so colourless, and the dark brow and hair such a contrast. I never see you without wishing to cry; if any painter could paint me that face as it is, I would give him anything I possess on earth." A touching letter—but what human being was ever touched by a passion of which he was the object?

At last she consented to accompany Lady Bessborough—and Byron breathed again. This had been his first adventure with a woman of rank, and a hateful experience he found it. This mistress of his, so greedy of his time and thoughts, had ended by infuriating him. And she, who had flung herself into this passion with heedless yet generous violence, emerged from it sick and dying. A girl cousin who was present at the arrival of the mother and daughter in Ireland described it thus: "my aunt looks stout and well, but poor Caroline most terribly the contrary. She is worn to the bone, and her eyes starting out of her head. . . . She appears to be in a state very little short of insanity, and my aunt describes it as at times having been decidedly so."

Byron, nevertheless, was writing to Lady Melbourne: "Dear Lady Melbourne—I presume you have heard and will not be sorry to hear *again,* that *they* are safely deposited in Ireland, and that the sea rolls between you and *one* of your torments; the other you see is still at your elbow. Now you will not regret to hear, that I wish this to end, and it certainly shall not be renewed on my part. It is not that I love another, but loving at all is quite out of my way; I am tired of being a fool, and when I look back on the waste of time, and the destruction of all my plans last winter by this last romance, I am—what I ought to have been long ago. It is true from early habit, one must make love mechanically, as one swims. I was once very fond of both, but now, as I never swim unless I tumble in the water, I don't make love till almost obliged."

Was he free of his mistress? She was writing dangerous letters from Ireland, reminding him that it needed only eight guineas, a post-chaise and a boat for her to reappear in London. If she did set fire to the powder and left her husband, Byron saw himself condemned by his code of honour to flee with her, *sans amour*. He was terrified, and strove to compose epistles worthy of the *Grand Cyrus;* he was ready to declare all the love she wanted, so long as he never set eyes on her again. Lady Melbourne treated the adventure with perfect detachment, as if it had been a question of being between two physicians and choosing the better remedy. She held Byron's kindness to be dangerous: "Do not, however, mistake me, I would not have you say a harsh sentence to her for the world, or anything that could be deemed insulting. I had not the least intention of advising you to do it; there is no kindness that I would not have you show her, but sacrificing yourself to her would only be romantic, and not kind— . . . for it must lead to unhappiness and misery. If a little trifling expression of coldness at present would prevent this *finale*, how much more kind, to give a little present pain, and avoid her total ruin. . . . I must, however, add that I think you attach too much blame to yourself—she was no novice. . . .

She knew enough to be upon her guard, and cannot be looked upon as the victim of a designing man." And, too expert in male credulity, Lady Melbourne ended: "If she thought her friends cared less she would be more likely to take some other fancy—the result of all this seems to me the best thing you can do is to marry, and that in fact you can get out of this scrape by no other means."

To marry . . . that accorded exactly with Byron's own desires. He believed in marriage. It was his last illusion. A young peer (and especially a Byron) ought to drink, gamble, and play with his neighbour's wife; and then, having taken his proper fill of adventure, should marry a woman of good birth and tolerable fortune, whom he did not love, and let her have a sufficiency of children to assure the future of his name. Such was the Convention, such the Newstead code.

To reassure Lady Melbourne once and for all, he made an astounding confession to her—that his keenest desire was to marry Lady Caroline's own cousin, the Miss Milbanke whom he had occasionally met at William Lamb's, and whose verses he had read. Nothing usually surprised Lady Melbourne, but this time she was taken aback. Could anyone imagine two creatures more divergent than the pious mathematician and Childe Harold? But it was just that contrast which took Byron's fancy, as well as the reserve of this girl, the only woman who had kept him at arms' length. "I know little of her, and have not the most distant reason to suppose that I am at all a favourite in that quarter. But I never saw a woman whom I *esteemed* so much. . . . My only objection would be to my Mamma, from whom I have already by instinct imbibed a mortal aversion." But to make up for that, he was enchanted by the idea of becoming Lady Melbourne's nephew. Decidedly he was destined for this family.

Lady Melbourne demanded some safeguards: "He was very changeable," she wrote to her "nephew"—"much like the man in the farce we saw together (the *Weathercock*)—do you recollect it? . . . Do you think you can manage both her and Caroline? Impossible. As a friend I say flirt as much as you please, but do not get into a serious scrape before you are safe from the present one." To which Byron answered: "You ask 'Am I sure of myself?' and I answer *No,* but *you* are, which I take to be a much better thing. Miss Milbanke I admire because she is a clever woman, an amiable woman, and of high blood, for I have still a few prejudices on the last score, were I to marry. As to love, that is done in a week (provided the lady has a reasonable share); besides, marriage goes on better with esteem and confidence than romance, and she is quite pretty enough to be loved by her husband, without being so glaringly beautiful as to attract too many rivals. . . ."

Love entered so little into this project of marriage that, in the letter in which Byron desired Lady Melbourne to transmit his request to Annabella's parents, he gave her a long description of his new passion for an Italian singer, "not very beautiful, but very much in the style I like. . . . She is very fond of her husband, which is all the better, as thus, if a woman is attached to her husband, how much more will she naturally like one who is *not* her husband." Fletcher, for his part, was anxious to marry his master to a Dutch widow "of great riches and rotundity." Fletcher, of course, was married, but, emancipated by the mosquitoes and siroccos of the Levant, he was enamoured of the widow's serving-woman;

he was hopeful that this union would advance his suit. The Dutch widow? Miss Milbanke? Caroline? The Italian singer? Byron waited in amusement for Fate or Lady Melbourne to make his choice for him. "Does Annabella waltz? It is an odd question, but a very essential point with me. I wish somebody could say at once that I wish to propose to her; but I have great doubts of her—it rests with herself entirely."

It was a terrible responsibility to put forward the claims of so wayward a suitor to one of the few persons of that age who still viewed marriage as a sacred and irrevocable act. Byron himself, in one of his sober moments, declared that she deserved a better heart than his. But Lady Melbourne was fond of the young man. She was touched when she heard, at the age of sixty, that she could still be preferred before all women. And perhaps she also reflected that it would be diverting to see this hesitant Don Juan taken in hand by her serious-minded niece. "Poor Annabella! her innocent eyes will improve *if* she should be in love with you. . . . Eyes require that sort of inspiration." Would Annabella suffer some pangs? That would do her no harm, thought Lady Melbourne, who was always annoyed by her apparent placidity, and she began to play her hand.

The girl was far from having forgotten Lord Byron. During her stay in London she had known the certainty of having interested him, almost the hope of saving him; but then the scandal of the liaison with Caroline had made her despair of saving this soul. Home again with her parents, she had once more found herself in the presence of the sea and sky. She enjoyed walking between these immensities. In this world which Byron saw as so stern and heedless of human sufferings, she believed that she could everywhere discern traces of the goodness of God: "I feel blessed in owning the benevolence of the Creator and I contemplate these scenes with the deepest happiness in thinking my Father made them all." In her diary she tried to sketch a word-portrait of Lord Byron: "The passions have been his guide from childhood. . . . Yet amongst his dispositions are many which deserve to be associated with Christian principles ('I love the virtues that I cannot claim'). . . . In secret he is the zealous friend of all the human feelings; but from the strangest perversion that pride ever created, he endeavours to disguise the best points of his character. . . . When indignation takes possession of his mind—and it is easily excited—his disposition becomes malevolent. He hates with the bitterest contempt. . . . He is inclined to open his heart unreservedly to those whom he believes *good*. . . . He is extremely humble towards persons whose character he respects, and to them he would probably confess his errors." She thought that she herself was one of those persons whose character he respected. She admired him, and was tempted; but she recognised the danger.

Byron was not very deft in his choice of Lady Melbourne as go-between, for Annabella had no high opinion of her judgment. She replied: "I should be totally unworthy of Lord Byron's esteem if I were not to speak the truth without equivocation. Believing that he never will be the object of that strong affection which would make me happy in domestic life, I should wrong him by any measure that might, even indirectly, confirm his present impressions. From my limited observations of his conduct, I was predisposed to believe your strong testimony in his favour, and I willingly attribute it more to the defect of my own feelings than of his character that I am not inclined to return his attachment. After this statement, which I make with real sorrow from the idea of giving pain, I must leave our future intercourse to his judgment. . . ." In fact, if Miss Milbanke was to be believed, she declined to be his wife because she did not love him. It was quite a fresh experience for the author of *Childe Harold*.

XVII

THE GODS IN LUCRETIUS

1812–1815

In her first passion Woman loves her lover,
In all the others all she loves is Love,
Which grows a habit she can ne'er get over,
And fits her loosely, like an easy glove. . . .

BYRON

HE had long abandoned the idea that he and Newstead should stand or fall together. His debts had reached a figure of £25,000. In September 1812 the Abbey was offered for sale. The faithful Hobhouse was sent to the auction, and under Hanson's direction, pushed the first lot up to £113,000, and the second to £13,000—which he found quite amusing, as he then possessed exactly twenty-one shillings and sixpence. The real sale took place privately, after the auction, and the estate was bought by a Mr. Claughton for the sum of £140,000. "I had built myself a bath and a *vault*," commented Byron, "and now I shan't even be buried in it. It is odd that we can't even be certain of a grave." Byron would henceforward have been rich if only Claughton had paid; but the new proprietor was not long in confessing that he had committed himself beyond his means. Hanson, that shrewd and cautious attorney, had made provision for a forfeit of £25,000 in the event of the total price not being forthcoming—which ruined Claughton in any case. But while the lawyers squabbled, Byron was once more short of ready cash.

He had been invited to spend the month of October with some new friends of his fame, the Jersey and Oxford families. Lady Jersey was one of those women whose fashionable success is such that the mere impossibility of leisure assures their virtue. She infused vitality into any society in which she happened to be. Her looks were charming, with her raven-black hair, creamy complexion and pink pearls, and she had no faults beyond her volubility, which had become notorious. Her friend Granville had given her the nickname of "Silence," and wondered how she contrived to be always in her own house and everyone else's at the same time. Byron told her that she spoiled her beauty by excessive animation; for her eyes, tongue, and arms were all in action at once. Under her roof at Middleton he passed what he termed "a week of chastity."

He then went on to Lady Oxford's at Eywood, in Herefordshire. He had met her in London during the winter, come across her again when taking the waters at Cheltenham after Lady Caroline's departure, and had instantly reached the mute understanding that unites a rather shy but ardent young man to a still beautiful woman of amorous fancy, who knows how to make the first approaches easy. Lady Oxford was forty. "She resembled a landscape by Claude Lorrain, with a setting sun, her beauties enhanced by the knowledge that they were shedding their last dying beams, which threw a radiance around. A woman is only grateful for her *first* and *last* conquest. The first of poor dear Lady Oxford's was achieved before I entered on this world of care; but the last, I do flatter myself, was reserved for me, and a *bonne bouche* it was."

Eighteen years earlier, she had married Edward Harley, Earl of Oxford, a man as ill-favoured in body as in mind, though sprung of a family in which wit had been honoured. An ancestor of his had formed one of the best of English libraries; its rare pamphlets had been published under the title of the *Harleian Miscellany*. And the same name had been applied to Lady Oxford's children, a delightful family, who were remarkably like the handsomest of their father's friends.

Lady Oxford had provided herself with a philosophy of tender frailty. Sacrificed by her parents in a shameful marriage to a man whom she could not love, she took more than one revenge. A more charming friend could not be imagined. In her large eyes there often brooded that look of soft, happy reverie that is ever a promise of pleasures to come; and she had both wit and intelligence. She read Lucretius, and worshipped physical love, treating sentimental love as a sickness, the symptoms and duration of which are perfectly known. She was no less changeable than lovable, and to one of her lovers who complained that she had broken his heart, she retorted that a broken heart was merely a sign of bad digestion.

She had invited Byron to visit her in her country-house of Eywood. There he spent the months of October and November 1812, and in the company of a tactful and tender woman, more cynical even than himself, was perfectly happy. Lady Oxford would read, and play music; and she never complained if her lover deserted her for his dreams. Lord Oxford (who was known as Potiphar) walked in the woods all day long, and showed himself a most discreet husband. Byron and his mistress lived like the Gods in Lucretius—"enjoying their immortality in a profound peace, far from the concerns of men and exempt from their cares, free from all peril, and rich enough in their own resources to have any need of others. . . ."

Nam privata dolore omni, privata periclis,
Ipsa suis pollens opibus, nihil indiga nostri. . . .

The Enchantress, a perfect Latinist, often read the lines to her young adorer, and he admired the pride of their epicureanism. Twice in his life already, on Harrow Hill and in the East, he had found happiness in detachment from human concerns. He was mortal and vulnerable, and relished these godlike interludes. The wildness of his heart had often clouded the lucidity of his mind. Lady Oxford seemed in his eyes girt with a prestige not unlike that of Lady Melbourne, and he enjoyed being guided by these bold and sceptical women. Sometimes, taken aback by the gentle apathy into which the Enchantress of Eywood cast him, he wondered into what animal this Circe would transform him. . . . A lazy one, in any case, for he scarcely worked at all, and spent the last of the fine days on the water or in the woods, with those angelic children whose features called up memories of so many charming sires. He was on the verge of falling in love with Charlotte, Lady Oxford's eldest daughter, already ravishly beautiful at eleven years old, and he composed for her a new dedication to *Childe Harold.* He was more contented with himself and with others than he had ever been in his life, and all his troubles seemed to be a thousand miles away. It was a triumph for pagan philosophy.

Meanwhile Lady Caroline Lamb had not accepted her defeat. She knew that Byron was at Eywood, and was

JANE ELIZABETH, COUNTESS OF OXFORD

After the Painting by Hoppner in the National Gallery

accordingly jealous. She was well acquainted with Lady Oxford. A few years earlier the two women had carried on a learned correspondence, discussing the problem of whether a knowledge of Greek purified the passions or inflamed them. In Lady Caroline's case, the answer admitted of no doubt. Every day brought its letters from her, either for Byron or for Lady Oxford: "My dearest Aspasia—only think, Byron is angry with me! Will you tell him I have not done one thing to displease him, and that I am miserable—tell him I wrote him a cross letter, I know. But I have a thousand times asked his pardon. He is tired of me, I see it by his letter. I will write no more—never teaze him—never intrude upon him, only do you obtain his forgiveness." Lady Oxford did not reply. Lady Caroline threatened to come—to write to Lord Oxford—to kill herself. The two lovers read these pathetic letters together with supreme scorn. To Lucretian philosophers their tone was intolerable.

Byron kept his great ally, Lady Melbourne, in touch with the enemy's movements: "Caroline threatens to revenge herself upon herself; this is her concern. . . . I cannot exist without some object of love. I have found one with whom I am perfectly satisfied, and who, as far as I can judge, is no less so with me; our mutual wish is quiet, and I find a double pleasure (after all the ridiculous display of last season) in repose. . . . I have much to do and little time to do it in; certainly not an instant to spare to that person. . . . The abhorrence I feel at part of her conduct, I will not trust myself to express. That feeling has become a part of my nature; it has poisoned my future existence. I know not whom I may love, but to the latest hour of my life I shall hate that woman. Now you know my sentiments; they will be the same on my death-bed. To her I do not express this, because I have no desire to make her uncomfortable; but such is the state of my mind towards her, for reasons I shall not recur to, and beg to be spared from meeting her until we may be chained together in Dante's *Inferno*."

Lady Melbourne approved this firmness, and denounced the vagaries of her daughter-in-law with implacable severity: "a servant brought me two letters from Caroline. If I know her, *vous n'en êtes pas quitte*. Both the letters are written the same day, one full of spirits, *gaieté,* dinners, parties, etc., etc., the other false, written to deceive one, talking of her unhappiness and affecting to be perfectly quiet and resigned. As this is not in her nature, you will most likely know the contrary by this time." It is only women who are ferocious in denouncing the lies of other women. If there lingered any pity or ingenuousness in Byron, it could not long withstand the disillusioned wisdom of Lady Melbourne.

For some time he replied courteously to Lady Caroline, and then, as the rash woman persisted in bombarding him with letters of mingled whines and fury, Byron grew exasperated, and wrote (probably under Lady Oxford's dictation) a stinging letter: "Lady Caroline—I am no longer your lover; and since you oblige me to confess it, by this truly unfeminine persecution . . . learn, that I am attached to another; whose name it would, of course, be dishonourable to mention. I shall ever remember with gratitude the many instances I have received of the predilection you have shown in my favour. I shall ever continue your friend, if your Ladyship will permit me so to style myself; and, as a first proof of my regard, I offer you this advice: correct your vanity, which is ridiculous; exert your absurd caprices upon others; and leave me in peace.—Your most obedient servant, BYRON."

Perhaps he might have treated her less cruelly if he could have seen her, for she was truly pitiable. She had the buttons of her servants' livery marked with the motto—*"Ne Crede Biron."* She imitated the handwriting of her former lover, and concocted forged letters to extort from the publisher Murray a portrait which Byron had refused to give her. At Brocket Hall she staged a curious ceremony in the course of which Byron was burnt in effigy, while the village girls, clad in white, danced round the pyre. She herself was dressed as a page, and, placing in the fire a basket containing locks of Byron's hair, books of his, and rings and copies of his letters, recited verses which she had composed for the occasion:

> Burn, fire, burn! These glittering toys destroy,
> While thus we hail the blaze with throats of joy.
>
> Burn, fire, burn! While wondering boys exclaim,
> And gold and trinkets glitter in the flame.
> Ah! look not thus on me, so grave, so sad:
> Shake not your heads, nor say the Lady's mad. . . .

And she was ingenuous enough to send an account of this ceremony to Byron himself, who passed it on to Lady Melbourne, endorsing it with this comment: "Long account of a bonfire, full of yeomanry, pages, gold chains, basket of flowers, herself, and all other fooleries."

In February 1813 Lady Bessborough, having returned to London, requested a conversation with Byron, and once again was dumbfounded at finding him so very matter-of-fact. A kind of inverse heredity always makes a mother partake to some extent of her daughter's folly. And although this mother regretted the adventure, still, the harm was done, and she wished the play to be well staged. A reasonable Byron was a disappointment. "Lady Bessborough," he remarked, "was a good deal horrified at my deficiency in Romance, and quite petrified at my behaviour altogether."

She was anxious to obtain an interview for her daughter; Lady Oxford, with great good sense, opposed the idea. William Lamb himself, finding his wife in tears, supposed that Byron was insulting *him* by his refusal to see her.—"Now this is really laughable; if I speak to her, he is insulted; if I don't speak to her, she is insulted." Lady Melbourne advised an interview in the presence of a witness, and Byron said he would agree to that, provited that the witness were Lady Oxford.

In the end the meeting took place unarranged, on July 6, 1813, at a ball at Lady Heathcote's. Lady Melbourne was present, with large plumes sweeping from her white hair; she was then sixty-one, and still one of the most fascinating women of the evening's party. Lord Grey and Sheridan were there. Suddenly the crowd parted, to watch with eager interest the entry of Byron, limping, pale, of an "almost sinister beauty." He found himself face to face with Caroline, who looked at him with haggard eyes.

At that moment the band was playing the first bars of a waltz, and the hostess, a trifle uneasy, spoke.—"Come, Lady Caroline, you must begin."—"Oh, yes! I am in a merry humour," said she, and leaning towards Lord Byron whispered: "I conclude I may waltz *now?*" (He had once made her vow never to waltz.)—"With everybody in turn," answered he sarcastically. "You always did it better than anyone. I shall have a pleasure in watching you."—She danced and then, feeling ill, went into a smaller room where supper was prepared. Lord Byron entered it with a lady on his arm, and seeing her remarked: "I have been admiring your dexterity." She seized a knife. "Do, my dear," said Byron, "but if you mean to act a Roman's part, mind which way you strike with your knife—be it at your own heart, not mine—you have struck there already."—"Byron!" she cried, and ran off, bearing the knife. Nobody saw exactly what happened. Some declared she cut herself, others that she was on the point of fainting, and, in trying to take a glass of water broke it, and wounded herself with the fragments. Whatever happened, she was covered with blood. Byron had meanwhile passed into a neighbouring room; when told of what had happened, he scornfully remarked: "Another of her tricks!"

But the story caused a great stir, and a journal called the *Satirist* published an account of it under the heading of "Scandalum Magnatum," to the effect that the preference of Lord B * * * n for another fair object had so enraged Lady C. L * * b that she had seized a knife in a paroxysm of jealousy and stabbed herself. This lady's husband, said the sheet, was to be pitied that the attempted suicide was not completely successful, as Lady C. L * * b was still alive.

A few weeks later she was bold enough to call upon Byron at his own house. He had gone out. But she had herself let in and, finding on the table a copy of Beckford's *Vathek,* wrote the words "Remember me" on the front page. On his return, Byron found the open book with the all too well-known handwriting, and on the spur of the moment he wrote the lines:—

Remember thee! remember thee!
  Till Lethe quench life's burning stream
Remorse and shame shall cling to thee,
  And haunt thee like a feverish dream!

Remember thee! Ay, doubt it not.
  Thy husband too shall think of thee!
By neither shalt thou be forgot,
  Thou *false* to him, thou *fiend* to me!

Nothing was more in character for Byron than this linking of husband with lover in the case against a woman whose worst crime had been the unpardonable one of loving him.

True, he had had enough of it. If love must bring adventures like these in its train, the only wise thing was to keep clear of women. The Enchantress herself, for all her wisdom, had sometimes made him suffer. She was free, and she never stood still; and while Lady Oxford still remained Byron's friend, she began to grow curious regarding another man. Whereupon Lord Oxford plunged deeper than ever into his woods, and Byron found himself for the time being set aside, with alarming frankness. He learned the truth through her each time, and was all the more sorry to lose her because he prized this wounding sincerity:

Thou art not false, but thou art fickle,
  To those thyself so fondly sought;
The tears that thou hast forced to trickle
  Are doubly bitter from that thought:
'Tis this which breaks the heart thou grievest,
Too well thou lov'st—too soon thou leavest.

They were forming pleasant plans for travelling *à trois* in Sicily when Lord Oxford, alarmed by an absurd family, took it into his head—as always happens—to grow jealous of Lord Byron just when the latter himself had the strongest reasons for jealousy. His wife had taken instant steps to calm the senile storm by reassuring lies, but it was decided that she would leave for the Mediterranean alone with her husband, and, as Byron wrote, that they would "live happy ever after." She left on June 28, 1813: "Lady Oxford sailed yesterday, and now, my dear Lady Melbourne, will you not mention her name to me? To tell you the truth, I feel more Carolinish about her than I expected."

XVIII

AUGUSTA

1813

Was there ever such a slave to impulse?
BYRON

IT had been agreed that he should accompany Lord and Lady Oxford to their vessel. But at the last moment he dropped the plan, because his sister Augusta had written saying that she was forced to leave home on account of her husband's money troubles, and was coming to stay with him in London. "My dearest Augusta," he wrote, "if you knew *whom* I had put off besides my journey—you would think me grown strangely fraternal. . . ."

He had not seen her since his return to England. She lived at Six Mile Bottom, in a country-house close to the Newmarket racecourse, with three children on her hands, and overwhelmed by money difficulties. Her husband, Colonel Leigh, was an unconscionable egotist, who spent his life in racing, piling up huge debts in consequence, and in running after servant-girls with his friend Lord Darlington. He hardly ever saw his wife, and only stayed with her during the Newmarket races. Augusta had the reputation of being faithful to him. She had been brought up by a pietistic grandmother, and she used a curious devotional jargon in place of any real morality. In the family it was known that a gift from Augusta Leigh would always be a Bible or a prayer-book. In any case, her household and maternal cares left her no time for thinking of other things. Tending her children, of whom at least one in the three was always ailing, staving off bookmakers and creditors, answering the letters of a husband who was incapable of penning one—her life was all taken up with this humble daily round. No one could live a more hand-to-mouth existence.

Byron received her in his Bennet Street apartments, in the early afternoon of Sunday, June 27, 1813. He was charmed by her. Physically she delighted him at a first glance. She did not look very pretty at a casual glance; her good looks depended as much on her carelessness in appearance as on her features, beautiful as they were. She had the Byrons' profile, their odd trick of not pronouncing an "r," their almost childishly pouting lips, their frowning eyebrows. For Byron, always so curious about himself, it was an astonishing and pleasant sensation to meet this other self, who turned out to be a pretty woman. In some ways they had points of moral likeness as well. She had the shyness of the Byrons, who had something of the wild creature in them. She and Byron were both silent in company, but found themselves delightfully free with each other when alone. Was it because of her being his sister, because he shared so many memories with her, from that fickle father of theirs to the Dowager of Southwell? However it might be, from the very first day their conversation was pleasant and animated. What a pity she was married! She would have come to live with him, and kept house for him—it would have been better for him than marrying some stranger. He hated strangers, creatures who know nothing of your life, of your sensitive spots, your wretched foot, your harsh childhood. With Augusta everything was so simple. You could let yourself go—completely. And for her "Baby Byron" Augusta had a soft-hearted indulgence. On that first Sunday, as soon as she left him, he wrote her a note asking her to go out with him that evening. "My dearest Augusta—If you like to go with me to Lady Davy's to-night, I *have* an invitation for you. There you will see the Staël, some people whom you know, and *me* whom you do *not* know—and you can talk to which you please, and I will watch over you as if you were unmarried and in danger of always being so. Now do as you like; but if you chuse to array yourself before or after half-past ten, I will call for you. I think our being together before 3d people will be a new *sensation* to *both.*"

He underlined the word *sensation;* doubtless he had already expounded to her his favourite doctrine that only powerful sensation can give us self-knowledge. But ideas expounded to Augusta were as water poured on a duck's back. In her muddled, see-saw mind ideas instantaneously slipped away into a limbo of vagueness. At first, out of sheer politeness, she asked to see any new verses of his; he replied that she would not understand anything about them; and she laughed, really satisfied. She had a childlike enjoyment of playing games. Gifted like all the Byrons with a very keen sense of the comical, she indulged in mimicry, to her brother's great delight. She spoke a queer language of her own, in which facts were wrapped in such a mist of parentheses, insinuations and incoherencies, that after five minutes listening to her one was no clearer as to what she was talking about. It was all "Oh, dear! Oh, dear!" . . . stories of children's ailments . . . suddenly an anecdote of Queen Charlotte, to whom she was a lady-in-waiting . . . and then some ridiculous memory that occurred to her . . . oh, dear! oh, dear! . . . and she burst into laughter. Byron adored this incoherence: the Augustan mysteries, he called it, and "her damned crinkum-crankum." He quickly came to adopt with her a tone of affectionate joking that was more like a lover's than a brother's.

All the early part of July she spent in London. She did not live at Byron's, but accompanied him to dance at Almack's or to the theatre, and she called on him daily in his Bennet Street rooms. He had an elderly housekeeper, Mrs. Mule, who looked like a witch and alarmed all his visitors, but worshipped her master, who was very kind to her. The housekeeper, the bachelor rooms, a lady's daily visits—it was the classic setting for a liaison, and from the very first there must have slipped into these "strangely fraternal" relations an element of sensuality, all the more ingratiating for its being at first unconscious.

Everything here was combining to seduce Byron. It was possible for this young woman who attracted him to visit him quite freely. They were not safeguarded against love, like normal brothers and sisters, by the wear-and-tear of their affection. "They had not been brought up together under the same roof in the unconscious innocence of childhood. . . . They rarely met." They had had neither the same mother nor the same family. Augusta, in Byron's eyes, retained all the glamour of a discovery. He believed in birth. He could not help admiring a half-sister of the Duke of Leeds, a lady-in-waiting to the Queen, who knew everybody in London and had rooms in St. James's Palace. It was flattering to display a new intimacy with such a woman. Not only could she attract him as any new woman friend could have done, but she was to tempt him further.

He had once written that he liked women to treat him "as a favourite and somewhat forward sister." And he knew himself thoroughly. He was seeking in love a blend of gay friendship, sensuality, an almost maternal tenderness. . . . A somewhat forward sister. . . . Once the thought had struck him, incest was to haunt him. Was it not enough for him to imagine a dangerous passion, to believe himself fated for it? Was he not born of the Byrons and the Gordons, whose history was as terrible as that of the Borgias? From childhood he had felt himself marked down, like Zeluco, for some monstrous crime that would set him above and beyond the pale of human law. In this adventure he had to feel himself guilty, and to find pleasure in feeling more guilty than he really was. It could almost be said that it was Byron, and he alone, who, by giving to this quite natural love for an unknown half-sister the name of incest, transformed the lapse into a crime. Even that inability to escape from himself, which isolated him so dangerously from others, was here serving him; for in this woman who was so like him, it was still himself that he sought. In his desire for her there lurked a kind of strange narcissism.

A couple of years earlier the shyness of a young and inexperienced male would perhaps have held him back. But thanks to Caroline Lamb, thanks to Lady Oxford, he was now an adept in that ritual of conquest which, by its almost fatalistic automatism, has such singular power over inexperienced women. As for Augusta, she was perhaps of all women the least capable of resisting him. Having neither will nor pride, she had been dominated by him from the start. He called her "Guss" or "Goose," and told her she was a little fool. And she laughed. Mrs. Leigh's religion was entirely superficial, and had not the slightest bearing on her actions. Her keenest sentiment was kindness, but it was a kindness so little regulated by the channels of moral or social rules, that she would have seen no harm in committing the most criminal act so long as she imagined it gave pleasure to someone she liked. Her mind was tolerably pure, and she was capable of committing the worst follies, and, no less, of instantly forgetting them.

Byron was soon telling his confidante, Lady Melbourne, of the matter, and stressed the fact that Augusta had yielded more from kindness than from passion. "By that God who made me for my own misery, and not much for the good of others, *she* was not to blame, one thousandth part in comparison. She was not aware of her own peril till it was too late, and I can only account for her subsequent *abandon* by an observation which I think is not unjust, that women are much more *attached* than men if they are treated with anything like fairness or tenderness."

This love yielded him a pleasure all the more sharp and penetrating for his sense of sin. Beside this mingled draught of joy and remorse all his past adventures seemed savourless. Incest, by its violation of one of the most ancient of human laws, seemed to lend to the joys of the flesh the splendour of Revolt. Augusta, a far simpler soul, just yielded. Oh, dear! oh, dear! . . . what an adventure for the mother of a family . . . and how ill-fitted her nature was for this tragedy! The strangest thing was that she still loved, in her way, that "impossible gentleman," her cousin and husband; but how could she refuse anything that her Baby Byron asked of her? Oh, dear! oh, dear! she was one of those women who believe that just by ceasing to think of it, an unpleasant past is wiped out. She hopped like a bird over the surface of her thought, picking up a comic detail here, a platitude there. Sometimes Byron, who relished the tart flavour of remorse, would try to make her share his brooding over their crime. But away she slipped, with a neat wriggle, and tried to make him laugh.

At the end of July she took him down to Newmarket with her to see the three children. It was a merry visit. The children liked their young uncle, and joyously shouted "Byron! Byron!" whenever he came into the room. Then Augusta returned to London with him. Colonel Leigh's financial situation was such that life was better anywhere than in that house of his. Brother and sister made plans for travel. Byron was disgusted with England. The Prince-Regent, whom he had thought a liberal, was daily becoming more and more despotic. Leigh Hunt, the man of letters, was imprisoned for criticising an eulogy of the Prince. Such a country horrified Byron. "What a fool I was to come back," he would say, and called to mind the scent of thyme and lavender, the sharp contours of mountains cutting an indigo sea, lands where you had no thought of anyone and no one had thought of you. Why not take Augusta away to Greece or Sicily?

But he could not hold his tongue, and began hinting to his friends, under a cloak of transparent mystery, the nature of his latest love. He wrote to Moore: "I have said nothing, either, of the brilliant sex; but the fact is, I am at this moment in a far more serious, and entirely new scrape than any of the last twelve months,—and that is saying a good deal. It is unlucky we can neither live with nor without these women." And Lady Mel-

AUGUSTA LEIGH

After a Drawing by Sir George Hayter in the British Museum

bourne herself received these confidences. She, notwithstanding her boldness, was startled; admittedly, she was no fanatic in morality, but the horror of incest goes beyond morality. "You are on the brink of a precipice, and if you do not retreat, you are lost for ever—it is a crime for which there is no salvation in this world, whatever there may be in the next." Byron was extremely proud of having been able to shock her: "she is a good woman, after all," he remarked, "for there are things she will stop at." But he obeyed her and dropped the Sicilian project. "Dear Lady Melbourne—Your kind letter is *unanswerable;* no one but yourself would have taken the trouble; no one but me would have been in a situation to require it. I am still in town, so that it has as yet all the effect you wish."

In town he certainly was, alone with Augusta in the desert of a London August, and very happy. "And now what are you doing? In this place we can only say what we are not doing. Town is empty, but not the worse for that; it is a delight of a place now that there is no one in it. I am totally and unutterably possessed by the ineffable power of indolence. I see no one; I say nothing, I do nothing; and I wish for nothing."

During the spring, before this liaison opened, he had published an oriental narrative poem, *The Giaour*, his only work since *Childe Harold*. It was a rather cold poem, of middling quality, dealing with a memory of Athens, the tale of a woman whom the Turks had wished to cast into the sea for her adultery. In the autumn, within a few days, he added five hundred lines to it, hammered out white-hot:

> Leila! each thought was only thine!
> My good, my guilt, my weal, my woe,

My hope on high—my all below.
Earth holds no other like to thee,
Or, if it doth, in vain for me:
For worlds I dare not view the dame
Resembling thee, yet not the same.
The very crimes that mar my youth,
This bed of death attest my truth!
'Tis all too late—thou wert, thou art
The cherish'd madness of my heart!

The cherished madness of his heart, his crime, his weal, his only hope on high and below—these were all Augusta. But he knew this madness could not last. Lady Melbourne, this time really anxious, was forced out of her usual indulgence. Convinced that Byron and his sister were both heading for disaster, she begged him to break the connection. He had not the courage to do so. Augusta spent the whole of August with him. And when she left him at the beginning of September, she was pregnant.

XIX

THE NEAREST PERCH

1813

My heart always alights on the nearest perch.

BYRON

IN his correspondence with Lady Melbourne, the heroines of Byron's love affairs were indicated by initial letters. Caroline was "C," Annabella Milbanke, "your A," and Augusta "my A," or sometimes, when he had to be more mysterious, was designated simply by a cross—"X." Lady Melbourne's sole wish, since the incest had come to pass, was to see a letter of salvation added to this dangerous alphabet. But was it possible? He wrote to her: "I have tried, and hardly too, to vanquish my demon; but to very little purpose, for a resource that seldom failed me before did in this instance. I mean transferring my regards to another, of which I had a fair and not discouraging opportunity. I willingly would, but the feeling that it was an effort spoiled all again; and *here* I am—*what* I am you know already. As I have never been accustomed to parade my thoughts before you in a *larmoyante* strain, I shall not begin now."

Immediately after Augusta's departure he had been invited to stay in the country with James Wedderburn Webster, a commonplace young man with a mop of tow-coloured hair, whom he had known in Cambridge days and met again later in Athens. Webster was a chatter-

box, indiscreet, awkward, always putting his foot in it—in a word, insufferable; but Byron was always indulgent to creatures of this species because of his sense of the comic. A year earlier Webster had married the youthful Lady Frances Annesley, and had now asked his illustrious friend to stand as godfather to his first child. Childe Harold was delighted. "If it is a boy . . ." Webster had written.—"And why not if it be a girl too?" answered Byron, vexed. It was a boy.

Lady Frances was very pretty, but had an air of fragility. Observing the pallor of her skin and the hectic gleam of her eyes, Byron wondered if she would live. Her sister, Lady Catherine Annesley, was no less frail, both of them blondes, with long upturning eyelashes, and mournful deeply ringed eyes. Webster, a plump jovial fellow, seemed out of place amid all these anæmic Graces. Several times during dinner his coarse jesting provoked faint movements of impatience from his wife and sister-in-law; and Byron, in silent amusement, lost not one of their soft sighs, and savoured them as a connoisseur. After dinner the men remained alone round the decanters. Byron paid high tribute to Lady Frances, and Webster expanded. He was very proud of his wife; but he was also very jealous. Lord Byron was beginning to know all the fashions and failings of the genus husband, and knew better than anyone how to tame the creature. During the whole of dinner he scrupulously avoided paying attention to his host's wife, and pushed indifference to the verge of discourtesy. Webster found him eminently tactful, this Don Juan of whom so much ill was spoken, and Byron really did feel lazily benevolent, with no desire to torment a husband.

Yet the latter played straight into his hands. He

asked Byron to invite him later to Newstead, where he had stayed for a short time a month before, and had admired at too close quarters the charms of one of the well-disposed nymphs of the Abbey. That evening Byron wrote to Lady Melbourne: "If I wanted to make mischief I could extract much good perplexity from a proper management of such events; but I am grown so good, or so indolent, that I shall not avail myself of so pleasant an opportunity. . . . He proposed to me, with great gravity, to carry him over there, and I replied with equal candour, that *he* might set out when he pleased, but that I should remain here to take care of his household in the interim; a proposition which I thought very much to the purpose, but which does not seem at all to his satisfaction. By way of opiate he preached me a sermon on his wife's good qualities, concluding by an assertion that in all moral and mortal qualities, she was very like Christ!!! I think the Virgin Mary would have been a more appropriate typification."

When Byron left Aston Hall on the following day, he was warmly invited to come again by the husband. The wife said nothing, but gave him a long look. Would he come back? "There will be no one to make him jealous of but the curate and the butler—and I have no thoughts of setting up for myself. I am not exactly cut out for the lady of the mansion. . . . She evidently expects to be attacked, and seems prepared for a brilliant defence; my character as a *roué* has gone before me, and my careless and quiet behaviour astonished her so much that I believe she began to think herself ugly, or me blind—if not worse."

Such praiseworthy abstention ought at least to have assured Byron of a peaceful stay. But men do not see real actions. In place of the veritable being, they gaze on the fictitious personage created by legend. Is he known for a man of wit? Then they laugh at his commonplaces. A great diplomat? His clumsiest moves seem to be deeply calculated. Does Don Juan abstain from eyeing a woman? Then the darkest designs are attributed to him. For once poor Byron wished to respect the peace of a friendly household, and the health of a frail woman; the husband grew nervous and irritable, and suspected that all this nonchalance must cloak dreadful projects. "Webster grows rather intolerable," wrote Byron to Lady Melbourne. "He is out of humour with my *Italian* books (Dante and Alfieri) and requests that *sa femme* may not see them, because, forsooth, it is a language which doth infinite damage!! and because I enquired after the Stanhopes, our mutual acquaintances, he *answers* me by another question: 'Pray, do you enquire after *my* wife of others in the same way?' So that you see my Virtue is its own reward—for never, in word or deed, did I speculate upon his spouse. . . . She is pretty, but not surpassing—too thin, and not very animated; but good tempered—and a something interesting enough in her manner and figure; but I should never think of her, nor anyone else, if left to my own cogitations, as I have neither the patience nor presumption to advance till met half-way."

It was perfectly true that Byron, who was neither a fool nor conceited, never made advances without knowing they would be met. He had been quite right in declaring that he had never seduced any woman. He had been a spectator no less surprised by his amorous than by his literary triumphs. The easiness of female virtue remained something truly astonishing for him, and, in his heart of hearts, something scandalous. From the moment of his arrival at Aston Hall he was persuaded that he barely interested this fair, quiet young woman who looked at him so coldly beneath her long lashes. But like most Elviras, Lady Frances was ready to go rather more than half-way. She contrived to remain alone with Byron in the billiard-room. "We were before long on very amicable terms, and I remembered being asked an odd question: 'how a woman who liked a man could inform him of it when he did not perceive it.' I also observed that we went on with our game (of billiards) without *counting the hazards;* and supposed that, as mine certainly were not, the thoughts of the other party also were not exactly occupied by what was our ostensible pursuit. Not quite, though pretty well satisfied with my progress, I took a very imprudent step with pen and paper, in tender and tolerably turned *prose periods*. . . . Here were risks, certainly: first, how to convey, then how would it be received? It was received, however, and deposited not very far from the heart which I wished it to reach, when, who should enter the room but the person who ought at that moment to have been in the Red Sea, if Satan had any civility. But *she* kept her countenance, and the paper. . . . My billet prospered, it did more, it even (I am this moment interrupted by the *Marito,* and write this before him, he has brought me a political pamphlet in MS. to decipher and applaud, I shall content myself with the last; oh, he is gone again), my billet produced an *answer,* a very unequivocal one, too, but a little too much about virtue, and indulgence of attachment in some sort of etherial process, in which the soul is principally concerned, which I don't very well understand, being a bad metaphysician; but one generally *ends* and *begins* with platonism, and, as my proselyte is only twenty, there is time enough to materialise. I hope nevertheless this spiritual system won't last long, and at any rate must make the experiment. I remember my last case was the reverse, as Major O'Flaherty recommends: 'We fought first and explained afterwards.' This is the present state of things: much mutual profession, a good deal of melancholy, which I am sorry to say was remarked by 'the Moor,' and as much love as could well be made, considering the time, place and circumstances. . . . Good evening, I am now going to *billiards.*

"P.S.—6 o'clock. This business is growing serious, and I think *Platonism* is in some peril. There has been very nearly a scene, almost an *hysteric,* and really without cause, for I was conducting myself with a (to me) very irksome decorum. . . . But these professions must end as usual, and *would* I think so now, had 'l'occasion' been *not* wanting. . . . Had anyone come in during the *tears,* and consequent consolation, all had been spoiled; we must be more cautious, or less *larmoyante.* P.S. second, 10 o'clock. I write to you just escaped from claret and vocification on G—d knows what paper. My landlord is a rare gentleman. He has just proposed to me a bet that *he,* for a certain sum, 'wins any given *woman,* against any given *homme* including *all friends* present.' . . . Is not this, at the moment, a perfect comedy?"

And so he found himself, having arrived there with his heart wholly taken up with another woman, caught up by a day of surprises in the most unexpected adventure, and—what was still more serious—in a platonic one. Lady Frances had said that, whatever the weakness of her heart might be, he would never have other proof of it than this avowal. He replied that he was entirely hers, that he accepted the given conditions, and would never without her permission take the slightest step to draw her beyond these promises. Entirely hers? Could he really be sincere? Had he forgotten Augusta so soon? He was amazed at it himself. But thus it was, and he of all men was the least able to deceive his own lucidity. He had been touched by this young woman, hardly more than a girl. A virgin at heart—for she had never known any man but this crude *marito*—she called forth the Mary Chaworth *motif*. He had written once of the sweet memory of a buried love. . . . Of those tombs amongst which he liked to live, the most precious to his heart were those of his dead loves. A sentimentalist beneath a cynic's mask, never completely cured of hope, he detested the hypocritical chastity which flees only to be pursued, but respected a tender emotion if he knew it to be sincere. An air of shyness, silence, and pallor, had more power over him than all the impassioned sentences of a Caroline Lamb.

Back at Newstead, and sitting opposite Webster, who had accompanied him, he wrote to the confidante: "Yesterday . . . has changed my views, my wishes, my hopes, my everything, and will furnish you with additional proof of my weakness. . . . For certain reasons, you will not be sorry to hear that I am anything but what I was. . . . Anything, you will allow, is better than the *last;* and I cannot exist without some object of attachment. You will laugh at my perpetual *changes,* but recollect the circumstances which have broken off the last, and don't exactly attribute their conclusion to caprice."

That evening the *marito,* all unconscious, described the joy of having in his wife a partner devoid of passion. And Byron, who was writing to Lady Melbourne, continued his letter before Webster's face: "I don't know, and cannot yet speak with certainty. . . . The only alarming thing is that Webster complains of her aversion from being beneficial to population and posterity. If this is an invariable maxim, I shall lose my labour. . . . I think her eye, her change of colour, and the trembling of her hand, and above all her devotion, tell a different tale."

Then, taking him back to Aston Hall, Webster borrowed £1,000 from Byron for the purpose of seducing a certain venal countess. Byron showed himself doubly generous, for he lent the thousand pounds but made no use of this weapon for the conquest of Lady Frances. Never had he spent such days as now. The pale young wife with the long dark eyelashes came and sat by his side, gazing passionately at him without a word. He too was silent. Their actions were hardly more expressive; sometimes hand pressed hand, with now and then a kiss. They both sat late into the night writing endless letters, and in the morning looked haggard as ghosts. She handed Byron her long letters in a book, or laid between sheets of music, and still met her husband's eyes with a gentle, dreamy gaze.

Byron's feelings were rather confused. He let himself be caught up more and more in the charm of this virginal sentimentality. She asked him for a lock of his hair, which he cut and gave her. Formerly, for Caroline Lamb, he had stopped short of this sacrifice and given her a lock from a manservant's head. That had greatly amused him; but to play such a trick on the delicate Lady Frances would have seemed monstrous.

Where was it all leading him? To a duel, or an elopement? He was prepared for either. He was enjoying the game enough to play his part to the end. Yet was it a part? Love comes by loving. "W. will probably want to cut my throat, which would not be a difficult task, for I trust I should not return the fire of a man I had injured, though I could not refuse him the pleasure of trying me as a target. . . . Ten days . . . —a week yesterday, on recollection: you cannot be more astonished than I am how all this has happened . . . she is, you know, very handsome, and very gentle . . . fearfully romantic, and singularly warm in her *affections;* but I should think of a *cold* temperament, yet I have my doubts on that point too; accomplished (as all decently educated women are) and clever, though her style a little too *German;* no dashing or desperate talker, but never—and I have watched her in *mixed* conversation—saying a silly thing (*duet dialogues* in course between young and Platonic people must be varied with a little chequered absurdity)."

Platonism has its charms. It lends value to little things, to flowers exchanged and whispered verses. It can draw infinite joys from a hand-clasp, a sigh, the brush of a gown spread further out than need be. Facility cheapens love as paper-money does a currency; and Byron, for all his disillusionment of mind, did not grow weary in this pastoral. The perils of a miniature conjugal war, the pleasures of being allied therein with somebody so graceful and sensitive, all kept him captive and intent.

But Don Juan after all was not the man to platonise for ever. Even had his temperament allowed it, his pride would not have borne it. The adventure lacked the seal of possession. Were it only for Lady Melbourne's sake, he must make the conquest. But Aston Hall, of all the country-houses of England, was the most ill-adapted for bringing matters to a head. The most that could be contrived was brief interviews, propitious for a mere fleeting kiss. Night-time remained, but topography did not permit of nocturnal visits.

For some time there had been talk of the whole Aston Hall party going over to spend a few days at Newstead Abbey, and Byron revived this partly forgotten scheme. He was strongly supported by the ladies, and Webster, attracted by the famous nymph, raised no objections.

At Newstead Byron was on his own ground. His glamour was heightened by that of his beautiful dwelling. He displayed his Gothic Abbey, his lake, the monks' avenue, the charming fountain in the cloister. Before the admiring eyes of Lady Frances he drained the brimming skull of wine. He took her walking in the park, where the deer and does stepped after them under the vast oaks. He could feel her respect and submissiveness, and in this house which he knew so well a secret *rendezvous* was easy. At midnight the blameless lovers met, alone, and far from everyone. "One day, left entirely to ourselves, was nearly fatal—another such *victory,* and with Pyrrhus we were lost—it came to this: 'I am entirely at your mercy. I own it. I give myself up to you. I am not *cold,* whatever I seem to others; but I know that I cannot bear the reflection hereafter. Do not imagine that these are mere words. I tell you the truth—now act as you will.' Was I wrong? I spared her. There was something so very peculiar in her manner—a kind of mild decision—no scene—not even a struggle; but still I know not what, that convinced me that she was serious. It was not the mere '*No*' which one has heard forty times before, and always with the same accent; but the *tone,* and the aspect—yet I sacrificed much—the hour *two* in the morning—away—the Devil whispering that it was mere *verbiage,* etc. And yet I know not whether I can regret it—she seems so very thankful for my forbearance—a proof, at least, that she was not playing merely the usual decorous reluctance, which is sometimes so tiresome on these occasions. You ask if I am prepared to go *all lengths*. . . . I answer, *Yes*, I love her."

For some days he was rent by a violent inward struggle. She yielded to his discretion: "Rather than you should be angry . . . rather than you should like anyone else, I will do whatever you please." He felt disarmed; he saw her there, so pale and fragile, and guessed that she was near to tears. What was he to do? He had pity and spared her. "She had so much more dread of the Devil; and I am not yet sufficiently in his good graces to indulge my own passions at the certain misery of another." Was this a mistake? Had he been the dupe of the finest feelings he had ever experienced? It was possible, and Lady Melbourne would doubtless be saying again that he did not know women. No matter: he did not pretend to know them. Virtue must be its own reward—and a good thing too, for it had no other. And one morning the lovers parted, Byron deeply moved, Lady Frances mysterious. As for James Wedderburn Webster, he presented Byron with a memento of this fortnight in the shape of a snuff-box—"with a flaming inscription."

XX

THE CORSAIR

1813–1814

> It is difficult to avoid seeing what the nineteenth century is seeking—an increasing thirst for strong emotions is its essential character.
>
> STENDAHL

REALLY, Satan was baiting too many hooks; and the soul he angled for was perhaps predestined to be his in any case. Byron had fought against incest, had tried to effect a transfer; and at the eleventh hour, just when he thought himself victorious, his good feelings had wrecked the scheme. Day and night he was tortured by regrets: regret for having lost Augusta, regret for having spared Lady Frances Webster, a vain brooding over the might-have-been, a vain remorse for what had been. Poetry, as he said, is the lava of imagination, whose eruption prevents an earthquake. At such moments, when the earthquake was imminent, he wrote spontaneously and without effort. Since the summer he had been pondering a new Turkish tale, *The Bride of Abydos* . . . Zuleika loved Selim, her brother. . . .

> Oh, Selim dear! oh, more than dearest!
> Say, is it me thou hat'st or fearest?
> Come lay thy head upon my breast,
> And I will kiss thee into rest. . . .
>
> . . . .
>
> Think'st thou that I could bear to part
> With thee, and learn to halve my heart?

Ah! were I sever'd from thy side,
Where were thy friend—and who my guide?
Years have not seen, Time shall not see,
The hour that tears my soul from thee:
Ev'n Azrael, from his deadly quiver
   When flies that shaft, and fly it must,
That parts all else, shall doom for ever
   Our hearts to undivided dust!

A tale of incest—it was an imprudent theme, but he could not keep his genius from prowling round such subjects. To calm the seething of his mind, on his return to London, he composed this twelve-hundred-line poem in four nights, and into it he wove his two obsessing images, Augusta and Lady Frances. "Had I not done something at that time, I must have gone mad, by eating my own heart—bitter diet."

To publish a poem on incestuous love was dangerous; to admit the connection of this poem with his own life still more so. He wrote to Galt that "the first part was *drawn* from *observations* of my life"; and to Lady Melbourne: "my new Turkish tale will be out directly. . . . It will for somc *reasons* interest *you* more than anybody. . . . I want to see whether you think my writings are *me* or not." Why these admissions? Why not keep silence? Why? What else could he do? He was far from having, like an Augusta, the faculty of oblivion. He was for ever chewing the cud of his errors and his thoughts. "I take up books and fling them down again. I began a comedy, and burnt it because the scene ran into *reality;* —a novel, for the same reason. In rhyme, I can keep more away from facts; but the thought always runs through, through . . . yes, yes, through."

Since returning he had kept a journal for his consolation. The complete and admirable contact of Byron's spirit with reality, the abrupt poetry of its brevities, made this journal a masterpiece. There he achieved in every line something which, in *Childe Harold,* had been the miracle of a few stanzas only—the total capture of his whole self. His egotism, "that cursed selfishness," made the impact of his thoughts on these pages no less forcible and truthful than on his spirit. His life now was simply a long dialogue of Byron with Byron. When he closed his journal at night, Byron was writing to Byron: "By the by, I am yawning now—so, good-night to thee, —Byron." External events he noted; but he did so as might a watchman from the summit of a rock, mingling in lofty indifference the tiger and elephant seen in some menagerie, with Shakespeare's Cleopatra, who struck him "as the epitome of her sex—fond, lively, sad, tender, teasing, humble, haughty, beautiful, the devil! —coquettish to the last, as well with the asp as with Antony."

Never had pen and paper revealed more sharply how stationary was Byron's soul. After fifteen years he was still brooding over his love for the child Mary Duff: "I should be quite grieved to see *her* now; the reality, however beautiful, would destroy, or at least confuse, the features of the lovely Peri which then existed in her, and still lives in my imagination." Outwardly Byron seemed to be living a life of gaiety, supping with Moore and Sheridan, or boxing with Jackson, or dodging Madame de Staël—who bored him. But the outward tokens of passion are easily missed. He was in pain . . . the thought always ran through, through. . . . Action! There perhaps might lie salvation. He had always believed himself born for action, not for poetry. "Who would write who had anything better to do? 'Action—

action—action,' said Demosthenes. 'Actions—actions' I say, and not writing,—least of all, rhyme. . . ." And yawning like some great wild beast behind the bars of Society, he went on from dinner-table to ballroom, thinking of the East and its silences. "Why should I remain or care? I am not, never was, nor can be popular. . . . I never *won* the world; and what it has awarded me has always been owing from its caprice. My life here is frittered away; there I was always in action, or, at least, in motion. . . . I am sadly sick of my present sluggishness, and I hate civilisation."

The ghost of Lady Frances was the first to be exorcised. Her letters to him had a surfeit of effusive soulfulness; their Carolinish style wearied him. "If people will stop at the first tense of the verb *aimer,* they must not be surprised if one finishes the conjugation with somebody else." "How soon you get the better of . . ." said Lady Melbourne.—"In the name of St. Francis and his wife of snow, and Pygmalion and his statue—what was there here to get the better of? A few kisses, for which she was no worse, and I no better." It was a small adventure, this Webster episode, but it confirmed him in his theory of women. No doubt Lady Frances would end by taking some lover bolder than himself. "It is impossible she can care about a man who acted so weakly as I did, with regard to herself."

And then, unhampered by another affection, he was once more gravitating towards Augusta when an unexpected letter reached him. It came from the Morning Star of Annesley, his M.A.C., "my old love of loves." A very short note:

"My dear Lord,—If you are coming into Notts, call at Edwalton near Nottingham, where you will find a *very old* and *sincere friend* most anxious to *see you.*

"Yours most truly,

"MARY"

These four lines conjured up all the enchanted regrets of old times. He knew she was unhappy. Jack Musters was a difficult husband. His farmers used to say he was the best of landlords, but they would have liked him better had he been less greedy of their daughters. The amazons of the hunting-field shared his heart with the farm girls, and his wife, sad and humiliated, had left Annesley. She was now staying with a friend in a small country-house not far from Newstead. Byron could not but feel the pity of it when he thought of life handling his Mary so rudely. A spoilt heiress, she had been adored by her mother, adored by the tenantry, adored by himself. How she must be suffering!

Should he reply? He knew now that she was not what he had boyishly thought her, a being with the divine essence in her. But he was bound to her by many memories. To see again one of those far-off smiles of hers. . . . But a wise instinct warned him that henceforth the real Mary Chaworth was the Mary of imagination. What could the other one want? Was she ready to love him? It seemed unlikely; she had the reputation of a very pure woman. Besides, in her next letter, she spoke of considering him "as a beloved brother," and added: "you would hardly recognise in me the happy creature you once knew me. I am grown so thin, pale and gloomy. You have indeed seen much of the world, I very little. The small portion I have had an opportunity of observing disgusts me; so much better did I expect to believe people in general, judging from my own heart." The phrases had a sad and graceful cadence; they were just what would touch him. "You have indeed seen much of the world, I very little. . . . " But what could he do for her? Was he to go and drag on "a sickly friendship" in the shires? What was the good?

Yes, he was tempted, as he always was when a woman made him the least advance. That heart which always alighted on the nearest perch was already trying its wings. Would she yield? It was hardly likely. There was "the beloved friend" with whom she lived,—some dreadful dragon of virtue, no doubt—and in her letters Mary spoke of Byron's terrible reputation. Yes: but notwithstanding this terrible reputation, she had certainly written to him. Was not this an avowal? Was she not like Lady Frances, like all the others, fleeing only to be caught? And if he joined in this sport, was he not risking another attack of his old trouble? When Lady Melbourne was consulted she declared she had lost her bearings: "You cannot expect me to understand and unravel the confusion that exists amongst all the different Ladies you allude to. You are accustomed to it; therefore to you I have no doubt it is clear."

Clear? To him? Not in the least. . . . He was weak. With the memory of Lady Frances fading away he was once more completely taken up with Augusta. He had almost forgotten her during his stay at Aston Hall, and had written so seldom that she thought he must be annoyed. In November, however, he sent her his portrait; and she, who had feared his love, and feared also the loss of his love, sent him a small packet containing a lock of her hair, with a note in French. . . .

Partager tous vos sentiments,
ne voir que par vos yeux,
n'agir que par vos conseils, ne
vivre que pour vous, voilà mes
vœux, mes projets, et le seul
destin qui peut me rendre
heureuse.[1]

Beneath the lock of hair she had written:

AUGUSTA

And Byron added:

La Chevelure of
the *one* whom I
most loved.

He gave up the struggle. "The kind of feeling which has lately absorbed me has a mixture of the terrible, which renders all other insipid to a degree; in short, one of its effects has been like the habits of Mithridates, who by using himself gradually to poison of the strongest kind, at last rendered all others ineffectual when he sought them as a remedy for all evils, and a release from existence."

He was working on a new poem, *The Corsair,* "written *con amore,* and much from experience," and it bore as epigraph a line of Tasso—"*I suoi pensieri in lui dormir non ponno.*" [2]

Although the poem was written "from experience," Conrad, the Corsair, was not Byron; but he was the Byronic hero of the authentic type, as portrayed by Byron to Hodgson in October 1811, as he had already painted

[1] "To share all your feelings, to see only through your eyes, to act only on your advice, to live only for you—these are my vows and projects, and the sole destiny that can make me happy."

[2] "His thoughts cannot sleep within him."

him in *The Giaour,* a fierce, outlandish, solitary man, driven by an inner fatality, a hurricane let loose upon the world like a simoon. No one knows whence he comes, nor whither he goes. He is wrapped in mystery. His past always contains a crime which is kept dark from us. "He knew neither repentance nor penitence nor expiation; what is done cannot be undone; the indelible cannot be wiped out; he will find no peace this side the tomb. Most often he is a renegade or an atheist—

> I would not, if I might, be blest;
> I want no Paradise, but rest. . . .

To find distraction from himself he rushes into action, into struggle; corsair or brigand, he declares war upon society, and chases after violent emotions. Even though he must die in this struggle, he must at all costs escape the ennui of life."

Between Byron and the Byronic hero the resemblances were manifest—noble birth, a tender and passionate mind in adolescence, disappointment, rage, crime, despair. . . . But the Byronic hero lived dramas which Byron only dreamed. Conrad was a man of action, a pirate chief; Byron regretted his indolence, but did not act. Conrad was strong, Byron lame; Conrad was swarthy, Byron pale. Conrad's laugh was terrible—

> There was a laughing Devil in his sneer,
> That raised emotions both of rage and fear. . . .

—but Byron's was gay and charming. There was something of the child in Byron. During his bursts of rage he became Conrad for a moment, but in everyday life Byron and the Byronic hero were hardly made to agree; and they made dangerous company for each other.

Byron, in spite of himself, lent much of his own weakness to the men he wished to be strong; the Byronic hero became for his creator a false and theatrical model which Byron felt obliged to imitate. In pleading for Conrad he was pleading for himself:

Yet was not Conrad thus by Nature sent
To lead the guilty—guilt's worst instrument:
His soul was changed, before his deeds had driven
Him forth to war with man and forfeit heaven.
Warp'd by the world in Disappointment's school,
In words too wise, in conduct *there* a fool;
Too firm to yield, and far too proud to stoop,
Doom'd by his very virtues for a dupe,
He cursed those virtues as the cause of ill,
And not the traitors who betray'd him still;
Nor deem'd that gifts bestow'd on better men
Had left him joy, and means to give again.
Fear'd, shunn'd, belied, ere youth had lost her force,
He hated man too much to feel remorse,
And thought the voice of wrath a sacred call,
To pay the injuries of some on all. . . .

"Doom'd by his very virtues for a dupe"—that was himself, the ingenuous adolescent. Mankind, and womankind especially, had trained him in Disappointment's school. And henceforth he would be the Corsair, the outlaw, the man of crime and love, chivalrous in his fashion, and the foe of all the human race save one single being—one, for Conrad loved a woman, to whom Byron gave first the name of Francesca in memory of Lady Frances, and then renamed Medora.

A curious subject for dissection they would have been, these heroines of the Byronic poems, projections in all their tender unreality of that *beau idéal* which their creator despaired of finding in real life. "A fine voluptuary will never abandon his mind to the grossness of reality. It is by exalting the earthly, the material, the *physique* of our pleasures, by veiling these ideas, by forgetting them altogether, or, at least, never naming them hardly to one's self, that we alone can prevent them from disgusting." Here was a surprising philosophy to find in a disciple of Lady Melbourne's. But those who hunger and thirst after diversion are erudite in the passions of love, for they have learned that naked sensuality is powerless to cure their ennui. In love, women have ever been the only realists, and, like his creator, Conrad loved the Peri of his fancy, Medora, with a chivalrous love.

Once the manuscript of *The Corsair* had been handed over to Murray, Byron left with his sister for Newstead, on January 17, 1814. Snow lay deep on the slopes and footpaths, and the Abbey was beautiful beneath this winter sky. He had thoughts at first of calling on Mary Chaworth, who was now so near. But the roads were in a bad state with the frost, and Newstead, with Augusta, left nothing to be desired. There was no need, as there had been with Lady Caroline, to be witty with every sentence: "We never yawn or disagree; and laugh much more than it is suitable to so solid a mansion; and the family shyness makes us more amusing companions to each other than we could be to anyone else."

The great vaulted halls echoed back their laughter. Byron gave Augusta Italian lessons. This was the first time that she had lived with her brother under one roof, and she was learning with astonishment what kind of man he was. She saw the loaded pistols that he placed by his bedside, and heard tell of his nightmares, so terrifying that he would sometimes call out for Fletcher to reassure him and soothe him down. In his sleep he gnashed his teeth with such violence that he placed a napkin between his jaws so as not to bite himself. When he was sleepless he would drink soda-water all night long, as many as twelve bottles, and was sometimes so thirsty that he smashed the necks of the bottles in his haste to open them. In the morning he took exaggerated doses of magnesia. This absurd régime made digestion a difficulty, and his troublesome stomach gave rise to fits of temper. The violence he could display over trifles was terrifying. Augusta recognised the temperament of Catherine Gordon in him, and reflected that if ever he married, his wife would have much to put up with.

Society was forgotten, except for Lady Melbourne, who kept sending warnings from afar: were not Byron and his sister going to return to a reasonable life? But Byron, as ever, defended Augusta:

"X is the least selfish person in the world; you, of course, will never believe that either of us can have any right feeling. I won't deny this as far as regards me, but you don't know what a being she is: her only error has been my fault entirely, and for this I can plead no excuse, except passion, which is none. . . . Excepting our one *tremendous* fault, I know her to be in point of temper and goodness of heart almost unequalled; now grant me this, that she is in truth a very *loveable* woman and I will try and not love any longer. If you don't believe me, ask those who know her *better.* I say *better,* for a man in love is blind as that deity. . . . As for me, brought up as I was, both physically and morally, nothing better could be expected, and it is odd that I always had a foreboding and I remember when a child reading the Roman History about a *marriage* I will tell you of when we meet, asking *ma mère* why I should not marry X?"

Towards the end of January Augusta's pregnancy was becoming advanced, and she had to return home.

Alone in the country with the being he loves, a man is rarely unhappy. That stay in a wintry Newstead had been an interlude of fondness and gaiety. But as soon as Byron returned to London he ran into a storm which assailed him from all quarters. The story of his affair with Augusta was getting abroad. There was something unparalleled in the incontinence with which he spoke of his private affairs and displayed other peoples' letters. He unbosomed himself to scores of confidants, sometimes most foolishly chosen. Caroline Lamb was chattering. Some boys at Eton who had read *The Bride of Abydos* asked a nephew of Mrs. Leigh's whether his aunt was Zuleika. Byron himself, in Lady Holland's drawing-room, could not hold his tongue, and kept putting forward the most brazen ideas regarding the relations of brothers and sisters. "There is a woman I love so passionately—she is with child by me, and if a daughter it shall be called Medora." And as people left Holland House, heads were shaken, and comments exchanged, over these all-too-obvious paradoxes.

The fact that he was violently disliked made people all the happier to find him guilty of a crime for which, as Lady Melbourne had said, there was no salvation. He had made himself unpopular by taking up an extreme Whig standpoint in the House of Lords. His admiration for Napoleon he had never concealed, and although the Allies had invaded France he continued to hope that his Bonaparte, "mine *Héros de Roman*," would thrash them all. He was in anguish at the prospect of a return "to the dull, stupid old system—balance of Europe—poising straws upon kings' noses." Ideas like this he maintained publicly in a country at war, where his talent and his love affairs had already made him a legion of enemies. Here was a poet who flourished in London's face the triple insolence of beauty, genius and free speech: against him was held in suspension so strong a rancour that the slightest shock would precipitate a most powerful solution of hate.

The pretext came. It was a small poem of eight lines which he had written over a year before against the Prince-Regent. At the time of the latter's desertion of his Whig friends, it had been said that his daughter, the Princess Charlotte, wept at the news, and to her Byron had addressed these anonymous lines:

Weep, daughter of a royal line,
  A Sire's disgrace, a realm's decay;
Ah! happy if each tear of thine
  Could wash a father's fault away!

Weep—for thy tears are Virtue's tears—
  Auspicious to these suffering isles;
And be each drop in future years
  Repaid thee by thy people's smiles!

No one had paid any heed to them, but when *The Corsair* was in the press Byron expressed his anxiety to add these eight lines to the volume and acknowledge their authorship. Murray wisely warned him of the danger. "I care nothing for consequences on this point," he answered. "My politics are to me like a young mistress to an old man—the worse they grow, the fonder I become of them." The two quatrains raised a newspaper storm of incredible violence. In the choice of arguments, the Jacobinism of the Moral Order has as few scruples as the other. The attack was directed not only on Byron's politics, but on his character, on his poems, even on his infirmity. Some of the articles were so violent that his friends wanted him to bring actions against his defamers. He retorted that he could feel hatred for an equal, but took no pleasure in tormenting earwigs.

These attacks raised his book, as they always do, to the highest peak of popularity. On the day of publication 13,000 copies were sold—an unprecedented figure for a poem. But the success was due not merely to the scandal; despite the strange theme (which then astonished nobody) this poetry impressed many with its direct and modern inspiration, something that echoed their own sentiments. "The lofty style, the scorn of what is mean and base, the courage—root of all virtues—that dares and evermore dares in the very last extremity, the love of the illimitable, of freedom, and the cadences like the fall of waves on a sea-shore, were attractive to them beyond measure." In the inevitable conflict between the Individual and Society, the Individual had found for more than a century past that the poets were in the camp of Society—and this was not their natural place. At last, for generations starved of strong sentiments, Conrad personified a being of true virility, with instincts unleashed. "Byron's influence was singular, beyond that of all predecessors and successors, in the wideness of its range. He was read by everybody. Men and women who were accessible to no other poetry were accessible to his, and old sea-captains, merchants, tradesmen, clerks, tailors, milliners, as well as the best judges in the land, repeated his verses by the page." The oriental background, a banality in later years, did not surprise the reader of 1814, because the Mediterranean countries, for him as for the author, were lands of fiercer and keener passions. Even more than *Childe Harold, The Corsair* made Byron the poet of all rebels, of everybody in

Europe who despaired of liberty, whether political or sentimental.

London . . . solitude amidst the mob . . . *Vanitas Vanitatum*. . . . "I wonder how the deuce anybody could make such a world; for what purpose dandies, for instance, were ordained—and kings—and fellows of colleges—and women "of a certain age"—and many men of any age—and myself, most of all! . . . is there anything beyond?—*who* knows? *He* that can't tell. Who tells that there *is?* He who don't know." Since January 22 he had been twenty-six, "six hundred in heart—and in head and pursuits about six." At twenty-six one ought to be something. But what was he? Who liked him? He was no longer the lion of the season, but he still received many invitations; yet he had no wish to see anyone. "Hobhouse says I am growing a *loup-garou,* a solitary hobgoblin—True. . . . The last week has been passed in reading—seeing plays—now and then visitors—sometimes yawning and sometimes sighing, but no writing,—save of letters—if I could always read, I should never feel the want of Society. Do I regret it?—um! 'Man delights not me,' and only one woman—at a time. . . . There is something to me very softening in the presence of a woman,—some strange influence, even if one is not in love with them—which I can not at all account for, having no very high opinion of the sex. But yet,—I always feel in better humour with myself and everything else if there is a woman within ken—Even Mrs. Mule, my fire-lighter,—the most ancient and withered of her kind,—always makes me laugh,—no difficult task when I am 'i' the vein' . . . Heigho! I would I were in mine island!"

King Lear, Hamlet, Macbeth—his evenings were passed in seeing Shakespeare. He knew Shakespeare by heart. He lived Shakespeare. He made frequent mention in his journal of the Prince of Denmark's brusque tone. And in that winter of 1814 life itself was Shakespearean. The drama of the Empire was rising to the climax of its last act. Hobhouse, supping at the Cocoa Tree, wagered a dinner that the Allies would be in Paris before the end of February; and Byron, faithful to his hero, took the bet. On the 28th Blücher was before Meaux and Byron won his dinner. In March the fighting at La Fère-Champenoise gave him hope for a week or two that he might see Blücher and Schwartzenberg, England's allies, defeated. Then everything went wrong. On April 9, he heard the news that his "poor little pagod," as he called Napoleon, had tumbled from his pedestal. "The thieves are in Paris," he remarked. On the 10th, came the news of the abdication, the choice of the Isle of Elba. Hobhouse and Byron went out to see London illuminated. On Carlton House, the Prince-Regent's, blazed triumphant lilies, and a huge inscription—"LONG LIVE THE BOURBONS!"

In his journal Byron noted: "I mark this day! Napoleon Bonaparte has abdicated the throne of the world. Excellent. Well. Methinks Sylla did better. . . . What! wait till they were in his capital and then talk of his readiness to give up what is already gone! . . . The Isle of Elba to retire to! . . . I am utterly bewildered and confounded. I don't know—but think *I* even *I* (an insect compared with this creature), have set my life on casts not a millionth part of this man's. But, after all, a crown may be not worth dying for. Yet, to outlive Lodi for this!!! . . ." And he wrote a contemptuous ode addressed to the hero who had failed him:

> 'Tis done—but yesterday a King!
>   And arm'd with Kings to strive—
> And now thou art a nameless thing
>   So abject—yet alive!
> Is this the man of thousand thrones,
>   Who strew'd our earth with hostile bones,
> And can he thus survive?
>   Since he who, miscall'd the Morning Star,
> Nor man nor fiend hath fallen so far.

Hobhouse, the big-game hunter of impressions, decided to cross to France and see the last footprints of the monster. He would gladly have taken his friend with him, but Augusta's confinement held Byron back. On April 15 she gave birth to a daughter to whom, with matchless imprudence, was given the name Medora. To Lady Melbourne, who had doubtless predicted that the fruit of an incestuous union would be a monster, he wrote: "Oh! but it is *worth while,* I can't tell you why, and it is *not* an *Ape,* and if it is that must be my fault; however, I will positively reform. You must, however, allow that it is utterly impossible I can ever be half so well liked elsewhere, and I have been all my life trying to make someone love me, and never got the sort that I preferred before. But positively she and I will grow good and all that, and so we are *now* and shall be these three weeks and more too." A few days after the birth he made Augusta—whose husband was still vexed—a gift of £3,000.

Certainly he loved her more than ever, with a love at once desperate and irresistible, and for her he wrote some stanzas which were possibly the most beautiful he had yet penned:

I speak not, I trace not, I breathe not thy name,
There is grief in the sound, there is guilt in the fame:
But the tear which now burns on my cheek may impart
The deep thoughts that dwell in that silence of heart.

Too brief for our passion, too long for our peace
Were those hours—can their joy or their bitterness cease?
We repent, we abjure, we will break from our chain,—
We will part, we will fly to—unite it again!

Oh! thine be the gladness, and mine be the guilt!
Forgive me, adored one!—forsake if thou wilt;—
But the heart which is thine shall expire undebased,
And *man* shall not break it—whatever *thou* mayst.

And stern to the haughty, but humble to thee,
This soul, in its bitterest blackness, shall be;
And our days seem as swift, and our moments more sweet,
With thee by my side, than with worlds at our feet.

One sigh of thy sorrow, one look of thy love,
Shall turn me or fix, shall reward or reprove;
And the heartless may wonder at all I resign—
Thy lips shall reply, not to them, but to *mine*.

What was she to think, poor muddled Augusta, of this impassioned cry? She too loved him—in her way. She could easily have done without having him as a lover. She would have liked to find him a wife, to put an end to it all, but her will was powerless before him. He was her brother; he was famous; he was rich. In her cramped and vexatious life he had suddenly appeared like a saviour. And she obeyed him.

The four thousand people who rule England by staying up (as Byron had remarked) when other people are in bed, were more excited than ever. Society was dancing to celebrate the peace as it had danced to celebrate the war. Balls were given for the Emperor of Russia, for the King of Prussia. Byron's club organised a fancy dress ball for the Duke of Wellington, at which Hobhouse wore an Albanian costume and Byron a monk's habit. "Isn't he beautiful?" said the women. Caroline Lamb, apparently consoled, was at her wildest, and forced an officer of the Guards to take off his scarlet uniform.

When Byron returned at dawn to the apartment he then occupied in Albany—that charming Piccadilly retreat—he sat down to work before going to bed. He began a poem, *Lara*, which for once he made no effort to transpose into an eastern setting. Lara belonged to no country, to no epoch; he was the pure Byronic hero. His character was generous, his heart fashioned for love yet withered in childhood, and he had at once a deep craving for the illusions of youth and too clear a comprehension of their folly. Such was Lara, who bore a strong likeness to Conrad, who bore a strong likeness to Childe Harold, who bore a strong likeness to Byron. In three of the strophes of *Lara* the author's portrait was painted with such transparent verisimilitude that it astonished even Augusta.

In him inexplicably mix'd appear'd
Much to be loved and hated, sought and fear'd;
Opinion varying o'er his hidden lot,
In praise or railing ne'er his name forgot:
His silence form'd a theme for other's prate—
They guessed, they gazed, they fain would know his fate.
What had he been? What was he, this unknown,
Who walked their world, his lineage only known,
A hater of his kind? Yet some would say,
With them he could seem gay amidst the gay;
But own'd that smile, if oft observed and near,
Waned in its mirth, and wither'd to a sneer;
That smile might reach his lip, but pass'd not by,
Nor e'er could trace its laughter to his eye:

Yet there was softness too in his regard,
At times, a heart as not by nature hard,
But once perceived, his spirit seem'd to chide
Such weakness, as unworthy of its pride,
And steel'd itself, as something to redeem
One doubt from others' half withheld esteem;
In self-inflicted penance of a breast
Which tenderness might once have wrung from rest;
In vigilance of grief that would compel
The soul to hate for having loved too well.

. . . .

There was in him a vital scorn of all:
As if the worst had fall'n which could befall,
He stood a stranger in this breathing world,
An erring spirit from another hurl'd. . . .

"A stranger in this breathing world. . . ." To this idea of himself he clung obstinately. He was the wandering spirit, the fallen angel, the being born for a superhuman existence but guided by destiny to deeds of evil. When a monster like Conrad has begun his life in virtue, his fury is heightened by tortures not of remorse only, but of envy too—an envy of those who, happier than himself, have contrived to wield their powers without coming into conflict with mankind, and a supreme envy of the man he could have been, the man that for an instant he was. As Lucifer in Hell is jealous of Lucifer in Heaven, so was Byron jealous of Byron. How few children had dreamed so nobly as the youthful god on Mount Ida! The Reprobate of Bennet Street could not console himself for that. Could he ever forgive the "ex-future Byron" his old enthusiasm, his old tenderness?

Summer came round again, and Byron took Augusta to the seaside. They spent the months of August and September at Hastings. The year was 1814: in Paris the soldiers were singing "*Il reviendra* . . ." and calling for the long grey greatcoat again. . . . Augusta and her brother were scribbling letters to each other, spattered with those childish crosses that stand for kisses.

XXI

BETROTHAL

1814

NEWSTEAD. For several months the purchaser's lawyers had been arguing with Hanson; but Hanson stood firm, and his contract likewise. Young Mr. Claughton had been forced to sell out, and Byron recovered his Abbey, plus the twenty-five thousand sovereigns of the forfeit—which enabled him to settle some of his debts. For a fortnight he was down there alone. True, he had invited Tom Moore: "the place is worth seeing, as a ruin, and I can assure you there *was* some fun there, even in my time; but that is past. The ghosts, however, and the gothics, and the waters, and the desolation, make it very lively still." But Tom Moore had not felt tempted by the gothics or the desolation, and Byron's sole companion at the beginning of this stay was the phantom monk in black, who passed close beside him in a corridor and looked at him, unhalting, with glittering eye.

Once he was alone at Newstead, Byron's thoughts turned to marriage. Why not? A melancholy place, this Abbey: "I should like to have somebody now and then to yawn with one." He did not enjoy solitude so much as the pleasure of telling a woman how much he loved solitude. Of all the forms of love, marriage was the only one he had left untried. He liked to astonish people, he liked to take risks. And for a man with his reputation, what was marriage if not astonishing?

The counsels of his intimates were pushing him towards it. Lady Melbourne wrote to him that a legitimate wife, and that alone, would be his salvation. Augusta proposed a young girl of her acquaintance. Byron wrote back to Lady Melbourne: "I do believe that to marry would be my wisest step—but whom? . . . I have no heart to spare and expect none in return—but, as Moore says: 'A pretty wife is something for the fastidious vanity of a *roué* to *retire* upon.' And mine might go as she pleased, so that she had a fair temper, and a quiet way of conducting herself, leaving me the same liberty of conscience. What I want is a companion—a friend rather than a sentimentalist. I have seen enough of love matches—to make up my mind to the common lot of happy couples. The only misery would be if I fell in love afterwards—which is not unlikely, for habit has a strange power over my affections. In that case I should be jealous, and then you do not know what a devil my bad passion makes me."

Whom was he to choose? There was Lady Catherine Annesley, the younger sister of Lady Frances Webster. She was pretty, very young, "and I think, a fool. But I have not seen enough to judge; besides, I hate an *esprit* in petticoats." There was Lady Adelaide Forbes, who was like the Belvedere Apollo. There was Augusta's friend, Lady Charlotte Leveson-Gower, with eyes like a gazelle's. There was that charming Miss Elphinstone with whom he kept up an intermittent flirtation, and who reproached him with his caprices. And above all there was Annabella Milbanke.

It was strange, but for two whole years now, this pair of beings, so widely different, had not been able to break away from each other. After his rejection by the Princess of the Parallelogram, Byron had made it almost a point of honour to show no trace of grievance. He did not know, he said, whether he was really above the common human prejudices of men on such occasions, but he was above showing them. But, "I must say," he added, "that I never can quite get over the 'not' of last summer —no—though it were to become 'yea' to-morrow." There lingered in him a trace of astonished respect for the only woman who had been so bold as to refuse him, a vague rancour, and some curiosity. Was she capable of love, this fair philosopher? It would be pleasant to humble so fierce a conscience.

The misfortune for her was that she, on her side, felt curiosity about this dangerous conquest. She was flattered of course by having attracted the lover for whom her wild cousin Caroline called so vainly; but she was also convinced that she alone could save this handsome sinner. Love will don strange disguises to slip into padlocked hearts. Her desire for sacrifice made Annabella vulnerable. Ever since that proposal, which had been an event in her calm life whose importance Byron, a prince of unrest, could not appreciate, she had been worried about his activities. She was troubled by the absurd and malicious rumours about Lord Byron that were always in London circulation. One story ran that he intended to take Lady Oxford's eldest daughter and bring her up himself on an island somewhere, and then marry her. It was also said that he had behaved badly towards young Claughton, the would-be purchaser of Newstead; Mr. Claughton had rashly made too high a bid and been cruelly ruined by Byron. And these tales saddened Annabella. She entrusted her aunt, Lady Melbourne, with messages for Byron: "As I shall not have an opportunity of seeing him again, I should be glad if you would tell him that I shall always have pleasure in hearing that he is happy, and if my esteem can afford him any satisfaction, he may rely on my not adopting the opinion of those who wrong him." She hoped to see him again: "I consider his acquaintance as so desirable that I would incur the risk of being called a Flirt for the sake of enjoying it, provided I may do so without detriment to himself."

At last, in August 1813, with a boldness astonishing in a girl, she had written to him herself, uninvited. Her former attitude she accounted for by another love (which was untrue, but the poor child thought it very adroit), offered her friendship, and gave some advice: "No longer suffer yourself to be the slave of the moment, nor trust your noble impulses to the chances of Life. Have an object that will permanently occupy your feelings and exercise your reason. Do good. . . . But to benefit man you must love him, and you must bear with his infirmities." Heigh-ho! The Corsair could not but smile. But he replied with an irreproachable letter couched in an almost solemn tone; she was the first woman, and probably the last, whom he had ever wished to lead to the altar. Lady Melbourne had been right in saying that he preferred her to all other women. It had been true, and it was so still. "But it was no disappointment, because it is impossible to impart one drop more to a cup which already overflows with the waters of bitterness. . . ." As for a friendship between them: "I doubt whether I could help loving you. . . . Whatever my feelings may be, they will exempt you from persecution." How submissive he was, how serious! Lady

Melbourne would hardly have recognised her friend in this style. Did he himself, as a matter of fact, know whether he was sincere or play-acting? Like all deeply imaginative creatures, he had something of the chameleon in him; and he conjured up this girl before him as he sat writing to her. He remembered her face, a trifle too round, but shapely, and he pictured her very pretty figure. Anxious to please, he assumed a form which could advance his design.

It was a frail, paradoxical friendship; but it endured, and Byron found it yielding a curiously pleasant savour. It was amusing to show Lady Melbourne her niece's weighty epistles. Annabella, in her heart-searchings, blamed herself for having refused him, and tried, without being as yet fully aware of it, to induce him to make a fresh offer of himself. How she blamed herself now for that tale of having loved another!

His reform she undertook as a matter of course. She had heard of the good qualities he sometimes showed, and knew his worth to be higher than his reputation. His laughter did not ring true; he was unhappy, she felt. Was it really possible that he was wholly an unbeliever? On this point Byron's frankness was complete: "I now come to a subject which, you have perceived, I always hitherto avoided—an awful one—Religion. I was bred in Scotland among Calvinists in the first part of my life, which gave me a dislike to that persuasion. Since that period I have visited the most bigoted and credulous of countries—Spain, Greece, Turkey. . . . My opinions are quite undecided. . . . I believe doubtless in God, and should be happy to be convinced of much more. If I do not at present place implicit faith in tradition and revelation of any human creed, I hope it is not from want of reverence for the Creator, but the creature." She advised him to read the works of Locke, and also not to attach so much importance to proofs. "If the system announced as divine were wholly comprehensible to finite capacity, it must on that account lose part of its credibility as an emanation of *infinite* intelligence." But Byron declined Locke and read Job and Isaiah, gloomier prophets.

He did not deny; he did not believe. "I have formed no decided opinion; but I should regret any *sceptical bigotry* as equally pernicious with the most credulous intolerance. . . . Why I came here? I know not. Where I shall go? It is useless to enquire. In the midst of myriads of the living and the dead worlds—stars—systems—infinity—why should I be anxious about an atom?" And by return of post she answered: "True, we are atoms in the universal, but is an atom nothing or worthless to the Infinite Being? It were to destroy that attribute of divinity to deny his power of embracing the infinitely little as the infinitely great." And rejoicing in her strength of mind and the power of her spirit, she proffered Byron moral counsel too: "Feel benevolence, and you will inspire it—you will do good. . . . Imperfect as my practice is, I have enjoyed the happiness of giving peace and awaking virtue."

She had the feeling of gravely approaching an invalid and tending him. Poor Annabella! The more she felt his distance from her, the more she persisted in writing to him. She could not thrust this astounding image from her mind. She read his poems—*The Giaour, The Corsair*. "Certainly he excels in the language of Passion. . . . The description of Love almost makes *me* in love." She talked of him to all her friends, and wrote of him to her aunt. In her inmost heart she was obsessed by him; but of that she had no suspicion. She was so certain of herself, so serious, and such a blue-stocking. Lord Byron was an unhappy and inoffensive creature whom she would lead back to the straight path. She pushed her boldness to the point even of having her parents invite him to Seaham: "I have to inform you that my father and mother, hearing that Lord Byron was likely to renew his Northern tour, have thought it advisable to invite him here. . . . I shall be very glad if he should avail himself of the invitation, which my father sends him by this post. . . . I am very indifferent about reports, and I know you think it the wisest plan to be so."

Outwardly, niece and aunt were on affectionate terms, but in reality they were not naturally sympathetic. Annabella regarded her aunt as frivolous and immoral; and Lady Melbourne did not like young girls to flit from mathematics to metaphysics. She was uneasy when a woman told her that her favourite authors were the Scottish philosophers, adding that she differed from many "in considering such books of great *practical* utility—even in the commonest circumstances of life." The old lady asked her niece to draw up for her a table of the qualities she required in a husband and received a communication in this form:

Husband

He must have consistent principles of Duty governing strong and generous feelings, and reducing them under the command of Reason.

Genius is not in my opinion *necessary*, though desirable if *united* with what I have just mentioned.

I require a freedom from suspicion, and from *habitual* ill-humour,—also an equal tenor of affection towards me, not that violent attachment which is susceptible of sudden increase or diminution from trifles.

I wish to be considered by my husband as a *reasonable adviser*, not as a guide on whom he could implicitly depend. . . .

Rank is indifferent to me. *Good connections* I think are an important advantage.

I do not regard *beauty*, but am influenced by the *manners of a gentleman*, without which I scarcely think that anyone could attract me.

I would not enter into a family where there was a strong tendency to insanity.

When Lady Melbourne read this document she shrugged her shoulders. What else could she do? To ask of a man whom one will love "dry Reason and cold Rectitude," and to demand from him neither "good-nature, openness, frankness and kindness of heart," seemed to her absurdities. She reproached her niece with going through life on stilts, and not on her legs like everyone else. "You are mistaken in thinking I meant to dispense with the amiable feelings. I thought those of 'good-nature, openness, frankness and kindness of heart' included under the term 'generous.' . . . So far from supposing that I could be attached by a character of *dry* Reason, and *cold* Rectitude, I am always repelled by people of that description. . . . After so full an explanation you will perhaps take me off my *stilts*, and allow that I am only *on tiptoe*."

She would have been greatly surprised if she could have seen the other side of the curtain, and read what Byron wrote to Lady Melbourne regarding this portrait, which she had sent on to him: "She seems to have been spoiled—not as children usually are—but systematically Clarissa Harlowed into an awkward kind of correctness, with a dependence upon her own infallibility which will or may lead her into some egregious blunder. . . . She talks of talking over metaphysics . . . seriously, if she imagines that I particularly delight in canvassing the creed of St. Athanasius, I think she will be mistaken. . . . I am not in love with her; but I cannot foresee that I should not be so, if it came 'a warm June' (as Falstaff observes), and, seriously, I do admire her as a very superior woman, a little encumbered with Virtue." And she would have been still more surprised had she known that, at the time when this correspondence began, Byron's main curiosity was to know whether or not Lady Frances Webster would decide to deceive her husband.

When Byron, down at Newstead in these early days of August 1814, began to wonder more seriously than ever before whether marriage was not becoming a necessity for him, he wrote to Miss Milbanke: "I did—do—and always shall love;—and as this feeling is not exactly an act of will, I know no remedy. . . . When our acquaintance commenced, it appeared to me from all that I saw and heard that you were the woman most adapted to render any man (who was neither inveterately foolish nor wicked) happy; but I was informed that you were attached, if not engaged. . . . It would be a very hard case if a woman were obliged to account for her repugnance. You would probably like me if you could; and as you cannot, I am not quite coxcomb enough to be surprised at a very natural occurrence." It was the most modest and engaging letter he had ever penned. But Annabella was incapable of dissociating her beliefs and her sentiments, a thing which most human beings do unconsciously. To an overture for which she had been waiting for months, she replied with one of her metaphysical epistles. She wondered if he were really "the person she ought to select as her guide, her support, her example on earth, with a view to Immortality." Byron was irritated, and authorised his sister, who had rejoined him, to make another proposal of marriage, this time to Lady Charlotte Leveson-Gower. But he regretted Annabella. As soon as the reply came from Lady Charlotte's parents, in the negative, he exclaimed that he would try his chance for himself; and on September 9, for a second time, he asked for the hand of Annabella Milbanke.

He wrote to her: "There is something I wish to say; and as I may not see you for some—perhaps for a long time—I will endeavour to say it at once. . . . Are the 'objections' to which you alluded insuperable? or is there any line or change of conduct which could possibly remove them? . . . It is not without a struggle that I address you once more on this subject. . . . With the rest of my sentiments you are already acquainted. If I do not repeat them it is to avoid—or at least not increase—your displeasure."

After writing this letter, he awaited the reply with impatience. Augusta was then at Newstead, and about the time the letter-carrier usually arrived, she saw Byron sitting on the Abbey steps looking out for him. One morning, when Byron and Augusta were seated at table, the gardener entered and produced Mrs. Byron's wedding-ring, which she had lost many years before; the man had just found it when digging beneath the window that had been the Dowager's. Byron detected an omen. Almost at the same moment he was handed a letter. "If it contains a consent," he said, "I will be married with this very ring."

It was from Annabella. "I am and have long been

pledged to myself to make your happiness my first object in life. *If I can* make you happy, I have no other consideration. I will *trust* to you for all I should look up to—all I can love. The fear of not realising your expectations is the only one I now feel. . . . There has in reality been scarcely a change in my sentiments. . . ." At the same time, in case he might be in London and not receive her letter soon enough, she had written another: "On the chance of sparing you a moment's suspense. . . . I hope you will find in my other letter *all you wish.*"

Triumphantly Byron handed the letter across the table to Augusta. She was perfectly heedless of the astonishing elements in the scene. "It is the best and prettiest I have ever read," she declared, and immediately felt her mind resolved to be the perfect sister-in-law, delighted to see Byron settled, and obliterating without any effort all memories of incest from her nebulous mind.

In sudden exaltation Byron wrote three letters to Seaham within three days: "Your letter has given me a new existence—it was unexpected—I need not say welcome—but *that* is a poor word to express my present feelings—and yet equal to any other—for express them adequately I cannot. . . . It *is* in your power to render me happy—you have done so already. . . ." And he explained how he was dying to see her, and at the earliest possible moment. "I feel more tremblingly alive to that meeting than I quite like to own to myself. When your letter arrived, my Sister was sitting near me and grew frightened at the effect of its contents—which was even painful for a moment. . . . You shall be my Guide, Philosopher, and Friend; my whole heart is yours. . . . This is my third letter in three days. . . ." And he ended: "With every sentiment of respect—and—may I add the word?—Love—ever yours."

Don Juan engaged! The novelty of the adventure fascinated him, and he really did hope for happiness to come of it. Hadn't he always longed for marriage, ever since Mary Chaworth's day? Didn't he need quietude? Could he find a better wife than this manifestly virtuous girl?—He didn't love her? But that can come in a couple of days; he was quick-handed in love. Lady Melbourne had to be informed—"My dear Aunt. . . ." It was delightful to become the nephew of his old friend. He pointed out that it was a pity her niece had not taken this decision sooner—how many torments and sins she would thus have spared other people! But all that was over and done with at last: "After all it is a match of *your* making. . . . My pride (which my schoolmaster said was my ruling passion) has at all events been spared. She is the only woman to whom I have ever proposed in that way, and it is something to have got into the affirmative at last. I wish one or two of one's idols had said *No* instead; however, all that is over; I suppose a married man never gets anybody else, does he? I only ask for information."

His friends also had to be informed. "My dear Moore,—I am going to be married—that is, I am accepted, and one usually hopes the rest will follow. My mother of the Gracchi (that *are* to be), you think too strait-laced for me, although the paragon of only children, and invested with golden opinions of all sorts of men." Odd sentiments: he, the Reprobate, was extremely proud of the spotless reputation of his betrothed. He informed Hobhouse and Scrope Davies. And all that remained was to dispose Annabella favourably towards Augusta: "It gives me much pleasure to hear that Augusta has written to you. She is the the least selfish and gentlest creature in being—and more attached to me than anyone in existence can be. She was particularly desirous that I should marry and only regretted that she had not earlier the pleasure of your acquaintance. . . . You ask me if Augusta is not *shy*—to excess. She is, as I tell her, like a frightened hare with new acquaintances, but I suppose she has made a grand effort to overcome it in this instance. She is now nursing, which will I fear prevent her accepting your father's very kind invitation. I wish with all my heart she could." Everything was shaping ideally. With sister on one hand, and wife on the other, he would spend delightful winters at Newstead.

Annabella, on her side, announced the great event to her family. "Dad" and "Mam" spoke with a slightly uneasy emphasis of their future son-in-law's great talents, and impatiently awaited the chance of weighing him up when he arrived at Seaham. To a friend of her childhood their daughter wrote: "It is not in the great world that Lord Byron's true character must be sought; but ask of those nearest to him—of the unhappy whom he has consoled, of the poor whom he has blessed, of the dependants to whom he is the best of masters. For his despondency, I fear I am but too answerable for the last two years. Yet I cannot reproach myself for having resisted my own wishes as well as his, until *thoroughly* convinced that their fulfilment would produce mutual happiness." Her ignorance of the character and life of her betrothed was rather pathetic. Byron's own diagnosis had been singularly correct when he remarked of her: "Her dependence upon her own infallibility will lead her into some egregious blunder." During that first week of their engagement she wrote further: "I have fixed with mature judgment on the person most calculated to support me in the journey to immortality." It is natural enough, alas, for girls still ignorant of their passions to mistake their desires for judgment.

To and fro shot the correspondence between London and Seaham. Byron had tried to reassure Miss Milbanke regarding his religious sentiments by telling her that, although no believer, he was ready to listen with an open mind to whatever arguments she might wish to advance; but she replied that she was in no hurry; this would all come straight easily enough if he loved her. "I was a little displeased not long ago by hearing that I meant to convert before I married you." Like all human beings, she was irritated by her own legend. She herself knew quite well that it was in no proselytising spirit that she loved her future husband. She knew that she was a woman, very much a woman, and in love with that beautiful face. Why did people call her cold? And she re-read the letters in which Byron told her of the beginnings of their love.

He had written to her: "You do not perhaps recollect the first time we ever met at Melbourne House. . . . I did not know your name, and the room was full of morning-visitors; I was myself almost a stranger and felt awkward and shy. . . . I set you down as the most puzzling person there. . . . There was a simplicity—an innocence—a beauty in your deportment and appearance which, although you hardly spoke, told me I was in company with no common being. . . . You say 'you will look up to me.' Were you my inferior I should perceive it—I should require it—but it is not so. . . . I do not mean that I should rely on you for that protection which it is *my* part to give . . . but that you should be not only my love, but my first friend, my adviser, my reprover when necessary. . . ."

And she had replied: "I remember indelibly every time that we have met—that first morning too, when our impressions so well corresponded. With you, and you only, I then felt *at home*—I cannot otherwise express it. Instead of being awed or repelled as others were, I could have told you my thoughts and perhaps your own also. . . . At one supper-party—when you sat between Lady Melbourne and me, but conversed only with her—I heard you say 'Thank God I have not a friend in the world.' You knew not the pang which you inflicted on a friend so near. Those words of bitterness chilled me. When I returned home to solitude, I wept over the recollections of them, and prayed that you might receive consolation from a friend below, as well as from a friend above."

Byron ought to have been touched by the beauty and sincerity of these lines. Perhaps for a moment he was; but before leaving Newstead for London, he carved on one of the trees in the park the initials of his own name entwined with those of Augusta.

XXII

MARRIAGE

1814–1815

Think you, if Laura had been Petrarch's wife,
He would have written sonnets all his life?

DON JUAN

HE was, then, not without pride in his conquest; but he could not bring himself to the point of starting for Seaham. Hanson was his excuse, Hanson the mistrustful lawyer, who insisted on a draft of settlement, properly drawn up. Byron, for all his pile of debt, did not desire to marry for money, although pleased enough to be adding something to his inadequate income, and his own proposed terms were very open-handed. Sir Ralph Milbanke, formerly a man of great wealth, had poured out money on his elections; and he was now giving his daughter a dowry of £1,000 a year, £300 of which was to go as pin-money to Lady Byron, and £700 to Lord Byron for life. Some day Annabella would inherit from Lord Wentworth £7,000 or £8,000 a year, which would be divided according to law between her and Lord Byron. But Byron, for his part, formally settled on his wife a capital sum of £60,000 to be secured on the Newstead estate, and valued at £2,000 a year.

All in all, these negotiations impressed Byron and his friends rather unpleasantly. Hanson and Hobhouse thought the Milbankes grasping; Lady Melbourne declared Hanson an intolerable fellow; and Byron fell back on the known fact that Miss Milbanke herself counted for nothing in these bickerings. At any rate he could not be said to be marrying her for her fortune, as his only gain from the match was an increase of income far less than the increase of expenditure which would be entailed in an establishment and in children. No, he was marrying her because it was a "sensation," because he felt the need of a "counsellor," and even because he believed, every now and then, that really—in his fashion—he loved her. But what could be more tiresome for him than the journey to Seaham, in distant Durham, to see his parents-in-law and play the suitor in the classic manner? "I wish I could wake some morning, and find myself fairly married." Shyness, it may be; a vague fear, too, of a future so different from all that had gone before; and an invincible distaste for abandoning what he held. But principally shyness: "the moment I can go to Seaham," he wrote to Lady Melbourne, "I will, and yet I feel very odd about *it, not her;* it is nothing but shyness, and a hatred of strangers, which I never could conquer."

Meanwhile, through that fine London autumn, he enjoyed his last bachelor days with childish pleasure. He was still living in Albany, that black-and-white cloister, but he supped nearly every evening with Douglas Kinnaird, a young banker who was a great friend of Hobhouse's. Tom Moore was there, and they would seat him at the piano to sing his Irish melodies. Kinnaird had an admirable brandy, and when Byron had emptied a few glasses of that he became sentimental. Moore would sing of "Love's Young Dream," and dreamily Byron would call to mind Augusta and Mary

Chaworth. Music, like scents, had the power of transporting him into the past and evoking its scenes so vividly as to blot out the present entirely. Poor Mary! He had sad news of her: for she was in the throes of a mental derangement, which had seized her at Hastings, just at the time of Byron's stay there with Augusta. She had been brought back to London, and it was said that the attack was serious, that she had to be put under restraint. . . . A conjugal Ophelia? Here was one more drama amongst the creatures whom he had loved; clearly, he brought them no luck. . . . Edmund Kean the actor gave imitations; he was amusing; Augusta too was clever at mimicry. . . . And Jackson, the gentleman boxer, turned up, bulging his muscles beneath his embroidered coat. In his company Byron became a child again, a pupil eager to please, bringing up the names of famous pugilists, trying to analyse their style. A glass of brandy. . . . Byron had tears in his eyes. . . . Kinnaird and Hobhouse were laughing uproariously. And in the small hours they set Moore at the piano again. He sang—

The time I've lost in wooing,
In watching and pursuing
  The light, that lies
  In woman's eyes,
Has been my heart's undoing.
Tho' Wisdom oft has sought me,
I scorn'd the lore she brought me,
  My only books
  Were woman's looks,
And folly's all they've taught me.

And are those follies going?
And is my proud heart growing
  Too cold or wise
  For brilliant eyes

Again to set it glowing?
No, vain, alas! th' endeavour
From bonds so sweet to sever;
  Poor Wisdom's chance
  Against a glance
Is now as weak as ever.

Poor Wisdom's chance. . . . There were depths beneath the seeming shallows in what Moore was singing. And he too, George Gordon Byron, the Wicked Lord, was about to join hands with Wisdom. Yet did he feel himself becoming another man? Not at all. He was beginning to feel really afraid that things might turn out very much awry.

At last, at the beginning of November, he made up his mind to start for Seaham. The place then was an insignificant seaport, a few fishermen's cottages overlooking a rocky beach; the Milbankes' house was not far from the sea. When Byron's carriage drew up before the door Annabella was in her room, with a book. Coming down, she found him alone in the drawing-room beside the fireplace. She held out her hand; he kissed it; they both remained silent. And at last, speaking in low tones, he said, "It is a long time since we met." She murmured something about fetching her parents, and left the room.

From the moment of their first encounter, the family life of Seaham roused Byron's keen sense of the ridiculous. In each other's company, these three people were natural, gay, and affectionate. But the happiness and simplicity of a group are often incommunicable, and Byron's humour, more akin to Dean Swift's than to the Vicar of Wakefield's, was something totally different from the cheerfulness of the Milbankes. Byron mocked at religion, at government, at the follies and vices of mankind. The Milbankes had a repertory of little domestic jokes, about fleas and legs and food. Sir Ralph, however, found some grace in his son-in-law's eyes. He was a bore, with those interminable stories of his, but he was "the perfect gentleman," and played the conventional rôle of father-in-law very well. Lady Milbanke, Byron had always disliked. He didn't know why, but it was so; and now, under her roof, he found her excitable and officious, difficult to get on with. Her bugbear was her sister-in-law, Lady Melbourne, Byron's dear friend. She liked to busy herself with outside matters, and wanted to rule her daughter and husband, who thereupon made common cause against her. To a great extent it was in reaction against her mother's excitability that Annabella had assumed her placidity of demeanour. But Byron was disappointed in Annabella herself. No sooner had he set eyes on her again, then he knew he had made a mistake. It was the old story; when far away from a woman, he wove a romance round her. So long as he did not meet her again, she stood tranquilly in her niche in that gallery of defunct divinities in Byron's soul; but if any woman had personally to play the usually superhuman part which he allotted to her, she was ruined. From Annabella—the devil alone knew why—he had expected the rôle of a woman at once strong and sensitive, capable of winning his love and of guiding him as well. More poets than one have dreamed this dream of someone who will combine the charm of a mistress and the gay wisdom of a comrade. But when a woman is in love, she is so with all love's weaknesses; and this was what Byron could not understand, particulaıly as regards Annabella.

She was silent, terribly silent, this fresh young girl, and not particularly pretty; and she kept watching him

ANNE ISABELLA, LADY BYRON

After an Engraving from a Painting by W. J. Newton

with a questioning look which he found most perturbing. She was seeking to match him with an abstract image of the man of genius, the man of virtue. He felt it, and was annoyed. Above all, she was too intelligent; she analysed every word he uttered, whereas he said whatever came into his head, anything at all, if only to prevent himself from yawning. From his rude outbursts, which a Lady Oxford laughed at and an Augusta never heeded, Annabella drew professorial deductions. The fair mathematician gauged every tiny variation in tone by a calculation of sentimental probabilities, and turned love into an equation. One moment their characters seemed too closely akin, the next they were not close enough. She overwhelmed him with waves of beautiful sentiments, described how she was attacked by scruples, wanted to break off the engagement, and, over and above all, was seized every other day with some incomprehensible illness. Byron's lucid, loveless scrutiny took her measure; "a perfectly good person," he judged her, but over-solicitous, fated to self-torment without end, and—his pet aversion in a woman—a weaver of romance. He had always declared that in marriage he wanted "a companion—a friend rather than a sentimentalist." But from morning to night in this household the talk ran on nothing but sentiments. He felt he had been switched back to the time of Caroline Lamb, and for a day or two he thought that the marriage would never come off.

With his old tactical adviser, Lady Melbourne, he had often analysed what they both laughingly called the "calming process," the only one, according to her, which can ever succeed with women, and consists of replacing words by gestures, an argument by a caress, a retort by a kiss. "In fact, and *entre nous,* it is really amusing; she is like a child in that respect, and quite caressable into kindness, and good humour. . . . Her passions stronger than we supposed. Of these last I can't yet as positively judge; my observations lead me to guess as much, however. She herself cannot be aware of this, nor could I, except from a habit of attending minutely in such cases to their slightest indications, and, of course, I don't let her participate in the discovery."

It was soon clear that the "calming process" had a certain effect on Annabella; it had, in fact, made her still more passionately in love with Byron. The world, and her aunt, had made a great mistake in supposing her cold because she was pure: cold women are those who make a plaything of love. A woman like Annabella, who has kept herself through all the years of girlhood for a sentiment which she desires to be unique and believes she has found at last, yields to it in the end with one splendid surrender, of body as of soul.

Her first letter after this visit was humble and passionate in the same breath: "My own Byron. . . . If I do repent you shall not have the satisfaction of knowing it. If our present and I hope last separation should spare you the anxiety which my troubled visage has sometime communicated, it is enough. . . . Are you quite sure that I love you? Why did you doubt it? It is *your* only trespass. As for *my* trespasses I must not think of them—I wish we were married, and then I could do my best, and not quarrel with myself for a thousand things that you would not mind. I expect you will write me a lecture—and it shall be studied *con amore*. . . . Will you take me to your heart, my home 'till Death do us part'—and don't turn me out of doors in revenge as you threatened. . . . Ever thine."—And again the next day: "My own Byron. . . . I certainly was not myself during your stay. . . . Before you pass sentence on me finally, wait to see *me myself*. Myself is by no means the grave, didactic, deplorable person that I have appeared to you. I am only sage under some visitation of anxiety. . . . Those who have seen me *quite* as a domestic animal have had more reason to complain of my nonsense than my sense. . . ."

Poor Wisdom, as Moore sang, poor Wisdom, ever seeking to please by donning that mask of Folly which so ill befits her. Annabella, the love-sick maid, signed herself—"Thy wife"; and the reply came back from Augusta's place at Six Mile Bottom, signed—"Your attached Byron." He asked her, while there was yet time, if she were absolutely sure of having no regrets. "I shall be too happy—there will be no reverse. . . . I wish for you, want you, Byron mine, more every hour. All my confidence has returned—never to sink again." So be it. The die was cast; she willed her ruin; he had given his word. *Crede Biron.*

He had told her at parting that this separation would be short, but one week passed over Seaham and then another, and Byron did not return. He was in London, drinking Kinnaird's brandy, and had now no excuse to offer. In vain did Annabella write that her father was composing an epithalamium, that all the Milbanke cousins had sent their wedding-gifts, even Caroline (*"Timeo Danaos et dona ferentes,"* commented Byron in reply), that the wedding-cake was baked, that all was ready for the great performance, and that if the bridegroom did not decide to come, it would doubtless be necessary to suppress his rôle, like that of the Prince of Denmark in *Hamlet*. In vain—grown very bold now—did she write that she would come and visit him in Albany one of these days if he persisted in staying away much longer. She was on fire to see him again. No longer were her letters those of a devout and cultivated girl; she could only repeat in a thousand guises the words *I love you*—"and when you were here, I so often appeared *the most silent woman in the world* because I could not think of anything else. . . ."

He had the wedding postponed, pleading in excuse Hanson's failure to find a purchaser for Newstead: one could not marry without an adequate income. That did not matter, protested Miss Milbanke; simple living called for no great fortune. Byron must come back. Her parents were beginning to think him a laggard, and Sir Ralph was for ever coming into his daughter's room to ask her for rhymes for his epithalamium. "Dad says 'Fly swiftly ye moments till Comus return'—and my mother stitches with much more alacrity since your mention of Saturday. Dearest—you and happiness will come together. . . ." —"With regard to happiness, it would be presumptuous enough to feel too certain of uninterrupted felicity, inasmuch as that depends not altogether on persons but things. . . ." A few days before the wedding he was still asking her to ponder well. And at last—on December 23—"Dearest Annabella,—if we meet let it be to marry. . . . With regard to our being under the same roof and *not* married—I think past experience has shown us the awkwardness of that situation. I can conceive nothing above purgatory more uncomfortable. If a postponement is determined upon, it had better have been decided at a distance."

Into these hesitancies, perhaps, there entered not a few regrets for the renunciation of Augusta, who continued to write him the fondest of letters, disjointed pages all peppered with symbolic crosses.

Byron had asked Hobhouse to be his best man, and to accompany him on his journey by post-chaise. Before setting off they went together to apply for the marriage licence, and when the registrar handed it to Byron, the latter asked him how many callers he had who wished him to make marriages for them, as against those who wanted them unmade.

Two days had been the agreed duration of the journey, but the bridegroom snatched at every chance of wasting time. Passing by way of Six Mile Bottom, he decided to stop for a day with Augusta, and, wishing to be alone with her, sent Hobhouse on to Newmarket. Thus he spent Christmas Day with his sister, and from her house wrote his last letter to Seaham: "I am thus far on my way and as warm as Love can make one with the thermometer below God knows what. . . . The licence is in my portfolio. It is a droll composition, but enables us to marry in the house—so pray let us. I am sure we shall both catch cold kneeling anywhere else. . . . Augusta is looking very well. . . . I wish you much merriment and minced pye—it is Christmas day!"

The friends set off again on the 26th, and spent four days in reaching Seaham in snow and rain—"the bridegroom more and more *less* impatient," said Hobhouse. The whole household was upset by their delay. Lady Milbanke, overcome by distress, had had to go upstairs and take to her bed. Annabella melted in tears when they did come in. The vexed Hobhouse sought for excuses in vain: the only one, indeed, was that his companion had been in no great hurry. To distract attention and break a louring silence, he unwrapped his own gift—the complete works of Byron, bound in yellow morocco. He was watching the bride with some curiosity. No great beauty, he thought: "Miss Milbanke is rather dowdy-looking, and wears a long and high dress, though her feet and ankles are excellent." She was noticeably and alarmingly silent, too; but she seemed modest and reasonable, and "dotingly fond" of Byron, whom she gazed at continuously in a dumb admiration. Lady Milbanke was unable to come down to dinner, and Sir Ralph was left to do the talking. Hobhouse thought him rather an old chatterbox, but a good fellow, and gifted with a certain sense of humour. There were also present two clergymen, the Rev. Mr. Wallace, vicar of Seaham, and the Rev. Mr. Thomas Noel, of Kirkby Mallory.

The talk ran upon ecclesiastical subjects. Sir Ralph told anecdotes of the Bishop of Durham and his snobbery, of how he had written to the son of a lord: "The friendship which I have for my Lord, your father, and the peculiar situation in which I stand with my Lord God. . . ." And then he spoke at great length of the Archbishop of Canterbury. Byron and Hobhouse exchanged glances. As they left the table, Byron told him how one day at dinner Lady Caroline Lamb had asked her husband, "William, what's the seventh commandment?" —"Thou shalt not bother," answered William.

Next morning, the last day of the year, Hobhouse came down first and went for a walk on the seashore. Sadly, on the fine clear winter's day, he watched the waves. He no longer foresaw any good from this marriage, but Annabella herself he was beginning to find more congenial; after an evening's scrutiny, he began to realise that a man could love her, or at least feel some tender interest in her. That night, the men of the party held a mock-marriage, in which Hobhouse played the part of Miss Milbanke, while Hoar the lawyer took that of Sir Ralph, and the Rev. Thomas Noel officiated. Close on midnight they went down to look at the sea, and then, after a very merry evening, wished each other a good new year.

On New Year's Day 1815 Byron and Hobhouse took a long walk together on the shore. The day dragged gloomily on, and at night, after dinner, Byron remarked: "Well, Hobhouse, this is our last night; to-morrow I shall be Annabella's." Next day, January 2nd, was the date fixed for the marriage, and when Byron woke to see his wedding clothes laid out by his valet, the sight cast him into a deep gloom. Coming down to breakfast, he found Mr. Noel clerically attired, and Lady Milbanke so excited and jumpy that she could not even pour out tea. A moment later Hobhouse arrived, in white gloves. In the drawing-room the servants were setting out kneeling-mats on the floor, two of them slightly in front of the rest, for the bridal pair. Byron went out for a stroll in the garden, saying he was to be called when the moment came. At last Annabella came down in a plain gown of white muslin, with her head bare. She seemed to be fully mistress of her feelings, and was accompanied by her governess, Mrs. Clermont. Byron was summoned. He entered and knelt beside his bride; the mats were hard, and he made a grimace that gave him a look of pensive devotion. The Rev. Thomas Noel read the service. Annabella was calm, turning her head and looking steadily at Byron.

He heard nothing, he saw nothing. A mist seemed to float before his eyes; he was thinking (Heaven knew why!) of the parting scene with Mary Chaworth, conjuring up that room at Annesley, the long terrace, the grassy fields, that lovely face now twitching with unbalanced fears. He was torn from his reverie by the words he had to speak: "With all my worldly goods I thee endow . . ."—and he glanced at Hobhouse with a half-smile. The bells pealed out from the little church of Seaham; a few firearms were discharged in the garden; the Rev. Thomas Noel became silent; and from voices that spoke congratulation and hands clasping his, Byron learned that he was married.

The new Lady Byron vanished for a moment to change her dress, and came back wearing a slate-coloured pelisse, trimmed with white fur. Sir Ralph's fiery features were tense with emotion, Lady Milbanke's eyes brimming with tears. Hobhouse, mindful of his duties, handed the bride into her carriage. "I wish you many years of happiness," he said to her.

"If I am not happy," she answered him, "it will be my own fault."

Then Byron stepped in, firmly clasping Hobhouse's hand. The footman closed the door. Byron seemed unable to bring himself to let go the hand of his faithful friend; he seized it again through the carriage-window; he was still gripping it when the horses moved off. And the dejected Hobhouse was left alone with Annabella's parents. Had she not behaved well, Lady Milbanke asked him, had she not behaved like the mother of Iphigenia? But Hobhouse was left with the feeling that he had buried a friend.

XXIII

THE TREACLE-MOON[1]

1815

I cannot now determine whether he was or was not an actor.

LADY BYRON

THE carriage rolled on towards Halnaby, the house lent by Sir Ralph for the honeymoon, bearing an anxious, eager wife, a nervous, exasperated man. Why, oh why, had he married? Was it to save Augusta? To make a break with her? To feed his pride? Now, to his dying day, he would have this grave, awkward, unknown creature beside him; already she was watching him, and judging him. There was something mad in the hatred that rose in his heart; and he began a wild singing, as was his way when he was unhappy.

They passed through the streets of Durham. The bells were ringing. "Ringing for our happiness, I suppose?" sneered Byron. Fields and woods were mantled in snow. And he began to talk. This marriage, he declared, was on his side merely an act of vengeance. This

[1] Our sole document on the nature of these first weeks of marriage is the evidence of Lady Byron. It is unpublished, except for the excerpts given by Miss Ethel Colburn Mayne. I have read the document. It is a moving piece of writing, with the ring of truth in it. Here I give only some unpublished passages, especially those touching on Lord Byron's beliefs. I have omitted certain painful features which added nothing to one's understanding of the subject. We have confirmation of the alarm which Lady Byron retained of this stay at Halnaby, in Hobhouse (II, 281), who cannot be suspected of partiality towards her; he says that Lady Byron always seemed terrified when speaking of her residence there.

was the new myth to which he was clinging in the break-up of his life: he had always found his needed support by seeing himself the hero of a romance. Was marriage, for a time at least, going to chain him to one woman and one only? Well, so be it: they would act the play out between them. It was untrue that he had married her in any spirit of revenge. The myth had been altogether different at the time of his first proposal; then, he had desired and hoped for happiness through the dominance of a woman over himself. But the real Annabella could not be that woman, and now he was casting her for the victim's part. This idea of a vengeance patiently planned since the first refusal was a fine theme for a Byronic frenzy; he had always liked that story of how Ali Pacha had captured and executed the ravisher of his sister after forty-two years. *Crede Biron.* A Byron never forgot. He brooded on, working himself up with his imaginings.

"Oh, what a dupe you have been to your imagination! How is it possible a woman of your sense could form the wild hope of reforming *me?* . . . You might have saved me once; now it is too late. . . . Enough for me that you are my wife for me to hate you—now. When I first offered myself, you had it all in your power. Now you will find that you have married a devil." And then, seeing her alarm, he laughed—so naturally that she was convinced he was joking. Annabella was losing that courage and authority which her relations had so much admired in her. How long, she wondered, would Byron treat her like this? "Just as long as you continue to notice it," Hobhouse would have answered, if she could have consulted him. But notice it, alas, she did. Her reading, her happiness, her spoilt-child successes, her dangerous self-confidence had not really trained her to understand and placate a Byron.

Towards evening the carriage drove up in front of Halnaby, the great empty house looming sinister in the dusk and falling snow. Annabella stepped out with the face and bearing of despair. During dinner he said to her: "Now you are in my power and I shall make you feel it." Talking of William Lamb, he remarked: "Caroline Lamb must be to her husband's heart like a perpetually falling drop of water. It ruins and petrifies"—and malignantly added that she would find that she had got just such a partner.

The period which followed he called their "treacle-moon"; and never was the inconstant moon at once more brilliant and more heavily clouded. Byron was the most terrible and yet the most engaging of husbands. For brief moments his evil humours lifted like a morning mist, and then their talk would be intimate and gay, and he would delight in making his wife chatter all kinds of childish absurdities. "Pippin," he called her, and twitted her with her calm; and for Annabella those moments of relief became memories the sweeter for their fewness—"springs in deserts found," as she used to say. But then, no sooner did certain turns of phrase startle him with the prospect of her relapse into what he called her "sermons and sentiments," than he became brutal. Wrought up by his own sound and fury, and incapable of self-control, he spoke out with cruel frankness. Annabella was twenty-two, and knew nothing of life; what she was now learning was something very different from her preconceived picture.

Her partner was a creature both phenomenal and

simple; he had a painful degree of susceptibility, and his physical and moral egotism was almost beyond belief. He would talk tirelessly of his health, of a fallen hair or a decaying tooth. Regarding his lameness, his *amour-propre* was extremely touchy, and during the early days he never once mentioned it to her. Her anxiety to free their common life from this embarrassment made her the first to raise the subject; she had been reading an article on diseased volition by Erasmus Darwin, in which he declared that a sufferer can be relieved by talking freely of his trouble. And thenceforward he really admitted that she knew, but always with a nervous laugh and some reference to "my little foot." When he took a stroll on the public road and heard the approaching footsteps of a passer-by, he would often stop dead and stand motionless, in case some stranger might see him limping, or else break into a run. He had a horror of being watched; any gaze that rested on him provoked a burst of rage.

He made immediate efforts to combat Annabella's moral sentiments. *"Ce n'est que le premier pas qui coûte,"* he told himself, and in the evening would try to prove to her that there was no truth in either religion or morality. He ended on a note of challenge—"Now convert me!" She tried to evade answering, assuring herself that forgiveness, resignation, courage, and gaiety, would be the best means of convincing him that men are not wholly bad. For what Byron called religion was all that gloomy doctrine of his childhood, and she was discovering that it had driven deep into his soul, and, in combination with his two years in lands of Islam, had produced his fatalism. Not thus had Annabella conceived the action of Providence: "I believed in the living presence of God with those who desired, not their own will, but His."

Before living with Byron, she had supposed him to be a Voltairean sceptic. But now she saw the truth to be far otherwise: in his intelligence, her husband was a Voltairean, but the recesses of his spirit were deeply imbued with a lurking Calvinism. No living being could be more overwhelmingly aware of a Divine Will; but it was a Will in which justice was tempered by no trace of pity. His religion was compact of fear, and was, consequently, rebellion. He believed that certain men were destined for Heaven, others for Hell, and that he was among the latter; and from this there sprang a natural fury against the Tyrant of the Universe, and likewise the debauchery of desperation. One day, after a violent argument, he sank into an arm-chair, saying to his wife: "The worst of it is I *do* believe!" When he thought of a God rejoicing in the sufferings of His creatures, perhaps even laughing at them, he raged. "All this hostility to the laws of morality was to be traced to his unhappy creed, which forbade the return of the Prodigal Son,"—as Annabella commented.

A tragic couple, in all conscience. The very qualities of each, in combination with the faults of the other, could produce nothing but misery. Annabella, with her speeches and her inborn habit of thought, brought Byron back to the serious side of his nature. But to force Byron to ponder the ordering of the universe was simply driving him to violence. There was good reason for his preference for pretty and frivolous women. Salvation would have lain in a lightheartedness of which Annabella was incapable. She was far from being deficient in psychological intelligence, and she analysed Byron's character to perfection: "His misfortune is an habitual *passion for Excitement,* which is always found in ardent temperaments, where the pursuits are not in some degree organised.—It is the Ennui of a monotonous existence that drives the best-hearted people of this description to the most dangerous paths, and makes man often seem to act from bad motives. . . . The love of tormenting arises chiefly from this source. Drinking, gaming, etc., are all of the same origin."

Sometimes he would expound to her the idea that nothing has any importance, that morality is merely dependent on climate or period; and she was anxious to be convinced. "I can remember," she said long afterwards, "wishing it to be right to give up all for him, even to be a slave and a victim. . . ." A woman, she thought, cannot love a man for his own sake unless she loves him even in his crimes; no other love was worthy of the name. But no: Annabella's incorruptible reason refused her the right to weakness, and her logical sense was something too strong for her heart to prevail against.

The superstitious side of his nature took her by surprise. In him there dwelt side by side an emancipated spirit and a victim of childish fears. He told her how terrified he had been, during his childhood in Aberdeen, living close to a graveyard. Every coincidence was a miracle; he believed in omens; to wear a black gown was dangerous; a bat flying into the room brought ill-luck. One night, standing in the snow-clad garden, they watched a woolly wisp of cloud coming close to the moon. If it crossed the moon, he declared, he would be ruined; if it didn't, all would be well. . . . The cloud crossed the moon.

The Dowager's wedding-ring proved to be too large, and Annabella had wound a black ribbon round it to make it hold. "A black ribbon!" cried Byron when he saw this, and insisted on her removing it. A few minutes later, standing against the mantelpiece, she put her hands behind her back, and the ring fell into the fire. The incident perturbed Byron for hours on end. So extraordinary were some of his beliefs that she often wondered whether he were serious. Perhaps he was only half in earnest; he had always liked mystification. He used to declare, for instance, that he was a fallen angel, not symbolically but literally, and told Annabella that she was one of those women spoken of in the Bible who are loved by an exile from Heaven. Even in his reading he would find omens. He had not forgotten Zeluco, and spoke of him to Annabella at great length. Zeluco ended by strangling his child—and so would it be for himself, said Byron: "I shall strangle ours." He believed in some invincible force that was driving him to evil. He often said: "I must return to the East, I must return to the East to die. . . ." To him, the face of the future was all outlined in advance in the constellations and portents. Mrs. Williams, the gipsy soothsayer, had said he would die at thirty-seven, and he believed it. Lady Byron, the student of science, often listened to her husband with amazed anxiety. Was he mad? Or feigning a comedy of madness? She could not tell.

But that was not all. Beneath that first layer of mystery, black though it was, Annabella now perceived the existence of a second, darker still. On the very first morning, Byron received a letter from Augusta, which he read to Annabella in a kind of exultant ecstasy:

"*'Dearest, first, and best of human beings . . .'*—what do you think of that?" he asked her.

A few days after their wedding he made her look into a mirror at Halnaby to point out a slight resemblance between them. "As like as if we were brother and sister," she said with a laugh. He caught her by the wrist. "When did you hear that?" he cried. Another day, unintentionally, but perhaps because some unconscious anxiety was forming in her mind, she spoke to him of Dryden's tragedy of incest, *Don Sebastian,* and again he burst into a rage. The subject seemed to horrify him; yet he was for ever harking back to it. Ingenuously the young woman made an attempt at understanding by using her class-room methods; her "reason and judgment" were in great measure unavailing, and she had to solve the unknown factor in a problem without having the necessary data. She had an impression that he had married her, not so much from motives of vengeance, as to hide some hideous crime, the nature of which she could not even imagine. Had he, she wondered, had as his mistress some woman whom he later identified as a natural daughter of his own father?

At night she saw him harassed by nightmares. He talked in his sleep. He got out of bed and strode up and down, brandishing pistols and daggers, and then lay down again gnashing his teeth. She came and laid her head on his shoulder to calm him. "You should have a softer pillow than my heart," he said one night. And she answered: "I wonder which will break first, yours or mine?" Once she asked him gently to tell her if he had seduced someone: "does Augusta know?" He confessed that he really did have a terrible secret in his life: "I shall tell you when you have had a child." Often she thought of flight, of leaving him; but she loved him and was sorry for him. "Then for the first time in my life I knew what it was to be alone with God."

And what of him? What did he think of this woman, so different from all who had been his before? Sometimes his heart was touched by her, and he told her that she was a strong argument for immortality. "If anything could make me believe in Heaven, it is the expression of your countenance at this moment. Poor little thing, you ought to have married a better man!" He pitied her, and yet was inexorable. Ever since *Childe Harold* he had been the play-actor of his own life, and never had he found a more credulous audience than this studious, startled girl. If she had only had the sense to smile, he would instantly have altered his rôle. What he needed at this time was the company of a woman of epicurean calm, like Lady Oxford; Annabella's gravity was his undoing. "I only want a woman to laugh," he told her, "and don't care what she is besides. I can make Augusta laugh at anything. No one makes me happy but Augusta."

How could he be so brutal, he who believed himself the gentlest of men, who could be pacified by the very presence of a woman, be she even old and plain, who had treated the frail Lady Frances with such fondness and delicacy? He himself could not comprehend. He was a Byron. A mad rage took hold of him. "You do not know what a devil any bad passion makes me!" He felt himself this woman's prisoner. He had asked her to break their engagement, but she had wanted to marry him and said she would have no regrets. And now here she was, a stranger planted in the midst of his life. Perhaps he might have pitied her if she had seemed weak, but she hid her weakness only too well. She had neither Augusta's troubled shyness, nor the scared fragility of Lady Frances; her demeanour was imperturbable, her cheeks plump and rosy. She laid down the law, she passed judgment, she solved problems. And she would be eating, slowly and methodically, when he himself had finished a whole meal in a moment or two. "Don't be sentimental!" he cried to her, hands flung heavenward. And she took everything literally. "If you wouldn't mind my words, we shall get on very well together." He needed calm and solitude; it was terrible to be perpetually two; he was for ever sending her out of the room with the words, "I don't want you," or else, "I hope we are not always to be together—that won't do for me, I assure you"; and another time, "one good thing in my marriage is that it will deliver me from my friends."

Already he foresaw the approaching end of his conjugal fidelity. He had once asked Lady Melbourne: "A married man never gets anybody else, does he?"—and now he was writing to her: "I cannot sufficiently admire your cautious styie since I became chickenpecked, but I love thee, *ma tante,* and therefore forgive your doubts which will last till the next scrape I get into." The old lady felt that Byron had brought scandals enough into this family, and was anxious that he should keep quiet. "I hope always to be your *corbeau blanc* (you remember Voltaire's tale). I wish you may hit as justly upon the *Corbeau Noir* and avoid him, . . ." he replied, "but I must still take omens from her flight. I can't help loving her, though I have quite enough at home to prevent me from loving anyone essentially for some time to come." *Essentially*—the word amused Lady Melbourne: "I am laughing now at your *essentially*. Was that word ever made use of before in such a sense?"

He had originally intended leaving Halnaby on January 20, so as to spend his birthday, two days later, with the Milbankes at Seaham. But discovering at the last moment that the 20th was a Friday, he declared he would not travel on that day; they would leave on the 21st. Lady Byron smiled faintly, and he peevishly explained that Friday was the Mohammedan sabbath, which he customarily observed. He was in fairly good humour, and told her during the drive that their life together would run along well enough. "I think you know pretty well what subjects to avoid," he added, looking straight across to her.

He was beginning to discern her qualities. During those cruel weeks at Halnaby she had worked for him, copying out the *Hebrew Melodies* which he was writing for the musician Nathan. They talked together of their reading. She was intelligent. If only she had not been his wife. . . . But how could she not be held responsible for the massive ennui of the marriage? What could be more hateful, for a man who had been free, than to find himself hobbled with parents-in-law when he had never been shackled even with parents of his own? It was not without alarm that Byron encountered "my papa, Sir Ralph," at Seaham once more. The rosy old baronet was cordial, but he had annoying tricks, and a really incorrigible taste for his little stock of endlessly repeated jokes. There was one about a shoulder of mutton, which Sir Ralph was so obstinately fond of that he had a shoulder served up several times a week for the sake of once more firing off his quip. Sitting on alone with Byron after dinner, he would recite for his benefit the speeches he had lately delivered to the Durham taxpayers. "I am listening," wrote Byron, "to that monologue of my father-in-law which he is pleased to call conversation; he has lately played once on the fiddle, to my great refreshment. . . . He is now, I believe, speaking it to himself (I left him in the middle) over various decanters, which can neither interrupt him nor fall asleep." And the son-in-law went off to dream in his room, until the tea-bell rang and he had once more to join the Family. "I must go to tea," he wrote to Moore, "damn tea, I wish it was Kinnaird's brandy." Augusta, jealous perhaps and certainly clumsy, made quite amusing fun in her letters of this domesticated Byron. In the evenings he yawned most dreadfully, in that drawing-room which had been the sanctuary of his marriage; for those evening hours which were the most enticing of all in London, were at Seaham the drowsiest.

If parents-in-law bored him, the force of contrast then made Annabella into an ally and a refuge. He had now baptised her "Pip."—"You are a good kind Pip—a good-natured Pip—the best wife in the world," he told her one night when she brought him his lemonade in bed. But there were still queer incidents from time to time. They had been playing crambo one evening and Byron proposed sending the papers to Augusta for her amusement, when his wife suggested that she would put crosses on his rhymes to distinguish them from hers. He turned pale. "For God's sake don't—it would frighten her to death!" All night long she lay wondering what these crosses could mean.

But on the sands he became a cheerful and artless companion for her, and they took regular walks over to a great rock known as "the Feather-bed"; he challenged her to scale it as quickly as he could, and he clambered up ahead of her with all the agility that was his when he could run. This was what she called his "child-side"—"a state of being, for brief intervals, resembling that of a guileless child." And frequently he would drop into the small child's way of talking to himself in the third person, saying, in his moments of misery: "Byron's a fool—yes, he *is* a fool!"—and then bitterly, "Poor Byron . . . poor Byron!" Annabella was touched by the despairing note in his voice at these moments. One night, near the end of their stay, he said to her: "I think I love you"—which was not at all improbable, for she was becoming what he most needed, a habit. She was familiar now with the hobbling gait, the bedside pistols, the forbidden subjects, and if he had stayed a few more months at Seaham he would perhaps have fitted himself into the daily round there, as formerly into others elsewhere.

He wrote to Moore: "I am in such a state of sameness and stagnation, and so totally occupied in consuming the fruits—and yawning—and trying to read old Annual Registers and the daily papers—and gathering shells on the shore—and watching the growth of stunted gooseberry bushes in the garden—that I have neither time nor sense to say more. . . . My spouse and I agree to—and in—admiration. Swift says 'no *wise* man ever married'; but, for a fool, I think it the most ambrosial of all possible future states. I still think one ought to marry upon *lease;* but am very sure I should renew mine at the expiration, though next term were for ninety and nine years."

The Byrons had arranged to leave for London in the spring, and on March 9, the carriage once more drove them away. Byron showed some desire to stop alone at Augusta's, at Six Mile Bottom, but his wife insisted on coming there with him. Mrs. Leigh wavered a long time before agreeing to entertain them—she had no room, it was a small house, she didn't know whether the colonel would be away from home; but in the end she did invite them. Byron showed a flash of ill-temper when the carriage left Seaham. "What on earth does your mother mean," he exclaimed, "by telling me to take care of you? I suppose you can take care of yourself? I didn't want you. . . ." Annabella said she was determined to visit Mrs. Leigh. "Augusta is a fool!" he answered, and then, in a gloomy tone: "Ah, yes! Augusta is a fool!" He became kindlier towards evening: "You married me to make me happy, didn't you? Well then, you do make me happy."

Augusta welcomed them calmly, saying hardly a word, and not kissing her sister-in-law. The two women went up to the bedrooms together, and there Annabella made the first move by embracing Augusta. After dinner Byron asked for brandy, began drinking, and advised his wife to retire. "We don't want *you,* my charmer," he told her, and later, on coming up to her room: "Now I have *her,* you will find I can do without *you*—in all ways. I told you you were a fool to come here and had better not." The scene struck Annabella as extraordinary; Byron, she thought, must have had a passion for Augusta and been repulsed by her. The next morning, Augusta greeted them both with her strange tranquillity. "Well, Guss," said Byron, "I am a reformed man, ain't I?" Augusta looked vexed. "I have observed some improvements already," she replied.

Throughout this visit Mrs. Leigh was very kind to

Annabella. It looked as if Byron were pressing her, and as if she, though seeking to escape him, were in terror of him. He delighted in making more and more direct allusions: "*We must fly, we must part*—you remember, Guss, I wrote these lines to *you.*" Annabella was struck by the peculiar beauty of his expression when he looked at little Medora. "You know that is my child?" he said, pointing to her. But Lady Byron refused to understand; she felt it her duty to stifle as far as possible so dreadful a suspicion of her husband, and experienced a sensation of "immeasurable horror and pity." And inwardly she solemnly vowed to act as if no such thought had ever crossed her mind.

Byron had had two brooches made in London, containing strands of his own and Augusta's hair entwined, and both marked with the letters—"A—B—+++." One of these he gave to Augusta, pointing to his wife with the words: "If she knew what these mean! Do you remember our signs at Newstead?"

However, the two A's took long, friendly walks together in the park, talking about Byron as they went. Notwithstanding her dark doubts, the despairing Annabella made Augusta her confidante, and the latter was astonished by the humility of the affection her sister-in-law showed. "You are kind to me because you do not know me," said Mrs. Leigh, and gave Annabella advice on the régime that Byron ought to be made to follow. Obedient to the nature of her mind, which made her always bring the most tragic events down to her own level, she believed that her brother's furies sprang from indigestion. He starved himself to keep slim, and then, famishing, devoured a heavy meal; then he suffered for it, and took overdoses of magnesia. That was the whole trouble, explained Augusta. Annabella said that Byron was a difficult husband, and that she had hopes of winning him over by her affection. High hopes, answered Augusta, for habit had immense power over Byron.

Notwithstanding Mrs. Leigh's quite genuine kindness, that stay was a nightmare for Annabella. Byron was irritated with himself, irritated with his wife, irritated with his sister, and a victim to the formidable frenzies of a man to whom an expected pleasure is refused. He drank to forget; his talk became the more violent in consequence; and he compelled Augusta to read out the letters which she had had from him during the past two years, letters in which he spoke cynically of his indifference to Annabella, and of his mistresses. And turning to his wife, he said: "And all the time *you* thought I was dying for you!" In the evenings he sent Annabella upstairs early, and sat on with Augusta for an hour or two. So wretched did Lady Byron feel that she could not eat; she was starving; and sometimes she locked herself in her room so that she could cry her heart out. "It is impossible . . . impossible . . ." she kept telling herself. One day she showed Augusta a quotation from Madame Necker: "Troubles in which one has had no part will always vanish, but epochs and sentiments are fixed by remorse." Augusta stared at her without a word, and Annabella felt that a silent understanding had been set up between them.

Nearer the end of the visit, when reality had become intolerable, Lady Byron sought refuge in contemplation and ecstasy. She read the Bible, where she found passages that accorded with her emotions, and achieved a state of mystical enthusiasm. She would appoint herself the guardian of these two lost souls, she would save them. . . . But how could you save a man whom you loved, and who hated you?

It was at Six Mile Bottom that Byron heard of the return from Elba, the desertion of the royal troops, the soaring of the Eagle! The news enraptured him. So his "little pagod" was not shattered after all. "And now if he don't drub the Allies, there is 'no purchase in money.' If he can take France by himself, the devil's in't if he don't repulse the invaders, when backed by those celebrated sworders—the Imperial Guard—it is impossible not to be dazzled and overwhelmed by his character and career."

London was dumbfounded and storm-tossed. At the Cocoa Tree they were taking odds of three to one on the Bourbons. Hobhouse staked on Napoleon. On the 23rd came news that the Emperor was in Paris; he had traversed France in twenty days. In the harbours facing the cliffs of Dover fluttered the tricolour. Twenty years of history were beginning again.

At any other time Byron would have been eager to discuss this news with Hobhouse and Kinnaird; but so gloomy a pleasure was he taking in "working them both well," these two women at Six Mile Bottom, that he would gladly have stayed on there. Augusta, however, would not have it, and on the 28th, he took Annabella away with him. She was presenting, in her husband's phrase, "gestatory symptoms." And she was broken.

XXIV

13 PICCADILLY TERRACE

1815–1816

The tragedy of the marriage, as of many another, is that what each saw in the other was not the whole truth.

H. J. C. Grierson

THEY had rented a handsome town house at Number 13 Piccadilly Terrace; they had a staff of servants; they had two carriages. What they lacked was a fortune. The rent was £700 a year, which took the whole of the income from Lady Byron's side, Byron's own revenue being quite negative, as the Newstead rent-roll did not even meet the interest on his debts. Almost immediately the duns began calling, attracted by the show of stylish living. Hobhouse came to see his friend before leaving for France, where he proposed taking notes on the return of the Emperor, and found him deep in gloom. Byron offered no complaint, but advised Hobhouse not to marry.

The first days were fairly happy—"for ten days he was kinder than I had ever seen him"—but Annabella had few hopes left. "Hope is nothing but the paint upon the face of Existence: the least touch of Truth rubs it off, and then we see what a hollow-cheeked harlot we have got hold of."—Was she too attaining that sour philosophy?

Byron was more handsome than ever. His face had taken on a certain loftiness, a look of restless grandeur, and the black clothes which he now wore heightened the impressive nobility of his appearance. Annabella never tired of gazing at him. She enjoyed going out with him when she went to buy gloves at Henderson's, and she "deposited" him at Leigh Hunt's house at Lisson Grove while she went shopping; and there the two men would discuss Lord Castlereagh's politics, Byron swinging to and fro on the little Hunts' rocking-horse. The Government and the Tory press wanted to come to the help of the Bourbons,—"How could they sit quiet whilst their neighbour's house was on fire?"—but Byron and his friends, of course, were against the war and for Bonaparte, protesting against England's participation in another country's civil war. On her way back, Lady Byron called for her husband, waiting at the door in her handsome carriage. On the front steps Byron stood playing with the Hunt children. Here, surely, was the very type and pattern of bliss! The smiling young wife, just a little plump, the husband on the steps bidding farewell to his friend, the spirited horses chafing and champing—what more was wanted for this sentimental mezzotint? Home at Piccadilly Terrace, and here was Byron working at his new poem, *Parisina,* and here was Annabella, the perfect author's wife, copying out the pages. The face of Existence was painted quite respectably.

But Lady Byron's sadness persisted. She did not recover her fresh, country-lass colouring, and she felt marooned. Byron's friends, Kinnaird and Hobhouse—"the Piccadilly crew" as she called them—were distasteful to her. Kinnaird had bought in Byron's name a share in the Drury Lane Theatre, so that his friend could be one of the managing committee, and Annabella did not care for that green-room society. What was more, she knew that Byron was frequenting Melbourne House again, which was disturbing, for her aunt was a dangerous counsellor. But what could she do? In the eyes of the outer world, the Melbournes and Lambs were relatives and friends of the Byrons. Caroline and William were cooing like turtle-doves; Byron was their unquestioned guest; things seemed to have a way of settling down. He kept groaning that Caroline was very tedious; but she attracted him as an old mistress can, as one with whom speech is free and confidence flattering. Lady Byron had gone once herself to Melbourne House, where, as ill-luck would have it, she met Mrs. Chaworth-Musters, the Morning Star of Annesley, who had now recovered from her nervous collapse. To Augusta, Annabella described the visit: "I never told you of my meeting with Mrs. Musters there. She asked after Byron. Such a wicked-looking cat I never saw. Somebody else looked quite virtuous by the side of her. O, that I were out of this horrid town, which makes me mad! . . . If I were in the country I believe I could regain my good looks and my good spirits wonderfully." And indeed there could be nothing more agonising for Lady Byron, so eager in her love, so sensitive in her pride and so chaste, than this London life in which she felt herself spied upon by these hostile women once loved by her husband, and where she was afraid of betraying any hint that her marriage was a failure.

Then, on top of everything else, there was Augusta. After an interval of ten days, Mrs. Leigh had come up to town and installed herself at Piccadilly Terrace. How did Annabella come to invite her? "It was hopeless to keep them apart—it was not hopeless, in my opinion, to keep them innocent. I felt myself the guardian of these two beings." Byron's first greeting of Augusta was one of his famous downcast glances, darting hatred; but in a few minutes he had recovered his zest in her. "You are a fool," he told his wife, "for letting her come to the house, and you'll find it will make a great difference to *you* in all ways." And to be sure, the life of Six Mile Bottom began once more. In the evening Annabella was sent up to her room, and lay there wakefully listening for Byron's footsteps. That tread foretold the state of mind in which he was coming to her. Sometimes he came upstairs with terrifying energy, a sign of anger; sometimes she would hear his steps mingling with Augusta's, and bursts of laughter as they came. The relations of these three people were truly extraordinary. Annabella was "Pip" and Augusta "Goose"; to his wife, Byron was "Duck," and to his sister, "Baby." There were still flashes of happiness. "If I had known you since I was five years old," said Byron to his wife, "I might have been happy." And again: "Well, poor thing, you are easily pleased, to be sure!" But some days were so dreadful that they drove Annabella into such a hatred of Augusta that she wanted to kill her. "I was almost mad—and to prevent myself in indulging the passion of revenge, I was obliged to substitute another—that of romantic forgiveness." She who in bygone days had defended Thermopylæ and tended the plague-stricken, now yearned to save this woman who caused her misery. And hatred was then transmuted into an ardent, despairing friendship. Like all women in love, she craved to possess the past of the man she loved. Augusta was the woman who knew. She was also the woman who shielded her when her presence exasperated Byron. Nevertheless, towards the end of June, Lady Byron made it quite clear to her sister-in-law that the visit had lasted long enough, and Mrs. Leigh went back to live at Six Mile Bottom.

Throughout that spring of 1815 Byron spent an hour or two every morning in John Murray's office. There he met one of the very few writers for whom he felt both esteem and admiration—Sir Walter Scott. Both men greatly enjoyed these conversations. Scott had been told that Byron was an extravagant young man, but this was by no means the impression he received. Nobody was more capable than he of appreciating all the nobleness in Byron's character. In religion as in politics, they stood in opposing camps, but Scott did not think that Byron's opinions on these subjects were very fixed: a few more years, he told him, and his feelings would change. "I suppose," retorted Byron quickly, "you are one of those who prophesy that I will turn Methodist?"—"No, I don't expect your conversion to be of such an ordinary kind. I would rather look to see your retreat upon the Catholic faith, and distinguish yourself by the austerity of your penances. The species of religion to which you must, or may, one day attach yourself must exercise a strong power on the imagination." Byron smiled gravely, and did not gainsay it.

They exchanged presents. Scott gave him a very handsome dagger, mounted in gold, which had been the property of the redoubtable Elfi Bey; and a few days later Byron sent him a large funerary urn in silver, filled with bones, and bearing an inscription of the lines of Juvenal:

Expende Annibalem: quot libras in duce summo
Invenies? . . . Mors sola fatetur
Quantula sint hominum corpuscula. . . .

Scott has been better able than anyone to pacify Byron and win his confidence. "He was often melancholy—almost gloomy," he wrote. "When I observed him in this humour, I used either to wait until it went off of its own accord, or till some natural and easy mode occurred of leading him into conversation, when the shadows almost always left his countenance."

If Lady Byron had had the same understanding of souls in torment, the house in Piccadilly Terrace might have known some peace; but Lady Byron was absolute, and she was in love—both dangerous obstacles on the path of wisdom.

June 1815. Annabella was now more than three months advanced in pregnancy. Hobhouse, over in France, was awaiting news of the armies. On the 20th a postmaster outside his inn informed him that Napoleon had been completely beaten at Waterloo. "Poor fellow!" he said; and Byron, on hearing the news, exclaimed: "Well! I'm damned sorry for it!" All the fashionable young Englishwomen were then in Belgium, tending brothers, or husbands, or lovers, and Caroline Lamb was among them, not without certain heartburnings at the triumph of Lady Frances Webster. Byron had been right in saying a bolder lover would have his way with that young woman; she had made notable progress since her mock battle with him; and it was rumoured that she had been the cause of Wellington's late arrival on the field of Waterloo. As for the *marito,* he was escorting his wife; and he composed a poem on the battle.

Hobhouse came home. Byron and he bewailed the tragic drama of the *Bellerophon,* and inveighed against the English admiral who addressed the Emperor as

"General." "Savage rascal!" exclaimed Hobhouse, and they were both delighted when they heard how Napoleon had been cheered by the English crowd at the moment of sailing. But this time the catastrophe was beyond curing; all Europe would be under the yoke of Metternich. "Every hope of a republic is over, and we must go on under the old system. But I am sick at heart of politics and slaughters; and the luck which Providence is pleased to lavish on Lord Castlereagh is only a proof of the little value the gods set upon prosperity when they permit such ——'s as he and that drunken corporal, old Blücher, to bully their betters. From this, however, Wellington should be excepted. He *is* a man,—and the Scipio of our Hannibal."

But was all this even worth thinking about? "When all is said and done," said Chateaubriand, "is there any single thing to-day for which we would willingly take the trouble to rise from our beds? We fall asleep to the sound of kingdoms crashing in the night, and every morning they are swept up before our doors." Oh, to be gone! To leave all the rottenness of the West behind! To find peace of mind, in Greece or Turkey! How splendid those hours had been when he galloped with Hobhouse, and the eminent Fletcher, under the blue dome of skies! This dull conjugality was growing intolerable. For a being so accustomed as he was to independence, the constraint was maddening. His diagnosis of Annabella had been right: she was infallible, even in failure, a creature of rules and principles, and thinking thereby to control events. And the more she believed this, the more he delighted in proving her impotence to her.

Marriage from love, like vinegar from wine—
   A sad, sober beverage—by time
Is sharpened from its high celestial flavour,
Down to a very homely household flavour.

There's doubtless something in domestic doings
   Which forms in fact, true love's antithesis;
Romances paint at full length people's wooings,
   But only give a bust of marriages;
For no one cares for matrimonial cooings,
   There's nothing wrong in a connubial kiss:
Think you, if Laura had been Petrarch's wife,
He would have written sonnets all his life?

He was annoyed when Murray congratulated him on the moral correctness of the two poems he had written since his marriage; and no less so when the publisher added, with an indulgent smile, that he would not have ventured to read them aloud to Mrs. Murray had he not recognised the delicate hand that had copied them.

Circumstances seemed to conspire to infuriate Byron. Lady Milbanke's brother, Lord Wentworth, died, leaving her the title of Lady Noel and a large income from the Kirkby Mallory estate, amounting to almost £8,000 a year; but nothing of this fortune could come to Annabella during her mother's lifetime, and as the estate ate up all its revenue and Sir Ralph was crippled with debts, Lady Noel could not come to her daughter's help. So the financial situation at Piccadilly Terrace was dangerous. Murray knew that his author was in difficulties, and sent him a cheque for £1,500; but Byron returned it. A bailiff was sleeping in the house, and the presence of this stranger became, in Byron's imagination, a veritable drama. He always needed one; Annabella, who now knew him well, passed the observation that bailiffs were "quite the subject of his romance at present."

All his misfortunes he laid at the door of the woman who, despite himself, had wished to share his life. He had told her that money would be short. And short it was; the duns were threatening to sell up the books and furniture. On the staircase resounded the tramp of the bailiff, overlord of a Byron's house. And that woman was perpetually there, with her offensive air of virtue. He knew he was treating her badly; he felt remorse, often keenly; but that very remorse was a fresh reason for hating her. She reflected once that had he felt worthy of her, he would have been good: it was as if she were his conscience. Lady Byron was often penetrating: yes, it was just that—she was there like an incarnate conscience, and there are times when one longs to escape from one's conscience. He was jealous of her, as he had been jealous of the other Byron. To find his peace of mind again he must see her no more, he must be off, set sail for Naxos, or send her home—"running back to your father like the spoiled child you are." The sight of the living Annabella brought forth a demon from within him. Like that forebear of his who had "an evil turn in his hand," he seemed to split in twain, to be looking on at the behaviour of a Byron who was almost dangerous. Anger is like inspiration; he relished the spectacle of his excesses, and enjoyed his surrender to a fury that seemed not far short of sacred. One day, in a burst of passion, he threw a clock on the floor and shattered it with blows of a poker. Had not his mother, Kitty Gordon, long ago, done the same thing in front of him at Southwell? Can any man hold back his ancestors from being reborn within him? Annabella, with only three months now before the birth of her child, saw a hostile force beside her, waxing greater and greater, and now beyond her power to control.

She was dismayed; and being reluctant to say anything disturbing to her parents, she had the idea of falling back on Mrs. Leigh. During August, Byron had drawn up a will, by which he left his sister all that he possessed, and it was Lady Byron who, with admirable disinterestedness, had informed her sister-in-law of the fact. "Dearest Lei," she wrote, "I must tell you how lovingly Byron has been talking of *dear Goose,* till he had half a mind to cry—and so had I. The conversation arose from his telling the contents of a will that he had just made,—as far as I can judge, quite what he ought to make. . . . And, dearest Augusta, believe that I know you too well to suppose what a certain person might suppose, or anything of the kind." (The "certain person" was doubtless Caroline Lamb, whose gossip about Byron and his sister had begun to filter through London society.) Annabella knew that Augusta, for all her failings, was capable of kindness, and invited her to come again and stay at Piccadilly Terrace, until her confinement. In these last stages of her pregnancy she clutched at every straw of help; alone with this man who seemed no longer master of himself, she was afraid; and she did not hesitate to summon the woman whom she most dreaded.

On her arrival, Augusta was startled by Byron's condition. He had had a liver attack which had turned his pallor yellow. Sick and unhappy, and having lost even his genuine pleasure in writing, he was taking laudanum to check his suffering, and had a small bottle of it always at his bedside. The drug soothed him for a short time, but then left him more violent than ever. Exasperated by the perpetual constraint of having under his roof a dulled and ailing woman, deprived of everything he was fond of—tranquillity, the poetic solitude of a great silent house,—and pestered by creditors, he was becoming like the Gordons of old, a wild beast. And this time, he ill-treated Augusta just as much as Annabella. He spoke to her with horror of her husband and her children; and when Augusta took the liberty of uttering the word *duty,* he bade her leave duty to God. Every day he inveighed against the hideous institution of marriage, swore to throw off its hateful bonds, and threatened both women that he would bring mistresses to live in the house.

Wife and sister had sorrowful conversations together. "Ah! You don't know *what* a fool I've been about him!" Why, yes, Annabella did know, and sometimes let it be understood, with an obscure rancour which perturbed her sister-in-law; and then their talk would glide into less perilous channels. But to what avail? Augusta was now the sole barrier between Annabella and fear. Those wifely confidences, those whisperings that stopped short when he appeared, infuriated Byron. Besides the two women, the house was now sheltering George Anson Byron, the heir-presumptive, whom Augusta had invited to stay there for their protection, and Annabella's governess, Mrs. Clermont. Byron believed that his wife was using the latter to spy on him; letters vanished from his drawers; the gynecœum was topsy-turvy like a stricken hive; he could see that his looks were being watched, that he was being kept furtively under observance. Did they think he was mad?

Madness, indeed, was the idea at which Annabella was now clutching. Surely he could not possibly hate an innocent woman so bitterly unless he were mad? Wasn't there often a fixed stare in his eye? And hadn't Augusta noticed his way of lowering his head and looking up from under his eyelids? That was one of the symptoms noticed in the King when his insanity developed. . . . Once in a box at the playhouse, he began talking to himself. A result of laudanum? Or of boredom? Or the unconscious murmur of a writer experimenting with subjects? The two women and George Byron, who were there with him, exchanged glances. The more he felt himself under observation, the stranger his behaviour became. Cousin George himself advised Lady Byron to leave the house. "If not," he said, "I shall be obliged to warn your father."

The child was born on December 10. It was a girl. He had not even the heir he wished for.

Hobhouse came and saw the infant, amused at the notion of the Corsair as father of a family. "Called on Byron—saw his child, Augusta Ada. The latter a name of someone who married into his family in the reign of King John." And leaving Piccadilly Terrace, Hobhouse went to dine at Holland House, where he sat next Caroline Lamb. She was in excellent humour that night, and defined Truth as "what one thinks at the moment." She had wit, had Lady Caroline; and Hobhouse looked at her, thinking how quickly one forgets. There she was, apparently quite happy, along with her mother-in-law and a fond husband, while the wretched Byron was furiously pacing his cage in Piccadilly Terrace. A strange thing, life. "If the whole creation is a speck," Hobhouse reflected in his journal, "all that I need think of it is that, upon this speck, I am found and must do the best for myself as long as the fact shall exist."

On December 28 Annabella received a letter from her mother inviting them all to Kirkby Mallory, her new property. Byron had no desire to go there himself—but why not take this chance of ridding himself of his encumbrances? On January 3, in Lady Byron's room, he spoke of his intention of installing an actress in the house, and then, for three days on end, did not come to see her or the child. On the sixth she had a note from him: "When you are disposed to leave London, it would be convenient that a day should be fixed, and (if possible) not a very remote one for that purpose.—Of my opinion on that subject you are sufficiently in possession; and of the circumstances which have led to it—as also to my plans—or rather intentions—for the future. When in the country I will write to you more fully. As Lady Noel has asked you to Kirkby, there you can be for the present—unless you prefer Seaham.—As the dismissal of the present establishment is of importance to me—the sooner you can fix on the day the better—though of course your convenience and inclination shall be first consulted.—The child will of course accompany you." She replied next day: "I shall obey your wishes, and fix the earliest day that circumstances will admit for leaving London."

Thinking him mad, and seeing that the madness had taken the form of a deep aversion to her, she thought it her duty to go. Consulting her own physician, Dr. Baillie, and Byron's, Dr. Le Mann, she was told that the nature of the affliction would no doubt show more clearly in the following few days, and that Lord Byron could then be taken to Kirkby under medical supervision. They also told her to avoid anything that might possibly irritate him, and to write to him cheerfully and affectionately.

On the eve of her departure, she asked to say good-bye to him. She was holding the baby Ada in her arms. He greeted her coldly. On the last night she slept well, but awoke exhausted next morning. The carriage was at the door. Annabella came down. In front of the door of Byron's room was a large mat on which his Newfoundland dog used to sleep. She was tempted to lie down there on the floor, and wait; but it was only for a moment, and she passed on.

From the first halt she wrote to Byron: "Dearest Byron,—the Child is quite well, and the best of Travellers. I hope you are *good,* and remembering my medical prayers and injunctions. Don't give yourself up to the abominable trade of versifying—nor to brandy—nor to anything or anybody that is not *Lawful and right.* Let me hear of your obedience at Kirkby—though *I* disobey in writing to you. Ada's love to you with mine.—PIP." And the next day from Kirkby: "Dearest Duck—We got here quite well last night, and were ushered into the kitchen instead of the drawing-room by a mistake that would have been agreeable enough to hungry people. Of this and other incidents Dad wants to write you a jocose account, and both he and Mam long to have the family party completed. . . . If I were not always looking about for Byron, I should be a great deal better for country air. Miss finds her provisions increased and fattens thereon. It is a good thing she can't understand all the flattery bestowed on her,—'Little Angel' and I know not what. Love to the good Goose, and everybody's love to you both from hence.—Ever thy most loving PIPPIN. . . . PIP . . IP."

XXV

"FARE THEE WELL . . ."

1816

THE doctors had supposed that, after his wife's departure, Byron would calm down; but Augusta and George Byron, who stayed on with him, found him still in a highly excited state. Augusta sent a daily bulletin to her sister-in-law: "Byron stayed at home yesterday evening—no brandy and both his medicines. He was well the beginning of the evening but towards the end grew *fractious,* and in a reply to a question from George of when he thought of going to Kirkby, he said, after a vacant stare: 'I go there? Not at all! I've no thought of it if I can help it.' From that moment he talked all sorts of strange things—fell on me as usual—abused my spouse, my children—in short, all as you know and have heard before." "Difficult"—Augusta spoke of her brother as a mother of her child, as a rock-climber of a peak. She viewed him as a phenomenon of nature, not as a responsible human being. And that may have been why he loved her.

But while the agonised, tyrannical Byron thought he was ruling the guests in Piccadilly, his own fate was being decided up at Kirkby. On arrival at her parents', Lady Byron was unrecognisable. Those round cheeks which had earned her the nickname of Pippin were pale and sunken; she could not sleep; thoughts and doubts and fears kept her awake and feverish. If she had indeed believed herself infallible, she must now have recognised her mistake. What was to be done? What was to be said? She loved Byron and would gladly have rescued him; too dogmatic to be tolerant, she held his actions and doctrines alike in horror. But he was mad—he could not be blamed—he must be looked after. The idea of Duty then returned to her; and as soon as an abstract duty appeared amongst the factors in the problem, she felt herself on solid ground.

So startled were her parents by her appearance, that she was forced to admit some part of the truth, but without a word of her suspicions regarding her sister-in-law. The worthy baronet was highly indignant. "You cannot think how severe my father is," wrote Annabella to Augusta. However, as she explained that her husband's health had broken down, her parents forgave, and suggested that he should come and be looked after at Kirkby. "Nothing can exceed their tender anxiety to do everything for the sufferer. My mother is quite composed, though deeply affected. . . . My father and mother agree that in every point of view it would be best for Byron to come here; they say he shall be considered in everything and that it will be impossible for him to offend or disconcert them after the knowledge of this unhappy cause. . . . It will be by means of the *heir* that it can be effected." Byron, in point of fact, had several times expressed his intention of resuming life with his wife until she bore a son (even if only to spite George Anson), and of subsequently leaving for the Continent.

Such were the first days. Later, as Annabella's account gradually revealed what her life had been like, her parents' anger increased. Lady Noel, ever a busybody, proposed going to London to take legal advice, and when she had gone Annabella herself was profoundly troubled by the news she received from Piccadilly. The malady, it appeared, had not defined itself, and Dr. Le Mann wrote: "With regard to the state of my patient's mind, I must say that I have discovered nothing like settled lunacy. There is an irritability of temper (probably depending on irregular action of the liver and other organs of digestion) that might by improper management be driven into a state of distraction very soon; but I think that may be easily overcome."

If he did prove to be sane, forgiveness was out of the question; and Lady Byron's faith, as well as her intellectual pride, thereupon dictated a choice both painful and necessary. Our life on earth, she believed, was only a preparation for immortality, and she did not admit the right of spending it with a damned soul who would drag her, with himself, towards punishment everlasting. She thus came to accept the idea of a separation as inevitable. Nevertheless, she was in despair.

Up in London, on the other hand, Lady Noel was feeling pleasantly important, as is the way of elderly women when, freed themselves from the torments of love, they can free a young woman likewise. She consulted an eminent jurist, Sir Samuel Romilly, and then Dr. Lushington, a brilliant young barrister who took her fancy much more. "I would not but have seen Lushington for the world—he seems the most *gentlemanlike,* clear-headed and clever man I have ever met with,—and agrees with all others that a proposal should be sent by your father for a quiet *adjustment*. . . . I have a great persuasion that Lord Byron will not oppose *the arrangement*. . . . But if he does, Lushington thinks that the Spiritual Court will grant a separation on the ground of *cruelty* and *temper.*" She was delighted when she heard of her daughter's decision.

On February 2 Sir Ralph wrote to Byron to propose a separation. The letter was intercepted by Mrs. Leigh, who sent it back in the hope of avoiding the fatal decision. Whereupon Sir Ralph went up to London, and a fresh letter was delivered into the proper hands, informing Lord Byron that his wife's parents felt it was wrong to allow her to return under his roof, and requesting him to name an attorney. Byron was dumbfounded and prostrate. He had Annabella's letters in his hands, as loving as could be, and written at the time of her journey north. What had happened in the meantime? He could not believe that the decision had been reached by Annabella. His character had caused her suffering, but she had forgiven. Augusta? But now the two sisters-in-law seemed to be in league against him. Perhaps he had taken a queer pleasure in making allusions which he naïvely supposed were unintelligible; but what proof could Lady Byron have brought forward—and in any case were not the facts all previous to marriage? It was impossible that a woman should cut free from him like this. Under the provocation of her presence, he could toy with the idea of a separation; but the actual fact horrified him. A chameleon in sentiment, he was already letting his thoughts run solely on their hours of happiness. Why, only the evening before, he had been calling on Lady Melbourne, and talking for a whole hour of Annabella's lovable qualities! "All I can say seems useless," he wrote to his wife, "and all I could say might be no less unavailing; yet I still cling to the wreck of my hopes, before they sink for ever. Were you then *never* happy with me? Did you never at any time or times express yourself so? Have no marks of affection, of the warmest and most reciprocal attachment, passed between us? Or did in fact hardly a day go down without some such on one side and generally on both?"

He was right in thinking that Annabella would be affected by this appeal. Fletcher's wife, who was then with her, was witness of her fits of despair. But she had the strength to stand fast. She knew that no conjugal life was possible with Byron; and the factor which he had chiefly neglected in his calculations was the certitude of Annabella's religious sense. He did not believe that she *could* be implacable. But how could anyone be otherwise who believed that her infallibility of judgment was divine inspiration? She wrote to Mrs. Leigh, saying that she regarded it her duty towards God to act as she had done. Byron played all his charms, his fascination, his eloquence, his childishness: "Dearest Pip, I wish you would make it up. I am dreadfully sick of all this." And then, seeing that she was unyielding, he made one of his fierce gestures and sent back to her one of her betrothal letters, in which she had said: *"I shall be too happy—there will be no reverse. . . ."* He underlined the words with a marginal note—"Prediction fulfilled. February 1816."—and at the foot of the page added three lines of Dante:

Or non tu sai com' è fatta la donna . . .
Avviluppa promesse—giuramenti;
Che tutta spargon poi per l'aria e venti.

In London the news spread fast. There were too many doctors and lawyers and servants cognisant of it. And now would begin that ordeal of questioning and counselling with which the inquisitive herd of friends will torment—for his own good, of course,—every hapless wretch who has not the good fortune to be alone.

"Dear Lord Byron," wrote Lady Melbourne, "there is a report about you, so much believed in town, that I think you should be informed of it. They say you and Annabella are parted. . . . In general, when reports are as false as I know this to be, I think the best way is to despise them. But really, it is so much talked about and believed, notwithstanding my contradictions, that I think you ought to desire her to come to town, or go to her yourself." Lady Caroline, too, officious and secretly triumphant, proffered "a sinner's advice." Augusta was uneasy, and wanted her brother to strike his flag. "It strikes me that if their *pecuniary* proposals are favourable, he will be too happy to escape the exposure. He *must* be anxious, dear Mr. Hodgson. It is *impossible* he should not be in some degree." Anxious indeed he was, and striving hard to reassure his friends. "I do not believe—and I must say it in all the dregs of this bitter business—that there ever was a better, or even a brighter, a kinder, or a more amiable and agreeable being than Lady Byron. I never had, nor can have, any reproach to make her, while with me." He explained that the cause of all the trouble had been his bad health, which had made him irritable, and, over and above that, the pressure exercised on Lady Byron by Lady Noel, who detested him.

When it was clear that neither Byron nor his friends could bend Annabella, the attorneys of the two families were left to confront each other alone. Hanson, of course, was Byron's defender, and pleaded that, although his client admitted bad behaviour during the period at

Piccadilly Terrace, he considered those facts condoned by the letter beginning "Dearest Duck. . . ." His opponent, Dr. Lushington, confined himself to the reply that he was informed by Lady Byron of facts too serious to admit of any possible reconciliation. Hanson asked what these arguments were; but he was told that they would be reserved in case of the matter coming before the courts. What Lushington actually had in his hands was a memorandum drawn up by Annabella in which, methodically classifying them in numbered paragraphs, Princess of Parallelograms even in the supreme tragedy of her life, she had detailed the secret reasons for her decision.

The faithful and clumsy Hobhouse was full of wrath against Lady Byron. He was familiar with all the eccentricities of his friend, and understood the upheavals which the annoyances of married life could cause in a creature so ingenuously wild as Byron; to him the real causes of the disagreement were obvious. There could be no doubt that Byron had showed himself, as he himself had often experienced, violent, irritable, and fantastic. Lady Byron had fancied herself the object of a passionate aversion and, hugging this dangerous idea to herself, had contributed by her very demeanour to accentuating the frenzies of which she complained. "What, then, is Lord Byron charged with?" wrote Hobhouse sternly. "Why, he got up late, dined alone, was generally out of spirits, and occasionally out of humour." When the rumours of incest reached his ears, he drew up a document of rebuttal, which he asked Lady Byron to sign. It was dated March 6, 1816: "Lady Byron solemnly affirms that her only motive or pretext in applying for a separation from Lord Byron is the conviction that, from diversity of habits and opinions, their mental happiness is not likely to be insured by any further continuance of matrimonial intercourse. . . . She in the same manner most solemnly and without the least reserve disclaims for herself and her family any participation of or belief in the scandalous and calumnious rumours tending to the total destruction of his lordship's character which have been propagated. . . ."

Lady Byron refused to sign. Byron's friends then drew up a less precise text, in which Lady Byron was no longer asked to declare that she did not believe the current rumours, but would only say that they were not of her propagation, and that she would not have used them in the event of a trial. This was dated two days later: "Lady Byron declares that she does not consider herself in any ways responsible for the various reports injurious to Lord Byron's character and conduct which may be circulated in the world. They certainly have not originated with or been spread by herself or those most nearly connected with her. And the two reports specifically mentioned by Mr. Wilmot do not form any part of the charges which, in the event of a separation by agreement not taking place, she should have been compelled to make against Lord Byron."

It was much less satisfactory than the Hobhouse document; but they had to be content with it, and there only remained for solution the problem of finance.

This was unfortunately important to Byron, who was at the moment penniless. So short of ready cash was he that, for the first time, and in spite of his prejudice against professional authorship, he accepted a cheque from John Murray. At last the lawyers reached an agreement. Of the annual £1,000 of Lady Byron's dowry, she would receive £500, Byron retaining the other

£500; on Lady Noel's death, an arbitrator would divide between husband and wife the incomes accruing from the Wentworth inheritance. So Byron kept his personal income, plus £500 a year and large expectations. Hanson had not played his cards badly.

The house in Piccadilly Terrace looked as woebegone as if someone lay dead upstairs. To and fro in the drawing-rooms stalked the bailiffs, piling up books in anticipation of a sale. This took place on August 6, when Murray bought most of the books, and also the large screen on which Byron had pasted the portraits of Jackson and Angelo, and prints of famous prize-fights.

Byron's bedroom was full of pills and potions against his liver attacks; here and there some forgotten object still recalled Annabella; and in this melancholy atmosphere Byron slowly settled into calm. Just as certain creatures bred in damp and misty climes can never thrive save in fogs and rain, so he could never endure the sunshine of happiness. Annabella was gone, was she? Like Edleston, like Matthews, like his M.A.C., like the strange Mrs. Byron herself, she had glided out of his life. Already she was partaking of that mysterious glamour which death and the shades held for him. Alone in the great house, he paced its rooms of an evening, and sat down at his writing-table with thoughts of certain hours that had been dear; of that head with its burden of thoughts, thoughts, thoughts, which so often had sought peace and quiet on his shoulder; and of the tiny girl whom he had called an "implement of torture," while she was there, yet found that he was growing fond of when he had her no more. He took up a sheet of paper; tears spotted it as he wrote; and once again he found the spontaneous flow of that simple, natural rhythm which grief, and grief alone, could bring him:

Fare thee well! and if for ever,
Still for ever, fare thee well:
Even though unforgiving, never
'Gainst thee shall my heart rebel.

Would that breast were bared before me
Where my head so oft hath lain,
While that placid sleep came o'er thee
Which thou ne'er canst know again. . . .

Though the world for this commend thee—
Though it smile upon the blow,
Even its praises must offend thee,
Founded on another's woe:

Though my many faults defaced me,
Could no other arm be found,
Than the one which once embraced me,
To inflict a cureless wound?

Yet, oh yet, thyself deceive not;
Love may sink by slow decay,
But by sudden wrench, believe not,
Hearts can thus be torn away.

And when thou would'st solace gather,
When our child's first accents flow,
Wilt thou teach her to say "Father!"
Though his care she must forego?

When her little hands shall press thee,
When her lip to thine is press'd,
Think of him whose prayer shall bless thee,
Think of him thy love had bless'd.

But 'tis done—all words are idle—
Words from me are vainer still;
But the thoughts we cannot bridle
Force their way without the will.

Fare thee well! thus disunited,
Torn from every nearer tie,
Sear'd in heart, and lone, and blighted,
More than this I scarce can die.

Sometimes a burst of anger ran away with him. He had conceived a particular hatred of Mrs. Clermont, whom he suspected, not without reason, of having induced Lady Byron to leave him; and against her he unleashed a terrible invective:

Born in the garret, in the kitchen bred,
Promoted thence to deck her mistress' head;
Next—for some gracious service unexpress'd,
And from its wages only to be guess'd—
Raised from the toilette to the table,—where
Her wondering betters wait behind her chair.
With eye unmoved, and forehead unabash'd,
She dines from off the plate she lately wash'd.

And the frightful portrait was developed:

A lip of lies; a face form'd to conceal,
And, without feeling, mock at all who feel:
With a vile mask the Gorgon would disown,—
A cheek of parchment, and an eye of stone.
Mark, how the channels of her yellow blood
Ooze to her skin, and stagnate there to mud. . . .

Exaggerated it may have been; yes, but he was no longer master of himself. He felt like a hunted beast with all the human pack on his trail. The political cabal which had attacked him at the time of *The Corsair* was again giving tongue, and furiously. With his usual rashness he had recently published some verses, disguised as a translation from the French, in which Napoleon was spoken of as "Freedom's son," and an ode *On the Star of the Legion of Honour*—

Star of the brave:—whose beam hath shed
Such glory o'er the quick and dead . . .

in which the tricolour flag was compared to—

A rainbow of the loveliest hue
Of three bright colours, each divine,
And fit for that celestial sign;
For Freedom's hand had blended them
Like tints in an immortal gem.

In publishing the *Domestic Pieces,* the newspaper *The Champion* remarked that its object in offering these to its readers was to show the nature of the moral habits which accompanied the noble lord's political opinions; and this campaign turned Byron into a traitor in the eyes of the populace. His chaste and discreetly silent spouse became a symbol of all the British virtues. It was almost a joy to discover his guilt. This poet, a libertine, a liberal, and a cripple, had never been a true "English figure."—"He had been posing as a rebel against all the domestic proprieties. So long as his avowed licence could pass for a literary affectation, or be condoned in the spirit of the general leniency shown to wild young men in the era of the Prince-Regent, the protest was confined to the stricter classes. But when Lara passed from the regions of fancy to 13 Piccadilly Terrace, matters became more serious," and middle-class opinion had risen against him.

On his way into the House of Lords he was insulted by some bystanders, and in the House itself no one spoke to him except Lord Holland. The Tory journals were comparing him to Nero, to Heliogabalus, to Henry the Eighth, to the Devil himself. Rogers assumed the duty of informing Byron regarding the most malicious of these articles, and came into Byron's room one day with a newspaper in his hand. He was sure, he said, there was yet another attack in it against him; but Byron should not take it seriously. And unfolding the sheet, he began reading out a paragraph, with occasional glances to see whether Byron showed signs of pain. The article went on to refer to that poetaster, that unpleasant individual, Mr. Samuel Rogers. . . . And Rogers stood up, throwing down the newspaper. "It must be that scoundrel Croker," he exclaimed, and advised Byron to challenge the writer.

Nor did the Whig drawing-rooms defend him. His life had been that of his caste and his times, but he had vaunted it. Formerly Lady Melbourne had managed to put him on his guard against cynicism; but even she could save him no longer. Lady Jersey, like the courageous friend she was, tried to make a stand against the flowing tide, and gave a ball to which she invited Byron and Augusta. But when brother and sister made their appearance, the rooms emptied before them. Poor Lady Jersey! Her cream-white complexion, her coral necklaces, the sparkle and movement of her eyes and tongue and arms, were all unavailing: that day's flood of hate she could not stem. Apart from her, the only woman who would converse with Byron and Augusta was the pretty red-haired Miss Elphinstone. The men were implacable, and some of them stepped aside to avoid shaking Byron's hand. He took up his stance in a corner, folded his arms, and gazed with disdain at the hostile crowd, observing exactly the attitude of everyone in it. From that evening his firmness became more marked; and he noted how curious it was that any kind of agitation always fired his courage anew and set him on his

SARAH, COUNTESS OF JERSEY

After the painting by Sir Thomas Lawrence

feet for a time. Great had been his fall; and the very grandeur of the crash gave him exactly what he needed —a great rôle to play, satanic though it might be. In this rejection by the whole of a society there was a certain beauty. Already chased forth from his inward paradise, he now saw himself as the exile driven from his own country by a social ostracism far more definite and brutal than any potsherd voting. So be it. If England declared it time for him to go, he would set forth again on his pilgrimage.

Of all the living souls from whom his exile would part him, Augusta was the only one he regretted. On Easter Sunday, April 14, she came to bid him farewell. Once more she was approaching a confinement and had to go home to Six Mile Bottom. She spent a melancholy evening with him, during which she spoke for the first time of her remorse, with many tears. After Mrs. Leigh's departure from town Byron wrote to Annabella commending his sister to her care: "More last words—not many—and such as you will attend to—answer I do not expect—nor does it import—but you will hear me. I have just parted from Augusta—almost the last being you had left me to part with. . . . Wherever I may go—and I am going far—you and I can never meet again in this world—nor in the next. . . . If any accident occurs to me—be kind to Augusta,—if she is then nothing —to her children. . . ."

The week preceding his departure was taken up with a new adventure, and one which was not to lessen his contempt for the facile virtue of women. He had for some time been bombarded by love-letters from a lady unknown. At first they were signed with fictitious names, and on two occasions Byron's servants had refused to admit this stranger. She then signed her real name, which was Clare Clairmont, and asked for a recommendation to the Drury Lane Theatre. Byron began by sending her to Kinnaird. She grew bolder: "You bade me believe that it was a fancy which made me cherish an attachment for you. It cannot be a fancy since you have been for the last year the object upon which every solitary moment led me to muse. . . . I do not expect you to love me; I am not worthy of your love. . . . Have you any objection to the following plan? On Thursday evening we may go out of town together by some stage or mail, about the distance of ten or twelve miles. There we shall be free and unknown; we can return early the following morning. . . ." And then, a few days later: "Where shall I meet you?—how and when? . . . On Monday you set out for Italy and I—God knows where. . . . Now pray answer me kindly, and do not put any little sarcastic speeches in it; but, if you stand in need of amusement and I afford it you, pray indulge your humour; I had rather any thing than contradict you." He was becoming bored, and the girl was young. She had a pretty voice; he needed some "sensation" in order to forget; and he agreed to spend a night with her.

That was the end. The packing was completed. He had acquired for the journey a superb carriage, copied from that of the Emperor Napoleon, and was taking along with him the philosophic Fletcher, and a young doctor, John William Polidori, who had studied medicine at Edinburgh. Polidori fancied himself as a writer; and when Murray offered him £500 for the manuscript of his travel diary, he made haste to purchase a stout notebook.

During these last days Polidori was hardly ever out of the Piccadilly house; Isaac Nathan, the Jewish musician to whom Byron had given the *Hebrew Melodies*, was also there; Leigh Hunt came frequently, and Hobhouse daily. Kinnaird brought a cake and two bottles of champagne for the journey. Then Hanson appeared, with a story of having seen Lady Byron, who seemed "all torn here," he said, pointing to his heart. Polidori kept butting into the conversations of all the visitors, an intolerable braggart, prating of the journal he would keep and the three tragedies he had written. The profoundly English Hobhouse disapproved this choice of a foreign doctor, and could not bear "Polly-Dolly"—as he called him—and told Byron he was wrong to take him. So what with discussions, visits and gifts, these last days were lively enough to mask something of their sadness. Two days before leaving, the deed of separation was signed, and Byron wrote four lines in its margin:

A year ago, you swore, fond she!
"To love, to honour," and so forth:
Such was the vow you pledged to me,
And here's exactly what it's worth.

Nathan, knowing that Byron had a fine taste for biscuits, sent him some cakes of the Jewish Passover, which was just then beginning. Here, said his letter, are "some holy biscuits, commonly called unleavened bread, denominated by the Nazarenes *motsas,* better known in this enlightened age by the epithet Passover Cakes. . . . As a certain angel, at a certain hour, by his presence, assured the safety of a whole nation, may the same guardian spirit pass with your lordship to that land where the fates may have decreed you to sojourn for a while!" To which Byron replied that the unleavened bread would go with him on his pilgrimage, and the *motsas* be a charm against the Destroying Angel.

At last, soon after dawn on April 24, the Pilgrim left that house which only a year before he had thought would mark the term of his wanderings. In front of the door a crowd of idlers had gathered round the imperial barouche, and Byron stepped in with Scrope Davies: Polidori and Hobhouse followed in another carriage. The French authorities had refused Byron passage through their country on account of his dangerous political opinions, so he had to make for Switzerland by way of Dover, Ostend and Belgium. As soon as they were getting clear of London, Dr. Polidori began his notes: "The plain, enamelled with various colours according to the different growth of the corn, spread far before our sight. . . . The Thames next, with its majestic waves, flowed in the plain below, bearing numerous fleets upon its flood. Its banks in many parts were beautiful. . . ." With a sigh, Hobhouse sank deeper into his corner.

At Dover they were rejoined by Fletcher, who did not leave Piccadilly until after his master. He told Byron how the bailiffs had entered the house immediately after their departure and seized everything, even down to a tame squirrel. The vessel was not sailing until next morning, and to while away the time Byron proposed a visit to the grave of Charles Churchill. He knew that this famous satirist of half a century ago, who, like himself, had been "the comet of a season" and had his *annus mirabilis,* was buried down here; and an aged sexton led them to the grave, a mound of ill-kept turf with a grey stone at its head. In answer to their questions, the guide admitted that he knew nothing about the person buried there. "He died before my day of sextonship, and I had not the digging of his grave," said the old man; and his reply, with its ring of the gravediggers in *Hamlet,* took Byron's fancy, and plunged him into one of those meditations so dear to him, on fame and the end of all things. And then, before the astonished eyes of his friends and the old sexton, he lay down, outstretched, on the turf of the grave.

That evening, his last in England, was spent in listening to one of Polidori's tragedies, read by its author. Hobhouse and Davies laughed a good deal, but as Polidori seemed hurt Byron re-read the best passages himself, kindly and seriously.

Curiosity in Dover was running high; a number of ladies disguised themselves as chambermaids, so as to stand in the passages of the inn. Next morning, April 25, Hobhouse rose very early, but there was no sign of Byron. He was in his room, writing a farewell poem to Tom Moore:

> My boat is on the shore
> And my bark is on the sea;
> But before I go, Tom Moore,
> Here's a double health to thee!
>
> Here's a sigh to those who love me,
> And a smile to those who hate;
> And whatever sky's above me,
> Here's a heart for every fate!

But there he had to stop. The captain of the ship was furious; he would wait no longer, he roared. Even the imperturbable Scrope Davies was agitated. At last Byron was seen coming along the quay, limping on Hobhouse's arm. He handed Hobhouse a small package intended for Miss Elphinstone. It was a beautiful Virgil which he had received as a prize in his Harrow days. And he added: "Tell her that had I been fortunate enough to marry a woman like her, I should not now be obliged to exile myself from my country." The noise and flurry of departure sustained him until he was actually on board; but once there, he looked very unhappy. Shortly after nine o'clock the gangway was pulled in. Hobhouse ran to the end of the wooden jetty. It was a rough sea, with a head wind. When the vessel came past the jetty, close in and already taking on a roll, Hobhouse saw "the dear fellow" standing erect on deck. Byron raised his cap and waved it in farewell to his friend. "God bless him," said Hobhouse to himself, "for a gallant spirit and a kind one!"

PART III

Life as it flows is so much time wasted, and nothing can ever be recovered or truly possessed save under the form of eternity, which is also the form of art.

SANTAYANA

XXVI

THE PAGEANT OF A BLEEDING HEART

1816

> Once more upon the waters! yet once more!
> And the waves bound beneath me like a steed
> That knows its rider. . . .

ALREADY the pangs of exile had been projected into a new Childe Harold. He had brooded too long over that drama of failure and disgrace, the scum of hatred, the fingers pointing at Augusta, the hostility of a united England. He had thought of it until his brain seemed nothing but "a whirling gulf of phrenesy and flame," and his need now was for refuge in some solitary, spirit-haunted retreat, for "creating to live a being more intense." For what was he, George Gordon Byron, in this month of April 1816? Nothing. Fond and vengeful, sad and glad, logical as Voltaire and wild as the wind. . . .

> What am I? Nothing: but not so art thou,
> Soul of my thought!

To become Byron again, he must become Harold again. The *Pilgrimage* should have a third Canto.

> Self-exiled Harold wanders forth again,
> With nought of hope left, but with less of gloom;
> The very knowledge that he lived in vain,
> That all was over on this side the tomb,
> Had made Despair a smilingness assume. . . .

Deep in the crucible of the stanzas the gloomy thoughts were circling, crushed together by the unseen worker seeking to give them form; yet on the upper surface an English gentleman was loftily and lightheartedly amusing himself with Dr. "Polly-Dolly" over the incidents of travel. And when this Byron reached Ostend, the first stage of the journey, he became, like his father the captain years before at Valenciennes, the lover of the chambermaid at the inn. Polidori, his eye firmly fixed on Murray's £500, began his Belgian diary: "*Antwerp:* went to the café and saw all playing at dominoes. . . . Read *The Times* till the 23rd. . . . Women better looking, at all the fountains Madonnas. . . . Van Dyck, in my opinion, much superior to Rubens. *Brussels:* The English women are the only good-looking women in Brussels. All sorts of disgusting books publicly sold; beastliness publicly exhibited on the public monuments; fountains with men vomiting with effort a stream of water; and still worse. . . ." Byron, always more deeply moved by the emotions of memory than by an actual spectacle, would not rest till he had seen Waterloo. There his "little pagod" had collapsed; here at Brussels, on the battle's eve, had slept some of his friends, young men and gay, fated to die on the morrow; and here, through a long, blood-red evening, the chaste Lady Frances had thrown fond glances at the Duke of Wellington. "There was a sound of revelry by night . . ."— and then, the guns. . . .

They hired a chaise to take them out to Waterloo. It broke down "by a damned wheel pertinaciously refusing its stipulated rotation." Byron had to hobble on to the battlefield on the doctor's arm, hunting for bones. A farmer sold him a Cossack horse, mounted on which he continued his expedition. Flowers were springing up, and the fields were already under the plough. "If it were not for the importunity of boys and the glitter of buttons in their hands, there would have been no signs of war." Byron and Polidori carved their names in the chapel at Hougoumont, the former describing the battle to his companion, and praising the courage of the French. Then going off by himself, he meditated. Here, in this commonplace scene, in one single day, had foundered the grandest of human destinies. Action was no less futile than glory. " 'Tis but a worthless world to win or lose. . . ." The sole wisdom lay in retreat, in silence, in scorn. "But quiet to quick bosoms is a Hell," and Bonaparte subdues a continent, and Byron writes *Childe Harold,* and humans turn this way and that like sick men thinking always to find coolness in movement, yet never finding it because their fever comes from within. . . . As dusk fell they left the battlefield, Polidori silent, Byron on his mount singing a Turkish horseman's song at the top of his voice.

France was closed to them, so they came down to Switzerland by way of the Meuse and Rhine valleys. Byron's imperial carriage was a magnet for beggars, who clamoured for ha'pence addressing him as "General" and as "King of Hanover." The designations tickled Byron, and filled the heart of his companion with gladness. "I am with him on the footing of an equal," he wrote, "everything alike. . . ." One day he asked Byron what there was, after all, that his lordship could do better than he.—"I think there are three things I can do which you cannot," said Byron. Polidori challenged him to say what they were. "I can swim across that river"—he answered. "I can snuff out that candle at the distance of twenty paces—and I have written a poem of which fourteen thousand copies were sold in one day." As for Fletcher—the man of learning, as Hobhouse called him—he was in high spirits, and commented on the resemblance he found between the Rhine, from Coblenz to Mayence, and certain valleys in Albania. But the food, he said, was better. He was getting stout.

Wherever they went, the travellers found traces of the Emperor. They were always asking who had built this monument, who had made that road, who had dug this canal; and always the peasants would answer, "Napoleon." Byron, ever fond of a coincidence, was delighted to find every edifice graven with the initials "N.B."—"Noel Byron."

Crags upholding their castles, the slopes covered with the vines. . . . These smiling landscapes of the Rhine valley were calling up pictures of Augusta, who now stood in Byron's mythical universe for Fidelity in Misfortune. He wrote to her with passionate tenderness, and composed a poem for her—

> The castled crag of Drachenfels
> Frowns o'er the wide and winding Rhine . . .

telling her of this scene, as fair as any in the world,

> . . . which I should see
> With double joy wert *thou* with me.
>
> . . . .
>
> Nor could on earth a spot be found
> To nature or to me so dear,
> Could thy dear eyes in following mine
> Still sweeten more these banks of Rhine!

And along with this poem he sent some flowers specially dried for her. But Augusta was already much farther away from him than he imagined.

They crossed the battlefield of Morat, where the Switzers had beaten Duke Charles of Burgundy. Bones of the dead were still to be found in the fields, and Byron, glory's pensive gravedigger, purchased a few for Murray. In the end, on May 25, 1816, they reached the shores of the Lake of Geneva and stopped at Dejean's hotel at Sécheron. On the register which the travellers had to sign, he entered his age—"100."

A few days earlier, the same hostelry had welcomed the young woman who had been Byron's last mistress in England—Clare Clairmont. She was accompanied by her step-sister, Mary Godwin, and a young man, Mary's lover, Percy Bysshe Shelley. Byron had never met Shelley, but had read and admired his poem *Queen Mab*. Clare introduced the two men to each other; and Polidori noted in his diary: "Percy Shelley, author of *Queen Mab,* came: beautiful, shy, consumptive, twenty-one; separated from his wife; keeps the two daughters of Godwin, who practise his theories; one Lord Byron's."

Shelley and Byron soon became intimate. Both were lovers of ideas, both were in sympathy with the liberal view of politics, and regarded Waterloo as the opening of an age of hateful reaction. They also had in common those simpler tastes which perhaps unite men even more. They enjoyed spending their days on the water. Shelley had already hired a boat, and every evening Polidori, the two poets and the two young women went rowing on the lake. In his unhappy and restless condition, Byron was sensitive to the peace and tranquillity of these waters that mirrored the grey twilit mountains, and the first peeping stars. One evening, when a strong current was running and the waves of the lake were dangerous, he grew animated: "I will sing you an Albanian song," he cried. "Now be sentimental and give me all your attention!" He let forth a strange, wild howl, and then, laughing at the disappointment of the women, who had been expecting some oriental pæan, declared this to be an exact imitation of the mode of the Albanian mountaineers. That night Clare and Mary dubbed him "Alba," and the nickname persisted in their little group. But more often he would just lean over the side of the boat, gazing at the water without a word. He loved that marvellous silence of "clear, placid Leman," when—

> It is the hush of night, and all between
> Thy margin and the mountains, dusk, yet clear,
> Mellowed and mingling, yet distinctly seen,
> Save darkened Jura, whose capt heights appear
> Precipitously steep; and drawing near,
> Then breathes a living fragrance from the shore,
> Of flowers yet fresh with childhood; on the ear
> Drops the light drip of the suspended oar,
> Or chirps the grasshopper one good-night carol more.

Sometimes they landed, and the quick-walking Shelley, unable to curb his pace, would instantly forge ahead with the two women, while Byron limped behind at a distance, leaning on his cane and muttering a stanza to himself.

After a fortnight the Shelleys took a small peasant's cottage on the other side of the lake, and Byron rented the charming Villa Diodati, just above them. It was an old house and well-placed, standing half-way up the slope of the hill, with grass and vineyards below, and it had a splendid view of the lake with its flowery shores, and across to Geneva and the Jura. Byron was pleased with the rustic dignity of this dwelling, the modest house of a man of standing, and was not slow to adopt a Diodati routine: late breakfast—a visit to the Shelleys—an expedition on the lake—dinner at five (so summary that he preferred taking it alone)—and then, if weather permitted, down to the boat again. In bad weather, the Shelleys would come up and spend the evening, and sometimes the night, at Diodati. To her dying day, Mary was to remember those two voices—Byron's grave and musical, Shelley's eager and shrill. . . . She loved to listen to them with closed eyes. When the one fell silent the other instantly resumed. . . .

At first Byron had viewed Shelley a little loftily and suspiciously, for he rather liked a semblance of the social virtues—in others. For Clare he felt neither esteem nor love, and on her account had been tempted to look down upon Shelley as being a friend of hers. But he had a shrewd eye for character, and soon came to admire in Shelley an intelligence livelier than either Hobhouse's or Matthews'. To those questions which Byron had been asking of the Universe since childhood, Shelley, in his piercing voice, brought answers of a subtle novelty. Byron wondered who had created this world, a God or a Devil; and Shelley, the atheist idealist, believed God and Devil to be projections of human tendencies. "To the pure all things are pure." Jove, the creator of hatred, owed his existence to the relics of hatred in the heart of Prometheus; the Christian Satan owed his to the wickedness of certain souls. Evil did exist, but not in nature; it sprang from that artificial and "conventional" ugliness which is the creation of men united in society, and to be found in marriage or soldiers, in judges, in monarchs. The sole natural reality in Shelley's eyes was Beauty, which was identifiable by Harmony, and was to be found, fragmentarily, in fine evenings on the lake, in birds, in stars, in the eyes of women.

Byron was no metaphysician, and he was both fascinated and amused as he listened to the shrill expounding of this pantheism of Love. When his own turn came to speak, he set forth a gloomier doctrine, "methodist, calvinist, augustinian." No, things were not so simple as Shelley wished and believed them to be. Evil did exist. Evil was Sin: within his own soul he beheld a conflict whose issue he could not perceive. To one woman after another he had brought disaster, though loving some and respecting others. He, for his part, knew very well that men are complex and unhappy. Shelley, with his excessive pureness of mind, knew neither men nor women. Less clearsighted than Byron, and perhaps less severe upon himself, he would fall to temptation and hail it as a Virtue. Byron's mind was far too definite to contrive to cloak his faults with gilded mists of doctrine. He knew that man is not good. Politically, he might agree with Shelley in desiring the liberty of the people, but did not believe that for their deliverance a vague general verbiage was enough. He desired action, heroic and definite, for a people known and visible. His horror of the social structure was something quite different from what Shelley felt. Shelley, the idealist even in his loathing, held in scorn a World of his own imagining, and did not know the World of the flesh. Byron, the realist, was in flight from a society which he had desired to conquer. "I have not loved the world," he could write, "nor the world me. . . ." To Shelley life was a straightforward problem: a struggle between the powers of Good, which he believed to be reigning within himself, and a world quite external to himself. He was not divided against himself; he knew one Shelley, and only one. Byron knew several Byrons, and his conflict was internal: a conflict of Mary Chaworth's Byron against Lady Melbourne's, of sentimentalist against cynic, of pride against tenderness, of orthodoxy against rebellion, of one of the most generous against one of the most cruel of beings. The stern destiny which had forced him to the actions he so bitterly regretted was no figment of his own mind. He did not believe, as Shelley did, in the omnipotence of man in re-creating the universe; he recognised that he was surrounded by divine and by diabolical forces. In the registers of inns Shelley would put down "atheist" after his name. For Byron the Creator existed, but the creation was bad. Cain was right in complaining of the God of Israel, Prometheus in his cursing of Jove; and he, George Gordon Byron, the innocent victim of his blood's fatality, he too belonged to this race of the great rebels.

In this way the two voices answered each other. Byron, while recognising the highest virtues in Shelley, was sometimes irritated by his misunderstanding of real problems. Shelley complained to Mary of the fashionable and aristocratic tinge which Byron's thought had preserved. But so inseparable had they become that Polidori grew jealous of the place taken by Shelley in Byron's life, and wanted to challenge him to a duel. Hobhouse had been right when he counselled Byron not to take "Polly-Dolly" along with him. The little doctor had become intolerable. He took it as his right to join in the loftiest discussion, and he ruined conversation. He picked quarrels with the Genevese, which Byron had to straighten out. Byron indeed showed uncommon patience with him, referring to him as "the child and childish doctor Polly-Dolly," and saying that a great part of his life was spent in looking after his own physician.

One day at the beginning of June, Shelley and Byron set off together on a cruise round the lake, and were luckily able to leave Polidori at the villa with an injured foot. During this expedition the two poets were caught unawares by a storm off Meillerie. Byron had already slipped off his clothes and, as Shelley could not swim, offered to save him. Shelley refused, and sat calmly in the bottom of the boat declaring that he would go under without even trying to struggle.

Together they traversed the haunts of Rousseau, and, considering the differing rhythms of their lives, they enjoyed each other's company fairly well. Shelley, up with the lark, hurried along the mountain paths, while Byron did not rise till noon and had no love of walking. But they enjoyed re-reading the *Nouvelle Héloïse* together in the very heart of the scenes which it described. They were particularly struck by the Castle of Chillon: "the most terrible monument," wrote Shelley, "of that cold and inhuman tyranny which man delights to exercise over man." In Bonivard's dungeon, where Byron carved his name, they heard the story of this victim of the tyrants, and Byron, in a single night, wrote *The Prisoner of Chillon,* while Shelley composed his *Hymn to Intellectual Beauty*. During this journey Byron added numerous stanzas to *Childe Harold.* Some of these were on Rousseau, and on Clarens:

> Clarens! sweet Clarens! birthplace of deep Love!
> Thine air is the young breath of passionate thought;
> Thy trees take root in Love; the snows above
> The very Glaciers have his colours caught,
> And sunset into rose-hues sees them wrought

By rays which sleep there lovingly; the rocks,
The permanent crags, tell here of Love, who sought
In them a refuge from the worldly shocks,
Which stir and sting the soul with hope that woos, then mocks—

and others on Gibbon's Lausanne and Voltaire's Ferney:

Lausanne! and Ferney! ye have been the abodes
Of names which unto you bequeath'd a name;
Mortals, who sought and found, by dangerous roads,
A path to perpetuity of fame:
They were gigantic minds, and their steep aim
Was, Titan-like, on daring doubts to pile
Thoughts which should call down thunder, and the flame
Of Heaven, again assail'd, if Heaven the while
On man and man's research could deign do more than smile.

In Gibbon's garden Byron plucked a sprig of the acacia under which the author had stood in contemplation of Mont Blanc after penning the last sentence of his history. Shelley declined to do likewise, fearing to offend the name, the greater name, of Rousseau.

Shelley's influence over Byron increased during their wanderings together. He treated him with "doses of Wordsworth," a poet whom Byron had always refused to read. But in these surroundings, soothed and won over by the kindliness of the lake, he developed a taste for this poetry, in which he could recognise the same pantheistic Love which was Shelley's religion. With this double influence working upon him, there now appeared in his verses themes that were new to him. The "vanity of vanities" which formed the *basso-profondo* of all Byronic poetry was blended with softer notes. Beside those peaceful waters, watching those splendid mountains, Harold himself believed that he had found peace. Solitude and nature—in these perhaps lay the secret of a happiness which hitherto he had deemed impossible.

Is it not better, then, to be alone,
And love Earth only for its earthly sake?
By the blue rushing of the arrowy Rhone,
Or the pure bosom of its nursing lake,
Which feeds it as a mother who doth make
A fair but froward infant her own care,
Kissing its cries away as these awake:—
Is it not better thus our lives to wear,
Than join the crushing crowd, doom'd to inflict or bear?

I live not in myself, but I become
Portion of that around me; and to me,
High mountains are a feeling, but the hum
Of human cities torture: I can see
Nothing to loathe in nature; save to be
A link reluctant in a fleshly chain,
Class'd among creatures, when the soul can flee,
And with the sky, the peak, the heaving plain
Of ocean, or the stars, mingle, and not in vain.

And thus I am absorb'd, and this is life:
I look upon the peopled desert past,
As on a place of agony and strife,
Where, for some sin, to Sorrow I was cast,
To act and suffer, but remount at last
With a fresh pinion; which I felt to spring,
Though young, yet waxing vigorous as the blast
Which it would cope with, on delighted wing,
Spurning the clay-cold bonds which round our being cling.

And when, at length, the mind shall be all free
From what it hates in this degraded form,
Reft of its carnal life, save what shall be
Existent happier in the fly and worm,—
When elements to elements conform,
And dust is as it should be, shall I not
Feel all I see, less dazzling, but more warm?
The bodiless thought? the Spirit of each spot?
Of which, even now, I share at times the immortal lot?

Are not the mountains, waves, and skies a part
Of me and of my soul, as I of them?

Is not the love of these deep in my heart
With a pure passion? should I not contemn
All objects, if compared with these? and stem
A tide of suffering, rather than forego
Such feelings for the hard and worldly phlegm
Of those whose eyes are only turn'd below,
Gazing upon the ground, with thoughts which dare not glow?

The form was still Byron's; the outline kept its clean precision. But, even without Wordsworth's slow and liquid form, this was in essence Wordsworth's vision of the world. That shrill, eager voice had traced its furrow across Byron's mind; and sometimes, at evening especially, in all the peacefulness of sky and earth, he would gaze on the star-strewn water and the vast shadows of the mountains, fancying he could feel the faint throbbing of mysterious, benevolent forces. But in Byron's mind such thoughts could only be transient. Forget his identity? Lose himself in the beauty of the Whole? How were such things possible for the Great Egotist?

The quick unfolding of scenes and pictures during a journey enabled him to forget for a moment his inner tragedy; once he had achieved the ordered peace of Diodati, he could bring back his phantom creatures to life again. Real life, after all, was so simple. Life—what was that? Those grassy slopes, this tranquil lake. . . . How far away seemed that Piccadilly bedroom, befouled by bailiffs and empty bottles! The absent are as good as dead to us. They are as the pale shades of the dead, and their features, like those of the dead, we forget. But like the dead, the absent can haunt us, can wrap their shrouds about us. Mary Ann . . . Augusta . . . Annabella . . . Just as in the days of *The Corsair,* "the thought ran through everything—yes, through." He had done great wrongs, and did not admit his guilt. His adolescent temper had been generous; the wickedness of mankind had made him a monster. How wanton this waste of virtue! The injustice, the cruelty of Destiny enraged him! In a waking delirium he evoked the long succession of the strands in this doom of his . . . Annesley. . . . He wrote a long poem on the loves of his childhood, *The Dream:*

> . . . the hill
> Was crown'd with a peculiar diadem
> Of trees, in circular array, so fix'd,
> Not by the sport of nature, but of man:
> These two, a maiden and a youth, were there
> Gazing—the one on all that was beneath,
> Fair as herself—but the boy gazed on her;
> And both were young, and one was beautiful:
> And both were young, yet not alike in youth,
> As the sweet moon on the horizon's verge,
> The maid was on the eve of womanhood,
> The boy had fewer summers. . . .

It was curious, this inability to free himself from so small an adventure. . . . And then some *Stanzas to Augusta:*

> Though the day of my destiny's over,
>   And the star of my fate hath declin'd,
> Thy soft heart refused to discover
>   The faults which so many could find;
> Though thy soul with my grief was acquainted,
>   It shrunk not to share it with me,
> And the love which my spirit hath painted
>   It never hath found but in *thee.*
>
> Though the rock of my last hope is shiver'd,
>   And its fragments are sunk in the wave,
> Though I feel that my soul is deliver'd
>   To pain—it shall not be its slave.

There is many a pang to pursue me:
They may crush, but they shall not contemn;
They may torture, but shall not subdue me;
'Tis of *thee* that I think—not of them.

Though human, thou didst not deceive me,
Though woman, thou didst not forsake,
Though loved, thou forborest to grieve me,
Though slander'd, thou never couldst shake;
Though trusted, thou didst not disclaim me;
Though parted, it was not to fly;
Though watchful, 'twas not to defame me,
Nor, mute, that the world might belie.

From the wreck of the past, which hath perish'd,
Thus much I at least may recall,
It hath taught me that what I most cherish'd
Deserved to be dearest of all:
In the desert a fountain is springing,
In the wide waste there still is a tree,
And a bird in the solitude singing,
Which speaks to my spirit of *thee*.

What was happening to Augusta, far away over the sea? He knew not. The silvery surface of the lake beneath his windows recalled the lake at Newstead; on other reed-rimmed banks he had been happy—with her. And he wrote touching letters to her: "Do not be uneasy, and do not 'Hate yourself.' If you hate either, let it be *me*—but do not—it would kill me. We are the last persons in the world who ought or could cease to love one another. . . ." And again: "What a fool I was to marry—and *you* not so very wise, my dear. We might have loved so single and so happy—as old maids and bachelors; I shall never find anyone like you—nor you (vain as it may seem) like me. We are just formed to pass our lives together, and therefore—we—at least I am—by a crowd of circumstances removed from the only being who could ever have loved me, or whom I can unmixedly feel attached to. Had you been a Nun and I a Monk—that we might have talked through a grate instead of across the sea—No matter—my voice and heart are ever thine. . . ."

She made hardly any response. Her obscure, breathless letters told how she was seeing much of Annabella, and that Annabella was very kind to her. Very kind? Lady Byron? Humph! That took his breath away. In his gallery of symbolic characters Annabella was becoming the Pitiless Spouse, his "moral Clytemnestra." Madame de Staël, whom he used often to visit at her house at Coppet, on the opposite shore, had thoughts of reconciling him with Annabella; she had made him write her a letter, but he knew it was vain. Annabella had broken his heart—that heart which he used once upon a time to boast was as hard as a Highlander's heel-piece; he now felt as if he had been trampled by an elephant. . . . Yes, Lady Byron had the right to reproach him; but after all she was his wife, she had taken him as her husband "for better or worse," she was not marked out by Providence to strike him. . . . One day the Fates would avenge him. To none of the ancient Divinities did he render such honour as to Nemesis, the Vengeance of the Gods. He voiced mysterious prophecies: "One day or another her conduct will recoil on her own head; *not* through *me,* for my feelings towards her are not those of Vengeance, but—mark—if she does not end miserably *tôt ou tard.* . . ." And again, hearing of her being ill, he wrote:

> And thou wert sick—yet I was not with thee;
> And thou wert sick, and yet I was not near;

Methought that joy and health alone could be
Where I was *not*—and pain and sorrow here!

. . . .

I am too well avenged!—but 'twas my right!
Whate'er my sins might be, *thou* wert not sent
To be the Nemesis who should requite—
Nor did Heaven choose so near an instrument.
Mercy is for the merciful!—if thou
Hast been of such, 'twill be accorded now.
Thy nights are banish'd from the realms of sleep!—
Yes! they may flatter thee, but thou shalt feel
A hollow agony which will not heal,
For thou art pillow'd on a curse too deep;
Thou hast sown in my sorrow, and must reap
The bitter harvest in a woe as real!

The visits to Madame de Staël were his only contact with outside life. He admired the little château of Coppet, and relished the charm of its brown tiles, its courtyard with the two turrets at one end, the romantic park, the waterfall, the ravine. Sometimes Byron would come across English visitors there; they eyed him as if he were the Prince of Darkness. A certain Mrs. Harvey actually fainted away when he entered the room—an incident which drew from Madame de Staël's daughter, the lovely and charming Duchesse de Broglie, the exclamation: "Really, that is exaggerating—at sixty-five!" The other guests at Coppet had no great fondness for him. The Duc de Broglie found his conversation to be "spiced with impious jesting and the commonplaces of a vulgar liberalism"; and Madame de Staël scolded him: "You ought not to have declared war on the world," she told him. "It's an impossibility. The world is too strong for an individual. I tried it myself when I was young—but it's impossible." She certainly seemed to be right. Byron had wished to storm the mist-wreathed hill-tops where sat the Britannic Conventions. But no man can attack unscathed the gods in whom he secretly believes; and now there he was, nailed down by hatred to his lonely rock, a comically comfortable Prometheus with a scanty chorus of Godwinian Oceanides.

It was from Madame de Staël that he heard how Caroline Lamb had recently published, on May 10, a novel in which he figured as hero. *Glenarvon* was its title, and its second edition bore an epigraph taken from *The Corsair:*

> He left a name to all succeeding times,
> Linked with one virtue and a thousand crimes.

Byron read the romance, not without difficulty, for it was an extremely tedious work, in which Lady Caroline had recounted her own life transparently disguised. The heroine at an early age married Lord Avondale, who was William Lamb. If Lord Avondale had a fault, it was the excessive goodness and greatness of his character, which led him to allow his frivolous helpmate to order and direct everything,—"You shall be my law," said Lord Avondale to his wife, "you shall be my mistress, my guide, and I a willing slave." Naturally, Lady Avondale drifted away from this weakling and loved Glenarvon, who was a blend of Byron, the Corsair, and Lara: "I am sick of life, of all society. Love, sentiment, is my abhorrence. Oh! Damn it! Don't talk about it!" Lady Oxford also played her part, drawn in unkindly lines: "she was no longer in the very prime of youth; a certain pedantry took off much of the charm of her conversation." Lady Caroline had even gone so far as to publish, in the guise of a letter from Glenarvon to Lady Avondale, the actual letter sent her by Byron at the rupture;

and in conclusion she made Glenarvon perish by drowning. She was on fire to know what Byron thought of her book. He composed the following verse:

> I read the *Christabel,*
> Very well:
> I read the *Missionary;*
> Pretty—very:
> I tried at *Ilderim;*
> Ahem!
> I read a sheet of *Marg'ret of Anjou;*
> Can you?
> I turn'd a page of Webster's *Waterloo;*
> Pooh! pooh!
> I looked at Wordsworth's milk-white *Rylstone Doe;*
> Hillo!
> I read *Glenarvon,* too, by Caro Lamb—
> God damn! . . .

And he expressed his opinion that if the novelist had written merely the plain truth, her tale would have been more romantic, and far more amusing. "As for the likeness," he added, "the picture can't be good—I did not sit long enough."

The absent are like the dead. . . . But there are times when we live far more with the dead than with the living. What was Clare, the mistress of to-day, beside more insistent shades? Every evening she came up to Diodati to join her lover, and left at break of day, down through the vines, back to the Shelleys' house. She was with child now, and in deep melancholy. She worked for Byron, copying *The Prisoner of Chillon* and the new stanzas of *Childe Harold.* He was bored and irritated by this humbly-born, shameless woman who had flung herself at his head in a blue-stocking caprice. . . . She was expecting a child by him, was she? Well and good.

He would bring up the child. A child was part of the Byron clan, and would also, perhaps, be treasured now that Ada was refused him. But the mother he did not wish to see again.

Shelley had a tender, brotherly affection for Clare, and the tone in which Byron spoke of her was intolerable to him. He still admired the poet, and was dazzled by his brilliance and his facility; but the man he found disturbing, and sometimes infuriating. Byron was a liberal in theory, but he attached importance to birth; the fact that Shelley was the son of a baronet was not a matter of indifference to him; he always let it be felt that he himself was a baron. When he talked of women, it was with a lofty detachment that shocked Shelley. Yet Byron, for his part, felt Shelley's logical certainties to be inhuman. That piercing voice fatigued him. With his usual suspiciousness, he was sometimes even doubtful of Shelley's pureness of heart. He called him the Serpent. . . . Goethe's Mephistopheles referred to the serpent which tempted Eve as his aunt, the famous serpent; and Byron always thought, he said, that Shelley was none other than one of Mephistopheles' nephews.

Hobhouse and Scrope Davies sent word of their coming. It would be refreshing to hear that irresistible stutter of Davies', to forget Wordsworth and the pantheism of Love, to talk of those evenings at Kinnaird's. On August 29, the Shelleys went off, taking Clare with them; and a few days later Byron wrote to Augusta: "Now, don't scold; but what could I do?—a foolish girl, in spite of all I could say or do, would come after me, or rather went before—for I found her here—and I have had all the plague possible to persuade her to go back again; but at last she went. Now dearest, I do most truly tell thee, that I could not help this, that I did all I could to prevent it, and have at last put an end to it. I was not in love, nor have any love left for any; but I could not exactly play the Stoic with a woman who had clambered eight hundred miles to unphilosophise me. . . . And now you know all that I know of that matter, and it's over."

XXVII

AVALANCHES

1816

HOBHOUSE and Scrope Davies, ambassadors of friendship, arrived at the end of August, and were delighted with the house and its view of the Jura. They had brought out some of the English products for which the exile kept asking in his letters—magnesia, a sword-stick, Mr. Waite's red tooth-powder—and were pleased with the appearance of their friend. He had lost that sallow colour which he had when he left England, and seemed to have calmed down; the almost excessive tranquillity of his manner was really evidence of his straining efforts to hide his still smouldering violence, but after all, the fact that he could restrain himself was something. London gossip declared that he was debauching the work-girls of the Rue Basse, and that Augusta was with him, disguised as a page. Hobhouse's observation showed that life at Diodati seemed to be the height of chastity, and sent a favourable bulletin to Mrs. Leigh: ". . . your excellent relative is living with the strictest regard to decorum, and free from all offence either to God, or man, or woman. . . . A considerable change has taken place in his health; no brandy, no very late hours, no quarts of magnesia, nor deluges of soda water. Neither passion nor perverseness, even the scream has died away; he seems as happy as he ought to be; by this of course you will see that I mean, as happy as it is consistent for a man of honour and common feeling to be after the occurrence of a calamity involving a charge, whether just or unjust, against his honour and his feeling."

Hobhouse, of course, wished to see something of the country, and the three musketeers of Trinity, with Polidori in tow, set off for Chamonix and Mont Blanc. Byron had some difficulty in scrambling over the glaciers. At the inn at Montanvers they found Shelley's name in the register, followed by the words "atheist and philosopher" in Greek characters. Byron thought he would be doing Shelley a service in effacing the words, and did so. On their return he took his friends over to Coppet; they enjoyed meeting Madame de Staël, Bonstetten and Schlegel. Hobhouse had lately read *Adolphe,* and told Madame de Staël that he had recognised sentences of hers in its pages; "like glow-worms amid dead leaves," he said, "their light serves only to show up the dryness of what lies around them." Madame de Staël turned to Bonstetten: *"Charmant, n'est ce pas?"* she said. Hobhouse was very fond of Coppet.

Not without shyness, Byron submitted the manuscript of *Childe Harold's* third Canto to his friends. Hobhouse, who had not lived with Shelley, was greatly surprised: "Very fine in parts," he said, "but I don't know whether I like it so much as his first cantos. There is an air of mystery and metaphysics about it." As for the *Stanzas to Augusta,* he found these intolerably plaintive, and parodied them mercilessly:

> Though a poet, you should not abuse us;
> Though a wit, have a truce with your jokes;
> Though you govern us all, yet excuse us
> If we think there's enough of this hoax.

Though trusted, no creditors touch thee;
Though parted, 'tis but from thy wife;
Though wakeful with Molly to much thee
'Tis not such a damnable life.

Talking sentiment to Hobhouse was no easy matter. . . .

Scrope Davies was the first to leave, and went laden with cut stones, agates and crystal necklaces, which Byron had bought at Chamonix for his Leigh nieces, and for his daughter Ada, "the love." Of all his creations, Ada was the most visionary, this tiny girl whom he had seen but twice, whom he loved in his fashion. A few days after Davies had gone, the wretched Polidori was sent off; he had his virtues, but his vanity made him insufferable. Hobhouse, who was pitiless in scoring the points, observed that he had foretold this, and then, being now alone with Byron at the Villa Diodati, proposed another tour in the mountains and a visit to the Jungfrau.

The deep green pastures, the blending cow-bells, the shepherds standing on peak after peak and seeming to belong rather to sky than to earth, the last drifts of darkened snow left unmelted by summer—all reminded Byron of his childhood's holidays in the Highlands. "It is like a dream," he said to Hobhouse, "something too brilliant and wild for reality." He delighted in the glaciers, their billowy surface seeming like a "frozen hurricane"; in the high waterfalls, with their manes of gleaming, shooting foam that reminded him of some gigantic white horse, the steed, as it might be, ridden by Death in the Apocalypse; and in the heavy, sulphurous clouds rolling beneath the precipices like the foam of some Infernal ocean. As he gazed on these wonders, it was to Augusta that his thoughts kept turning, and throughout the expedition he kept a diary for his sister's benefit:

"Yesterday September 17th, 1816—I set out (with H.) on an excursion of some days to the mountains. I shall keep a short journal of each day's progress for my sister Augusta. . . .

"The music of the Cows' bells . . . in the pastures (which reach to a height far above any mountains in Britain), and the Shepherds' shouting to us from crag to crag, and playing on their reeds where the steeps appeared almost inaccessible, with the surrounding scenery, realised all that I have ever heard or imagined of a pastoral existence . . . this was pure and unmixed—solitary, savage, and patriarchal. . . . As we went, they played the 'Ranz des Vaches' and other airs, by way of farewell. I have lately repeopled my world with Nature. . . . Nine o'clock—going to bed. H. in next room knocked his head against the door, and complained of course against doors; not tired to-day, but hope to sleep nevertheless. Women gabbling below; read a French translation of Schiller. Good Night, Dearest Augusta. . . .

"Arrived at the Grindenwald. . . . Starlight, beautiful, but a devil of a path! Never mind, got safe in; a little lightning. . . . *Passed whole woods of withered pines,* all withered; trunks stripped and barkless, branches lifeless; done by a single winter,—their appearance reminded me of me and my family. . . .

"From Bern to Fribourg; different Canton—Catholics: passed a field of Battle. . . . Bought a dog—a very ugly dog, but *'très méchant'*; this was his great recommendation in the owner's eyes and mine. . . . He hath no tail, and is called Mutz. . . .

"September 29. . . . In the weather for this tour (of 13 days) I have been very fortunate—fortunate in a companion (Mr. H.)—fortunate in our prospects. . . . I was disposed to be pleased. I am a lover of Nature and an admirer of Beauty. I can bear fatigue and welcome privation, and have seen some of the noblest views in the world. But in all this—the recollections of bitterness, and more especially of recent and more home desolation, which must accompany me through life, have preyed upon me here; and neither the music of the Shepherd, the crashing of the Avalanche, nor the torrent, the mountain, the Glacier, the Forest, nor the Cloud, have for one moment lightened the weight upon my heart, nor enabled me to lose my own wretched identity in the majesty, and the power, and the Glory, around, above, and beneath me.

"I am past reproaches; and there is a time for all things. I am past the wish of vengeance, and I know of none like for what I have suffered; but the hour will come, when what I feel must be felt, and the—but enough.

"To you, dearest Augusta, I send, and *for* you I have kept this record of what I have seen and felt. Love me as you are beloved by me."

During the month of August he had had a visit at Diodati from Matthew Lewis, author of *The Monk,* who translated for him some passages from Goethe's *Faust*. Here was a theme to touch his heart! These age-old questions asked by Faust of the universe, the pact with the Devil, the loss of Margarita—was not this his own story? But if Byron himself had been the creator of Faust, he would have painted him both bolder and more tragic. Why tremble before the spirits? A man, a true man, defies them and defies Death.

A work of art is always born of a shock that fertilises a fruitful soil. In Byron the soil was ready; it held a burning mass of repressed feelings; horror, love, desire, regret,—a lava-flood which once again threatened to engulf him. From the shock that came from the reading of *Faust* and from these Alpine landscapes, there emerged a great dramatic poem—*Manfred*. Its first two acts he composed in twelve days, while still travelling. The landscapes sketched in prose for Augusta became, with a slight transposing of key, the fragments of the new drama, and were mingled therein with avowals of distress. All the actual scenes of the tour, a meeting with a huntsman, another with a shepherd singing the *Ranz des Vaches,* were instantly thrust into this poem. Its subject was vague enough to find room for everything.

Manfred, the overlord of a feudal township in the Alps, has practised the magical arts; he is rich and a man of learning, but his soul is apparently tortured by the memory of a great crime. In a very Faust-like opening scene he evokes the Spirits of Earth, Ocean, Air, Night, Mountains and Wind.—"What wouldst thou with us, son of mortals—say?" they ask. "Forgetfulness."—"Of what—of whom—and why?"—"Of that which is within me . . ." answers Manfred. What is within him? He lets us divine it. . . . Regret for a woman, Astarte, lost and now yearned after; and desire, desire to be avenged on another woman whom he does not name. Against the latter a tremendous incantation is recited by a mysterious voice, and because Byron is powerless to escape from himself and forget his identity,

—because, too, the allusions are clear and the symbols tranparent, we become aware that Manfred is Byron, that Astarte is Augusta, that the object of the incantation is Annabella:

When the moon is on the wave,
And the glow-worm in the grass,
And the meteor on the grave,
And the wisp on the morass;
When the fallen stars are shooting,
And the answer'd owls are hooting,
And the silent leaves are still
In the shadow of the hill
Shall my soul be upon thine,
With a power and with a sign.

Though thy slumber may be deep,
Yet thy spirit shall not sleep;
There are shades which will not vanish,
There are thoughts thou canst not banish;
By a power to thee unknown,
Thou canst never be alone:
Thou art wrapt as with a shroud,
Thou art gather'd in a cloud:
And for ever shalt thou dwell
In the spirit of this spell.

From thy false tears I did distil
An essence which hath strength to kill;
From thy own heart I then did wring
The black blood in its blackest spring;
From thy own smile I snatch'd the snake,
For there it coil'd as in a brake;
From thy own lip I drew the charm
Which gave all these their chiefest harm:
In proving every poison known,
I found the strongest was thine own.

By thy cold breast and serpent smile,
By thy unfathom'd gulfs of guile,
By that most seeming virtuous eye,
By thy shut soul's hypocrisy;

By the perfection of thine art
Which pass'd for human thine own heart;
By thy delight in others' pain,
And by thy brotherhood of Cain,
I call upon thee, and compel
Thyself to be thy proper Hell!

Manfred then beseeches a sorceress to conjure up Astarte for him; he describes her to the witch—and it is Augusta:

Manfred. She was like me in lineaments—her eyes,
Her hair, her features, all, to the very tone
Even of her voice, they said were like to mine;
But soften'd all, and temper'd into beauty:
She had the same lone thoughts and wanderings,
The quest of hidden knowledge, and a mind
To comprehend the universe: nor these
Alone, but with them gentler powers than mine,
Pity, and smiles, and tears—which I had not;
And tenderness—but that I had for her;
Humility—and that I never had.
Her faults were mine—her virtues were her own—
I loved her, and destroy'd her!

Witch. With thy hand?

Manfred. Not with my hand, but heart—which broke her heart—
It gazed on mine and wither'd. I have shed
Blood, but not hers—and yet her blood was shed—
I saw—and could not stanch it.

"I loved her, and destroy'd her!"—that was the secret of Manfred's despair, as of Byron's; and through Manfred's lips Byron was crying aloud his suffering. It had been too well masked beneath the tranquillity of the host of Diodati, the politeness of the visitor to Coppet.

My solitude is solitude no more,
But peopled with the Furies,—I have gnash'd

My teeth in darkness till returning morn
Then cursed myself till sunset;—I have pray'd
For madness as a blessing—'tis denied me.
I have affronted death—but the war
Of elements the waters shrunk from me,
And fatal things pass'd harmless—the cold hand
Of an all-pitiless demon held me back,
Back by a single hair, which would not break.

But in vain do the infernal powers evoke Astarte for Manfred. She appears, but stands dumb, just as the slowly fading image of Augusta in Byron's memory was facing him with lips sealed.

Thou lovedst me
Too much, as I loved thee; we were not made
To torture thus each other, though it were
The deadliest sin to love as we have loved.
Say that thou loath'st me not—that I do bear
This punishment for both—that thou wilt be
One of the blessed—and that I shall die;
For hitherto all hateful things conspire
To bind me in existence—in a life
Which makes me shrink from immortality—
A future like the past. I cannot rest.
I know not what I ask, nor what I seek:
I feel but what thou art—and what I am;
And I would hear yet once before I perish
The voice which was my music.—Speak to me!
For I have call'd on thee in the still night,
Startled the slumbering birds from the hush'd boughs,
And woke the mountain wolves, and made the caves
Acquainted with thy vainly echo'd name,
Which answer'd me—many things answer'd me—
Spirits and men—but thou wert silent all.
Yet speak to me! I have outwatch'd the stars,
And gazed o'er heaven in vain in search of thee.
Speak to me! I have wander'd o'er the earth,
And never found thy likeness.—Speak to me!

She swoons away, vouchsafing no answer, and the Spirits gaze almost with terror on Manfred's despair—

AVALANCHES

> Had he been one of us, he would have made
> An awful spirit. . . .

The lava had poured forth superbly. *Manfred* was still without a third act, but Byron did not write it immediately. He had gone back to Diodati with Hobhouse, and the mountain spells were already broken.

One of the deepest roots of Manfred's anguish lay in the silence of Astarte. Why did Augusta reply to Byron's appeals with nothing better than a few commonplace letters? Why should her annoying incoherence, charming though it was to Byron's fancy, change into platitudes and moralisings? Byron grew anxious as he began to discern through the foggy phrases of his sister the influence of a very different spirit, one that he recognised only too well. But he was far from imagining what exactly had passed between the two women since his departure.

When Byron left England, Lady Byron had for some weeks been living in London, to keep within reach of her legal advisers; and on the day of his departure she went back to the country to rejoin little Ada. She was twenty-four. Life seemed to be ended for her. Her feelings against Byron were violent; she had loved him too well not to hate him now, yet still without any abatement of her love. Augusta saw her before she left, and found that she had the terrifying calmness of one who is dead.

The moral problems torturing the scrupulous conscience of this stricken casuist were in no way ended by the departure of her husband. How ought she to behave towards Augusta?—As a friend? But this would invalidate her most serious ground of complaint, if ever she had to state her case against Byron in the course of her daughter's upbringing.—Or, as the lawyers wanted, as a foe? But this would only confirm the rumours which Caroline Lamb and so many others were circulating; and it would also make life impossible for Mrs. Leigh in England. "For if Augusta fled to Byron in exile, was seen with him as *et soror et conjux,* the victory remained with Lady Byron, solid and final. . . . But with her the romance of self-sacrifice was all-powerful." She did not seek the ruin of her sister-in-law, judging it her duty as a Christian to save Augusta's soul, and if possible, though she no longer believed it so, Byron's as well. This double goal could only be reached by preventing the guilty parties from ever meeting again. Respect for their liberty would make her an accomplice in their damnation.

Such were the subtle paths by which duty ordered that the guilty woman should be pursued; spite or jealousy might have acted similarly; and beneath the mask of duty, no doubt, there slipped into the conscience of this woman of scruples a more disturbing, yet very natural sentiment—the need to *know.* Only certainty can stay jealousy. And regarding the terrible adventure which had been the real cause of the ruin, Annabella had no real certainty. From her wedding-day she had caught glimpses of incest prowling about her house, but did those signs that met her eye relate to a passion that was already old, extinct, exorcised? Or, on the other hand, had this monstrous love persisted even after her marriage? She did not know, and longed passionately to understand. Augusta now held a place in her thoughts which might have been surprising, if it were not for the fact that we always cling, with a tenacious anxiety almost akin to tenderness, to anyone who holds the secret, be it even one of dread, which we crave to know.

In all this confusion, Lady Byron had managed to find a confidante. One of Augusta's intimate friends, Mrs. George Villiers, had asked her to support her sister-in-law against the current calumnies, whereupon Annabella had paid her a visit and told her the truth. Mrs. Villiers, a woman of high character, was at once stupefied and deeply interested. Augusta had always spoken to her of the separation and the current reports in a tone of such outraged innocence that she had difficulty at first in believing Lady Byron's account. But once convinced, she was furious. Forgiveness might have been possible, she said, for a sorry and penitent Augusta, but this frivolous pride in wrongdoing was intolerable. These were exactly Annabella's feelings. Just as some men enjoy helping a friend in distress provided he gives not the faintest sign of pleasure or consolation, so these two women were ready to give a helping hand to the sinner —provided always that she humbled herself. Byron too was a sinner, but at least he knew what sin was. Augusta seemed never to give it a thought. "I have always observed," wrote Annabella, "the remarkable difference, that his [Lord Byron's] feelings—distinct from practice —were much more sensitive and correct on all moral questions than hers. She did not appear to think these transgressions of *consequence*."

Mrs. Villiers was at one with Lady Byron in believing that Augusta *must* be led back from pride to penitence. Mrs. Leigh seemed to think it quite natural that friendly relations between herself and her sister-in-law should continue for the world to see. It was important to make her feel that she was henceforth outside the pale. "My dear Augusta," Lady Byron wrote early in June, "before your confinement I would not risk agitating you, but having the satisfaction of knowing you are recovered, I will no longer conceal from yourself that there are reasons founded on such circumstances in your conduct, as (though thoroughly convinced they have existed) I am most anxious to bury in silence, which indispensably impose on me the duty of limiting my intercourse with you. . . ."

With fond anxiety the two virtuous ladies wondered how their erring sister would react to this threat. "I think her first feeling," Annabella opined, "will be terror—her second, pride—and under what influence she may reply I cannot conjecture. . . ." But Augusta's answer was one of humility. "The tide of public opinion has been so turned against my Brother that the least appearance of coolness on your part towards me would injure me most seriously—and I am therefore *for the sake of my children* compelled to accept from your compassion the 'limited intercourse' which is all you can grant to one whom you pronounce no longer worthy of your esteem or affection!"

The next step towards completing this moral cure was to obtain from her, first, a confession of her fault, and then, an undertaking never to see Byron again. Letters accordingly passed to and fro between the sisters-in-law, and little by little the weaker of the two began, willy-nilly, to drift into implicit avowals. She first of all admitted that guilty relations had existed before the marriage, but swore with all the accents of sincerity that after the marriage she had resisted.[1] Then the question-

[1] *Lady Byron to Mrs. Leigh:* "As you do not, and never have attempted to deceive me respecting *previous* facts, of which my conviction is un-

ing became more detailed. Two people will sometimes agree to leave some grave and painful subject in prolonged oblivion; but when at last they decide to lance the spiritual abscess, they often find a mingled pain and zest in the operation, and an uneasy pleasure in the joint study of the details which to both have been the core of so many solitary broodings. Annabella explained to Augusta how, on the day of the very first visit to Six Mile Bottom, everything seemed to rouse her suspicions, and Augusta very complacently dissected her own illusions and her foolish belief that Annabella was hoodwinked.

Sometimes the sinner had relapses. On July 18, 1816, Mrs. Villiers told Lady Byron how she had seen Augusta on the previous evening, and how the whole of their conversation "turned on Gauzes and Sattins. . . . I thought her looking quite stout and well . . . and perfectly cool and easy, having apparently nothing on her mind." A little later, fortunately, she appeared to be preoccupied and dejected. But the good work was not yet completed.

The danger was that Byron might resume his sway over her. He wanted her to rejoin him in Switzerland or Italy; and there was reason to believe that she was sorely

alterable, I rely the more on your assertion of having never wronged *me* intentionally. . . ."

Mrs. Leigh to Lady Byron: "The delusion to which I alluded was an entire unsuspicion—that you *even suspected*—that *I* caused or added to your misery. . . ."

Lady Byron to Mrs. Leigh: "It seems to me that you dwell too much on the pain you occasioned *me,* and not enough on the irreparable injury you did *him* by the voluntary sacrifices (for, to principles and feelings like yours, they must have been entirely sacrifices) which you once made to his immediate indulgences. . . ."

Lady Byron to Mrs. Villiers: "I have an answer—all that it ought to be or that I could desire.—It thoroughly convinces me of her innocence in regard to all the period with which I was concerned. . . ."

tempted, all the more so because Colonel Leigh, deeper in ruin than ever, was quite capable of consenting to her departure. Her brother had only to speak his unhappiness and she was ready for any folly. In vain did Annabella describe the awful agonies of remorse which she had seen Byron going through. "I never witnessed," replied Augusta, "anything like what you have, alas! and describe to have been *his* Agonies. . . . If I did but know how to contribute to his ULTIMATE good! but Alas! I do not. . . ." There were moments when Lady Byron would gladly have pinned on her sister-in-law's breast the label "Heretic and Relapsed."

Finally, in August 1816, she came up to stop in London in order to see Mrs. Leigh again. In preparation for this decisive cross-examination, she followed her usual custom of drawing up a catechetical memorandum: "Do you sorrow most for the sin or for the consequences?—for the offence towards God—or the injury towards your fellow-creatures? . . . Do you sufficiently feel that every *thought* associated with such sin, is sinful, that the heart may be criminal though the actions are innocent? . . ."

During the first half of September the two women saw each other daily.[2] These long conversations ended in Augusta's surrender to a stronger personality, and she abdicated the ordering of her own soul in favour of Annabella promising for the future to show her all

[2] *Statement of Lady Byron:* "Augusta made full confession of the previous connection—any subsequent to my marriage being stoutly denied. . . . She acknowledged that the verses (*'I speak not, I trace not, I breathe not thy name . . .'*) were addressed to her. She told me that she had never felt any suspicions of *my* suspicions, except at the time, in the summer of 1815, when I evidently wished she would leave us. . . ."

Mrs. Villiers to Lady Byron: "I spoke very strongly of those *lines* to her. I wonder whether *he* still possessed many of her former letters to him? They alone would be proof positive."

Byron's letters and to reply to her brother only in a tone of coolness. Lady Byron did not insist on her abandoning all exchange of letters with him. "I should not advise you for his sake to restrict your correspondence further than by keeping always in view to *rectify* instead of *soothing* or *indulging* his feelings—by avoiding therefore all phrases or marks, which may recall wrong ideas to his mind . . . and let me also warn you against the levity and nonsense which he likes for the worst reason, because it prevents him from reflecting seriously. . . ." Note the instinctive cleverness of woman! She was robbing Augusta of her one peculiar charm. . . .

At Geneva the weather was turning cold and rainy. Byron was anxious to leave Switzerland. From Sécheron, on the shore of the lake, English tourists were pointing their spy-glasses across to his balcony in the hope of catching a glimpse of a petticoat. He was sensitive, like all who have been persecuted, and felt that even into this far retreat he was being pursued by that hatred which had accompanied his departure. He wanted to cross the mountains, to reach the Adriatic, like a stag at bay taking to the water.

Early in October he left Diodati with Hobhouse, to reach Milan by way of the Simplon. They were accompanied by the admirable Fletcher who delighted Hobhouse by his skill in transposing everything he saw into English imagery: the famous cataract of Pissevache reminded Fletcher of old Mr. Becher's white wig. A team of six horses dragged Byron's carriage to the top of the Simplon Pass; they passed through the successive belts of pine trees, of barren rock, of eternal snow. Unable to find any wall at the summit on which to carve their names, they wrote them on a piece of paper which they carefully concealed beneath a stone. Then, coming down again from the snow to the wilderness of rocks, and from there down to the pine trees, they descended at last into the valley of Domodossola, with its white church towers gleaming here and there on the vine-clad slopes.

Fletcher was ordered to prepare carbines, daggers, and pistols, for the two Englishmen had been told it was a dangerous part of the country. Napoleon's downfall had brought this hapless Italy back under foreign domination. The Holy Alliance, a "league of dynasties," had made Lombardy into an Austrian kingdom which Metternich, the Divine lieutenant, ruled through his police. Spies were everywhere; informers were paramount even within the family. Liberals and patriots banded together in secret societies, and at Milan Byron immediately found himself in touch with Italian liberal circles. He had an introduction from Madame de Staël to Monsignor Ludovic de Brême, chaplain to the former King of Italy. Thanks to him Byron met the Marquis de Brême, who had been minister of the interior under Eugène de Beauharnais, and likewise Monti, the most famous living Italian poet, and the writer Silvio Pellico. He liked the country. The peasant women had lovely dark eyes. Every face was lit up by courage and love.

He was delighted by the Ambrosian Library, where he was shown the relics of Lucrezia Borgia and Cardinal Bembo, a lock of her long, beautiful hair, and certain letters, "so pretty and so loving that it makes one wretched not to have been born sooner to have at least seen her. And pray what do you think is one of her *signatures?*—why this +, a Cross—which she says 'is to stand for her name, etc.' Is not this amusing? I suppose you know that she was a famous beauty, and famous for the use she made of it; and that she was the love of this same Cardinal Bembo (besides a story about her papa Pope Alexander and her brother Cæsar Borgia—which some people don't believe—and others do)—and that after all she ended with being Duchess of Ferrara, and an excellent mother and wife; so good as to be quite an example."

In the Brêmes' box at the Scala, Hobhouse and Byron met a Frenchman, Monsieur de Beyle, a former official in the Imperial commissariate, who told them some astonishing stories. He told them that he had been Napoleon's private secretary, and in attendance on the Emperor during the retreat from Moscow. "Napoleon had then completely lost his head," said Beyle. "He used to sign his decrees with the name of 'Pompey.' " Beyle had said to him: "Your Majesty has made a slip of the pen here," and the Emperor looked at him with a horrible grimace saying, "Oh, yes. . . ." In the course of one day Beyle had seen eighty-four generals arrive at headquarters in tears, crying: "Oh, my division! . . . Oh, my brigade! . . ." When the Emperor left, Beyle had taken duty with Murat, who sat weeping bitterly on his bed. And then Monsieur de Beyle spoke of Talleyrand, saying that a jury would have convicted him, and that from being cruel, Napoleon was not cruel enough. He also recounted how Madame Ney was at Milan, and how she had had her husband's tomb engraved with the words—"Thirty-five years of Renown—one day of Error." An astonishing fellow, this Monsieur de Beyle; he had always been present in person on the most remarkable occasions. "I have every reason to believe," wrote Hobhouse, after making careful note of these precious anecdotes, "that

Beyle is a trustworthy person. . . . However, he has a cruel way of talking, and looks, and is, a sensualist."

At Milan Byron and Hobhouse ran across the hapless Polly-Dolly again. He had a quarrel with an officer, and Byron had once more to intervene to save him. The little doctor was now a candidate for the post of physician to the Princess of Wales. "Poor thing," said Hobhouse when he gave him a letter of recommendation, "she must be mad!" But Luigi de Brême, less unjust than that violent xenophobe Hobhouse, was a better judge of the poor doctor, and wrote to Madame de Staël that one would seldom find a more honest man than Polidori, or one more artless and sincere.

On Byron himself, Luigi de Brême added a judgment which was all the more interesting as it confirmed that of Sir Walter Scott: "Lord Byron is an altogether lovable man. When an opportunity occurred of showing his good will to Polidori, he seized it straightforwardly and eagerly. Dare I tell you this? I think there are men who . . . may not always have a *social* bent, but yet are eminently *humane.* Lord Byron is gifted with a variety of qualities for which it is quite natural that those who are in touch with him, in his own country or his family circle, do not give him credit, as he is lacking in others which are customarily held essential. . . . We have let him feel how remote we are from all the opinions that have been formed regarding himself, and that it depends entirely on him to form one for us. So keenly are his works relished by those of his friends who know English that, without ever mentioning it, we are endlessly showing him our private admiration, and this results in a mutual and habitual bond of understanding which leaves him perfectly at his ease amid this society with which I have surrounded him." Those who can console tortured souls have their reward: they are alone in understanding them.

Byron's Italian friends showed him all the sights of Milan. He heard the echo of Simonetta and viewed the Duomo by moonlight. Monsieur de Beyle noted the astounding impression made on Byron by a painting of Danieli Crespi's, representing a canon lying in a coffin in the middle of a church while the burial service was sung over him, and suddenly lifting the pall and emerging from the coffin with the exclamation—"I am damned by a just judgment!" Byron could not be torn away from this picture. He was moved even to tears, and his companions, respectful of genius, silently mounted their horses again and rode off to await him a mile or so away.

At last, on November 4, Byron and Hobhouse set off for Venice. They passed through Brescia, and through Verona, where Byron enjoyed recapturing the memory of Juliet, and through Vicenza; and then one night, asleep in a gondola beneath a darkling sky, they suddenly woke amid the lights of Venice. The echo of the oars told them that they were under a bridge. "The Rialto!" cried their gondolier. A few minutes later they were disembarking at the Hôtel de la Grande Bretagne, on the Grand Canal, and were being shown up a lordly staircase into gilded apartments hung with painted silks.

XXVIII

"A FAIRY CITY OF THE HEART . . ."

1816–1818

A COUPLE of weeks later Byron was writing to Murray: "Venice pleases me as much as I expected, and I expected much. It is one of those places which I know before I see them, and has always haunted me the most after the East. I like the gloomy gaiety of their gondolas, and the silence of their canals. I do not even dislike the evident decay of the city, though I regret the singularity of its vanished costume; however, there is much still left; the Carnival, too, is coming." And to Tom Moore: "It is my intention to remain at Venice during the Winter, probably as it has always been (next to the East) the greenest island of my imagination. It has not disappointed me. . . . I have been familiar with ruins too long to dislike desolation."

He enjoyed the Venetian dialect, and the ochreous colouring of the Venetian houses, the sonorous names and the pink marbles of the Palazzi, and the funereal beauty of the black gondolas. At every turn in this city of the Merchant and the Moor, of Portia and Desdemona, he could in fancy encounter the ghost of Shakespeare. And his lameness seemed a lessened evil in a city where the slow gliding of the gondolas took the place of walking.

The Venetian Republic existed no longer; the winged lions of St. Mark's guarded neither Doge nor Council of Ten; the Bucentaur had been burnt by the French; and at Milan, an Austrian governor ruled as representative of Metternich. But the city remained a place of indulgence and gaiety. The cafés on the Square of St. Mark's were crowded, and Venice had eight theatres—more than either London or Paris could boast. The Italian society met at *conversazioni,* the most brilliant of which was that of the Countess Albrizzi, whom the Venetians called "the Italian Madame de Staël," and who lost no time in being presented to "the leading poet of England." A few gentlemen and some ladies were sipping water in a small room. Hobhouse judged this *conversazione* a poor imitation of the salon at Coppet, but the lady struck him as an agreeable person.

On December 4 the two friends parted company, Hobhouse leaving for Rome while Byron stayed on in Venice. He had there found a lodging and a mistress at one and the same time, under the roof of a certain Signor Segati. This man was a cloth-merchant who owned a shop in the Frezzeria, the long narrow street adjacent to St. Mark's. It bore the sign of "The Horn"—and very soon his apprentices were able to add the qualification "English," for although Segati's trade languished, his wife was young and pretty. Besides, she sang marvellously well, and by favour of her voice the Segatis were received by the Venetian aristocracy. Marianna Segati contrived to give Byron, so ingenuous under his roué's mask, the illusion that he was her first lover. She had the name in Venice of being greedy and easy, but he was enchanted by her. He had loved her from the first week of his stay, he wrote, and continued to do so because she was amiable and pretty—"not two-and-twenty, with great black, Eastern eyes, and a variety of subsidiary charms, etc., etc."—because he was diverted by her Venetian dialect, because she was artless, and because he could see her and make love to her at any time, which suited his temperament.

At heart he loved her, in his half-sentimental, half-scornful way, as he loved a faithful dog, or a horse, or a song of Tom Moore's. She was a nice submissive animal, gay when he wanted, silent if he were sad; and with her beside him he grew slowly calmer. The Alps, the writing of *Manfred,* and the novelty of Italy, had united to still that inner seething into which, back at Diodati, he had hardly dared to peer. If he had not ceased to suffer, he at least had made an end of enjoying his suffering; and that was a great step forward. The chattering of this foreigner in her "bastard Latin" was a useful stupefiant. And for tiring his limbs, a sound remedy against the passions, he had procured four horses from the Austrian commandant of a fort and took daily gallops on the Lido, along the narrow strip of land, with the Adriatic waves plashing the fetlocks of his mount.

Daily, too, he moored his gondola outside the Armenian convent, where he had made friends with the fathers, and took pleasure in visiting them in that islet of theirs planted with cypresses, oranges and Judas trees. Crossing their flowery cloister, he entered a room all covered with sacred images, where he helped Father Pascal Aucher in the composition of an English-Armenian grammar. He admired the olive complexion of the father, and the long black beard that gave him the air of a high-priest in the temple of Solomon. Armenian was a stiff language, but its very difficulty was an attraction to Byron. "I found that my mind wanted something craggy to break upon: and this—as the most difficult thing I could discover here for an amusement—I have chosen, to torture me into attention."

He was asked how long he would be staying in Venice, and replied that Marianna and the Armenian alphabet "would probably carry him through the winter." He was glad to converse with the fathers, and felt a certain envy of their solitude, their withdrawal, their peace of mind. Father Aucher described Armenia to him, and declared that all biblical authority pointed to its having been the site of the Earthly Paradise. Heaven knew where Byron had been seeking that! Had he found it at last—in Venice? Sometimes he thought so. The gondola, the morning gallop, the Armenian lessons, and Marianna's embraces, were all keeping the great enemy, Boredom, at safe distance. For the evening there were the salons. The Venetians were already viewing him as an accepted ornament of their city; and, thanks to the *Divine Comedy* and young Nicolo Giraud of Athens, he spoke Italian fairly well.

> I've taught me other tongues, and in strange eyes
> Have made me not a stranger. . . .

Just as in Greece, years ago, he was escaping his native conformity by being uprooted from his own soil; and safe from English onlookers he was sometimes able to forget the English law that lived in his heart. "If I could but remain as I now am," he wrote to Kinnaird, "I should not merely be happy, but *contented,* which in my mind is the strangest, and most difficult attainment of the two—for anyone who will hazard enough may have moments of happiness. I have books—a decent establishment—a fine country—a language which I prefer—most of the amusements and conveniences of life—as much of society as I choose to take—and a handsome woman, who is not a bore—and does not annoy me with looking like a fool, setting up for a sage. Life has little left for my curiosity; there are few things in it of which I have not had a sight, and a share—it would be silly to quarrel with my luck because it did not last—and even that was partly my own fault. If the present does—I should fall out with the past; and if I could but manage to arrange my pecuniary concerns in England . . . you might consider me as *posthumous,* for I would never willingly dwell in the 'tight little Island.'"

Carnival came round, the great season in Venice, the time of routs and mysteries, the time less liked by husbands than by lovers, the time when women, before their Lenten devotions, laid in store of matter for penitence. Byron was beginning to know something of these dark-eyed women of Venice. They all had at least one *amoroso* apiece; those who had but one were regarded as virtuous, and changed him at the Carnival season. Marianna Segati, content with her Englishman, was alone in thinking only of keeping hers.

Brightly coloured costumes—Turkish, Jewish, Greek and Roman—gleamed in the dark coffins of the gondolas, and Byron surrendered to the dancing rhythm of the life. His letters to Tom Moore twanged like the Venetian guitars:

> What are you doing now,
> Oh Thomas Moore?
> What are you doing now,
> Oh Thomas Moore?
> Sighing or suing now,
> Rhyming or wooing now,
> Billing or cooing now,
> Which, Thomas Moore?

But the Carnival's coming,
Oh Thomas Moore!
The Carnival's coming,
Oh Thomas Moore!
Masking and humming,
Fifing and drumming,
Guitarring and strumming,
Oh Thomas Moore!

From the dark streets rose the sounds of singing and kissing, right on till dawn. All night long Marianna and Byron wandered through the city, whilst the Merchant of Venice slept on at the sign of the "English Horn." For a few days this was delightful, but then the nocturnal life tired Byron. His health was giving way. The fever of those stagnant waters, perhaps? A touch of malaria, like that which nearly killed him at Patras? Or old age already? He had just passed the turning-point of twenty-nine; "the sword outwears its sheath," he sang; and to Marianna he addressed those tired and lovely lines:

So, we'll go no more a-roving
So late into the night,
Though the heart be still as loving,
And the moon be still as bright.

For the sword outwears its sheath,
And the soul wears out the breast,
And the heart must pause to breathe,
And love itself have rest.

Though the night was made for loving,
And the day returns too soon,
Yet we'll go no more a-roving
By the light of the moon.

He spent the Lenten season in bed, rather ill, and in his feverish broodings the pictures of the past again became dangerously vivid. What was happening to Augusta? He could not understand a word of this devout new jargon of hers. "I have received all your letters I believe, which are full of woes, as usual, megrims and mysteries; but my sympathies remain in suspense, for, for the life of me I can't make out whether your disorder is a broken heart or the earache—or whether it is you who have been ill or the children—or what your melancholy and mysterious apprehensions tend to, or refer to, whether to Caroline Lamb's novels—Mrs. Clermont's evidence—Lady Byron's magnanimity—or any other piece of imposture; I know nothing of what you are in the doldrums about at present. I should think that all that can affect *you* must have been over long ago; and as for me, leave me to take care of myself. . . ." Again, a fortnight later: "I repeat to you again and again—that it would be much better at once to explain your mysteries—than to go on with this absurd obscure hinting mode of writing. What do you mean? What is there known? or can be known? which *you* and *I* do not know much better? and what concealment can you have from me? *I* never shrank—and it was on your account principally that I gave way at all—for I thought they would endeavour to drag you into it—although they had no business with anything previous to my marriage with that infernal fiend, whose destruction I shall yet see. . . ." This letter was sent on to Lady Byron, with Augusta's comment: "a more melancholy one I can't imagine—such anger and hatred and bitterness to *all*—only fit for the fire—in short, it's plain to me that he is angry with *himself,* poor fellow!"

During his illness he had finished the third act of *Manfred.* It was rather a skimped act, for Byron had not Goethe's gift for handling the supernatural in vast blocks; but doctrinally it was interesting. It showed Manfred face to face with Death. An Abbot was trying to reconcile him with himself, and the scene was perhaps an echo of Byron's conversations with the Armenian fathers. The Catholic priest offered penitence and pardon—

My son! I do not speak of punishment,
But penitence and pardon;—with thyself
The choice of such remains—and for the last,
Our institutions and our strong belief
Have given me power to smooth the path from sin
To higher hope and better thoughts; the first
I leave to Heaven—"Vengeance is mine alone!"
So saith the Lord, and with all humbleness
His servant echoes back the awful word.

But Manfred answered him:

Old man! there is no power in holy men,
Nor charm in prayer—nor purifying form
Of penitence—nor outward look—nor fast—
Nor agony—nor, greater than all these,
The innate tortures of that deep despair,
Which is remorse without the fear of hell,
But all in all sufficient to itself
Would make a hell of heaven—can exorcise
From out the unbounded spirit, the quick sense
Of its own sins, wrongs, sufferance, and revenge
Upon itself: there is no future pang
Can deal that justice on the self-condemn'd
He deals on his own soul.

In the closing scene the Demons sent from Hell sought to drag Manfred back with them. But he routed them:

Back to thy hell!
Thou hast no power upon me, *that* I feel;
Thou never shalt possess me, *that* I know:

What I have done is done: I bear within
A torture which could nothing gain from thine:
The mind which is immortal makes itself
Requital for its good or evil thoughts—
Is its own origin of ill and end—
And its own place and time—its innate sense,
When stripped of this mortality, derives
No colour from the fleeting things without;
But is absorbed in sufferance or in joy,
Born from the knowledge of its own desert.
Thou didst not tempt me, and thou couldst not tempt me;
I have not been thy dupe, nor am thy prey—
But was my own destroyer, and will be
My own hereafter,—Back, ye baffled fiends!
The hand of death is on me—but not yours!

Thus, under Shelley's impetus to metaphysical reflection, Byron was striving for the first time to reconcile his invincible sense of sin with that sceptical philosophy which rejected the orthodox notions of Hell and Punishment. And by a wonderfully Byronic solution, he contrived to turn himself, and himself alone, into the centre and the whole of the system. Byron alone had been Byron's tempter. Byron alone would chastise Byron in Byron. Byron alone, Byron's destroyer, would be the Byron in the world to come. Hell exists—but not the childish Hell of Mary Gray. Hell exists—but it is *within* us, and the living plunge into it themselves.

"Old man! 'tis not so difficult to die"—those were Manfred's last words to the Abbot; and in them, as Byron wrote to Augusta, lay the whole moral of the poem. Not all men are afraid of death. Some fear it because they love this life, others because they dread a future life. But human existence is a stern struggle, and there are some beings, conscious of an inner battle which can never be decided, to whom death appears as a welcome repose. Of these Byron was one. Too brave to flee from life, but too weary to be afraid at the end, he kept death ever in his thoughts, even in the midst of the unwonted carnival. Along the painted friezes of his Venetian retreat, as once over the grey walls of Newstead, there flitted a Dance of Death.

That third act cost him many pangs to write. A first version forwarded to Murray struck his friends as weak, and he refashioned it. In the end the drama was published in England in June 1817. Its appearance boded no good for Augusta, who, in the eyes of the public, was unmistakably denounced by Manfred's love for Astarte. "No avowal can be more complete," wrote Mrs. Villiers. "It is too barefaced for her friends to attempt to deny the allusion. . . . Did you see the newspaper called *The Day and New Times* of June 23? There is a long critique on *Manfred* ably done, I think, but the allusions to Augusta dreadfully clear." As for the last-named, she was completely tamed, and wrote to Annabella, asking what she ought to say regarding *Manfred* if she were questioned about it. "You can only speak of *Manfred,*" wrote Lady Byron, "with the most decided expressions of your disapprobation."

In the spring, when Byron's health was on the mend, the doctors advised a change of air; a healthier climate would rid him of his fevers. Hobhouse, who had been archæologising in Rome for five months past, summoned his friend. Byron hesitated. It was childish, perhaps, but the idea of parting from Marianna made him quite "Carolinish." She had nursed him well during his illness. He had not been absolutely faithful to her, but he had become attached to her. He had only to love a woman to be seized with a ludicrous hope of disclosing a beautiful soul in her. At the moment it was Marianna Segati's turn, and this indulgent wife of a Venetian draper, was unexpectedly becoming an incarnation of the *beau idéal.*

However, a journey to Rome would be an opportunity for adding a fourth Canto to *Childe Harold,* and he decided to obey the doctors. He passed through Ferrara, where he wrote *The Lament of Tasso* and saw the tomb of Ariosto, and through Florence, where he noted that one of the women in a painting of the Massacre of the Innocents was remarkably like Lady Ponsonby. (Like Fletcher, he was for ever finding English likenesses.) Then, on the road to Rome, he passed close to Lake Trasimene. In his childhood the minister Paterson had described to him the ground there covered with corpses, the stream running red with the blood of Romans and Carthaginians. The peasants showed him that stream: it was still called the Sanguinetto. The lake was like "a sheet of silver," and the peaceful scene was framed by well-tilled fields and clumps of trees.

In Rome, as always, he lived on two planes—the Byron plane, and the Childe Harold plane. On the former, he rode frequently, revised that confounded third act of *Manfred* which Murray's circle persistently refused to approve, and wrote to Moore: "Of Rome I saw nothing; it is quite indescribable and the Guide-book is as good as any other. I dined yesterday with Lord Lansdowne . . . but there are few English here at present. . . . I have been on horseback most of the day, all days since my arrival, and have taken it as I did Constantinople. But Rome is the elder sister, and the finer. . . . As for the Coliseum, Pantheon, St. Peter's, the Vatican, Palatine, etc., etc.—as I said, vide Guide-book. They are quite inconceivable, and must *be seen.* The Apollo Belvedere is the image of Lady Adelaide Forbes—I think I never saw such a likeness. I have seen the Pope alive, and a cardinal dead,—both of whom looked very well indeed. . . . Here is Hobhouse, just come in, and my horses at the door; so that I must mount and take the field in the Campus Martius. . . ."

The sculptor Thorwaldsen, for whom he posed at the recommendation of the Countess Albrizzi, had the privilege of catching the transition from Byron to Childe Harold. Seated in the artist's studio, Byron put on an expression quite different from his usual one. "Will you not sit still?" said Thorwaldsen, "you need not assume that look."—"That is my expression," said Byron.—"Indeed?" said the sculptor, and portrayed Byron as he himself saw him. When the bust was finished, Byron complained that it was not at all like him: "my expression is more unhappy," he maintained.

For Childe Harold's contemplations, Rome was the perfect setting. Nowhere in the world could there be a richer store of Byronic themes. Grandeur and decadence, ruin and beauty—the sublime commonplaces rose up at every turning. . . . He meditated upon the tomb of Cecilia Metella:

> But who was she, the lady of the dead,
> Tomb'd in a palace? Was she chaste and fair?
> Worthy a king's—or more—a Roman's bed?
> What race of chiefs and heroes did she bear?
>
> . . . .
>
> Was she as those who love their lords, or they
> Who love the lords of others? such have been
> Even in olden time, Rome's annals say.
> Was she a matron of Cornelia's mien,
> Or the light air of Egypt's graceful queen,

Profuse of joy—or 'gainst it did she war,
Inveterate in virtue?

. . . .

Perchance she died in youth: it may be, bow'd
With woes far heavier than the ponderous tomb
That weigh'd upon her gentle dust, a cloud
Might gather o'er her beauty, and a gloom
In her dark eyes, prophetic of the doom
Heaven gives its favourites—early death; yet shed
A sunset charm around her, and illume
With hectic light, the Hesperus of the dead,
Of her consuming cheek the autumnal leaf-like red.

Perchance she died in age—surviving all,
Charms, kindred, children—with the silver grey
On her long tresses. . . .

He had so sensuous a taste for death that his heart melted for this dead incognita. . . .

And then upon the Palatine he dreamed again, whilst the night-birds hooted to each other amid the ivy-clad ruins of what once had been the palace of the Emperors:

There is the moral of all human tales,
'Tis but the same rehearsal of the past,
First Freedom, and then Glory—when that fails,
Wealth, vice, corruption—barbarism at last.
And History, with all her volumes vast,
Hath but *one* page,—'tis better written here,
Where gorgeous Tyranny hath thus amass'd
All treasures, all delights, that eye or ear,
Heart, soul could seek, tongue ask. . . .

Rhetorical? Certainly—but rhetoric has its uses. . . . There was one clear moonlight night in the Coliseum, when the stars quivered up through those arches fringed with wild flowers, and standing in that magic circle haunted by the great dead, he invoked Nemesis, his favourite goddess, and avenging Time against all who had made him suffer, against his "moral Clytemnestra," against the revilers of his exile:

> And thou, who never yet of human wrong
> Left the unbalanced scale, great Nemesis!
> Here, where the ancient paid thee homage long—
> Thou, who didst call the Furies from the abyss,
> And round Orestes bade them howl and hiss
> For that unnatural retribution—just,
> Had it but been from hands less near—in this
> Thy former realm, I call thee from the dust!
> Dost thou not hear my heart?—Awake! thou shalt and must.

The fourth Canto of *Childe Harold* was not yet written; but Byron had the material, and now he could go. Hobhouse was going to stay at Naples, and would gladly have taken him on there; but Byron was unhappy at being so far from Marianna. He wrote to her to come and meet him, and returned with her to Venice.

It was the hot season. Byron was afraid of the fever. He rented for the summer a villa at La Mira, on the Brenta, some distance out of Venice; and there, with the well-paid consent of the draper, Marianna came to stay with him. The villa had formerly been a convent, the chapel of which had disappeared. Under one pointed arch there was a stone let into the wall bearing this inscription:

HIC SAEPE LICEBIT
NUNC VETERUM LIBRIS
NUNC SOMNO ET INCERTIBUS HORIS
DUCERE SOLLICITAE
IUCUNDA OBLIVIA VITAE.

The neighbours were not troublesome. Opposite there lived a Mexican marquis, ninety years old, and on one side a Frenchman who had known Voltaire. The Brenta mirrored the loveliest sunsets in the world. Hobhouse came to rejoin Byron after returning from Naples, and together they passed industrious days. It was a strange life, noted Hobhouse, very calm and comfortable: "I saw my friend well and in good spirits. . . . Byron talked to me about family affairs to-night. He does not care about his wife now—that is certain." Byron was writing the fourth Canto of *Childe Harold;* Hobhouse, precise and erudite, was boring him with scholarly topography, and compiling his *Notes in Illustration of Canto IV of Childe Harold*. Frequently they crossed the lagoon to go riding on the Lido, and Hobhouse in his turn enjoyed the matchless joy of these gallops along the breaking waves. "Went with Byron to Lido. Lovely day. Recollect the glee inspired by galloping along the beach. A light breeze. Byron told me Lady Byron thought he did not like me. At another time said I had no principle, because Byron used to say I should laugh at some fine sayings of hers. Poor, dear, contradictory thing." And thus passed five perfect months.

On January 2, his wedding anniversary (he attached great importance to the date), he dedicated the fourth Canto of *Childe Harold* to "John Hobhouse, Esq., A.M., F.R.S.,— . . . one whom I have known long and accompanied far, whom I have found wakeful over my sickness and kind in my sorrow, glad in my prosperity and firm in my adversity, true in counsel and trusty in peril—to a friend often tried and never found wanting." Nevertheless, this last Canto of *Childe Harold* had not gained by its being written under the immediate patronage of John Hobhouse, Esq., A.M., F.R.S. The third, with Shelley as its inspirer, had been more poetical. But it had great beauties: a bewitching picture of Venice, a heart-felt remembrance of England, some profound and melancholy stanzas on the subjectivity of love:

> O Love! no habitant of earth thou art—
> An unseen seraph, we believe in thee,—
> A faith whose martyrs are the broken heart,
> But never yet hath seen, nor e'er shall see,
> The naked eye, thy form, as it should be;
> The mind hath made thee, as it peopled heaven,
> Even with its own desiring phantasy,
> And to a thought such shape and image given,
> As haunts the unquench'd soul—parch'd—wearied
>   —wrung—and riven.
>
> Of its own beauty is the mind diseased,
> And fevers into false creation;—where,
> Where are the forms the sculptor's soul hath seized?
> In him alone. Can Nature show so fair?
> Where are the charms and virtues which we dare
> Conceive in boyhood and pursue as men,
> The unreach'd Paradise of our despair,
> Which o'er-informs the pencil and the pen,
> And overpowers the page where it would bloom
>   again?

And what was true of love was true also of ambition. Human desires did not always accord with the nature of things. . . . We long for perfection, yet bear all the while the indelible stigmata of sin. We dream great deeds, and are victims of petty cowardice. Byron himself, alas, had experienced how far mean perfidies can go towards spoiling a life that should have been one of beauty:

> But I have lived, and have not lived in vain:
> My mind may lose its force, my blood its fire,
> And my frame perish even in conquering pain;
> But there is that within me which shall tire

Torture and Time, and breathe when I expire;
Something unearthly, which they deem not of,
Like the remember'd tone of a mute lyre,
Shall on their soften'd spirits sink, and move
In hearts all rocky now the late remorse of love.

A Promethean stanza, prophetic and full of just pride. Faced with this poverty of things human, what could one do? Nothing, save to give the power of reason sway over this mediocrity of condition, and seek in Nature the happiness which society makes impossible. He rounded off the Canto with a description of the one faithful friend—the sea:

And I have loved thee, Ocean! and my Joy
Of youthful sports was on thy breast to be
Borne, like thy bubbles, onward: from a boy
I wanton'd with thy breakers—they to me
Were a delight; and if the freshening sea
Made them a terror—'twas a pleasing fear,
For I was as it were a child of thee,
And trusted to thy billows far and near,
And laid my head upon thy name—as I do here.

Thus was *Childe Harold* completed. But it was not the only work of those five months at La Mira. Lord Kinnaird, brother of Douglas, had come to Venice, and brought Byron a new poem by John Hookham Frere, a light satire imitated from the Italian poets, and in particular from Pulci. It delighted Byron, and he began a Venetian tale in the same manner, which he called *Beppo*. The tone suited his new frame of mind. It was good-humoured, and it was cynical, even regarding its own lines; whenever a stanza began to soar into the lyrical, the hand of the ironic bird-catcher pulled it back. . . .

England! with all thy faults I love thee still,
  I said at Calais, and have not forgot it;
I like to speak and lucubrate my fill;
  I like the government (but that is not it);
I like the freedom of the press and quill;
  I like the Habeas Corpus (when we've got it);
I like a parliamentary debate,
  Particularly when 'tis not too late;

I like the taxes, when they're not too many;
  I like a seacoal fire, when not too dear;
I like a beefsteak, too, as well as any;
  Have no objection to a pot of beer;
I like the weather, when it is not rainy,
  That is, I like two months of every year,
And so God save the Regent, Church, and King!
  Which means that I like all and everything.

Our standing army, and disbanded seamen,
  Poor's rate, Reform, my own, the nation's debt,
Our little riots just to show we are free men,
  Our trifling bankruptcies in the Gazette,
Our cloudy climate, and our chilly women,
  All these I can forgive, and those forget,
And greatly venerate our recent glories,
  And wish they were not owing to the Tories.

Some time later, a young Frenchman, Alfred de Musset, was to catch that tone from Byron, as Byron had caught it from the Italians.

His love for the Signora Segati did not last so long as the sojourn at La Mira; and it was Marianna's fault. She could not hide her greed. She sold the diamonds her lover had given her. He knew it, bought them back, and gave her them again—not without twitting her on this romantic fondness for his gifts. The *marito* Segati, whose honour gave him periodic twinges, was decidedly too expensive that winter. And as the final touch to make this liaison just like an unhappy marriage, Marianna showed symptoms of jealousy.

Byron was slipping away from her. During one of their rides along the Brenta, Hobhouse and he had noticed two magnificent girls in a group of country-folk. Byron proposed a rendezvous to one of them, Margarita Cogni. She replied that she was quite ready to love him, as she was married and all married women did so, but that her husband, a baker, was a man of some ferocity. Byron dubbed this baker's wife "La Fornarina," and conquered her by force of sequins. She was twenty-two, and could neither read nor write. He had never before come across a woman so primitive; and he liked her for being so.

But the gossips of La Mira told tales to Marianna, of how Byron's horse had been heard neighing out in the country, late at night. The reigning sultana grew anxious, hunted out her rustic rival, and insulted her to her face. Margarita threw back the white kerchief which she wore on her brow, and answered: "You are not his wife. I am not his wife. You are his *donna,* and I am his *donna.* Your husband's a cuckold, and so is mine. So what right have *you* to reproach me?" After which neat little speech she departed, leaving Signora Segati to her own thoughts. When the latter tried to complain to Byron, she realised that she was beaten.

In the course of January 1818 Hobhouse had to return to England and on the eve of his departure the two friends gave a fête worthy of eighteenth-century Venice. To go over to the Lido they engaged two singers, who sat one at the prow and the other at the stern of the boat, and, leaving the Piazetta, sang fragments of Tasso, the *Death of Clorinda,* and the *Palace of Armida,* just like the gondoliers of the past. On retiring, Hobhouse felt melancholy, as he always did on parting with this strange and fascinating personality, and wrote in his journal: "Passed the evening with Byron, who put the last hand to his *Childe Harold*, and took leave of my dear friend, for so I think him, at twelve o'clock. A little before his going he told me he was originally a man of a great deal of feeling, but it had been absorbed. I believe the first part of what he said literally. God bless him!"

With Hobhouse there disappeared once more the Onlooker, and Byron was left in dangerous independence. The period which followed was that of his most extreme debauchery, and the causes of his moral confusion are fairly clear.

There was first of all the weak restraining-power of a foreign society, whose judgments were indifferent to him. In this land of easy morals, far from the one human pack of which he felt himself really a responsible member, he reverted to the status of a solitary animal, with no aim beyond the satisfying of its desires. His last remaining English friend was the Consul, Richard Hoppner, a son of the painter, a clever little man who had married a charming Swiss. But the Hoppners, proud of being Lord Byron's familiars, dared not tell him the truth, and they did not take the place of Hobhouse.

Secondly, there was the fact of Marianna's reign being over. He still lived at the Segatis' house in the Frezzeria, but his admiration for Margarita Cogni was rising. He described her to Moore: "a Venetian girl, with large black eyes, a face like Faustina's, and the figure of Juno—tall and energetic as a pythoness, with eyes flashing, and her dark hair streaming in the moonlight—one of these women who may be made anything. I am sure if I put a poniard in the hand of this one, she would plunge it where I told her,—and into *me,* if I offended her. I like this kind of animal, and am sure that I should have preferred Medea to any woman that ever breathed."

He liked that kind of animal, but he was not faithful to it. The gentle, shy woman, with the eyes of a gazelle, always held him more firmly, always made him more happy.

A third cause was the high purchasing-power of his English income on the markets of Venetian vice. At a thousand guineas the Canto, his poems would have sufficed to keep him, but on top of that he had Annabella's annual £500, and Newstead had recently been sold for the large sum of £94,500 to an old Harrow friend, Major Wildman ("Tom Wildman on my left hand, Long on my right . . ."). So Byron's account with his friend and banker, Douglas Kinnaird, had now a credit balance.

One curious trait, inherited from Catherine Gordon, showed itself now that he had money. He became miserly—not meanly so, and still remaining open-handed—but niggardly in his mother's way. She had been capable of giving to her husband, and then to her son, almost everything she had, and yet could torment herself over some outlay of a few shillings. There Byron resembled her. He had always had a taste, hereditary perhaps, for a kind of elementary asceticism. He liked to know that his food was only costing him a few crowns, to cut down his housekeeping bills, to check Fletcher's accounts minutely. With the savings thus gained he filled a money-box, and enjoyed the sight of the golden coins accumulating.

Over his love affairs he was no haggler. He now knew the resources of Venice thoroughly. Having almost forsaken the literary salon of the Countess Albrizzi, he was now frequenting the Countess Benzoni's who received a somewhat freer circle. But he chiefly sought out women of the people. "It is a very good place for women," he wrote to Rogers. "I like their dialect and their manner very much. There is a *naïveté* about them which is very winning, and the romance of the place is a mighty adjunct; the *bel sangue* is, not however now amongst the *dame* or higher orders, but under *i fazzioli,* or kerchiefs, a white kind of veil which the lower orders wear upon their heads." He admired these vigorous women, fit mothers for gladiators, as he said, and saw a great number of them. He received them in a very discreet *casino,* for these encounters had to be concealed from Margarita Cogni, who would probably have disfigured her rivals. The Venetians used to declare that he entertained as many as nine Muses in this *casino.* But that was doubtless legendary: when Dante was exiled to Ravenna, did not the passers-by point to the poet's beard and see it singed by the flames of Hell?

In April 1818 came news of the death of Lady Melbourne. "The time is past," he wrote to Murray, "in which I could feel for the dead—or I should feel for the death of Lady Melbourne, the best and kindest and ablest female I ever knew—old or young. But I have 'supped full of horrors,' and events of this kind leave only a kind of numbness worse than pain—like a violent blow on the elbow or on the head. There is one link less between England and myself."

Another death which powerfully impressed him, and

confirmed his belief in Destiny was that of Sir Samuel Romilly, Lady Byron's legal adviser, and one of the prime movers in the separation. In the magic circle of the Coliseum, Byron had invoked the vengeance of Nemesis upon all those who had acted against him in this affair. And now he wrote to Lady Byron: "Sir Samuel Romilly has cut his throat for the loss of his wife. It is now nearly three years since he became . . . the advocate of the measures and the Approver of the proceedings, which deprived me of mine. . . . This Man little thought, when he was lacerating my heart according to law, while he was poisoning my life at its sources, aiding and abetting in the blighting, branding, and exile that was to be the result of his counsels . . . that in less than thirty-six moons—in the pride of his triumph as the highest candidate for the representation of the Sister-city of the mightiest of Capitals—in the fullness of his professional career—in the greenness of a healthy old age—in the radiance of fame and the complacency of self-earned riches—that a domestic affliction would lay him in the earth, with the meanest of malefactors, in a cross-road with the stake in his body, if the verdict of insanity did not redeem his ashes from the sentence of the laws he had lived upon by interpreting or misinterpreting, and died in violating. . . . It was not in vain that I invoked Nemesis in the midnight of Rome from the awfullest of her ruins."

From England came occasional letters from the Shelleys. The child Clare had been expecting when she left Byron at Diodati was born on January 12, 1817. Mary announced the birth to the father at the same time as her own marriage, and Shelley wrote soon afterwards to say that, pending Byron's decision regarding a name,

Mary and Clare had called the little girl Alba. "She is very beautiful," wrote Shelley from Marlow, "and although her frame is of somewhat a delicate texture, enjoys excellent health. Her eyes are the most intelligent I ever saw in so young an infant. Her hair is black, her eyes deeply blue, and her mouth exquisitely shaped. She passes here for the child of a friend in London, sent into the country for her health. . . ."

Shelley was quite used to shouldering the burdens of his friends' follies, but none the less he began to wish, after a few months, that Lord Byron would remember his promise to take charge of his daughter. Byron was always curious regarding his own blood, and was perfectly willing to bring up the child. But his letters on this topic to Kinnaird contrasted painfully with the airy sweetness with which Shelley wove little Alba's cradle: "Shelley has written to me about my daughter (the last bastard one), who it seems is a great beauty; and wants to know what he is to do about sending her . . . will you think of some plan for remitting her here, or placing her in England? I shall acknowledge and breed her myself, giving her the name of Biron (to distinguish her from little Legitimacy), and mean to christen her Allegra, which is a Venetian name." And in March 1818, when asking Hobhouse if he would not soon be sent the purchase-deeds of Newstead for signature, he said: "A clerk can bring the papers (and, by-the-bye, my *child* by Clare, at the same time. Pray desire Shelley to pack it carefully), with *tooth-powder, red only;* magnesia, soda-powders, tooth-brushes, diachylon plaster, and any new novels good for anything." The cynical tone, no doubt, was only to shock Kinnaird or Hobhouse.

When the Shelleys came to Milan, a Swiss nurse, Elise,

brought the little Allegra to her father's. Byron found her pretty and intelligent, and was very proud of seeing her a great favourite with the Venetian ladies. "But, what is more remarkable," he wrote to Augusta, "she is much more like Lady Byron than her mother—so much so as to stupefy the learned Fletcher and astonish me. Is it not odd? I suppose she must also resemble her sister Ada: she has very blue eyes, and that singular forehead, fair curly hair, and a devil of a spirit—but that is papa's." He was quite happy to see a Byron again—even a bastard one.

XXIX

PALAZZO MOCENIGO

1818

> The professional Don Juan destroys his spirit as fatally as does the professional ascetic, whose looking-glass image he is.
>
> ALDOUS HUXLEY

SIR,—With great grief I inform you of the death of my late dear Master, my Lord, who died this morning at ten of the Clock of a rapid decline and slow fever, caused by anxiety, sea-bathing, women, and riding in the Sun against my advice. . . ." So began the tragi-comical letter which Byron wrote to Hobhouse towards the end of July 1818, signing it "Fletcher."

He was only half joking. When he broke with Marianna Segati he had left the house in the Frezzeria and took one of the three Mocenigo palaces, on the Grand Canal, at a yearly rental of 4,800 francs. He now had his own house, like a Venetian born, and his gondola was moored to its posts with their painted spirals of blue and white, the Mocenigo colours; the green waters of the canal lapped the flight of steps, where the visitor was confronted by the gondolier Tita Falcieri, a giant with immense mustachios, who was equally adept in finding strong rowers and weak wives. From the vent-holes rose the barking of dogs, the squeal of monkeys, the singing of birds, and above all other noises rose the powerful voice of Margarita Cogni and the childish treble of Allegra, who shared the management of this menagerie with the Fornarina.

Margarita Cogni, at first a mere bird of passage, had gradually settled herself there. One night Byron found her on the steps of the Palazzo Mocenigo, refusing to go back to her husband. And Byron, ever the indolent fatalist, would always, after a burst of temper, submit to the creatures who insisted on his accepting their love. Margarita set him off laughing with some nonsense in the Venetian dialect, and stayed.

He soon regretted his weakness. The Fornarina slapped the other women, intercepted his letters, learned to read so as to decipher them, and filled both Tita and Fletcher with profound terror. The whole household complained of her. Byron forgave. She kept his accounts, halved his expenses, and loved him—great and rare virtues all. The fierce joy she displayed when her lover came home made Byron think of a tigress returning to her cubs; but he did not dislike tigresses. Quite the contrary. It was just the primitive, animal character of this life, and its comparative innocence, which kept him from excessive shame for a life of rather coarse debauchery. Through the finer feelings, he had known suffering and caused suffering.

His philosophy of life had greatly altered since his exile. *Manfred* was the last outburst of revolt, the last cry forced from the individual vanquished by the universe; and with *Childe Harold* there died the dolorous Byron of adolescence. He now looked askance on *The Corsair* and *Lara,* unable to comprehend how the public had managed to stomach these false and inflated characters. For several months his favourite reading had been Voltaire. There Byron again found his own pessimism, but viewed from a comical angle. Candide might well have been *Childe Harold* if Voltaire had not dominated Candide, if Voltaire had not passed judgment on Voltaire. Human destiny appears tragic if the spirit become identified with a single being, an Othello, a Hamlet, or a Conrad, and shares its sufferings and its rage. It is comic if the observer is made aware simultaneously of the incredible exaltation in the hearts of these characters, and of that uniform mechanism of the passions which is common to all mankind. Byron had always been a humourist of genius in his letter-writing, but hitherto he had held a tight rein on the emergence of this quality in his verse. In *Don Juan,* on which he had been working for a year, he had at last found a free outlet for that mixture of Voltaire and Ecclesiasticus which was the natural form of his thought.

> My poem's epic, and is meant to be
> Divided in twelve books; each book containing,
> With love and war, a heavy gale at sea,
> A list of ships, and captains, and kings reigning,
> New characters; the episodes are three:
> A panoramic view of hell's in training,
> After the style of Virgil and of Homer,
> So that my name of epic's no misnomer.
>
> All these things will be specified in time,
> With strict regard to Aristotle's rules,
> The *Vade Mecum* of the true sublime,
> Which makes so many poets and some fools;
> Prose poets like blank verse, I'm fond of rhyme,
> Good workmen never quarrel with their tools;
> I've got new mythological machinery,
> And very handsome supernatural scenery.

Never had Byron's spirit been more clear, his form more supple and vigorous. The tone was that of *Beppo,* a poetry mocking at itself, and masking a strong and bitter philosophy beneath lighthearted gaiety and whimsical rhymes. He had long made total surrender to the currents of his sensibility. As distance brought tranquillity, judgment resumed her sway. The cries and plaints were over. Byron naturally remained a more complex and sensitive creature than Voltaire had been. His theoretic philosophy, like Voltaire's, was a rational deism; but Voltaire had not been tormented either by memories of a calvinistic childhood, or by the conflict of a sensual temperament with a naturally religious soul. His field of thought was narrow and clear. In Byron the luminous zone was surrounded by vast tracts of *terræ incognitæ,* darksome regions peopled with monsters. Voltaire was perfectly content with himself when he had "crushed a mystery beneath ten truthful brevities." Byron, having known the sense of sin, retained the sense of mystery. But the site of the mystery had been shifted; it was now not so much the destiny of George Gordon, Lord Byron, as the mystery of human destiny. And it thereby became universal and classic.

Only the first Canto remained autobiographical, yet not with the earlier bitterness. The first lines brought Annabella on to the stage. Don Juan's mother, Donna Inez, was portrayed from her:

> Her favourite science was the mathematical,
> Her noblest virtue was her magnanimity;
> Her wit (she sometimes tried at wit) was Attic all,
> Her serious sayings darken'd to sublimity;
> In short, in all things she was fairly what I call
> A prodigy; her morning dress was dimity,
> Her evening silk, or, in the summer, muslin,
> And other stuffs, with which I won't stay puzzling.

2. 10. Canto 1st.

Meantime – Sir Laureate – I proceed to dedicate –
In honest simple verse this song to you –
And if in flattering strains I do not predicate –
'Tis that I still retain my "Buff and blue"
My Politics as yet are all to educate –
Apostasy's so fashionable too,
To keep one's creed's a task grown quite Herculean
Is it not so my Tory Ultra=Julian?

I want a hero – an uncommon want –
When every Year and Month sends forth a new one
Till after cloying the Gazettes with cant
The Age discovers he is not the true one
Of such as these I should not care to vaunt
I'll therefore take our ancient friend Don Juan –
We all have seen him in the Pantomime
Sent to the Devil – somewhat ere his time.

2 VI

Most epic Poets plunge in "Medias res"
Horace commends it as the safest road –

PAGE FROM THE MANUSCRIPT OF *DON JUAN*

Courtesy of the Pierpont Morgan Library

She liked the English and the Hebrew tongue,
  And said there was analogy between 'em;
She proved it somehow out of sacred song,
  But I must leave the proofs to those who've seen 'em,
But this I heard her say, and can't be wrong,
  And all may think which way their judgments lean 'em,
'Tis strange—the Hebrew noun which means "I am,"
The English always use to govern d—n.

Some women use their tongues—she look'd a lecture,
  Each eye a sermon, and her brow a homily,
An all-in-all sufficient self-director,
  Like the lamented late Sir Samuel Romilly
The law's expounder and the State's corrector. . . .

. . . .

In short she was a walking calculation,
  Miss Edgeworth's novels stepping from their covers,
Or Mrs. Trimmer's books on education,
  Or "Cœlebs' Wife" set out in quest of lovers;
Morality's prim personification,
  In which not Envy's self a flaw discovers;
To others' share let "female errors fall."
For she had not even one—the worst of all.

Oh! she was perfect, past all parallel—
  Of any modern female saint's comparison;
So far above the cunning powers of hell,
  Her guardian angel had given up his garrison:
Even her minutest motions went as well
  As those of the best time-piece made by Harrison.
In virtues nothing earthly could surpass her,
Save thine "incomparable oil" Macassar!

But the poem very quickly took on breadth and serenity. Why be angry with the world? The earth is bound to turn on its axis, and humanity along with it. One must live, die, make love, pay taxes. It is all amusing, dangerous, melancholy, inevitable.

No more—no more— Oh! never more on me
  The freshness of the heart can fall like dew,
Which out of all the lovely things we see
  Extracts emotions beautiful and new,

Hived in our bosoms like the bag o' the bee:
  Think'st thou the honey with those objects grew?
Alas! 'twas not in them, but in thy power
To double even the sweetness of a flower.

No more—no more— Oh! never more, my heart,
  Canst thou be my sole world, my universe!
Once all in all, but now a thing apart,
  Thou canst not be my blessing or my curse:
The illusion's gone for ever, and thou art
  Insensible, I trust, but none the worse,
And in thy stead I've got a deal of judgment,
Though Heaven knows how it ever found a lodgment.

My days of love are over; me no more
  The charms of maid, wife, and still less of widow,
Can make the fool of which they made before:
  In short, I must not lead the life I did do;
The credulous hope of mutual minds is o'er,
  The copious use of claret is forbid, too;
So far a good old-gentlemanly vice,
I think I must take up with avarice.

Ambition was my idol, which was broken
  Before the shrines of Sorrow and of Pleasure;
And the two last have left me many a token,
  O'er which reflection may be made at leisure. . . .

. . . .

What is the end of Fame? 'Tis but to fill
  A certain portion of uncertain paper;
Some liken it to climbing up a hill,
  Whose summit, like all hills, is lost in vapour:
For this men write, speak, preach, and heroes kill,
  And bards burn what they call their "midnight taper."
To have, when the original is dust,
A name, a wretched picture, and worse bust.

. . . .

But I, being fond of true philosophy,
  Say very often to myself, "Alas!
All things that have been born were born to die,
  And flesh (which Death mows down to hay) is grass;

You've pass'd your youth not so unpleasantly,
And if you had it o'er again—'twould pass—
So thank your stars that matters are no worse,
And read your Bible, sir, and mind your purse."

In some respects this newly attained wisdom of Byron's had resemblances to the wisdom of Shakespeare. For Shakespeare too had learned by living that all human desires, love and ambition, are but illusion. Prospero knows that life is a dream, yet still can respect and enjoy the spectacle of youthful love. Byron, though persuaded that he was purged of all illusions, continued to regard the illusions of youth as things of beauty and necessity,—

But sweeter still than this, than these, than all,
Is first and passionate love—it stands alone,
Like Adam's recollection of his fall:
The tree of knowledge has been pluck'd, all's known—
And life yields nothing further to recall
Worthy of this ambrosial sin, so shown,
No doubt in fable, as the unforgiven
Fire which Prometheus filch'd for us from heaven.

Therein Don Juan was more of the sentimentalist than Candide. The new Byron was converted from one form of romanticism, but clung impenitent to another.

The Hoppners wrote to Shelley telling him that Byron was determined to leave Venice if Clare should come there, but that if she liked she could see Allegra without her former lover knowing it. For the child was no longer at the Palazzo Mocenigo. Hoppner had hinted to Byron that to have a child living in such surroundings was something of a scandal, and offered to take charge of her. Accordingly, it was to the consul's house that Shelley accompanied Clare in the month of August.

Whilst she was with her daughter, Shelley paid a visit to Byron, who took him out in his gondola to the Lido, where horses were waiting. In *Julian and Maddalo* Shelley portrayed the essence of his conversation with Byron. They spoke of God, of free will, of destiny. Byron of course took the side of fatalism, the impotence of mankind, and Shelley answered him:

> ". . . it is our will
> That thus enchains us to permitted ill—
> We might be otherwise—we might be all
> We dream of happy, high, majestical.
> Where is the love, beauty, and truth we seek
> But in our minds? and if we were not weak
> Should we be less in deed than in desire?"
> "Ay, if we were not weak—and we aspire
> How vainly! to be strong," said Maddalo:
> "You talk Utopia."

It was that same endless debate of theirs, with Shelley believing that things are dependent on man, that a man's life is of his own making, and Byron urging that evil is an external reality against which all human effort must shatter itself. Calvinism versus radicalism.

During a second trip to Venice the Shelleys saw the Fornarina at Byron's. Their judgment was sternly adverse. Shelley could not, like Byron, admire a fine animal; he respected love too highly to endure the sight of its degradation into sensuality. Mary Shelley, of course, was even more merciless. From the very first day, on the shores of the Lake of Geneva, she had been horrified by Byron's attitude towards women, and there was scorn in the thin smiling lips of her face, with its frame of long brown ringlets. Nothing is more secret or more uneasy than the feelings of the honest woman towards Don Juan. It may be that when Mr. and Mrs. Shelley tossed their heads on leaving the Palazzo Mocenigo, there was the faintest hint of complacence, and of that vague envy which rebels can inspire. But facts soon justified them. The weakness of the epicurean idea lies in its assumption that man, unhampered by spiritual checks, is capable of moderation in his pleasures. By the autumn Byron's health had again broken down. Under doctor's orders he showed his mistress the door: not without difficulty, for she first of all stabbed herself, as Caroline Lamb had done, and next flung herself into the canal, whence she was fished out by the gondoliers.

During December Hanson came to Venice accompanied by his son, to obtain his client's signature for the sale of Newstead. He found Byron in sorry plight. Amazed to be gliding along between the rose-flushed palaces, the two attorneys from the distant island arrived in a gondola, laden with papers and parchments, tooth-brushes and red powder. They climbed the steps of the Palazzo Mocenigo, flanked by dogs and birds, a fox and a caged wolf, and then, passing up a staircase of marble, were led to Byron's apartment. "Well, Hanson!" said Byron, "I did not think you would have ventured so far!" His eyes were wet with tears. "In common with all poets . . . a strong burst of deep feeling"—was young Hanson's astonished comment. Byron asked innumerable questions about London and about his friends, biting his nails the while—a trick he had kept from boyhood.

Money matters were going well for him. The Abbey had been sold for ninety thousand guineas. A sum of £12,000 would be needed to pay the money-lenders; Lady Byron had the settlement money, amounting to £66,000, and Hanson himself brought a note of his own fees, totalling £12,000. Thus there remained no ready money, but the interest on Lady Byron's settlement brought Byron an annual revenue of £3,300. Adding to that his income from his poems (and since 1816 he had received over £7,000 from John Murray), he was one of the richest men in Italy. He was glad of that, he told Kinnaird, "for money is power and pleasure, and I like it vastly."

White hairs were creeping into his rich brown locks. His face was pale, bloated, and sallow, and his hands swollen with fat.

XXX

CAVALIERE SERVENTE

1819

Men are often more happy than they would wish.

ALAIN

ONCE again spring chased forth the fevers from Venice. The faintly stirring waters of the Grand Canal lapped against the blue and white spirals of those mooring-posts. Fletcher was getting stout. Two new bulldogs had been added to the menagerie, and in the treasure chest the gold sequins were heaped higher than ever. Already the heart of the Sentimentalist was fluttering, seeking whereon it might perch. Byron was tempted by one Venetian maiden, and fell into the canal whilst trying to scale her windows. The family, one of the high nobility, sent a priest and an officer of police to call upon him; he offered them both coffee; everything was straightened out. The young lady, for her own part, was eager that he should repudiate his mathematician. Did she want him to poison her? asked Byron. She was silent. He paused in wonder at the passions of these lands of sunshine, and turned back into the world of fashion, in quest of a prey.

At the Benzoni *conversazione* a certain Countess Guiccioli was presented to him. She was very young, with Titian hair, beautiful teeth, and large ringlets; her legs were rather short, her bosom was perfection. For a year past she had been married to a gentleman in his sixties, and Byron remembered having met her once before, only three days after the marriage. She had not seemed to take any notice of him on that occasion; it was customary for a young wife to wait for a year before taking a *cicisbeo*. But her second encounter left her instantly vanquished. "I was more fatigued than usual that evening," she wrote, "and went with great reluctance to this party, and purely in obedience to Count Guiccioli. . . . Lord Byron's noble and exquisitely beautiful countenance, the tone of his voice, his manners, the thousand enchantments that surrounded him, rendered him so different and so superior a being to any whom I had hitherto seen, that it was impossible he should not have left the most profound impression on me."

As Byron left the Countess Benzoni's drawing-room he slipped a piece of paper into Teresa Guiccioli's hand. It was a rendezvous. She kept it, and from that moment they met every day.

She regarded herself as free. In that field the unwritten laws of marriage were clearly defined. A girl was confined to a convent until the age of sixteen; a rich husband was then sought for her, the older the better, and the young lady saw her betrothed occasionally in the convent parlour. She was overjoyed to gain her liberty at the price of her body; no question of love entered on either side. Count Guiccioli was sixty when he married Teresa, who was sixteen. From the first they had occupied separate rooms, and she had not ceased to address him as "Sir." He was quite a pleasant old man, although reported to have poisoned his first wife and to have been the murderer of Manzoni. A man of culture, and a friend of the poet Alfieri, he was something of an intriguer, and was the wealthiest landowner in Romagna.

But an elderly man, however cultured, could not suffice this young woman. "Love," observed Byron, "is not the same dull, cold, calculating feeling here as in the North. It is the business, the serious occupation of their lives; it is a want, a necessity. Somebody properly defines a woman, 'a creature that loves.' They die of love; particularly the Romans; they begin to love earlier, and feel the passion later than the Northern people." The young Countess had completed her novitiate of fidelity; the husband was trustfully relaxing his vigilance; the time was ripe for taking a lover.

In more ways than one the affair recalled that of Caroline Lamb. The Guicciolis were of older nobility than the Melbournes; Teresa, a finer beauty than the Englishwoman, showed the same violence of feeling and the same scorn for public opinion. She had been well brought up, spoke French as well as Italian, had read widely, recited poetry, quoted the Latin historians, and painted pictures—all rather childishly, but in quite a pleasing way. At first she insisted on a platonic mode, not withholding the fullest hopes, but only seeking safeguards.

Loyal to the amorous code of her society, she was in search of no fleeting adventure, but of a *cavaliere servente.* It was a serious problem for a young woman. One could take a husband in a moment; but to pick a lover needed thought. Before long her husband would be taking her away to Ravenna and Bologna, where he owned estates. Would Byron follow her? A *cavaliere servente* would have to follow. Don Juan was rather embarrassed, and wrote to Hobhouse: "I have hopes, sir—hopes, but she wants me to come to Ravenna, and then to Bologna. Now this would be all very well for certainties; but for mere hopes; if she should plant me, and I should make a 'fiasco,' never could I show my face on the Piazza. It is nothing that money can do, for the Conte is awfully rich, and would be so even in England. . . . She is pretty, but has no tact; answers aloud when she should whisper—talks of age to ladies who want to pass for young; and this blessed night horrified a correct company at the Benzoni's by calling out to me *'mio Byron'* in an audible key, during a dead silence of pause in the other prattlers, who stared and whispered their respective *serventi.* One of her preliminaries is that I must never leave Italy. I have no desire to leave it, but I should not like to be frittered down into a regular Cicisbeo. . . ."

A few days before her departure for Ravenna, she became his mistress. So proud was she of the fact that she proclaimed it openly in all the *conversazioni,* which electrified the Benzoni and Albrizzi salons for a few nights, and was rather embarrassing for Count Guiccioli, a man of modest feelings. Fortunately the couple had to leave Venice for the whole of the summer, and the Count took his wife away with him, leaving Byron once again truly in love, tender, melancholy and cynical—and delighted to be so.

Hardly had she arrived at Ravenna when she had a miscarriage. During the journey she had written to him every day. She adored him, and now that she was ill, begged him to come to her. He hesitated, rather mistrustfully, wondering whose child this could have been. . . . Not his, for certain. The Count's? It was possible. She promised that if Byron came she would receive him in her own house; and notwithstanding all

TERESA, COUNTESS GUICCIOLI

After a Sketch by Count D'Orsay, October 17, 1839

his experience of women and women's follies, he was taken aback by this boldness: "Now to go to cuckold a Papal Count . . . in his own house is rather too much for my modesty, when there are several other places at least as good for the purpose. . . . The Charmer forgets that a man may be whistled anywhere *before,* but that *after*. . . . She should have been less liberal in Venice, or less exigent at Ravenna."

But if Byron was skilled in rousing female will-power, he was less skilled in withstanding it. He had already started for Ravenna. The weather was hot, the roads dusty. "If I was not the most constant of men," he said, "I should now be swimming from the Lido, instead of smoking in the dust of Padua." Yes, but he *was* the most constant of men; and grumbling in a mixture of annoyance and contentment, he cast his eye on the women of Bologna, admired the scarlet stockings of the Cardinal-Legate, and was especially delighted by the simplicity of two epitaphs which he discovered in the graveyard of the Certosa at Ferrara.

Ravenna was bound to please him, a mysterious little town wrapping the relics of a barbarian empire amid the folds of her cool, narrow streets. Here Francesca had lived, hither Dante had been exiled. A few yards from the inn the poet's remains lay beneath a commonplace cupola. For riding, there was a great pine forest stretching right down to the seashore, clothing ground that once had been covered by the sea, where the Roman fleets had lain at anchor. It was the Pineta of Boccaccio, the "immemorial wood" of Ravenna, where the hounds of the phantom huntsman for ever chased the lady who had scorned love. And Byron could appreciate this solitude of woods and sea, quivering with the whirr of the cicada.

His advent had made a stir in the town. The Count called on him at the inn, and very politely invited him to pay a visit to his wife; his lordship could perhaps divert her thoughts from a trouble which seemed, alas, to be serious. The Palazzo Guiccioli was a large grey house situated a few hundred yards from the inn. Byron went, and was captured. Nothing could bind him more firmly to a woman than her weakness. Teresa was in bed, coughing, and spitting blood. He installed himself at her bedside and became the most attentive of nurses. But he was a trifle anxious, always expecting a stiletto in his throat at the hands of one of the Count's *sbirri*. But what matter? Death was bound to come one day or another, and it would not have been distasteful to die for Teresa. He was enslaved—and happy. When he left Venice, Mrs. Hoppner had predicted to him that he was once again about to fall under a woman's dominion. He had a taste for prophecies; and this one was fulfilled.

His only fear was lest Teresa should die. "I greatly fear that the Guiccioli is going into a consumption. . . . Thus it is with every thing and every body for whom I feel anything like a real attachment:—'War, death, or discord, doth lay siege to them.' " And again: "If anything happens to my present *Amica,* I have done with the passion for ever—it is my *last* love. As to libertinism, I have sickened myself of that, as was natural in the way I went on, and I have at least derived that advantage from vice, to *love* in the better sense of the word. *This* will be my last adventure. . . ." He summoned his friend Professor Aglietti from Venice, to examine the Countess's lungs. The professor ordered a continuance of the treatment. The treatment was Byron's visits. And, as the Countess afterwards wrote, the inexpressible joy which she found in Lord Byron's company was so beneficial to her health that she again became, in fact, capable of being his mistress. This took place in the *palazzo* itself, a maid, a negro boy, and a woman friend all lending their complicity. It was bold, but dangerous, for the Count found a drawn bolt—and was astonished.

But Count Guiccioli was a man of mystery. In spite of this incident he continued to pay the most courteous visits to Byron, and went out driving in a superb coach-and-six. The inhabitants of Ravenna passed ironic, not to say scornful, remarks on this friendship: the Count was the richest man in Romagna, but not the most popular.

But a fig for the Count! Byron had brought his own horses and rode in the forest daily. He saw his lady at all hours, suitable and unsuitable. He gladly welcomed days which, all in all, were pleasant, and had no mind to think of the future. When the Signora Guiccioli was feeling better, she had a pony saddled and came out riding with him, wearing a sky-blue habit and a hat like Mr. Punch's. She was artless and pious, and she taught Byron to stop and say a prayer when the bells of the old basilicas rang out the hour of the Angelus—

> Ave Maria! blessed be the hour,
> The time, the clime, the spot, where I so oft
> Have felt that moment in its fullest power
> Sink o'er the earth so beautiful and soft,
> While swung the deep bell in the distant tower,
> Or the faint dying day-hymn stole aloft,
> And not a breath crept through the rosy air,
> And yet the forest leaves seem'd stirr'd with prayer.

He liked having a mistress who was a Catholic and a believer. Sir Walter Scott had been right when he divined affinities between the needs of Byron's soul and the ceremonies of the Church of Rome. He had his daughter Allegra reared as a Catholic. When Teresa stood silent and motionless at the sound of the Angelus, he himself stood listening with religious happiness to the song of the Pineta's cicadas all around, to all the soft stirrings of the Romagna countryside. When the Countess Guiccioli became acquainted with the *Lament of Tasso,* written at Ferrara, she commanded a poem on the exile of Ravenna; and Byron, the submissive lover, composed the *Prophecy of Dante.* After finishing it he made a pilgrimage with his mistress to the tomb of the great Florentine. The Countess went in black, Byron in a broidered uniform. They entered the chapel, and Byron deposited one of his books and stood with folded arms, gazing fixedly on the tomb while his lover knelt in prayer.

He was growing attached to her. She was an honourable conquest, the Countess Gamba by birth, pretty and very amorous, no fool—or such at least was Byron's opinion—and even quite well-informed for a girl scarcely out of the convent. Perhaps he might have judged her more severely if she had not been a foreigner; for there is always a pleasure of the exotic which makes even platitudes seem delightful in an unfamiliar tongue. As a matter of fact she knew hardly any English, and did not grasp a word of his poetry. But in her eyes he was the Poet, the man of love. She had fashioned a heroic image of him, and this image she loved. Refusing to regard him as a cynic, she would have him chivalrous, fond, unreal—everything that women have always wished their lovers to be. And he played up to this, with some fear of looking ridiculous, it is true, but also with a certain pleasure: because, really, the Countess Guiccioli's Byron was rather like that other Byron of Harrow and Newstead, the Byron whom he himself had loved long ago. He was prepared even for long-enduring follies. "If you see my spouse," he wrote to Augusta, "do pray tell her I wish to marry again, and as probably she may wish the same, is there no way in *Scotland,* without compromising her immaculacy?" But if deceiving her husband seemed to Teresa a duty, leaving him would have seemed a crime.

At last the Guicciolis left for Bologna, as the Count had to continue the tour of his domains. The well-drilled Byron followed them next day, and picked up the threads of the same life at Bologna. There he rented an apartment in a *palazzo,* and had Allegra fetched from Venice to keep him company. The child amused him. She spoke a comical Italian: *"Bon di, Papa!"* she would say. And she was a real Byron, with Augusta's inability to pronounce the letter "r," pouting like Byron and his sister, with a dimple in her chin, the eyebrows usually drawn into a little frown, a very white skin, a soft voice, a curious love of music, and in everything a will of iron. It was amusing to watch a new plant of this curious genus growing so close to one. Byron played with her. He rode on horseback, strolled in the garden beneath a purple canopy of ripening grapes, sat beside the fountain, talked with the gardener, and then went to gossip with the gravedigger at the Campo Santo, whose daughter was the prettiest girl in Bologna. "I amuse myself with contrasting her beautiful and innocent face of fifteen with the skulls with which he has peopled several cells, and particularly with that of one skull dated 1766, which was once covered (the tradition goes) by the most lovely features of Bologna—noble and rich. When I look at these, and at this girl—when I think of what *they were*, and what *she* must be—why, then, my dear Murray, I won't shock you by saying what I think. It is little matter what becomes of us 'bearded men,' but I don't like the notion of a beautiful woman's lasting less than a beautiful tree—than her own picture—her own shadow, which won't change so to the Sun as her face to the mirror."

Melancholy thoughts, but he *was* melancholy. . . . Bologna after Ravenna. . . . He was beginning to tire of this profession of *cavaliere servente*. If, as he said, he spent his days "viciously and agreeably," he had a growing sense of the vanity of this life. It was no fault of Teresa's. She was young, amiable and faithful, but he had a bitter awareness that a man ought not to use up his days at the knees of a woman and a foreigner. . . . He was thirty-one, and what was he doing? Making love? Making a third Canto for *Don Juan?* "Alas! I have been but idle, and have the prospect of an early decay, without having seized every available instant of our pleasurable years. . . ." Action . . . action . . . action. . . . But how?—what?—where? Should he busy himself in England with the Reform agitation? In that country which had driven him forth he counted for nothing. He wanted to make one last journey thither, in the spring, and then go and live in South America. He clipped from newspapers the offers made by the government of Venezuela to foreigners desirous of settling there; and Bolivar, the liberator, was one of his heroes.

"I assure you that I am very *serious* in the idea, and that the notion has been about me for a long time, as you will see by the advertisement.—I should go there with my natural daughter, Allegra,—now nearly three years old and with me here,—and pitch my tent for good and all. I am not tired of Italy, but a man must be a Cicisbeo and a singer in duets, and a connoisseur of operas—or nothing—here. I have made some progress in all these accomplishments, but I can't say that I don't feel the degradation. Better be an unskilful Planter, an awkward settler,—better be a hunter, or anything, than a flatterer of fiddlers, a fan-carrier of a woman. I like women—God he knows—but the more their system here developes upon me, the worse it seems, after Turkey too; here the polygamy is all on the female side. I have been an intriguer, a husband, a whoremonger, and now I am a *Cavalier Servente*—by the holy! It is a strange sensation. . . . I want a country, and a home, and—if possible—a free one. I am not yet thirty-two years of age. I might still be a decent Citizen, and found a house, and a family as good—or better—than the former. . . . There is no freedom in Europe—that's certain; it is besides a worn-out portion of the globe. . . ."

Hobhouse was told of these projects by Murray, but was not inclined to take him seriously. "Our poet is too good for a planter. . . . It is the wildest of all his meditations—pray tell him. . . . No toothbrushes, no *Quarterly* Reviews. In short, plenty of all he abominates, and nothing of all he loves." Hobhouse liked Byron, but he treated him like a child. He was exasperating.

Seeking distraction in a simulacrum of action, Byron had become a member of the Società Romantica, a small group of Italian friends of liberty, and his presence at Bologna was a source of much inquietude to the spies of the "paternal" government of the Papal States. There were countless reports from the head of the police in

Bologna to the chief commissioner of police in Rome. They contained records of the unusual friendship between Count Guiccioli and Lord Byron, a person who was "not unknown as a man of letters, and in his own country has the reputation of being a fine poet. . . . This gentleman is especially dangerous because his abilities and abundant wealth enable him to assemble at his house persons of the most cultured class." "He never leaves the house, but is always writing," noted the police, suspiciously; and one secret agent added: "you deceive yourself if you believe that he is occupied only in putting horns on Guiccioli's head. He is libidinous and immoral to excess . . . but at the same time, in politics he is not so inconstant. Here he is an Englishman in the fullest sense of the term. . . ."

As the end of August approached, the Guicciolis left him for a few days alone with Allegra, and in their absence he took close measure of the emptiness of his life. He wandered sadly in their garden, where he found a copy of Madame de Staël's *Corinne* on a table, and on its last page he wrote these words: "My dear Teresa—I have read this book in your garden;—my love, you were absent, or I could not have read it. It is a favourite book of yours, and the writer was a friend of mine. You will not understand these English words, and *others* will not understand them—which is the reason I have not scrawled them in Italian. But you will recognise the handwriting of him who passionately loved you, and you will divine that, over a book which was yours, he could only think of love. In that word, beautiful in all languages, but most so in yours—*Amor mio*—is comprised my existence here and hereafter. I feel I exist here, and I fear that I shall exist hereafter,—to *what* purpose you will decide; my destiny rests with you, and you are a woman, seventeen years of age, and two out of a convent. I wish that you had stayed there with all my heart,—or, at least, that I had never met you in your married state. But all this is too late. I love you, and you love me,—at least you *say so,* and act as if you *did* so, which last is a great consolation in all events. But *I* more than love you, and cannot cease to love you. Think of me sometimes, when the Alps and the ocean divide us, but they never will, unless *you wish* it."—She had only been away for three days; but that had been enough to make him feel "Carolinish" about her.

When the Guiccioli household returned to Bologna, the Count had word that his presence was again required in Ravenna. The Countess told her husband that her state of health now called for a breath of Venetian air, and that if he himself could not follow her there, Lord Byron would gladly act as her escort. Count Guiccioli consented, and the two lovers left Bologna together on September 15, 1819. It was a happy journey. On her arrival in Venice, the doctors prescribed country air for the Countess, and Lord Byron, who still kept his villa at La Mira, was kind enough to place it at her disposal, and to come and join her under its roof.

Just as in Marianna Segati's time, the dark-tinted waters of the Brenta mirrored the loveliest of sunsets. But the evenings dragged. At Ravenna, the novelty, the amusement of a foreign tongue, the fear of being surprised, had all made the days pass quickly. But solitude will rob people of any adventitious glamour, and a young woman of seventeen soon exhausts her fund of knowledge. "What you say," wrote Byron to Hoppner, "reminds me of what Curran said to Moore—'So—I hear—you have married a very pretty woman—and a very good creature too—an excellent creature—pray—um—*how do you pass your evenings?*' It is a devil of a question that, and perhaps as easy to answer with a wife as a mistress; but surely they are longer than the nights. I am all for morality now, and shall confine myself henceforward to the strictest adultery, which you will please recollect is all that virtuous wife of mine has left me." But adultery, like marriage in days gone by, sometimes left him yawning.

Luckily he had a visit from Tom Moore, who was making a tour with Lord John Russell and arrived, alone, at La Mira on October 8. Byron was in his bath, and Moore was received by his old friend Fletcher. At last Byron appeared, overjoyed to see a friend of his young days. He was cordial and gay, but looked so much older that Moore was taken aback. He had lost that "spiritualised look" which had been so noticeable in the old days. He wore side-whiskers because Teresa had told him he had a musician's head, and had let his hair grow long at the back, which helped to give him a foreign appearance. Handsome he still was; but his face seemed to have taken the same path as his poetry, and now expressed the humour and wisdom of Don Juan rather than the sombre romanticism of Manfred or Childe Harold. He offered Moore hospitality at the Palazzo Mocenigo, and to take him over to Venice immediately; but first he introduced him to the Countess Guiccioli, whom Moore found both pleasant and intelligent. The gondolier Tita, with his rich livery and prodigious mustachios, sat on the box of the carriage, and at Fusina ferried the two friends across the lagoon.

Moore was moved by the sight of Venice, Byron by the

sight of Moore. All the incidents of London life, gay or ridiculous, were recalled—the roystering evenings at Kinnaird's, the brandy, the Irish songs. . . . Byron was like a child finding another child to play with. And then they reached the steps of the Palazzo Mocenigo. "Keep clear of the dog!" called Byron; and a few paces farther on, "Take care, or that monkey will bite you!"—and then kicked open a door (the key had been mislaid), saying to Moore: "These are the rooms I use myself; and here I mean to establish you." During the whole of Moore's stay in Venice, Byron spent his days with him, and only went back to La Mira at night to keep his *amica* company. The Venetians implored Moore to persuade Byron into moral courses, for he was outraging the local code by actually living with his mistress. "You must really scold your friend," said the Countess Benzoni. "He conducted himself *so* well, until this unfortunate affair!"

For Byron, Moore's stay was a time of holiday. On the last evening, coming over from La Mira to dine, he told Moore with the glee of a schoolboy who has been given a holiday, that the Countess had "given him leave to make a night of it," and that not only would he go to the opera, but also take supper, as in the good old days. After the opera they went and drank brandy-punch on the Square of St. Mark's, and sat on until the bronze figures of the great clock hammered forth their two strokes after midnight; and then, in the moonlight, Byron and Moore walked together through Venice. The scene was one of solemn beauty. This silent city of palaces, asleep upon the waters in the gleaming calm of the night, touched Moore profoundly, and Byron himself passed from hilarity into a gentle, peaceful sadness.

Next day Moore went to take leave of his friend at

La Mira. Byron came in carrying a small white leather bag. "Look here," he said, "this would be worth something to Murray, though *you,* I dare say, would not give sixpence for it." "What is it," asked Moore. "My life and adventures," said Byron. "It is not a thing that can be published during my lifetime, but you may have it—if you like—there, do whatever you please with it." Moore thanked him warmly, adding: "This will make a nice legacy for my little Tom, who shall astonish the latter days of the nineteenth century with it. . . ." When the time came for Moore to go, Byron ordered his horses and accompanied Moore's carriage for some distance into the country.

His domestic affairs were going none too well. Up to the present Count Guiccioli had seemed not perhaps to be blind to, but at least to connive at, his wife's liaison. But in November 1819, the Count intercepted a letter from Teresa's father, counselling prudence to his daughter, and arrived in Venice in high dudgeon. Then he found his wife in excellent health, and hating him so cordially that they had a violent quarrel. This time he gave her the choice—husband or lover, but not both. She chose "lover," and begged Byron to flee with her. "The lady was for leaving him, and eloping or separating; and so should I, had I been twenty, instead of thirty and one years of age, for I loved her; but I knew the event would for her be irreparable, and that all her family—her sisters particularly and father—would be plunged into despair for the reputation of the rest of the girls; so I prevailed upon her, with great difficulty, to return to Ravenna with her husband, who promised forgetfulness, if she would give me up." Count Guiccioli, his tears overflowing, came in person to talk to Byron. "If you abandon your wife," he told the Count, "I will take her undoubtedly; it is my duty, it is also my inclination in case of such extremity; but if as you say, you are really disposed to live with, and like her as before, I will not only not carry further disturbance into your family, but even repass the Alps; for I have no hesitation in saying that Italy will be now to me insupportable."

He was touched by Teresa's grief. "I pray of you, I implore you," he wrote to her, "to be comforted, and to believe that I cannot cease to love you but with my life. . . . I am going away in order to save you, and leaving a country which has grown insufferable to me without yourself. . . ." He was determined to stay in Italy no longer. He would go first to England, and then (who could tell?) to France, to America, to the United States, to Venezuela. He would take Allegra, the only creature left to him. Passing through England, he would see Augusta and try to find out what had happened to that incomprehensible woman.

He had written to her: "My dearest Love—I have been negligent in not writing, but what can I say? Three years' absence—the total change of scene and habit make such a differcncc—that we have now nothing in common but our affections—our relationship.—But I have never ceased nor can cease to feel for a moment that perfect boundless attachment which bound and binds me to you—which renders me utterly incapable of *real* love for any other human being—for what could they be to me after *you?* My own X X X X we may have been very wrong—but repent of nothing except that cursed marriage—and your refusing to continue to love me as you had loved me—I can neither forget nor *quite forgive* you for that precious piece of reformation. . . . It is heartbreaking to think of our long Separation—and I am sure more than punishment enough for all our sins—Dante is more humane in his 'Hell' for he places his unfortunate lovers (Francesca of Rimini and Paolo whose case fell a good deal short of *ours*—though sufficiently naughty) in company—and though they suffer—it is at least together. . . . When you write to me speak to me of yourself—and say that you love me—never mind commonplace people and topics—which can be in no degree interesting—to me who see nothing in England but the country which holds *you*—or around it but the sea which divides us.—They say absence destroys weak passions—and confirms strong ones—Alas! *mine* for you is the union of all passions and of all affections. . . ." [1]

During the two weeks that followed Teresa's departure, his mind was made up to leave Italy. Moore's visit had made him home-sick for England and for his friends; even the details of everyday life filled him with a yearning for the familiar soil. He would go and have his teeth seen to by Mr. Waite—they needed attention badly; he would buy toothbrushes, soda, magnesia—all the things which he kept vainly asking for in his letters

[1] The authenticity of this letter—an admirable one—has never been disputed. Its destination has been questioned, and it has been maintained that the letter was not addressed to Augusta. This theory seems to me indefensible, for the phrase "precious piece of reformation" is repeated and commented upon in a letter of June 27, 1819, from Lady Byron to Mrs. Leigh: "this letter is an ample testimony of . . . the prior 'reformation' which was sufficiently evidenced to *me* by your own assertion and the agreement of circumstances with it." The whole of this letter can be read in *Astarte* (page 85). It proves (*a*) that Lady Byron regarded Byron's letter as having been written to Augusta; (*b*) that Augusta herself admitted this, and communicated the letter to Lady Byron as having been addressed to herself. The letters of Augusta preceding and following this one should particularly be read. For a fuller discussion, *vide The Byron Mystery,* by Sir John Fox, pp. 137 *et seq.*

and were never sent. But then everything seemed to conspire against this journey. He had a fresh bout of his fever, which Allegra caught, then the nurse, a gondolier, a domestic servant. Through the Palazzo Mocenigo he wandered in solitary gloom, turned now into a child's sick-nurse. One day he thought of postponing the trip until the spring, next day until the Greek calends. Scant encouragement came from England. Augusta was in a quandary. Lady Byron commanded her not to see her brother again; but Augusta knew that if he did come back she would not have the courage to close her door against him, and did not want to have to face the temptation. "I fear the return is but too decidedly and certainly intended," she wrote to John Murray. "Let him *come* and *go* (if possible) like other people! or else he may share the fate of his odious DON. . . ." And strings of exclamation marks emphasised her fears.

From Ravenna, on the other hand, Teresa was beckoning. She had straightened everything out—heaven alone knew how! Ill again, she could only recover if Byron were with her; her father had talked to her husband; her husband had given his consent. She was awaiting her Byron. But the day appointed for the departure for England had arrived, and the baggage-laden gondola was swaying on the waves of the Grand Canal in front of the Palazzo Mocenigo. Byron was ready—he had put on his gloves; Allegra had embarked; they were only waiting for himself and his armoury. And at that moment he declared that if one o'clock struck before his swords and pistols were in the gondola, he would not leave. The hour struck, and Byron stayed. He wrote to Teresa Guiccioli: "Love has gained the victory. I could not summon up resolution enough to leave the country where you are, without at least once more seeing you. . . . I am a citizen of the world—all countries are alike to me. You have ever been, since our first acquaintance, *the sole object of my thoughts*. My opinion was, that the best course I could adopt, both for your peace and for that of all your family, would have been to depart and go far, *far* away from you. . . . You have however decided that I am to return to Ravenna. I shall accordingly return—and shall *do*—and *be* all that you wish. I cannot say more."

XXXI

ARSENAL IN THE PALAZZO GUICCIOLI

1819–1821

> Italia! oh Italia! thou who hast
> The fatal gift of beauty. . . .
>
> Byron

He was glad to see his peaceful Ravenna again, Ravenna with its narrow streets and mysterious palaces, the basilicas with their tiled roofs, the lines of the countryside stretching away into infinity, and that glorious forest, so dense and so living. Snow lay a foot deep in the streets. Teresa welcomed him with the simple joyousness of a sick child whose parents have allowed the visit of a cherished playmate to help its convalescence. The Count was reserved, but not hostile. The Gambas, hitherto seeming to disapprove of the liaison, now treated Byron as one of the family; and Count Pietro Gamba in particular, Teresa's brother, an ardent and lighthearted youth, showed every sign of friendliness. The *cicisbeo* was looked upon as a brother-in-law.

Byron had taken rooms at the Albergo Imperiale, an inn with nothing imperial about it save the name. Would he be staying a day—a week—a year? He knew not. . . . The ordering of his life lay with Destiny. He had come because a woman had summoned him, and he would go if his going became desirable. His attachment had neither the violence of the early days of a passion, nor the metriculous strictness of a rupture. He let himself drift, dropping the tiller, down the lazy, caressing currents of La Guiccioli's whims.

Allegra was with him, in the care of her nurse and surrounded by masses of toys which the Hoppners had brought her on the day of the departure. It was rather troublesome to live at the inn with a child, and Byron would have preferred an apartment. He had begun to look for one when Count Guiccioli offered to let him rent an empty floor of his palazzo. It was a surprising, but useful, offer; Byron sent for his furniture from Venice, and once again settled under the same roof as his mistress. Really, this husband was a ticklish man to understand.

As for the Countess, all her pride was in her fine English lover, and her keenest desire seemed to be to show him off as much as she could. From the very first week, she made him don an embroidered uniform, and she dragged him, sword at his side, to a ball at her uncle's, the Marquis Cavalli. She wanted to make her entrance on the poet's arm. With recollections of Lady Jersey's party, Byron dreaded some outburst, but the Marquis, the Papal Vice-Legate, "and all the other vices," were as courteous as possible. Byron was delighted by the beauty, the intelligence, and the diamonds of the ladies of Ravenna, and a trifle alarmed by the scandal. It was all crazy, but it was agreeable—the devil take England and its morality! He fancied he was beginning to understand the code of this country, where the commandments, in essence, were transformed into—"Thou shalt commit adultery. . . . Thou shalt covet thy neighbour's wife. . . ." But one must covet *only* her, and she, forsooth, will be as jealous as a fury, insistent on a lover's fidelity as on a debt of honour. "You hear a person's character, male or female, canvassed, not as depending on their conduct to their husbands or wives, but to their mistress or lover." The *cavaliere servente* had to treat the husband with great respect; a stranger's first impression always was that they were kinsmen. The danger was that a *relazione* or *amicizia* lasted from five to fifteen years, after which a widowhood generally turned it in the end into a *sposalizio*. A man was reduced to the rôle of a trinket in a woman's life. Romance was triumphant . . . but at what a price! Occasionally Byron railed at himself, with a biting humour—"I am drilling very hard to learn how to double a shawl, and should succeed to admiration if I did not always double it the wrong side out. . . ." It was a sorry end for a man who, in his day, had dreamed of glory and heroic deeds. He would have lost all his self-respect in this Guicciolian bed of roses had it not just then happened, in the nick of time, that Italian politics offered him a chance of danger.

For some months he had been dabbling in the current of Italian politics; and for the freedom of Italy he was ready to give his life, chiefly because he loved Italy and lived freedom, and in some measure because he did not love life. At Bologna he had become a member of the Società Romantica, and by now was fully initiated as a Carbonaro. Nay more, his prestige as a great English nobleman, and, as a foreigner, his comparative immunity from police interference, led to his recognition by the Carbonari as leader of their Ravenna group, the *Americani*.

It was the year 1820, and Europe, stunned at first by the bludgeon of the Holy Alliance, was beginning to recover consciousness. Spain, by a revolution which had only needed "six years of patience and one day of explanations," had just won a constitution, and her example was an incitement to the subjects of the Pope, of the King of Naples, and of Metternich. At Naples, a few score of soldiers shouting "Long live King and Constitution!" had sufficed to terrify the King, and on July 6, 1820, he had signed a proclamation granting a constitutional government. At Ravenna the walls of the town were everywhere scrawled with "Long live the Republic! Down with the Pope!" The Cardinal of Ravenna turned pale beneath his purple. The carbineers complained of the livery of Byron's servants, who wore military epaulettes; Byron retorted that this livery had been that of his family since the year 1066, and ordered his men to fire if they were attacked. The children in the Ravenna streets screamed "Long live Liberty!"—and when Byron rode out into the Pineta he met the Americani drilling and singing—"Soldiers of liberty are we. . . ." They acclaimed him as he passed, and he returned their salute as he rode on. This, he noted, showed the spirit of Italy of the day; and writing to all his friends bidding them send him swords and gunpowder, he organised an arsenal of a hundred and fifty guns at the Palazzo Guiccioli. All of which needed courage, for anonymous letters advised him to drop his rides and to beware of the police of the *Buon Governo*.

Count Guiccioli was a man of wealth, and being therefore vulnerable, was prudently respectful of established authority, whatever its form. He was beginning to think his wife's lover a man of deplorable breeding. Whoever heard of a *cavaliere servente* piling up firearms in his bedroom and compromising a respectable house? He had leased this foreigner a floor of his palace, and he let him go out with his wife; Byron's ingratitude struck him as abominable. There was nothing but conspirators in his house now, conspirators all the time. Every drawer was crammed with explosive proclamations. The Government had seized the translation of *Childe Harold,* and people were quoting Byron's poem on Dante as a hymn of revolution. In a secret report to the Austrian police the Governor of Rome described Count Guiccioli as "well known to be one of the fiercest disturbers of the public peace, and closely allied [*strettamente legato*] with the said Lord Byron. . . ." "*Strettamente legato*" was good!

Once again the Count ordered his wife to choose between himself and Byron. She was indignant. Choose? Who had ever obliged a woman to choose? Byron implored Teresa to be prudent; the Count might ask for a separation, and the status of a wife in that plight was difficult in Romagna, where the ecclesiastical authorities did not allow a woman parted from her husband to live with her lover. But the subtle moral reflections of Don Juan were all in vain. Teresa was obdurate. "I will stay with him," she answered her husband, "if he will let you remain with me. It is hard that I should be the only woman in Romagna who is not to have her *amico*. . . ."

The whole of Ravenna sided with the lovers: the Gamba family because they hated Guiccioli, the people and the women because, as Byron said, they always take the side of those in the wrong, and also because he was adored by the poor folk of the city. He was always helping the poor in the district, giving money to the old crones he met carrying faggots on the Pineta road, giving to churches, giving to monasteries. If an organ was damaged, it was Byron who paid for its mending; if a campanile must be restored, it was Byron who offered it to the town. Besides, it was well known that he favoured a free Italy. Public opinion awarded him his case.

Comedy broke in when a separation was eventually asked for, not by the Count, but by the Gambas, on grounds of grave insult, and when Guiccioli, for his part, opposed it, so as to avoid refunding the dowry. The suit came before the pontifical courts and occasioned much talk; it was the first case of its kind in the Ravenna courts for two hundred years. The advocates refused to plead for Guiccioli, saying that he was either a fool or a knave—a fool, if he took eighteen months to notice an unconcealed liaison, a knave if he put up with it. The upshot of it was that in July the Pope pronounced a separation. The Countess was to live under the roof of her father Count Gamba, and Byron was only to see her under very restricted conditions. He had offered to make her an allowance, but the decree laid it down that Count Guiccioli ought to provide for his wife's needs, and Teresa was perfectly disinterested.

In days gone by, Lord Byron had denounced and affronted those mist-wreathed goddesses, the British Conventions; and now, by order of the pontifical court, he was becoming a victim of their sisters. The Countess Guiccioli was of good birth, and through Byron's fault (in so far as, in such adventures, it is ever the man's fault) she had lost a husband. He held himself in honour bound to marry her, if circumstances allowed him, just as formerly he had regarded himself bound to Caroline Lamb.

He wrote to Augusta: "This is positively the last time of performance (as the playbills say), or of getting into such scrapes for the future. Indeed—I have had my share. But this is a finisher; for you know when a woman is separated from her husband for her *Amant,* he is bound both by honour (and inclination—at least I am), to live with her all his days; as long as there is no misconduct.

"So you see that I have closed as papa *begun,* and you will probably never see me again as long as you live. Indeed you don't deserve it—for having behaved so *coldly—when I was ready to have sacrificed everything for you.*— It is nearly three years that this 'liaison' has lasted. I was dreadfully in love—and she blindly so—for she sacrificed everything to this headlong passion. That comes of being romantic. I can say that, without being so *furiously* in love as at first, I am more attached to her than I thought possible to be to any woman after three years—(except one and who *was she* can you *guess?*) . . . If Lady Byron would but please to die, and the Countess Guiccioli's husband (for Catholics can't marry, though divorced), we should probably have to marry—though I would rather *not*—thinking it the way to hate each other—for all people whatsoever. . . .

"PS.—*You* ought to be a great admirer of the *future* Lady Byron for three reasons, Firstly she is a grand patroness of the present Lady Byron, and always says 'that she has no doubt that' she was exceedingly ill-used by me.—Secondly she is an admirer of yours; and I have had great difficulty in keeping her from writing to you eleven pages, (for she is a grand Scribe), and thirdly, she having read *Don Juan* in a *French* translation—made me promise to write *no more* of it, declaring that it was abominable, etc., etc. . . . She had a good deal of *us* too, I mean that turn for ridicule like Aunt Sophy and you and I and all the Byrons."

Perhaps the astonishing constancy of Byron in this adventure could have been partly explained by this "Byron side" which he found in Teresa. It was unexpected, but doubtless quite real.

The separation decree obliged the Countess to live at her father's, and on July 16, 1820, she left for the villa owned by Count Gamba in the neighbourhood of Ravenna. It may have been in the cardinals' minds to separate her from her lover in this way, but the Gambas, father and son, liked Byron, shared his political views, and shielded the affairs of his heart. He was made welcome at their country-house, to which he went out on horseback several times a month throughout the summer. And when Teresa returned to Ravenna in the autumn, he was able to see her every evening at the Gambas'.

It was not an unpleasing situation. The mystery and difficulty of his visits, the blending of conspiracy and adultery, kept weariness from creeping into his liaison. Byron passed the long, cold winter of 1821 alone in the Palazzo Guiccioli. The roads were deep in snow; the horses stamped in their stalls; and he sat at home, reading and staring into the fire. But what was there to be found in books? "What can anybody say, save what Solomon said long before us?" He had again begun keeping a diary, and the present one was perhaps even more remarkable than that of 1813. Like the Grecian sunlight, Byron's mind illuminated objects and feelings so sharply that their shape stood out with implacable accuracy. He described them as he saw them, telling as few lies about himself as about others, and giving to events as to men an appearance of being phenomena of nature, all uniform beneath his world-weary gaze. Under

BYRON

At Venice, 1820

After a drawing by G. H. Harlow

that strange compulsion of his to record everything that went to make up himself, he still noted every moment of this existence: "Dined *versus* six o' the clock. Forgot that there was a plum-pudding . . . and had dined before I knew it. Drank half a bottle of some sort of spirits, probably spirits of wine. . . . Did *not* eat two apples, which were placed by way of dessert. Fed the two cats, the hawk, and the tame (but not tamed) crow. Read Mitford's *History of Greece*—Xenophon's *Retreat of the Ten Thousand.* Up to this present moment writing, 6 minutes before eight o' the clock—French hours, not Italian."

The journal kept that fascination of folly—Shakespearean in its way, for like the Elizabethan buffoons, Byron glided without transition from a lyric couplet to a jest, from the universal republic to the health of his pet crow. "Stayed at home all the morning—looked at the fire—wondered when the post would come. Post came at the Ave Maria, instead of half-past one o'clock, as it ought. Galignani's Messenger, six in number, a letter from Faenza, but none from England. Very sulky in consequence. . . ."—"Wrote five letters in about half an hour, short and savage, to all my rascally correspondents. . . ." "Hear the carriage—order pistols and great coat as usual, necessary articles. Weather cold—carriage open, and inhabitants somewhat savage—rather treacherous and highly inflamed by politics. Fine fellows though—good materials for a nation. . . . Clock strikes—going out to make love. Somewhat perilous but not disagreeable. Memorandum—a new screen put up to-day. It is rather antique, but will do with a little repair. Thaw continues—hopeful that riding may be practicable to-morrow. . . ."

"11 o'clock and nine minutes. Visited La Contessa G[uiccioli] *nata* G[hisleri] G[amba]. . . . Talked of Italy, patriotism, Alfieri, Madame Albany and other branches of learning. Also Sallust's *Conspiracy of Catiline,* and the *War of Jugurtha.* At 9 came in her brother, Il Conte Pietro—at 10 her father, Conte Ruggiero. Talked of various modes of warfare—of the Hungarian and Highland modes of broadsword exercise. Settled that the R[evolt] will break out on the 7th or 8th of March, in which appointment I should trust had it not been settled that it was to have broken out in October 1820. But those Bolognese shirked the Romagnuoles. . . . Came home—read the *Ten Thousand* again, and will go to bed."

"January 6, 1821. Mist—thaw—slop—rain. No stirring out on horseback. . . . At eight went out to visit. Heard a little music—like music. . . . Thought of the state of women under the ancient Greeks—convenient enough. Present state a remnant of the barbarism of the chivalric and feudal ages—artificial and unnatural. They ought to mind home—and be well fed and clothed—but not mixed in society. Well educated too, in religion—but to read neither poetry nor politics—nothing but books of piety and cookery. Music—drawing—dancing—also a little gardening and ploughing now and then. I have seen them mending the roads in Epirus with good success. Why not, as well as hay-making and milking?

"Came home and read Mitford again, and played with my mastiff—gave him his supper. . . . To-night at the theatre, there being a prince on his throne in the last scene of the comedy,—the audience laughed and asked him for a *Constitution*. This shows the state of the public mind here as well as the assassinations. It won't do. There must be a universal republic,—and there ought to be.

"The crow is lame of one leg—wonder how it happened—some fool trod upon his toe, I suppose. The falcon pretty brisk—the cats large and noisy—the monkeys I have not looked to since the cold weather, as they suffer by being brought up. Horses must be gay—get a ride as soon as weather serves. Deuced muggy still—an Italian winter is a sad thing, but all the other seasons are charming. . . ."

It was very nearly the tone of the London journal in the days of *The Corsair*. Nearly—but not quite. The flow of lava had cooled, the inward battling was less fierce, Byron more resigned. The absurdity of life was taken for granted, and ennui likewise. He still craved for excitement, but he no longer sought it in amorous adventuring; his temperament was calmer, his hair turning grey. "What is the reason that I have been, all my lifetime, more or less *ennuyé?* and that, if anything, I am rather less so now than I was at twenty, as far as my recollection serves? I do not know how to answer this, but presume that it is constitutional,—as well as the waking in low spirits, which I have invariably done for many years. Temperance and exercise, which I have practised at times . . . make little or no difference. Violent passions did;—when under their immediate influence—it is odd, but—I was in agitated, but *not* in depressed spirits. A dose of salts has the effect of a temporary inebriation, like light champagne, upon me. But wine and spirits make me sullen and savage to ferocity. . . . Swimming also raises my spirits—but in general they are low, and get daily lower. That is *hopeless;* for I do not think I am so much *ennuyé* as I was at nineteen. The proof is, that then I must game, or drink, or be in motion of some kind, or I was miserable. At present, I can mope in quietness. . . .

"What I feel most growing upon me are laziness, and a disrelish more powerful than indifference. . . ." Nothing now quickened him into strong feelings. He remained too English to take his Italian life seriously, and England itself was but a distant dream. Sometimes a sound, a scent, a page in a book, would call up the past. A line of Cowley's—

> Under the glassy, cool, translucent wave,

—evoked for a fleeting moment the quivering, watery image of that fantastically shaped tree-trunk which he had found in the depths of the Cam, when he was diving with Long. . . . "Oh! there is an organ playing in the street—a waltz too! I must leave off to listen. They are playing a waltz which I have heard ten thousand times at the balls in London, between 1812 and 1818. Music is a strange thing." Ghosts were passing. Caroline Lamb waltzing. . . . He had heard how this year she had gone in fancy dress to Almack's, as Don Juan, with a train of attendant demons. For Caroline the drama was ending with a masquerade. As for Lady Byron, he had been outraged by the news that she was a patroness of some charity ball. Patroness of a ball—while her husband, in exile, was risking his life for a foreign people! He felt very bitter about that, for several hours.

Yet, if he could have read the journal which Annabella was keeping at that time, he would have read how she went out early to look at her old home in Piccadilly Terrace, and looked up from the street at the room where she had so often sat with him. She felt, she said, as if she had lived there once with a friend long dead to her. There was no sense of her past agony, but simply a gentle mournfulness. Byron likewise had sometimes felt as if their letters were Dialogues of the Dead. But he still continued to commend Augusta to her care: whatever she might be, or might in the past have been (he wrote), Lady Byron had never had grounds of complaint against her—quite the contrary. Lady Byron could not know her debt to her. Augusta's life and his, Annabella's life and his, were two perfectly distinct things; when one ended, the other began; and now both were ended. . . .

His friends were far away. Hobhouse had entered Parliament as an extremely advanced Radical, and had also got himself into prison—news which Fletcher discovered in an Italian news-sheet. Byron laughed! Laughed, because "Rochefoucault" (as he wrote it) was right—the misfortunes of our friends always make us laugh; but also because he found demagogy as repellent as tyranny, of which it is merely one form. He wrote a humorous ballad on Hobhouse's imprisonment, much to the annoyance of his friend:

When to the mob you make a speech,
  My boy Hobbie O,
How do you keep without their reach
  The watch within your fobby O?
But never mind such petty things,
  My boy Hobbie O;
God save the people—damn all Kings,
  So let us crown the Mobby O!

Scrope Davies had "down-diddled" himself with gambling, and been forced to flee abroad. What could London be like without Scrope's stuttering? "Brummel at Calais, Scrope at Bruges, Buonaparte at St. Helena, you in your new[gate] apartments, and I at Ravenna, only think! So many great men! There has been nothing like it since Themistocles at Magnesia, and Marius at Carthage. . . ."

On January 22, 1821, he was thirty-three. "To-morrow is my birthday—that is to say, at twelve o' the clock, midnight, i.e. in twelve minutes, I shall have completed thirty and three years of age! ! !—and I go to bed with a heaviness of heart at having lived so long, and to so little purpose.—It is now three minutes' past twelve. ' 'Tis the middle of the night by the castle clock,' and I am now thirty-three!

> *"Eheu, fugaces, Posthume, Posthume,*
> *Labuntur, anni . . .*

but I don't regret them so much for what I have done, as for what I might have done.

> "Through life's road so dim and dirty,
> I have dragged to three and thirty.
> What have these years left to me?
> Nothing—except thirty-three."

And on the following day he wrote the epitaph of the dead year—

> 1821
> Here lies
> Interred in the Eternity
> of the Past,
> from which there is no
> Resurrection

for the days—whatever there may be
for the Dust—
the Thirty-Third Year
of an ill-spent Life,
Which, after
a lingering disease of many months,
sunk into a lethargy,
and expired,
January 22nd, 1821, A.D.,
Leaving a successor
Inconsolable
for the very loss which
occasioned its
Existence.

During these months at Ravenna he had worked hard. *Don Juan* had been interrupted at the fifth Canto by the Countess Guiccioli: "I have agreed to a request of Madame Guiccioli's not to continue the poem further" he told Hobhouse early in July. "She has read the French translation, and thinks it a detestable production. This will not seem strange even in Italian morality, because women all over the world retain their freemasonry, and as that consists in the illusion of the sentiment which constitutes their sole empire (all owing to chivalry and the Goths—the Greeks knew better), all works which refer to the *comedy* of the passions, and laugh at sentimentalism, of course are proscribed by the whole *sect*. I never knew a woman who did not admire Rousseau, and hate Gil Blas, and de Grammont and the like, for the same reason. And I never met with a woman, English or foreign, who did as much by D[on] J[uan]. As I am docile I yielded. . . ."

The Countess Guiccioli, rigid in her defence of traditional romance, tolerated no breath of heresy against the religion of love's supremacy in the world. When Byron told her one day that love was not the loftiest theme for authentic tragedy, her indignation was great, and she overwhelmed him with arguments. He had never shone in discussion, especially with a woman; he capitulated at once, and made Sardanapalus a lover.

For in default of *Don Juan* he was working on tragedies, some inspired by Venetian history—*Marino Faliero, The Two Foscari,*—others by classical and biblical history. The idea of writing verse tragedies had come to him from his new familiarity with the works of Alfieri; and it was, of course, his anti-romantic ideal to save English tragedy by a return to the unities.

But in his hands a subject, even an historical one, and a tragedy, even a classical one, always became an agent of self-liberation. If his thoughts ran on writing a *Tiberius,* it was in the hope of expressing personal feelings: "Pondered the subjects of four tragedies to be written, . . ." he noted, "to wit, Sardanapalus, already begun; Cain, a metaphysical subject, something in the style of Manfred, but in five *acts,* perhaps with a chorus; Francesca of Rimini, in five acts; and I am not sure that I would not try Tiberius. I think that I could extract a something of *my* tragic, at least out of the gloomy sequestration of old age of the tyrant—and even out of his sojourn at Caprea—by softening the *details,* and exhibiting the despair that must have led to those very vicious pleasures. For none but a powerful and gloomy mind overthrown would have had recourse to such solitary horrors,—being also, at the same time, *old,* and the master of the world."

Again, if he composed a *Sardanapalus*, he was pleading a brief *pro domo.* Sardanapalus led precisely the life that Byron led at the Palazzo Mocenigo, and answered his friends' reproaches with a eulogy of pleasure:

Sardanapalus. Shame me! By Baal, the cities though
well built,
Are not more goodly than the verse! Say what
Thou wilt against me, my mode of life or rule,
But nothing 'gainst the truth of that brief record.
Why, those few lines contain the history
Of all things human: hear—"Sardanapalus,
The king, and son of Anacyndaraxes,
In one day built Anchialus and Tarsus.
Eat, drink, and love; the rest's not worth a fillip."

Salemenes. A worthy moral, and a wise inscription,
For a king to put up before his subjects!

Sardanapalus. Oh, thou wouldst have me doubtless set
up edicts—
"Obey the king—contribute to his treasure—
Recruit his phalanx—spill your blood at bidding—
Fall down and worship, or get up and toil."
Or thus—"Sardanapalus on this spot
Slew fifty thousand of his enemies.
These are their sepulchres, and this his trophy."
I leave such things to conquerors; enough
For me, if I can make my subjects feel
The weight of human misery less, and glide
Ungroaning to the tomb; I take no license
Which I deny to them. We are all men.

But of all his dramas, *Cain* was the most revelatory. From childhood he had been haunted by this theme of the First Predestinate, the man damned by God *before* the crime. Cain was an attempt to transpose into dramatic form his impassioned protest against the existence of evil in a divine creation. The first scene portrayed Adam and his children after the Fall, all adoring Jehovah save Cain, who remains silent. Cain has not forgiven God. What, he asks, has been Adam's fault?—

The tree was planted, and why not for him?
If not, why place him near it, where it grew,
The fairest in the centre? They have but
One answer to all questions, " 'Twas *His* will,
And *He* is good." How know I that? Because
He is all-powerful, must all-good, too, follow?
I judge but by the fruits—and they are bitter—
When I must feed on for a fault not mine.

Then Lucifer appears, proclaiming himself the equal of God, and offering Cain to show him the true world that lies beyond appearances. Cain is reluctant to leave his sister Adah, who is also his wife.

Adah. . . . Cain, walk not with this spirit,
Bear with what we have borne, and love me—I
Love thee.

Lucifer. More than thy mother, and thy sire?

Adah. I do. Is that a sin, too?

Lucifer. No, not yet:
It one day will be in your children.

Adah. What!
Must not my daughter love her brother Enoch?

Lucifer. Not as thou lovest Cain.

Adah. Oh! my God!
Shall they not love, and bring forth things that love
Out of their love? have they not drawn their milk
Out of this bosom? was not he, their father,
Born of the same sole womb, in the same hour
With me? Did we not love each other? and
In multiplying our being multiply
Things which will love each other as we love
Them?—and as I love thee my Cain! go not
Forth with this spirit; he is not of ours.

Lucifer. The sin I speak of is not of my making
And cannot be a sin in you—whate'er
It seems in those who will replace ye in
Mortality.

Adah. What is the sin which is not
Sin in itself? Can circumstance make sin
Or virtue?

After the death of Abel, the Angel comes to brand Cain. He submits to the punishment, but denies the fault.

Cain. It burns
My brow, but nought to that which is within it.
Is there more? let me meet it as I may.

Angel. Stern hast thou been and stubborn from the womb,
As the ground thou must henceforth till; but he
Thou slewest was gentle as the flocks he tended.

Cain. After the fall too soon was I begotten;
Ere yet my mother's mind subsided from
The serpent, and my sire still mourn'd for Eden.
That which I am, I am; I did not seek
For life, nor did I make myself. . . .

It was the cry of Byron himself, his brow branded, as he believed, with the mark of Cain, and condemned like Cain to wander over the face of the earth. He too had slain a younger brother—the earlier Byron. But was he responsible for that? That which he was, he was; he had not made himself; he could not have acted otherwise. And in the face of an unjust God he cried aloud: "Why hast thou done this thing to me?"

Sir Walter Scott, to whom he had dedicated *Cain: a Mystery,* courageously accepted the dedication, but attempted to plead the Creator's cause: "The great key to the Mystery is, perhaps, the imperfection of our own faculties, which see and feel strongly the partial evils which press upon us, but know too little of the general system of the universe, to be aware how the existence of these is to be reconciled with the benevolence of the great Creator."

Cain was violently attacked, especially from the point of view of religious orthodoxy. Certainly, it was not the work of an atheist, as Byron was tirelessly insistent in pointing out, but it was the work of a heretic. From Kentish Town to Pisa, clergymen preached against this calvinistic Prometheus. The tragedies disappointed Byron's English readers (they were more romantic than he was), and this saddened him.

"You see what it is to throw pearls to swine," he wrote. "As long as I write the exaggerated nonsense which has corrupted the public taste, they applauded to the very echo, and, now that I have really composed, within these three or four years, some things which should 'not willingly be let die,' the whole herd snort and grumble and return to wallow in their mire. However, it is fit I should pay the penalty of spoiling them, as no man has contributed more than me in my earlier compositions to produce that exaggerated and false taste."

He had been the most modest of authors in the hey-day of the Byron craze; and he was beginning to worry about public opinion now that it showed signs of looking in another direction. But now, as always, he faced the situation boldly.

England was looking away from the poet. There remained the man of action. Oh, if he could only show Hobhouse, so proud of himself for having been both in

Parliament and prison, and for having written (anonymously) anti-Canning tracts, that he, Byron, was not content with such substitutes for courage! His greatest hope now was for an Italian revolution in which he might play a leading part.

All through the winter, with Pietro Gamba and his *Americani* brotherhood, he conspired; and he paid both with his person and his purse. Had they bayonets, or muskets, or cartridges to conceal? Had they to hold a secret meeting? He offered the Palazzo Guiccioli. "It is a strongish post," he commented, "—narrow street, commanded from within—and tenable walls." Did they need money? He gave it. He knew he was exposing himself to death, but he held the cause to be worth it. "Only think—a free Italy!!! Why there has been nothing like it since the days of Augustus."

It was a characteristic trait of Byron's that enthusiasm and physical courage went hand in hand with mental prudence and inexhaustible common sense. He was doubtful of the success of the Italians if they could not achieve unity among themselves, and he was constantly exhorting them to a systematic activity. His ideas on local strategy were sound: "I have advised them to attack in detail, and in different parties, in different *places* (though at the same time), so as to divide the attention of the troops, who, though few, yet being disciplined, would beat any body of people (not trained) in a regular fight—unless dispersed in small parties, and distracted with different assaults."

Unhappily, events justified his forebodings only too well. Early in March the Neapolitans were routed by the Austrian troops, and the constitution was repudiated by the monarch who had granted it. All the minor insurrections were crushed. The people of Ravenna, like the rest, had to abandon their plan; and, as always happens, the abortive revolt was the most harshly suppressed. The Papal police drew up lists of suspects. Byron they dared not touch, but in July 1821, in order to reach him, they banished the Gambas.

The Countess Guiccioli accepted exile, but not the loss of her lover. Whither would he follow her? She proposed Switzerland. But Switzerland contained too many English waiting to point their spy-glasses at Lord Byron. . . . While still hesitating, he received a letter from Shelley announcing a visit. Shelley was worried about Allegra and wished to talk with him. At the time of the conspiracy Byron had felt it imprudent to keep his little girl in a house that was becoming an arsenal, and in front of which there was murder done in broad daylight. He had long been determined that she should be a Catholic and marry an Italian; and, no doubt on Teresa's advice (she was convent-bred), Byron had placed Allegra with the nuns of Bagnacavallo, close to Ravenna.

Clare was frantic. She wrote him suppliant letters, begging him to restore Allegra to the Shelleys if he did not wish to keep her himself. But Clare, like Annabella, was one of that breed of women who had the misfortune to excite the cruelty in Byron. She had that shamelessness with which he had taunted Caroline Lamb, side by side with the "sermons and sentiments" of Lady Byron; and, as had happened to both of these, he did not pardon her for the cruelty she provoked in him. In any case, he despised her too much to entrust her with a young Byron. "Clare writes me the most insolent letters about Allegra," he told Hoppner. "See what a man gets by taking care of his natural children! Were it not for the poor little child's sake, I am almost tempted to send her back to her atheistical mother, but that would be too bad; you cannot conceive the excess of her insolence, and I know not why. . . . If Clare thinks that she shall ever interfere with the child's morals or education, she mistakes; she never shall. The girl shall be a Christian and a married woman, if possible. . . ." The words cast a revealing light on that stern instinctive moralist who had so long been kept lurking in the farthest recesses of his soul.

Shelley arrived on August 6. Not having been in personal touch with Byron since Venice, he was greatly surprised by the moral and physical improvement he found in him. "He has in fact completely recovered his health, and lives a life totally the reverse of that which he led at Venice. He has now a permanent sort of liaison with Contessa Guiccioli, who is now at Florence, and seems from her letters to be a very amiable woman. . . . Fletcher is here, and as if like a shadow, he waxed and waned with the substance of his master: Fletcher also has recovered his good looks, and from amidst the unseasonable grey hairs, a fresh harvest of flaxen locks put forth." And a few days later: "Lord Byron is greatly improved in every respect. In genius, in temper, in moral views, in health, in happiness. The connection with la Guiccioli has been an inestimable benefit to him. . . . He has had mischievous passions, but these he seems to have subdued, and he is becoming what he should be, a virtuous man. The interest which he took in the politics of Italy, and the actions he performed in consequence of it, are subjects not fit to be written, but are such as will delight and surprise you. . . . He has read to me one of the unpublished Cantos of *Don Juan,* which is astonishingly fine. It sets him not only above, but far above, all the poets of the day—every word is stamped with immortality."

This letter betokened a loyal anxiety to induce in Mary a more favourable view of Byron. In the Geneva and Venice days the Shelleys had been severe. Breaking away for a few days from the influence of "the absurd womenkind," Shelley showed more equable judgment. Not that he felt himself the friend of Byron: friendship calls for more freedom of spirit. Even to a man so selfless as Shelley, Byron's renown, contrasted with his own unmerited obscurity, was a stumbling-block. Bad feeling lurked between the two men. Shelley thrust it aside, surmounted it even, but strove in vain against his uneasiness. Byron recognised in Shelley the most remarkable man he knew, the best judge of poetry, and the most generous. Shelley's presence was like a clear, living flame. Those who warmed themselves at it were perforce to regret it all their lives. But at the same time Shelley was a living reproach. With his ardour and energy, he knew what he wanted; he even seemed to know what was right and what was wrong. Byron admired him, envied him, and sometimes watched him surreptitiously with a secret longing to catch him out. What would "Rochefoucault" have thought of this version of an atheist? And if Shelley himself were a hypocrite. . . . But even under the harsh light of Byronic analysis, Shelley remained unassailable.

Life during this visit followed Byron's usual round—morning sleep and afternoon breakfast, rides in the forest, readings in the evening, talks at night. Shelley wandered with amusement through the vast palazzo, meeting on the great staircase five peacocks, three guinea-fowl, and an Egyptian crane, witnesses of the "unarbitrated" quarrels of the monkeys, the cats, the crow and the falcon. In the course of their talks, Shelley was able to mention their mutual friend, Leigh Hunt, who was in sore straits in England and whom Shelley would have liked to bring to Italy. How could he be employed out here? Byron had an idea. For some time he had not been on good terms with Murray, and had been thinking of founding a review with Tom Moore and publishing his works therein; but Moore had not agreed. Why not suggest to Hunt the joint foundation, with Shelley and Byron, of a liberal review? An association with Byron would have made Leigh Hunt's fortune. And Shelley, without giving his host time to change his mind, made haste to write to Hunt, pressing him to come.

He was also charged by Byron to write to the Countess Guiccioli (whom he did not know) to ask her to abandon the Swiss project and choose Pisa as a residence. Teresa accepted, ending her letter with an anxious and moving paragraph—"Signor, your kindness makes me impatient to ask a favour of you. Will you grant it me? *Non partite da Ravenna senza Mylord.*" Not to leave Ravenna without Lord Byron . . . so she knew how dangerous it was to leave Byron alone! But the one person in the world who had least confidence in Byron was still Byron himself. He knew himself, he feared his own weakness, and foresaw that if he lived on at Ravenna with neither Shelley nor the Countess, he would relapse into debauchery of some kind. For a time he was insistent that Shelley should remain with him. But Shelley had come to see Allegra. He went off to visit the child at the convent, and then left for Pisa.

There the Countess Guiccioli and the Gambas soon

followed her, and approved Mary's choice of the Palazzo Lanfranchi, which she had taken for Byron. But he kept them waiting nearly three months. Once again, as in the days of his betrothal, he was "more and more less impatient." He had no luck: whenever he grew fond of a country, a town, or a house, some woman or other took him away from it. He had come to love Ravenna; the common people there had venerated him; the priests there protected him, because he hung out his tapestries for feast-day processions; he wrote there with enjoyment; he felt well there. From one week to the next, he kept postponing his departure. The Countess Guiccioli had won the heart of Mary Shelley, who was sorry for her. Shelley described her as "a very pretty, sentimental, innocent Italian, who has sacrificed an immense fortune for the sake of Lord Byron, and who, if I know anything at all of my friend, of her, and of human nature, will hereafter have plenty of opportunity to repent her rashness."

Meanwhile, at the Palazzo Guiccioli, Byron was working on *Heaven and Earth, a Mystery,* based on the biblical legend of the fallen angels who loved the daughters of the Earth. Those fallen angels, like Cain, were one of his oldest and foremost concerns. The furniture had already been carted off to Pisa, and Byron had nothing left but a table and a mattress; but amid the dust and din of packing he composed choruses of Spirits and an Archangel's song. At last, on October 29, he had to resign himself to leaving the Palazzo Guiccioli and to rejoining the lady who had been its mistress.

On the way from Ravenna to Pisa he was deeply moved, indeed stupefied, by a chance encounter at Bologna with his boyhood friend, Lord Clare. "This meeting," he afterwards said, "annihilated for a moment all the years between the present time and the days of Harrow. It was a new and inexplicable feeling, like rising from the grave, to me. Clare, too, was much agitated—*more* in appearance than even myself; for I could feel his heart beat to his fingers' ends, unless, indeed, it was the pulse of my own which made me think so. . . . We were but five minutes together, and in the public road; but I hardly recollect an hour of my existence which could be weighed against them."

A strange dream, is life. . . . Figures flit past that fill our days, and kindle jealousy, or love, or rage. They fade away. We think they are effaced. Then up they rise again, quickened suddenly into life between two post-chaises on a foreign road in the dusty swelter of the sun.

In the course of the same journey he also met the cadaverous Rogers. They visited the museums of Florence together; but Byron did not care for museums and was annoyed by the curiosity of the English tourists. On the way through Bologna he took Rogers to the graveyard of the Certosa, where dwelt the sexton with the pretty daughter. The man "looked at him very *hard*," wrote Byron to Hobhouse, "and seemed well disposed to keep him in his skull-room."

Shelley, at the moment of departure, had again written to Byron, begging him to bring Allegra. She would now be left at Bagnacavallo, far from all who loved her. But Byron arrived alone.—No, not quite alone: for he was accompanied by a flock of geese in a cage suspended beneath the carriage. For all his mockery of England, he clung pertinaciously in little things to the old customs of his country. He liked having hot-cross buns on Good Friday, and a roast goose at Michaelmas. He had therefore bought a goose, and in case it should turn out to be too lean he had fed it with his own hand for a whole month in advance. But this made him grow very fond of his goose, and when the day came round he refused to have it cooked. Another was bought for him, and the favourite goose accompanied him on all his journeys. He then felt that his bird should not be deprived of the joys of family life, and thereafter travelled with four geese. It was like Schopenhauer, the misanthrope, standing at the Frankfurt fair, with his heart melting over the sorrows of an orang-outang.

XXXII

SHIPWRECKS

1821–1822

> You were all brutally mistaken about Shelley, who was, without exception, the best and least selfish man I ever knew. I never knew one who was not a beast in comparison.
>
> BYRON

TO those branded with the mark of Cain, solitude is the least of misfortunes. At Pisa Byron was never happy in the way he had been at Ravenna. Romagna had given him the *Americani,* the old women in the Pineta, and the Gambas, enough to keep him occupied without perturbing him. In Pisa he was once more back in a small English community who immediately became his judges. Shelley's presence was no vexation to him; on the contrary, the more he saw of Shelley, the more he respected him. He admired his courage, and enjoyed seeing him steer his boat against the headlong currents of the Arno, rather as in life he battled against the world of men; indeed he had need of Shelley, who was ever ready to decide things for the indecisive. And, above all, there was the fact that Shelley admired him. "Space wondered less at the swift and fair creations of God," he wrote, "than I at the late works of this spirit of an angel in the mortal paradise of a decaying body." But Shelley was surrounded by a whole world of stern Abels, devoid of genius, who accepted the poet in Byron but were taken aback and misled by the man. He was too human, and they resented the externals of his life, despising his style of living, his palace, his liveried servants, his dinners. His cynicism had always shocked Mary Shelley, and to the Pisa group Clare had drawn his portrait making no allowances. He felt that all this was so, and felt likewise his inability to reveal to them that hidden Byron whom they might perhaps have liked. His conversation, so straightforward with Shelley, with them became brilliant and bitter. And so, unable to destroy his legend, he undertook to live it.

The Palazzo Lanfranchi, overlooking the Arno, was large enough to house a garrison, and was so full of ghosts that Fletcher several times asked leave to change his room. In the morning Byron strolled with Teresa under the orange trees in the courtyard, and in the afternoon she drove out with Mary Shelley, whilst Byron went out riding in company with Shelley, Captain Williams, the Irishman John Taaffe—translator of Dante, and as bad a horseman as a poet,—Prince Mavrocordato—who taught Mary Shelley Greek,—and Shelley's cousin, Thomas Medwin, a lieutenant in the Dragoons. The riders went as far as a certain farm, the owner of which had authorised Byron to come and practise pistol-shooting there. A silver coin served them as target, and it was afterwards given to the farmer. Coming home, Byron played billiards, or worked. After dinner, as at Ravenna, came a visit to the Gambas, and work until three o'clock in the morning. On certain evenings, too, Teresa Guiccioli and her brother would go up to the top-floor of the Tre Palazzi, where the Shelleys had a small apartment, and spend the evening there listening to Shelley reading poetry. On those evenings Medwin went alone to Byron's, and afterwards made notes of each conversation he had with him. Byron was aware of this, and liked his artless listener, to whom he never tired of telling stories of his younger days.

For Medwin all the rolled wrappings of the mummy, scored with hieroglyphs, were unwound. . . . Mary Chaworth . . . the theme of the subjectivity of love. . . . "Those were days of romance! She was the *beau idéal* of all that my youthful fancy could paint of beautiful; and I have taken all my fables about the celestial nature of women from the perfection my imagination created in her. I say *created,* for I found her, like the rest of the sex, anything but angelic."—"She had scarcely any personal attractions to recommend her. Her figure, though genteel, was too thin to be good, and wanted that roundness which elegance and grace would vainly supply."—"I never felt a stronger passion. . . . She gained (as all women do) an influence over me so strong, that I had great difficulty in breaking with her, even when I knew she had been inconstant to me."

Then Annabella . . . the omen theme . . . "the first time of my seeing Miss Milbanke, I remember that in going upstairs I stumbled, and remarked to Moore, who accompanied me, that it was a bad omen. I ought to have taken the warning. . . . It had been predicted by Mrs. Williams that twenty-seven was to be a dangerous age for me. The fortune-telling witch was right. . . . I shall never forget the 2nd of January! Lady Byron ("Byr'n," he pronounced it) was the only unconcerned person present; Lady Noel, her mother, cried; I trembled like a leaf, made the wrong responses, and after the ceremony called her: Miss Milbanke."

In the course of these excursions, Medwin always rode at Byron's elbow. He talked on and on, throwing an occasional glance at his Boswell to take the measure of his credulity. On December 10, he declined to shoot, and appeared to be depressed. "This is Ada's birthday, and might have been the happiest day of my life: as it is . . . I have a great horror of anniversaries. . . . Several extraordinary things have happened to me on my birthday; as they did to Napoleon." The next day he showed Medwin a letter from England. "I was convinced something very unpleasant hung over me last night; I expected to hear that somebody I knew was dead;—so it turned out! Poor Polidori is gone! When he was my physician, he was always talking of Prussic acid and compounding poisons. He has prescribed for himself a dose whose effect, Murray says, was so instantaneous that he went off without a spasm. . . . It seems that disappointment was the cause of this rash act." On January 28, he had word of the death of Lady Noel. "I am distressed for poor Lady Byron! . . . The world will think I am pleased at this event, but they are much mistaken. I never wished for an accession of fortune. . . . I have written a letter of condolence to Lady Byron, you may suppose in the kindest terms." A legal arbitration shared the income of the Wentworth inheritance between himself and his wife, and his own revenue was now swollen to more than £7,000 a year. Annabella's first act on coming into her Kirkby inheritance was to send Augusta some game.

Medwin was not alone in making notes on Byron. In mid-January a curious personage attached himself to the English group in Pisa. His name was Edward John Trelawny, and he had led the most story-book life, having been sailor, deserter, and pirate. The Shelleys liked him: "He is six feet high; raven-black hair, which curls thickly and shortly like a Moor's; dark-grey expressive eyes; overhanging brows." Trelawny felt the same liking for the Shelleys; but his relations with Byron were strained. Byron, meeting with a life-size Corsair, had at first made a point of being pleasant to him. He had treated this nautical specialist, as formerly he treated Jackson the boxer, with all the deference of the amateur towards the professional, and commissioned him to build boats for Shelley and himself. But Byron had a horror of people who resembled the Byronic heroes of his early manner. The "Conrad side" of Trelawny infuriated him; and Trelawny, for his part, was deeply disappointed. This small, limping, melancholy man, with his anecdotes of actors and boxers and how he had swum the Hellespont, seemed to him quite unworthy of Childe Harold. Then Byron, discovering that Trelawny did not always tell the truth, murmured that if their new acquaintance could be taught to wash his hands and not tell lies, there were the makings of a gentleman in him. The remark came round to Trelawny, and from that day forward he hated Byron.

In a circle of pseudo men of letters, where people dissected each other and remarks were quick on the wing, Byron felt his own weakness. He knew that the life he led was not the life expected of him. Although not unhappy with Countess Guiccioli, he wondered whether the liaison were not becoming rather ridiculous. In speaking of her, he used the words "my *amica*" with a light irony in his manner, the tone he used to assume in mentioning "my little foot." She too was an infirmity, this all-too-faithful mistress of his, with whom he sat so conjugally beneath the meagre orange trees of the Palazzo Lanfranchi.

Action . . . action . . . action. . . . During March 1822, Prince Mavrocordato learned that the Greek rising had hopes of success, and set off to place himself at the head of the insurgents. Byron envied him.

One result of the latent ill-humour engendered in Byron by the Pisa group sounded the note of tragedy. He had not brought his little Allegra with him. He had not even been to see her. *"Caro il mio pappa,"* wrote little Allegra, *"essendo tempo di fiera desiderai tanto una visita del mio Pappa."* But Byron's comment was simply that she wanted to see him because there was a fair, and she wanted some paternal gingerbread. . . . He was applying his beloved La Rochefoucauld even to five-year-olds. Clare, who had been assured by well-informed friends that the climate of Bagnacavallo was dangerous, and that the convent was not even heated, sat watching the winter blaze on her Florentine hearth, and thinking that her child was cold. Once again she begged Byron to lodge Allegra with some respectable family, no matter where, but in a healthy climate. She pledged her word never to go and see her. "I assure you I can no longer resist the internal inexplicable feeling which haunts me that I shall never see her any more. I entreat you to destroy this feeling by allowing me to see her." But Clare was violent and clumsy. She might be an atheist, but she remained English, Protestant, Pope-fearing. She used arguments that pained Byron and could only harden his heart. "I represent to you that the putting of Allegra at her years, into a convent, is to me a serious and deep affliction. . . . I have been at some pains to inquire into their system, and I find that the state of the children is nothing less than miserable. . . . Every traveller and writer upon Italy joins in condemning them, which would be alone sufficient testimony, without adverting to the state of ignorance and profligacy of the Italian women, all pupils of convents. They are bad wives, most unnatural mothers; licentious and ignorant, they are the dishonour and unhappiness of society. . . . This is the education you have chosen for your daughter. . . . Allegra's misfortune in being condemned by her father to a life of ignorance and degradation, in being deprived of the protection and friendship of her parents' friends, by the adoption of a different religion and of an education known to be contemptible, will be received by the world as a perfect fulfilment on your part of all the censures passed upon you. How will Lady Byron—never yet justified for her conduct towards you—be soothed, and rejoice in the honourable safety of herself and child, and all the world be bolder to praise her prudence, my unhappy Allegra furnishing the condemning evidence!"

Thus the question of the convent became for Byron both personal and doctrinal. The attack upon convent-bred women seemed to him to be a thrust at Teresa, and the onslaught upon religious education had always annoyed him. He did not reply. This time Shelley vehemently supported Clare, and was indignant at Byron's attitude. He had now but one desire—to leave at the earliest possible moment the town inhabited by Lord Byron. The Williamses and Clare were commissioned to go to the coast and find a house for the summer. Hardly had they left Pisa when the Shelleys learned, through Byron, that Allegra was dead.

Byron had wished to thwart an insolent woman, and to impose his authority because he knew that all eyes were upon him, but he certainly had never thought that he was condemning his daughter to this fate. He had loved Allegra, in his own way, and had tried to bring her up; it had pleased him to find her reproducing the Byron beauty and the Byron failings; he had thought of taking her abroad with him and making her the sole companion of his old age. He was unhappy, in his own way too, furious in his egotism. The Countess Guiccioli naïvely recorded how, when she told him of Allegra's death, "a mortal paleness spread itself over his face, and he sunk into a seat. . . . He did not shed a tear; and his countenance manifested so hopeless, so profound, so sublime a sorrow, that at the moment he appeared a being of a nature superior to humanity. . . . I found him on the following morning tranquillised, and with an expression of religious resignation on his features." "She is more fortunate than we are," he said, "besides, her position in the world would scarcely have allowed her to be happy. It is God's will—let us mention it no more."

Clare could not be expected to feel so tenderly towards Byron as the candid Teresa. Shelley wrote to him that he had been compelled by circumstances "to tell Clare the real state of the case. I will not describe her grief to you; you have already suffered too much. . . . She wishes to see the coffin before it is sent to England. . . . She also wishes you would give her a portrait of Allegra, and if you have it, a lock of her hair, however small. . . . This letter will, I fear, infect you with the melancholy that reigns here. But Nature is here as vivid and joyous as we are dismal, and we have built, as Faust says, 'our little world in the great world of all,' as a contrast rather than a copy of that divine example."

Inevitably, Byron's grief took the form of a reverie on the emotions of his past: "I wish her to be buried in Harrow Church: there is a spot in the Churchyard, near the footpath, on the brow of the hill looking towards Windsor, and a tomb under a large tree (bearing the name of Peachie, or Peachey), where I used to sit for hours and hours when a boy: this was my favourite spot; but, as I wish to erect a tablet to her memory, the body had better be deposited in the Church. Near the door, on the left hand as you enter, there is a monument with a tablet containing these words:

"When sorrow weeps o'er Virtue's sacred dust,
Our tears become us, and our Grief is just:
Such were the tears she shed, who grateful pays
This last sad tribute of her love and praise.

I recollect them (after seventeen years), not from anything remarkable in them, but because from my seat in the Gallery I had generally my eyes turned towards that monument: as near it as convenient I could wish Allegra to be buried, and on the wall a marble tablet placed, with these words:

"In memory of
ALLEGRA
daughter of G.G. Lord Byron,
who died at Bagnocavallo,
In Italy, April 20th, 1822,
aged five years and three months.

I shall go to her, but she shall not return to me.
2ND SAMUEL, xii, 23."

But the Churchwardens of Harrow deemed it unfitting to admit the body of a natural child inside the church, and in the little graveyard that crowns the hill there was only a rose tree planted in the turf to mark (as still it does) the resting-place of Byron's daughter.

Failing action, the sole specific against ennui and sorrow was work. Byron worked hard at Pisa. He wrote a Faust-like drama entitled *The Deformed Transformed,* which Shelley declared detestable, but was nevertheless an interesting document. Interesting first because of its subject, which was so directly linked with Byron's own life: the hunchback Arnold sells his soul to the Devil for a healing of his deformity, and for being made like other men and capable of being loved. Interesting, secondly, because of the famous opening line, when Arnold's mother cries to him: "Out, hunchback!"—and he replies: "I was born so, mother!" An authentic retort, it was said, made by Byron to his own mother. And thirdly, because of a very curious note of Byron's on an unfinished third act, to the effect that Arnold was jealous of himself in his earlier shape, and jealous of the intellectual force which had then been his . . . —a note which proves that Byron was pondering the problems of personality, and that no one was more conscious than he of the successive existence of several Byrons.

He had also resumed *Don Juan:* "It is not impossible that I may have three or four cantos of *Don Juan* ready by autumn, or a little later, as I obtained a permission from my Dictatress to continue it,—*provided always* it was to be more guarded, and decorous, and sentimental in the continuation than in the commencement. How far these conditions have been fulfilled may be seen, perhaps, by and by; but the embargo was only taken off upon these stipulations."

Now that he was often alone in the Palazzo Lanfranchi he was working all the better. The hapless Gambas had once again been expelled. In the course of a rumpus with an insolent sergeant-major, Byron's porter, a gold-laced young hothead, had made the mistake of striking this non-commissioned officer with a fork, and breaking a rib. The affair had caused a stir, and Tita and another innocent party were arrested. The upshot of it was that Tuscan justice, timorous of touching Byron, had struck at the Gambas, and Byron had to lease a villa for them at Montenero, near Leghorn. Nearly every week he went over there to see Teresa, whom these persecutions had reinvested with a certain glamour in his eyes. Women's greatest strength, he said, lay in their being absent; and he felt her to be less wife-like when he was parted from her.

On July 1 he was at Montenero with the Gambas, when Leigh Hunt was announced. In the previous year Hunt had enthusiastically accepted the proposal forwarded by Shelley. Not that he had any strong feeling of friendliness towards Byron: Hunt was a poet with no malice in him, but was dominated by his wife, Marianne, who had had an aversion to Byron ever since he used to visit her husband at Lisson Grove in 1815. She had been piqued because Lady Byron remained outside in her carriage and never asked to be introduced. With his books under his arm, she said, Byron was only a lord and an amateur giving himself the airs of a man of letters. At a moment when the Hunts had their backs to the wall, this lord had appeared as the only possible chance of further battling, and had saved them.

It had been a troublesome journey for Mr. and Mrs. Hunt with their six children in tow. Marianne Hunt arrived ill. At Leghorn they were met by the sombre and mustachioed Trelawny, very much the knight-errant, who guided them to Montenero. On their arrival there a violent quarrel had just broken out between the Gamba servants and the Byron servants. Poor Hunt thought he had fallen headlong into a melodrama. He did not recognise Byron in that plump figure with the long ringlets and open shirt-front. Everything seemed new, outlandish, and violent. Count Pietro Gamba had tried to intervene and received a stab with a dagger; Countess Guiccioli, flushed and dishevelled, was screaming; the bloodstained Gamba was threatening his assailant; and Byron was watching the scene with an air of luxurious indolence. The police, weary of this turbulent group, were threatening this time to banish the Gambas and all their connections from the whole of Tuscany. On Trelawny's arrival, all the actors in the scene, paying no heed to Hunt, bombarded him with contradictory orders. He was to sail Byron's schooner *Bolivar* on the Lake of Geneva—to France—to America. . . . In his desperation, Leigh Hunt supposed that Byron was going to abandon him, alone in Italy, on the very day of his arrival.

That evening Shelley turned up aboard the *Ariel* from Casa Magni. In action Shelley was admirable; he sailed up against the current of human wills just as, in his cockleshell of a boat, he did the stream of the Arno. Byron *must* remain in Italy; he *must* keep faith with the newspaper; he *must* give a poem for its first number. Shelley took the offensive on his own shoulders. Overwhelmed by the onset, Byron yielded all along the line.

Without leaving him time to recover, Shelley hurried off the Hunts to the Palazzo Lanfranchi. This time it was with them that he had to battle. They complained about everything: Lord Byron was lodging them in a damp ground-floor; he kept all the other floors for himself; the furniture which Shelley had bought for them, with Byron's money, was shoddy. . . . Shelley settled them in and calmed them down. Hunt, with thoughts of Shelley, noted in his journal that evening: "A truly divine religion might be established if charity were really made the principle instead of faith."

Shelley had to stay at Leghorn, where he wanted to see a notary to make his will, and was then returning to Casa Magni on board the *Ariel,* with his friend Captain Williams.

Three days later, about two o'clock in the morning, there was a knocking at the door of the Palazzo Lanfranchi. The Countess Guiccioli's maid cried out: *"Chi è?"* It was Mary Shelley and Jane Williams. Hunt was in bed, so the two women were brought up to Lord Byron. Painfully they climbed the staircase. Teresa came smiling towards them. Breathlessly Mary Shelley gasped out: "Where is he? *Sapete alcuna cosa di Shelley?"* But neither Teresa nor Byron knew anything. Shelley had left Pisa on the Sunday, and embarked on the Monday. There had been a storm on Monday evening. . . .

After Shelley's death the Pisan group was bereft of its soul. It disintegrated. Trelawny and Medwin went elsewhere, and the sole survivors who remained in Byron's orbit were Mary Shelley, who could not muster courage enough to leave Italy, and on the ground-floor of his palace, that strange legacy of Shelley's—the Hunt family.

For the hapless Leigh Hunt, Shelley's death had added the last twist of nightmare to his exile. The transition from smoky London to the dazzling sunlight of Leghorn had already dazzled and unsettled him. Only a few days after his arrival, the almost god-like friend whom he had come to join had disappeared. Hunt had seen that marvellously living body half-eaten by fish. He had seen the leaping flames of a funeral pyre on the sand of an Italian beach, and Byron, sated with horrors, diving naked into the sea and swimming—as once, during the burial of the Dowager, he had boxed. That day Hunt and Byron had come back together in a carriage, and driving through the forest they sang like madmen. . . . Yes, it was all a nightmare, illumined by the relentless gleam of white, sunstruck sands—but a nightmare with no awakening.

Hunt had instantly fathomed the extent of his loss in Shelley. Henceforth there would be no shrill, compelling voice to mediate in the bickerings of eagle and sparrow. Cut off in a foreign land, tied to a man who was almost a stranger to him and with whom he had not a taste in common, saddled with an ailing wife and six children, Hunt often felt dizzy as he peered over the abyss at the brink of which he stood committed.

For some weeks the situation was just tolerable. Byron was loyal to Shelley's memory. It could not be said that he mourned him. In Byron's eyes the violent deaths of the beings he loved were merely so many episodes in the long war waged between Destiny and George Gordon Byron. All those to whom *he* was attached were *bound* to vanish. Shelley was drowned, after Matthews and after Long . . . it was all in the order of things. Once again he must resume the melancholy routine of life, thinking that some day it would be upon himself that the invisible hand would fall. Defiance, then, rather than sadness. . . . But he defended Shelley's memory—"the best and least selfish man I ever knew"—and Hunt in the Palazzo Lanfranchi was sheltered by that noble shade.

Moreover, Byron believed in the success of the *Liberal.* Hobhouse and Moore twitted him with his association with the author of *"Rimini-Pimini";* he hoped to show them that his name was enough to make the success of a newspaper, whatever it might be like. Having lost Shelley, he was not displeased at lodging in his palace a writer and critic to whom, every morning, he could show the stanzas he had composed overnight. But Hunt was already tired of this exigent patron. Their ideas concerning the *Liberal* were divergent. Hunt was a polemist, Byron a man of genius. Hunt wished the review to be a lever for the toppling-over of Mrs. Grundy and John Bull, whilst Byron simply wanted to publish all that he might write. Byron's crotchets, which to his mind were laws of the universe, were irritating to Hunt. The latter used to work at the Palazzo Lanfranchi in a small room looking out on the orange trees of the courtyard, and every morning he heard Byron rise, take his bath, and dress, singing an air, loudly but out of tune, nearly always of Rossini's. A little later Byron would call out beneath Hunt's windows: "Leontius!"—a Latinisation of Leigh Hunt invented by Shelley. Hunt rose with a sigh, said good morning, and came down into the courtyard. The Guiccioli, if she were at Pisa, then joined the two men, her hair twisted in matutinal plaits, and Hunt had perforce to listen to the alternating grumbles of Byron on her jealousy, and hers on Byron's brutal language.

The two lovers by now knew each other too thoroughly for Teresa to go on turning "her poet" into the hardly flesh-and-blood hero of a Petrarchine romance. To Byron a fact was a fact, and when once a woman had consented to be his mistress, he spoke of her to all and sundry with a detailed frankness which left no doubt as to the nature of their relationship. This realism hurt the Countess Guiccioli. Byron, on his side, deemed her faithful, unselfish, and loving, but afflicted with the inevitable failings of "the absurd womankind"—jealousy and sentimentalism.

To this discontented couple Hunt was no kindly confidant. The Countess Guiccioli had not sought an introduction to Mrs. Hunt any more than Lady Byron had. The two women never spoke. Marianne Hunt treated Byron with effrontery, and ordered her children to keep away if he came near them, alleging that his conversation was dangerous to youthful minds. Byron was aware of this, and the harsh judgment of a woman living beneath his own roof had shocked him. This was surprisingly ingenuous in a disciple of "Rochefoucault," who ought to have been familiar with the natural results of benefits conferred. But all the Hunts were odious to him. He wrote to Mary Shelley: "I have a particular dislike of anything of Shelley's being within the same walls with Mrs. Hunt's children. They are dirtier and more mischievous than Yahoos. What they can't destroy with their filth they will with their fingers." At the entrance to his floor of thc palazzo, a bull-dog was stationed to keep them at a distance. "Don't let the Cockneys pass our way!" said Byron to this sentinel, patting its head. Ground-floor and first-floor of the Palazzo Lanfranchi were almost in a state of war. Hunt spoke scornfully of the unpoetic poet, the undignified lord. A few weeks later and Byron was forced, for a third time, to follow the tracks of the Gambas, who were now banished from the whole of Tuscan territory; he was exasperated at having to drag the Hunts along with him, with "their kraal of Hottentots." He was not quite hard-hearted enough to cut them adrift at Pisa, but as he hurriedly scribbled stanzas of *Don Juan* on the corner of the last table left by the furniture-removers in the Palazzo Lanfranchi, he cursed them with all his heart.

XXXIII

A NOSTALGIC GENTLEMAN

1822–1823

> Martin concluded that man is made to live in the convulsions of anxiety, or in the lethargy of ennui.
>
> VOLTAIRE

"ONCE more upon the waters! yet once more!"—but how ridiculous he felt this third pilgrimage of Childe Harold to be! Once again the Solitary had allowed a heterogeneous and troublesome accretion to fasten on to him, and once again he lacked the courage to shake off the human barnacles. He now required a flotilla to transport his illicit family, his clients, and his retinue from Lerici to Genoa. Lord Byron, Teresa, and the Gambas made the passage in the *Bolivar;* Leigh Hunt, Marianne Hunt, and the pack of little Hunts in another boat; in a third was Trelawny, the excited and self-important admiral of the Squadron, taking charge of papers and instruments with blustering and domineering conceit; and the domestics and animals were crammed into a felucca. "It was pretty to see the boats with their white sails, gliding by the rocks, over that blue sea," said Hunt. And for him, who had no responsibility for this wandering tribe, it may well have been a delightful sight; but for Byron, who would have to provide its maintenance and hear its complaints, the spectacle had less charm.

Mary Shelley had been entrusted with the billeting—the Shelleys' traditional rôle—and had rented two houses in the Albaro quarter, on a hill overlooking the gulf. There was a great barracks of forty rooms for herself and the Hunts; and for Byron an aristocratic rose-coloured villa, the Casa Saluzzo. Its good-sized garden contained a pavilion and an alley of cypresses, in the shade of which Byron took to reading, and the sea view was admirable. Fletcher was ordered to hang a small portrait of Ada, and also an engraved portrait of Byron himself, in the bedroom. On the upper floor was installed the Countess Guiccioli, *nata* Gamba, and all her family.

For Byron the Casa Saluzzo, like the Palazzo Lanfranchi, was an ill-fated abode. Right at the beginning he had determined to swim across the Gulf of Genoa; there was a blazing sun, and the expedition made him ill; his skin peeled; he could not get over it. The first issue of the *Liberal* had caused a scandal, and Hobhouse and Kinnaird had written letters of remonstrance. Some scandals, when they raise wide issues, are definitely desirable—but this one was merely laughable. Moore, Kinnaird, Hobhouse, were Liberals; but they were men of the world too, and shrugged their shoulders at the sight of Byron in partnership with Hunt. Byron was annoyed, and explained that he had acted only out of charity, that since Shelley's death Hunt was entirely dependant on him, that the poor fellow had a wife and six children. Murray, in defence of his author, had shown this letter, and word of it came back to Leigh Hunt. The whole forty-roomed house crashed on Byron's unhappy head.

With an exasperating blend of deferential kindness and vague moral reproach, Mary Shelley had written to him:

"When Hunt reflects that his bread depends upon the success of this journal, and that you depreciate it . . . that you depreciate him as a coadjuter, making it thus appear that his poverty and not your will consents—all this dispirits him greatly." Really, this cant was intolerable to Byron! Of course he had had no intention of insulting Hunt's poverty; he had known poverty himself, and respected it. But still, he had to speak the truth: would he have founded a journal with Hunt if Hunt had been a rich man? Obviously not. . . . "I have always treated him, in our personal intercourse, with such scrupulous delicacy, that I have forborne intruding advice which I thought might be disagreeable, lest he should impute it to what is called taking advantage of a man's situation." He was right; but Hunt did not forgive him. If the break was not a complete one—for Hunt could not do without Byron—their meetings became few and strained.

Gloomily Hunt paced the cobbled alleys, his thoughts full of Shelley. Almost his sole topic of conversation now with Byron was Dr. Johnson. Byron enjoyed imitating Johnson, and blurting out "Why! Sir," with a sweeping glance; and the overworked pleasantry annoyed Hunt almost as much as Byron's singing of Rossini airs in his bath. Visits to the Casa Saluzzo became rarer still. Hunt preferred sending a letter—almost always one asking for money in a tone of resentful irony: "I must trouble you for another cool hundred of your crowns, and shall speedily, I fear, come upon you for one more. . . ." He had dropped "my dear Byron," and taken to "dear Lord Byron." "Dear Lord Hunt," replied Byron. And then direct communications broke off, and the crowns were remitted weekly to the Hunt tribe through the agency of Byron's steward, Lega Zambelli. One more grievance.

Life at the Casa Saluzzo was woefully petty and unexciting. Byron had loved Teresa Guiccioli, especially during that time at Ravenna when he rode out to see her, not without danger, between a conspiratorial visit and a secret-police assassination. A little later, during the Montenero exile, she had taken on, in his own eyes at any rate, the aspect of a martyr in the cause of Liberty. When Leigh Hunt saw her for the first time, "fancying she walked, in the eyes of the whole world, a heroine by the side of a poet, she was in a state of excitement and exaltation, and had really something of this look." In a few months, from Pisa to Genoa, Teresa suddenly altered and aged; her face lost its look of passionate frankness, and she seemed to be overwhelmed by a secret sorrow. Her lover was still "exceedingly governed and kept tight in hand" by her, but he was tired of the whole thing. He felt that existence had grown even gloomier that when he used to shut himself up at Newstead, young and unknown, to yawn in his solitude. His only friends in the world in those days were Hanson and Dallas, kinsman and attorney,—the two last links of every man with humanity. Then he had been the "lion" of London, the most famous writer in the world; people could talk quite seriously of "Napoleon and Byron." Gradually the magic circle faded, and beneath this harsh light he was left alone. From solitude to solitude, his life had gone full circle.

And if he now took his bearings, in that almost cruelly, clear-sighted way of his, what notes would there be for his log? . . . March 1823, eleven hours and ten minutes "o' the clock," a rose-coloured palace in an unknown town, a mistress whose love was already four years old, the aged father of this woman, some dogs, Fletcher. . . . Nothing else in the world. . . . Yes, really life was more hollow than during the worst moments of adolescence. Was it for this he had suffered? . . . And yet—there was a force within him. . . . His thoughts turned back towards England. Why was he not living as a peer of its realm? Why could not England's politics be the legitimate aim of his activity?

Time was when he had regretted the landscapes of the East—now he regretted those of the North. He dreamed of a grey sky, of great clouds hurrying before the wind, as one sees them in Scotland. He sent off Don Juan to England, and described with a kind of loving fondness his hero's first glimpse of the cliffs of Dover:

> At length they rose, like a white wall, along
> The blue-sea's border; and Don Juan felt—
> What even young strangers feel a little strong
> At the first sight of Albion's chalky belt—
> A kind of pride that he should be among
> Those haughty shopkeepers, who sternly dealt
> Their goods and edicts out from pole to pole,
> And made the very billows pay them toll.

And through the garden-like meadows, Juan drove on by way of Canterbury towards—

> A mighty mass of brick, and smoke, and shipping,
> Dirty and dusky, but as wide as eye
> Could reach, with here and there a sail just skipping
> In sight, then lost amidst the forestry
> Of masts; a wilderness of steeples peeping
> On tip-toe through their sea-coal canopy;
> A huge, dun cupola, like a foolscap crown
> On a fool's head—and there is London Town!

Ah, how he envied Juan that journey!

Could he possibly make it himself some day? All depended on Annabella. She it was who had been the pretext of his exile by an unwritten decree. If he could return to London as father and husband, all would be forgotten. The image of his wife's personality was altering in his mind. He recognised her sincerity, her great qualities, the genuineness of her piety, her very real virtue. Why should she not forgive him? His heart grew soft towards her in his loneliness, and he made inquiries of a great friend of Lady Byron's then passing through Genoa, Colonel Montgomery, whether he could not obtain a portrait of her. He had no memento of his wife, hardly a letter—he who loved his nightly visits to the museum of his past. . . . Sometimes he would open the little account-book, his sole relic, which contained one word written twice in her hand—"Household. . . ." That was all. No—there was something else. During his sojourn at Pisa she had sent him a lock of Ada's hair, beside which she had written the date. Was that an encouragement? Who could say? He drafted a reply:

"I have to acknowledge the receipt of Ada's hair, which is very soft and pretty, and nearly as dark already as mine was at twelve years old. . . . But it don't curl,—perhaps from its being let grow. I also thank you for the inscription of the date and name, and I will tell you why;—I believe that they are the only two or three words of your handwriting in my possession. For your letters I returned, and except the two words, or rather the one word *Household,* written twice in an old account-book, I have no other."

He had not sent this letter, uncertain of how it would be received, but his desire to recover his place in the world, through Annabella and with her, was pressing. He confided it, with many other revelations of his character, to an English friend who came to Genoa in 1823, the famous Lady Blessington.

Byron had known Lord Blessington in London in 1812, and used to meet him fairly frequently at Watier's or the Cocoa Tree. In those days Lady Blessington was an obscure Irishwoman, leading a difficult life, and she had only married Lord Blessington in 1818, after Byron's departure. But he had often heard of her, and knew that Lawrence had painted a portrait of her which had been the rage of London society, that she had written three books, and that Tom Moore admired her. When the two visiting-cards of Lord Blessington and Count Alfred d'Orsay were brought up to him in his Albaro villa on April 1, 1823, he was at once disquieted, intimidated, and pleased. Count d'Orsay, as Byron said, was a Frenchman, and a friend of the family, "very young and a beauty." Lady Blessington, "entirely bored with her Lord," could not dispense with her Parisian paladin. The two men told Byron that her ladyship was in her carriage at the door. He hastened down with his troublesome limp, made his excuses, and bade her come in.

She had been looking forward to this meeting impatiently for several days, and had fears of being disappointed. She was. Looking forward to the sight of a tall figure of dignity and authority, she found herself facing a well-chiselled head with very expressive eyes, but a small, slight, almost childish frame. He had grown thin again since his sunstroke, and his clothes, apparently too big for him, looked as if they had been bought ready-made. His movements had the awkwardness that came from a consciousness of his infirmity. Next day the Blessingtons saw him arriving, a little out of temper but very friendly, at their hotel; and Lady Blessington, who was a practised man-tamer, soon detected that nobody could be easier to win over than Byron. No spirit of flirtation spoiled their friendship; her ladyship, as Byron said, was very well safeguarded "by her Parisian appendage." Byron believed in friendship between man and woman, so long as love did not take a hand; and finding Lady Blessington intelligent, he talked to her very openly, either during their rides, or at the luncheons at which they met in the villas of the neighbourhood. She made notes of these conversations, and it turned out, after a few weeks, that in so doing she had written one of the truest and most living books ever written about Byron.

She had grasped him, in all his complexity, most admirably. His essential trait struck her as being a generous and rather unhealthy sensibility, which ought in youth to have formed the substance of a fine character. The premature chill of perverseness had nipped the germinating seeds, but had not quite killed them. When Byron declared that he was a fallen angel, he was right. There did exist within him all the elements of the angel, but so cruel and so false had he found men that a horror of hypocrisy had emerged as his dominant sentiment.

She frequently heard him analyse the feelings of others, and his own too; like another La Rochefoucauld, but even more merciless, he discovered self-interest and falsehood everywhere. He seemed to take particular joy in the ridicule of romantic sentiments, and, a moment later, would display the self-same sentiments so unmistakably that tears stood in his eyes. She realised that he had taken to mocking this thing in order to cure it in himself, and observed that when reciting pathetic verses, he always did so with an air of mockery and a humorous emphasis, setting up a barrier against possible emotion. He refused to recognise the greatness in his own character, and dilated with relish on his failings.

In religious matters she found he was not an unbeliever, but sceptical, and in any case a deist. "A fine day, a moonlight night, or any other fine object in the phenomena of nature, excites strong feelings of religion in all elevated minds." But he was more superstitious than religious, and seemed offended when this weakness was not shared by others. He told Lady Blessington with great solemnity that the ghost of Shelley had appeared to a woman, in a garden. He still kept his dread of a Friday. He was startled by spilt salt or a broken glass.

And yet the most striking trait that she found, after Byron's innate goodness of heart, was his common sense —an anti-romantic, anti-individualist common sense which was prodigiously surprising in one who, according to his own legend, was the least social of all human beings. Rarely had a man spoken of marriage with such respectable, conventional wisdom. He told Lady Blessington that no real happiness existed outside of marriage. "If people like each other so well as not to be able to live asunder," he said, "marriage is the only tie that can ensure happiness. . . . I put religion and morals out of the question, though of course the misery will be increased tenfold by the influence of both; but, admitting persons to have neither, still liaisons that are not cemented by marriage, must produce unhappiness, when there is refinement of mind, and that honourable *fierté* which accompanies it. The humiliations and vexations a woman under such circumstances is exposed to cannot fail to have a certain effect on her temper and spirits, which robs her of the charms that won affection; it renders her susceptible and suspicious; her self-esteem being diminished, she becomes doubly jealous of that of him for whom she lost it, and on whom she depends. . . . He must submit to a slavery much more severe than that of marriage, without its respectability."

A portrait, no doubt, of Teresa Guiccioli, who was in fact becoming increasingly jealous, and was so even of Lady Blessington. But it was chiefly upon himself that Byron's power of observation was turned, and he knew himself through and through. "I often look back on the days of my childhood and am astonished at the recollection of the intensity of my feelings at that period;—first impressions are indelible. My poor mother, and after her my schoolfellows, by their taunts, led me to consider my lameness as the greatest misfortune, and I have never been able to conquer this feeling. It requires great natural goodness of disposition to conquer the corroding bitterness that deformity engenders in the mind, and which sours one towards all the world."

He was one of those men who can never be consoled for the loss of youthful illusions, and he would say that it was erroneous to hope for a respite from the passions with advancing age. The passions only alter form; love gives way to avarice, confidence to suspicion: " 'tis what age and experience brings us. No; let me not live to be old: give me youth, which is the fever of reason, and not age, which is the palsy. I remember my youth, when my heart overflowed with affection towards all who showed any symptoms of liking towards me; and now, at thirty-six, no very advanced period of life, I can scarcely, by raking up the dying embers of affection in that same heart, excite even a temporary flame to warm my chilled feelings."

How pleasing, how affecting, the young woman must have found this schoolboy of thirty-five, the incorrigible sentimentalist vainly striving after cynicism! "Poor Byron!"—used he not to say that to Annabella in his childish moods? And now in her turn Lady Blessington was saying the same thing, thinking of poor Byron, so conscious and so weak, so rich in worth and so cruelly calumnied,—poor Byron, who with all his genius, his rank, his fortune, was poor. . . .

During these two months, April and May 1823, Byron's relations with the Blessingtons became increasingly intimate. Count d'Orsay made a portrait of him, and also one of Pietro Gamba. Lady Blessington's conversation gave him a rest from the somewhat soured chatter of his mistress. He was sad when his friends had to go. On his last visit he bought a little memento for each of the trio. Tears filled his eyes. He brushed them away, with a sarcastic remark about his own emotion.

Don Juan seemed to thrive on Byron's boredom and moral solitude. At Pisa, and then at Genoa, he had written ten Cantos with a facility, a variety of key, and a suppleness of form that were truly amazing. The poem had broadened its scope. Juan was still its hero, but his adventures were now but a pretext for its real theme, which was like *Gulliver's Travels* or *Candide,* a satire on the ruling classes of Europe. These classes Byron had never liked. He had been reared in a puritan—that is to say, an opposition—atmosphere, and had only entered the House of Lords to address a few stern reproofs to

LORD BYRON

After a Sketch by Count D'Orsay, May, 1823

his fellow peers. In society, even in the days when he seemed to be living the life of a great eighteenth-century gentleman, he had felt a stranger. The storm that drove him forth battered him, but did not surprise him. And looking now from a more detached vantage-point upon the Europe fashioned by these stern men, he delighted in pointing out to them the bloodstained collapse of their doctrines.

Was he accused of scoffing at human virtue?—

> Good God! I wonder what they would be at!
> I say no more than hath been said in Dante's
> Verse, and by Solomon and by Cervantes,
> By Swift, by Machiavel, by Rochefoucault,
> By Fénélon, by Luther, and by Plato;
> By Tillotson, and Wesley, and Rousseau,
> Who knew this life was not worth a potato.

Neither the scrutinising of Nature, nor that of our own thoughts, will enable us to deduce a certainty. . . . One system devours another, as old Saturn his children:

> For me, I know nought; nothing I deny,
> Admit, reject, contemn; and what know you,
> Except, perhaps, that you were born to die?
> And both may, after all, turn out untrue.

This, Byron had been saying ever since *Childe Harold*, but in the days of *Childe Harold* the folly of religions and systems had made him doubt also the utility of human effort; at that time he had spoken of captive Greece only to despair of the fate of Greece. But now, perhaps under the spell of his recent Italian plotting, perhaps from some desperate craving for action, he was linking universal doubts with a definite political faith. He was finding out that metaphysical scepticism need not involve political scepticism. On the contrary, if we are all—

wretched humans that we are!—engaged in some dreadful, meaningless adventure, let us help each other in trying, as Shelley had said after Goethe, to build our little world in the heart of the mighty universe. Voltaire, the sceptic, had battled for the victimised Calas, and he, Byron, was eager to fight for liberty:

And I will war, at least in words (and—should
My chance so happen—deeds), with all who war
With Thought; and of Thought's foes by far most rude,
Tyrants and sycophants have been and are.
I know not who may conquer; If I could
Have such a prescience, it should be no bar
To this my plain, sworn downright detestation
Of every despotism in every nation.

It is not that I adulate the people:
Without me, there are demagogues enough,
And infidels, to pull down every steeple,
And set up in their stead some common stuff.
Whether they may sow scepticism to reap hell,
As is the Christian dogma rather rough,
I do not know:—I wish men to be free
As much from mobs as kings—from you as me.

Above all, he belaboured war. He sent Juan to the siege of Ismail during the Russo-Turkish campaign, in order to show the cheapness of human life to these leaders of ours whose "trade is butchery." He scoffed at military glory, at the men who run after ranks and ribbons, who lose their life for a gold stripe or a mention in despatches—

I wonder (although Mars so doubts a God I
Praise) if a man's name in a *bulletin*
May make up for a *bullet in* his body?
I hope this little question is no sin . . .

for the advancement of a Souvaroff or a Wellington:

The drying up a single tear has more
Of honest fame than shedding seas of gore.

He made mock of the national hero himself, the great Duke—

Call'd "Saviour of the Nations"—not yet saved,
And "Europe's Liberator"—still enslaved. . . .

Though Britain owes (and pays you, too) so much,
Yet Europe doubtless owes you greatly more:
You have repaired Legitimacy's crutch,
A prop not quite so certain as before. . . .

The tone was loud, and pitched to stir the feelings of a continent filled at that time with half-pay soldiers. This "modern" poetry would go straight to the hearts of all who had fought, all who had suffered through the monstrous egotism of their masters—

For I will teach, if possible, the stones
To rise against earth's tyrants. Never let it
Be said that we still truckle unto thrones:—
But ye—our children's children! think how we
Show'd *what things were* before the world was free!

It was not without a deep-lying cause that *Don Juan* contained a long eulogy of Don Quixote. Sancho's good sense was not wanting in Byron; but age, which teaches most men the lessons of doubt and irony, seemed to extirpate these from Lord Byron. Don Quixote's failure now struck him as painful rather than amusing:

Of all tales 'tis the saddest—and more sad
Because it makes us smile; his hero's right,
And still pursues the right;—to curb the bad
His only object; and 'gainst odds to fight,
His guerdon: 'tis his virtue makes him mad!
But his adventures form a sorry sight;—
A sorrier still is the great moral taught
By that real epic unto all who have thought.

Redressing injury, revenging wrong,
To aid the damsel and destroy the caitiff;
Opposing singly the united strong,
From foreign yoke to free the helpless native:—
Alas! must noblest views, like an old song,
Be for mere fancy's sport a theme creative,
A jest, a riddle, Fame through thick and thin sought!
And Socrates himself but Wisdom's Quixote?

And so Byron paced his garden with its dark lines of cypresses, the prisoner of Sentimentalism, the eternal adolescent of the spirit, and dreamed of a liberal chivalry, adventures, and glory. Was not his duty to show to John Bull something of the plight of this pitiful world? Through a few stanzas he might be Juvenal or Ecclesiasticus. Then his taste for the past would draw him away, and following his Juan, he once more entered the drawing-rooms wherein he had reigned, and satire drifted into a "ballade of lovers of long ago."

What did he want to be? Hamlet—or Don Quixote? The passionate lover of justice who dares, fails, and regrets not his failure,—or the dreamer spoiled for action by thought? Did he himself know? He was changeable, still mingling the illusion of childhood with the most disillusioned wisdom. Sometimes he longed to model the universe, and sometimes he gazed with resignation on the eternal, insensate flux:

Between two worlds life hovers like a star,
'Twixt night and morn, upon the horizon's verge.
How little do we know that which we are!
How less what we may be! The eternal surge
Of time and tide rolls on, and bears afar
Our bubbles: as the old burst, new emerge,
Lash'd from the foam of ages; while the graves
Of empires heave but like some passing waves.

XXXIV

HERO AND SOLDIER

1823

If anything was more characteristic of Byron than another, it was his rude common sense.

DISRAELI

THE great events in our lives are often prepared by facts so trifling that we hardly notice them; we are caught up by our actions, our words, in an ever finer network; one path, and one only, is left open; and the moment comes when we have to give our lives for our formulas. It is a turning-point reached by nearly all great men, and heroism consists in refusing to let the flesh renounce the boldness of the spirit.

For two years Byron had followed with a melancholy, intermittent interest the progress of the Greek insurrection. When Mavrocordato left Pisa to join the insurgents, Byron had told all his circle that he would gladly have followed the Prince. He wrote it to Moore, and repeated it to Gamba, to Medwin (who noted the exact phrase: "I mean to return to Greece, and shall in all probability die there"), and to Trelawny, who did not believe him. The truth was that nobody in the Pisan group took any project of Byron's seriously, whatever it might be. How often had he veered from Venezuela to the United States, from England to Greece, his imagination landing for a moment on each of those dreams! Then a woman would grow plaintive, a poem would hold him back, an omen would alarm him—and he stayed. In his friends' eyes his reputation was ready-made: he was feminine, weak and sensitive—at every point the reverse of the man of action.

Yet this Greek project seemed more enduring than the others. Not that Byron had any hatred of the Turks; indeed he retained the warmest recollection of those white-bearded pachas who had made him welcome in 1810. In those days he had bewailed the enslavement of Greece, yet the slavery seemed to him beyond all curing. But now the insurrection was apparently succeeding. The Turks had not managed to clamp their governance securely to the country, where they formed, as had been said, a camp provisionally pitched in Europe; but a camp can always be taken by storm, and it was comparatively easy to chase them out.

Why had not the Greeks shaken free earlier, in the eighteenth century? There was a good reason. Of all human forces, only the spiritual are efficacious; to rebel, one must believe in rebellion; and it was only through the French Revolution that the Greeks, like the Poles and the Italians, learned the words, Liberty, the Rights of Peoples. The Marseillaise was translated for them. By his stanzas in *Childe Harold,* Byron made Europe interested in their lot. They ceased to regard their slavery as a law of nature, and in so doing ceased to be slaves.

The movement had begun with secret societies, which had at first hoped for Russian support. But the vigilant Metternich pointed out to the Tsar "the revolutionary signs in the happenings in Greece." England was no less hostile than Austria. Pitt's explicit refusal to deal with anyone who did not admit the necessity, for British interests, of the Ottoman Empire's integrity, remained one of those magical, and usually outworn, formulas by which he so often shaped British foreign policy. France, still a tutelary of the Holy Alliance, could only provide isolated volunteers. The Greeks had to fall back upon themselves.

With the year 1821 several beacons blazed out. The Archbishop of Patras, the soldier-priest Germanos, took to the hills, and captured Patras; on the same day a local chieftain, Colocotronis, raised the Morea; another insurgent, Odysseus, seized a part of Eastern Greece. In Western Greece, events were being controlled by Prince Mavrocordato. There was a sharp contrast, and a difficult alliance, between this cultured young European with his frock-coat and gold spectacles, and the mountaineer bandits like Odysseus and Colocotronis; rifts between the Greek leaders saved the Turks from disaster. But abroad the Greek victories had kindled enthusiasm amongst the liberals of every nation. Old Napoleonic officers, students from Jena, and mystics from Switzerland were arriving to fight for Greece.

In England the Government was hostile, but when a Greek deputy, Andreas Luriottis, arrived in January 1823, to plead his nation's cause, a certain number of advanced Whigs saw an opportunity of making that cause a useful cat's-paw in domestic politics. They accordingly founded a "Greek Committee," which met at the Crown and Anchor Tavern, and, like most committees, published useless documents, gave excellent dinners, and did very little. It included the astonishing Jeremy Bentham, inventor of the words "international" and "codify," and reformer of the laws of logic, prisons, and universities, together with radical members of Parliament like Sir Francis Burdett and Hobhouse, and bankers like Kinnaird; and as Secretary it had Mr. John Bowring, a disciple of Bentham and a polyglot.

At the committee's opening meeting it was decided to send to Greece, for purposes of investigation and report, one Edward Blaquiere, the author of several books on the Mediterranean. When Trelawny, who was acquainted with Blaquiere, wrote to him in February that Byron frequently spoke of going himself to Greece, Hobhouse and Kinnaird smiled; the "dear fellow" was no commander-in-chief. But his name might be useful. Blaquiere informed Byron that he would stop at Genoa to see him on his way to Greece. And so it was that Byron found himself caught up in the turning gears of action.

In April, Blaquiere and Luriottis climbed the hill to the Casa Saluzzo, and Byron made them an offer to go to the Levant in July, if the committee considered it useful. . . . And why shouldn't he go? The move appealed to his craving for sensation, starved by the jog-trot life of Genoa, and no less to his ambition to show that he was something besides a versifier. "To be the first man (*not* the Dictator), not the Sylla, but the Washington, or Aristides, the leader in talent and truth, is to be next to the Divinity." The words were his; and he still believed them. He was for ever tempted to do things that few men, if any, had done before. And now the *Liberal's* collapse, the comparative failure of his recent publications, everything was driving him to feel that public opinion must be reconquered. The poet had ceased to please—and perhaps England was right. He himself believed that his real qualities would emerge rather in the life of action. He had always regarded himself as a soldier or a statesman, barred by bodily infirmity from the life for which he was intended. He wanted now to devote himself to "politics and decorum." "If I live ten years longer, you will see that it is not over with me. I don't mean in literature, for that is nothing; and—it may seem odd enough to say—I do not think it was my vocation. But you will see that I shall do something—the times and fortune permitting—that will puzzle the philosophers of all ages."

But it was not only redemption in the eyes of the world for which he hoped from such a sacrifice. It was above all the salvation of Byron in Byron's own soul. He had shown in *Manfred* how, for him, Hell was an inward drama; and the conflict which from adolescence has raged between the Byron that he might have been and the Byron that he had been, could be resolved in favour of the passionate schoolboy by the force of a great heroism. He scrawled a few lines in a notebook, the opening of an unfinished Canto:

> The dead have been awakened—shall I sleep?
> The world's at war with tyrants—shall I crouch?
> The harvest's ripe—and shall I pause to reap?
> I slumber not; the thorn is in my couch;
> Each day a trumpet soundeth in mine ear,
> Its echo in my heart.

"Poeshie," as he mockingly said; and none knew better the gap between the real sentiments, as dissected by his scoffing common sense, and those expressed in verse. But however merciless his dissection, and however ironic his smile when one of his companions spoke of "the Cause," he was well aware that love of liberty and the desire to do great deeds were real and potent elements within him.

In the course of his life he had encountered so many hindrances to action that he dreaded those which still barred his path. He knew well the tenacity of "the absurd womankind," and his own weakness before that race. "Madame Guiccioli is of course, and naturally enough, opposed to my quitting her; though but for a few months; and as she had influence enough to prevent my return to England in 1819, she may not be less successful in detaining me from Greece in 1823." But even before talking Teresa over, he had to settle a question still more pressing, and for him, more painful. Did the committee of Philhellenes in London really desire his collaboration? Ever since the proscription of 1816 he had felt, as regards anything English, as nervously apprehensive as a pariah. Unseen foes are always the most terrible to the imagination. He still believed the English to be violently up in arms against him, and was determined never to ask anything of them, lest he give an opening for a rebuff. The modesty of his offer to Hobhouse was perfect, and he was delighted when, after a rather protracted and irritating silence, he was elected a member of the committee. His letters about this time show him in his best light,—generous (he instantly announced his readiness to pay out of his own pocket, and began by sending at his expense medical stores and gunpowder), straightforward, and most notably and surprisingly business-like.

The letter Mr. Bowring had written him contained the usual clichés about "the classic land of freedom, the birthplace of the arts, the cradle of genius, the habitation of the Gods, the heaven of poets, and a great many such fine things,"—all in the tone that Byron most hated in prose. "Enthusiasm," he said with disgust, and replied by reporting on the actual situation of the Greeks in a style worthy of a highly capable chief-of-staff. "The material wanted by the Greeks appears to be, first, a pack of field artillery—light, and fit for mountain service; secondly, gunpowder; thirdly, hospital or medical stores." And in four pages of facts he pointed out the requirements, the best modes of transport, the addresses of eventual correspondents. It was all Kitty Gordon's hard sense, reckoning the expenses of Newstead, and in piquant contrast to the futile rhetoric of the committee.

Was he, then, notwithstanding his friends' ideas, the man of action he believed himself to be? The truth was not quite so simple as that. Endowed with the gifts for a life of action, having at once courage, realism and clear-headedness, Byron had been doomed to dreaming by reason of his indecision. He had desired to be at one and the same time a liberal, a defender of the peoples, and a great libertine nobleman,—a husband and a Don Juan,—a Voltairean and a Puritan. He had fought English society, and he had desired its favours. Neither Tory nor Radical, he had been in English politics that most luckless, because most self-divided of animals—a Whig. He had always been lacking in that unity of thought and conduct which alone fosters great designs.

But in this Greek adventure everything was straightforward. His high-born prejudices did not conflict with his desires for the freeing of a foreign race. On the contrary, he felt that if he played this hand out, he would have, for certain deep, obscure reasons, compounded of classical memories and heroic legend, the support of English public opinion. Henceforth his pacified spirit was working at its highest capacity, his lucidity and caution came into play, and he became a desirable leader. His old friend ought to have appreciated this change, but Hobhouse, "sceptical, prosaic, and a little jealous, was incapable of visualising the enterprise in its wider and more tragic contours. He was so fully occupied himself with party business, and the views of Mr. Bentham, and the future of J. C. Hobhouse, that he could pay but a superficial, although an affectionate and very tolerant, attention to the actions of Byron. And the latter, meanwhile, mortified but undeterred, proceeded with the detailed preparations for his departure."

Summer wore on, and his old foe Destiny seemed more kindly disposed than usual. Count Gamba was recalled from exile, and authorised to return to Ravenna on condition of bringing back his daughter with him. The Pope and Count Guiccioli were anxious for his return. "Her husband would forgive," said Byron (who was always very fair to the husbands of his mistresses), "provided that I (a very reasonable condition) did not continue his sub-agent." Teresa's brother, Count Pietro, of whom he grew more and more fond for his fascinating courage, was keenly desirous of accompanying Byron to Greece, and conspired with him in preparation for their setting-off. Father, mother, husband, lover, everybody (it was like the old story of Caroline Lamb), were at one in advising Teresa to make a reconciliation with her husband. Feminine passion once again raised unanimity against her. But Teresa, leaning upon Sentiment, stood firm, as Byron said, against the will of half of Romagna, with the Pope at its head,—and this, he added with alarm, after a five-year-old liaison.

If he wanted to go to Greece, said she, let him go—and she would follow; it would not be the first time she had shown that she could fight for liberty. "Of course the idea is ridiculous, as everything there must be sacrificed to seeing her out of harm's way. It is a case hard to deal with; for if she makes a scene, we shall have another romance, and tale of ill-usage, and abandonment, and Lady Carolining, and Lady Byroning, and Glenarvoning, all cut and dry. There never was a man who gave up so much to women, and all I have gained by it has been the character of treating them harshly. However, I shall do what I can, and have hopes. . . . If I left a woman for another woman, she might have cause to complain, but really when a man merely wishes to go on a great duty, for a good cause, this selfishness on the part of the *feminie* is rather too much."

At last, early in June, everything seemed to be straightening out. Countess Guiccioli was led away in a frenzy of tears by her father. The Hunts' fate was arranged for, Byron paying their journey to Florence, and for the future ceding to them his share in the *Liberal* and his copyright in the poems published therein. From Greece, Blaquiere was summoning Byron, and the departure had now to be hurried forward. Young Gamba was entrusted with the chartering of a vessel. He was a charming youth, Pietro, but he had what the Italians call the *"mal occhio."* "He would grapple earnestly and conscientiously with some problem, would write it all down in the most careful and exact memoranda, each illegible page beginning in the fashion of Bologna University, with the word *Considerando.* And then it would all go wrong."

The vessel which he chose, the brig *Hercules,* was an unseaworthy old tub. Ordered to engage a physician, he took a young man named Bruno, full of good intentions but totally inexperienced, and terrified by Lord Byron. Bruno later admitted that he had heard it said that, if he committed the least mistake, Lord Byron would have him torn to pieces by his dogs, or brained by his Tartar. The said Tartar was the worthy Tita, and the dogs were harmless; but these unavowed fears made Dr. Bruno extremely nervous, and during the rest of this history, whenever one of the members of the party felt sick, Bruno burst into tears, waved his arms, and completely lost his head. Byron desired to take Trelawny, who arrived on this invitation from Florence. This was not a happy choice; Trelawny had no love for Byron, and was no loyal follower, for he admitted that his real object was to use Byron's name to enter Greece, and once there to act on his own account.

For himself and for Trelawny he designed two helmets "of homeric proportions, and on the lines of that which, in the sixth book of the Iliad, had so dismayed the infant Ăstyanax. Below the nodding plume figured his own coat-of-arms, and the motto *Crede Biron,* while the whole was secured by a wide chin-strap of a very menacing aspect." But when Trelawny arrived he refused to don his, and the two helmets were left at Genoa.

On July 13, 1823, they were all aboard. In spite of his superstitions, Byron had agreed to set off on a Friday, the 13th. Besides Trelawny, Bruno, Gamba, and eight servants, including Fletcher and Tita, he took along five horses, arms, ammunition, two small cannon, and fifty thousand Spanish dollars. There was a blazing sun, and the air was so still that setting sail was out of the question. The town spread out its curving tiers beneath the blinding glare. Towards evening Byron came ashore, and dined beneath a tree on cheese and fruit. At last, about midnight, a wind sprang up. The *Hercules* stood up to it very poorly. The horses were terrified by the storm and kicked down the partitions of their stalls; the vessel had to be put into port again. Byron had spent the whole night amongst the horses. He said he regarded a bad beginning as a good omen, but he seemed to be pensive. He admitted to his banker, Charles Barry, that he felt very nearly inclined to give up. But Hobhouse and the others would scoff at him. . . . He felt a desire to go up and see the Casa Saluzzo once more, and on entering said to Gamba, "Where shall we be in a year?" He asked to be left alone, and spent a few hours meditating in the empty rooms.

His feelings were confused. He had longed to be out of this house, he had not been happy in it; yet he was regretting it, dreading the sadness of things that are ending. Sometimes he imagined what life would be after a triumph in Greece, a redeeming of the past by a victory; but more often his thoughts turned to the prophecies of Mrs. Williams the soothsayer. He really believed that he was heading for death.

Had he been able to take himself seriously and see this death as heroic, that would still have sustained him, but his redoubtable humour was turning upon himself. He had said to Lady Blessington: "Is it not pleasant that my eyes should never open to the folly of the undertakings passion prompts me to engage in, until I am so far embarked that retreat (at least with honour) is impossible, and my *mal à propos sagesse* arrives, to scare away the enthusiasm that led to the undertaking and which is so requisite to carry it on. It is all an uphill affair with me afterwards: I cannot for my life *échauffer* my imagination again: and my position excites such ludicrous images and thoughts in my own mind, that the whole subject, which, seen through the veil of passion, looked fit for a sublime epic, and I one of its heroes, examined now through reason's glass appears fit only for a travestie. . . . Well, if I do (and this *if* is a grand *peut-être* in my future history) outlive the campaign, I shall write two poems on the subject—one an epic, and the other a burlesque, in which none shall be spared, and myself least of all. . . ."

Toward nightfall he came down into the town again, took a hot bath, and re-embarked on the *Hercules*. At last they caught a favouring wind. On calling at Leghorn, Byron had the pleasurable surprise of finding some verses which Goethe had addressed to him in token of admiration; there too he received one of the first copies of the *Memorial of St. Helena,* sent by Augusta, which naturaly became his favourite reading. On board ship he was an easy and cheerful companion. "He boxed with Trelawny; he fenced with Gamba; he dined alone on cheese and pickled cucumbers and cider; he fired at the gulls with his pistols; he bathed when they were becalmed; he played with his dogs; and he chaffed the experienced, but drunken, Captain of the *Hercules*."

The captain, Scott by name, had made friends with Fletcher, and once when these two heroes were sipping their grog, Byron overheard their conversation. "What is your master going to such a wild country of savages for?" asked Captain Scott.—Fletcher wondered likewise. "It's all rocks and robbers," he said. "They live in holes in the rocks, and come out like foxes; they have long guns, pistols and knives. We were obliged to have a guard of soldiers to go from one place to another." Fletcher had retained the very worst memories of Greece and the Greeks, he was a Pro-Turk.—"The Turks are the only respectable people in the country. If they go, Greece will be like bedlam broke loose. It's a land of flies, and lice, and fleas, and thieves. What my Lord is going there for, the Lord only knows, I don't."—And just then noticing that his master was overhearing he added: "And my master can't deny what I have said is true."—"No," said Byron, "to those who look at things with hog's eyes, and can see nothing else."

The confusion of factions made it impossible to choose a port of disembarkment, and it had been wisely decided that the expedition should halt for some time in the Ionian Islands, to await the more definite information that Blaquiere was to bring. The Republic of the Seven Islands was under a British protectorate, and formed neutral territory; but the neutrality would be favourably inclined towards Byron. The chosen goal had originally been Zante, but an Englishman encountered during the voyage advised Cephalonia, because the British resident there was Colonel Napier, a remarkable man and a warm friend to the Greeks. On August 1 the *Hercules* dropped anchor at Argostoli, the chief port of Cephalonia. But here Byron had a great disappointment. Blaquiere had left for England a fortnight before without leaving any message. Really, these people on the English committee were intolerably careless. They had made him give up his home, his work, and his mistress, and were now leaving him on an unknown island with no instructions, no information, no purpose.

For three weeks he lay off Argostoli, aboard the *Hercules*. He was nervous about resuming contact with English officials. There were officers there—how would they receive him? He was convinced, in his morbid, self-centred way, that "he had become an object of loathing and ridicule to every Englishman, and he shrank with feminine timidity from exposing himself to any converse with them." He was quite amazed when the officers of the Eighth (King's) Regiment of Foot, invited him to dine in their mess, and still more when they rose after dinner to drink his health. He responded with feeling, and then leaned over to the colonel to ask whether he had said the right thing. He was rather alarmed, but extremely pleased.

If the English made him welcome, the Greek refugees on the island clung to him as to a saviour. They knew that he was rich and renowned. The Suliotes, in particular, crowded the deck of the *Hercules,* warriors of that almost savage tribe whose memory he fondly cherished because of their hospitality long ago, during his first pilgrimage. Their picturesque appearance so delighted Byron that he engaged forty of them to serve as his private bodyguard. He quickly repented. Gamba, who took charge of them with his kindly, busy incompetence, discovered that most of them were neither Suliotes nor Greeks, and after a few days' trial Byron gave his bodyguard two months' wages, paid their passage to Missolonghi, and was heartily glad to be rid of them.

Throughout this stay in Cephalonia, Byron's generosity was unbounded. Rochdale had been sold in June 1823 for £34,000, and he had resolved, if necessary, to spend this fortune for the cause of Greece. "My own personal wants are very simple, and my income considerable for any country but England (being equal to the President's of the United States! the English Secretaries of States or the French Ambassador's at the greater Courts)."

But although Byron was more decided than ever to give his all for Greece, he was anxious to do so reasonably. Trelawny, who was more of an adventurer and comic-opera hero than a soldier, could not understand why Byron did not start for Greece at once. "What Greece?" retorted Byron. Should he join Colocotronis in the Morea, Botzaris the Suliote at Missolonghi, or Odysseus the brigand of Athens? Nobody knew. Every bandit who could muster twenty men behind him dispatched an emissary to Byron. Blaquiere, who had at last sent a letter, advised that he should hold his hand. Colonel Napier, who was well acquainted with Greece, was not encouraging. It was hard enough to enter Greece, he said, but harder still to get out of it; and he further declared that nobody should take the lead in Greek affairs without two European regiments and a portable gallows. Besides, the Turks were in strength, and their fleet was blockading the coasts. Captain Scott refused to risk his ship on a sea patrolled by the Ottoman fleet. What could be more foolish for Byron than letting himself be captured? In the third week of August he decided to stop on in Cephalonia and took a house in a small village on the Island of Metaxata.

On Metaxata Byron found a paradoxical happiness. Never had his life been simpler. He wanted to follow a soldierly régime; asceticism had always given him both health and self-contentment. Gamba and Dr. Bruno were his only friends, but he did see something of a Cephaloniote, the Count Delladecimi (whom he nicknamed *"Ultima analisi,"* because he always began his sentences with "in the final analysis . . ."), and he also found a little Greek page, Loukas, a new Edleston.

Byron worked in the morning, took a cup of tea, went out riding, dined lightly on cheese and fruit, and in the evening read the *Memorial of St. Helena,* or a life of General Marceau, also a gift of Augusta's. Greek delegations waited upon him daily; refugees asked for help, and it was always forthcoming. At night, in the clear serenity of the moonlight, he stood watching the islands, the mountains, the sea, and far off, the rugged line of the coast of Greece.

Happiness? Yes, certainly this was happiness. No passion vexed the calm of his spirit, no critical eye spied upon him. Indeed, what reproach could have been levelled at him? He was there to behave as a man of honour. At the end of a long letter to Augusta, in which he had tried to show what stores of patience and philosophy were needed to straighten out the local intrigues, he added: "If you think this epistle or any part of it worth transmitting to Lady Byron, you can send her a copy. . . ." Perhaps she would approve of him at last—that obdurate Annabella for whose judgment he had such respect.

Except for an expedition into Ithaca, which ended rather badly with an attack of delirium in Lord Byron, his sole adventure during that stay was a spiritual one. There lived on the Island a certain Dr. Kennedy, a deeply religious Scotsman, who was striving hard to spread the Bible among the Greeks of the Ionian Isles. Soon after Byron's landing the worthy doctor had a religious argument with a group of Voltairean officers, and undertook to prove to them the truth of the Scriptures by processes as irrefutable as the theorems of Euclid.

A meeting was organised, and Byron asked to be allowed to attend. Naturally his presence excited much curiosity. A friend who met him riding to the meeting expressed the hope that his lordship would be converted. "I hope so too," he answered gravely. He sat on a sofa at Kennedy's, the others formed a circle round the table, and the doctor began his exposition.

His first theme was the difference between the Christianity of the Bible and the Christianity of men. Byron had promised to listen patiently, but all eyes were on him, and he soon began to talk. He had been brought up, he said, on very religious lines by his mother; questions of religion had always been passionately interesting to him; he had read numerous works of theology; but he could not understand the Scriptures. Sincere believers, he added, he would always respect and trust more than he would other men; but he had met too many pious people whose conduct was far other than the principles they professed.

Then, after a few words about his old friends, Eve and the Serpent, he returned to the difficulty which had always dogged him—the existence in the world of dreadful and meaningless evils, a fact which could not be reconciled with the existence of a benevolent Creator. For instance, he said, he had made a point of talking with nearly all the bodily infirm whom he had met, and had generally observed that their story was one of misery and sadness almost from birth. "How had these offended their Creator to be thus subjected to misery? and why do they live and die in this wretched state, most of them without the Gospel being preached to them? And of what use are they in this world? Many are constantly suffering under bodily evils and pains; many are suffering from the constant pressure of poverty; many are doomed to incessant toil and labour, immersed in ignorance and superstition, and neither having time nor capacity to read the Bible, even if it were presented to them."

The doctor declared that this question of the origin of Evil would open too wide a field, that it was the result of impiety, and moreover that unhappiness in this life led the spirit to the hope of a better world. When Kennedy was talking of the sovereignty of God and the old image of the potter and the clay, Byron exclaimed that if he himself were broken in pieces, he would certainly say to the potter, "Why do you treat me thus?" Byron's pleading seemed to interest the listeners more than the doctor's did, and the latter, after Byron's departure, rebuked his friends for having let themselves be influenced by the rank and fame of their guest.

But Kennedy, worthy man, bore no rancour. He went to call upon Byron, at his modest dwelling on Metaxata and resumed the discussion. He was amazed at the biblical erudition of his interlocutor. "I read more of the Bible than you are aware," said Byron. "I have a Bible which my sister gave me, who is an excellent woman, and I read it very often." Going into his bedroom, he brought out the finely bound pocket Bible which Augusta had given him. In the course of discussion, when Kennedy was vainly seeking a text to support his argument, Byron laid his finger on it instantly. He asked Kennedy astonishing questions about the Devil, and the Witch of Endor: "I have always thought this the finest and most finished witch-scene that ever was written or conceived," he said. "It beats all the ghost-scenes I ever read. The finest conception on a similar subject is that of Goethe's devil,

Mephistopheles; and though of course *you* will give the priority to the former, as being inspired, yet the latter, if you know it, will appear to you one of the finest and most sublime specimens of human conception." The doctor smiled at this odd association, admitting that he had never thought of regarding the Bible as literature. He then laid stress on the importance, for Byron, of amending his way of life. "I am now in a fairer way. I already believe in predestination, which I know you believe, and in the depravity of the human heart in general, and of my own in particular. Thus you see there are two points in which we agree." Then, as Kennedy was praising his open-handed charity and his lavish acts of kindness all around him, he went on: "You cannot expect me to become a perfect Christian at once. . . . What would you have me to do?"—"Begin this very night to pray that God would pardon your sins."—"That would be asking too much, my dear doctor," said Byron.

News from Greece was both heartening and disheartening. The Greeks were gaining victories over the Turks but could not agree amongst themselves. The London Committee sent word of a vessel with a consignment of artillery, and particularly of Congreve fuses, a new device of which wondrous reports were given. But pending the arrival of this Argo, Byron received from England nothing but maps and trumpets—estimable objects, but of small use in a country where the soldiers were as ignorant of topography as of music. The gentlemen of the Crown and Anchor had promised to send out an officer to direct operations, and Byron would have liked them to choose Colonel Napier. But the colonel did not share the Committee's views on Greek questions, being convinced that so long as one Turkish soldier remained in Europe, the Greek Government ought not to trouble about a constitution—a sentiment hardly likely to attract a Liberal committee. Colonel Stanhope, whom the London people did send out, made no favourable impression on Byron, for he was a Benthamite, and more of a politician than a soldier. It would be plain enough when the time came.

Napier at least helped Byron to make a choice among the factions. He strongly favoured Mavrocordato, the only revolutionary leader, he said, who was an honest and serious statesman. From the island of Hydra, where he then was, Mavrocordato got into touch with Byron, letting him know that he was prepared to bring out the Greek naval squadron, force the blockade, and proceed to Missolonghi to direct operations from there, provided that Byron, pending a loan which he was negotiating in London, could advance him £4,000 to pay the ships' crews. It was a large sum, but Byron produced it. He rather enjoyed being a plain citizen maintaining an army and a navy. He was amused when he noticed, in reading the *Memorial,* that the sums he had already given to Greece exceeded those with which Bonaparte had begun the Italian campaign. The Missolonghi Suliotes were asking him to put them on his pay-roll and become their leader. Despite his mortifications, he was tempted; for they were splendid fighting-men, and it would be superb to have a whole tribe under his orders. Who could tell? When Greece had been liberated, he could perhaps tilt at other windmills with his Suliotes? Already he caught glimpses of himself as a chieftain redressing wrongs in all quarters of the globe. . . .

Towards the end of the year, thanks to Byron's monetary aid, the Greek fleet was fitted out, and first Mavrocordato, then Stanhope, were able to cross to Missolonghi. Thence they begged Byron to come and join them. Mavrocordato wrote to him expressing eagerness for his arrival, and assuring him that his advice would be listened to like an oracle. And Stanhope wrote: "All are eager to see you. . . . The Prince is in a state of anxiety. . . . I walked along the streets this evening, and the people asked me after Lord Byron!!!"

It was perhaps still premature to take a hand, but Byron knew that in England the committee men were making fun of his long stay on the Island. He had been offended by a letter from Moore, which seemed to insinuate that instead of pursuing heroic adventures, he was lingering in a delightful villa, in course of continuing *Don Juan.* It was untrue. He had not continued *Don Juan,* or any other poem. "Poetry," he said to Gamba, "should only occupy the idle. In more serious affairs it would be ridiculous." He saw plainly that the adventure was perilous, "for it shall never be said that I engaged to aid a Gentleman in a little affair of Honour, and neither helped him off with it nor on with it. . . . For my part, I will stick by the cause while a plank remains which can be honourably clung to."

On December 27 he informed Moore that, twenty-four hours later, he would be embarking to join Mavrocordato at Missolonghi. "The state of parties has kept me here till now; but now that Mavrocordato (their Washington or their Kosciusko) is employed again, I can act with a safe conscience. I carry money to pay the squadron, and I have influence with the Suliotes. It is imagined that we shall attempt either Patras or the castles on the Straits; and it seems that the Greeks, at any rate the Suliotes, who are in affinity with me of bread and salt,—expect that I should march with them, and—be it even so! . . . I have hopes that the cause will triumph; but whether it does or no, still honour must be minded as strictly as milk diet. I trust to observe both."

XXXV

HAMLET AND DON QUIXOTE

1823–1824

The road of Excess leads to the Palace of Wisdom.

BLAKE

MAVROCORDATO and Stanhope had promised that the Greek squadron would safeguard his passage to Missolonghi; but Stanhope and Mavrocordato were no great organisers, and all that the two vessels bearing Byron and his fortunes fell in with was the Turkish fleet. Gamba's vessel was captured and taken off to Patras to be searched; Byron's managed to escape northward, and after a risky chase found shelter behind some rocks off Dragomestri. The Turks could easily have followed up, and he had with him only four men capable of fighting. He sent a message to Colonel Stanhope asking to be sought out and given safe escort. He wrote: "I am uneasy at being here, not so much on my own account as on that of a Greek boy with me, for you know what his fate would be; and I would sooner cut him in pieces, and myself too, than have him taken out by those barbarians." The Greek boy was Loukas, the lad he had brought from Cephalonia.

He waited for three days on Dragomestri. Fletcher had caught a violent cold in the head, and Byron had given up the ship's sole mattress to him. It was for such attentions that Fletcher used to say, "My lord may be very odd, but he has such a good heart." There Byron spent January 2, his wedding anniversary, always a day of memories for him, and on the 4th Mavrocordato had him escorted down to Missolonghi.

The town of Missolonghi lies on the edge of a shallow lagoon, only navigable by small flat-bottomed boats. A string of narrow islets bars the lagoon from the sea; Vassilidi, the most important of these, was fortified. On the morning of January 5, Byron donned a handsome scarlet uniform, borrowed before leaving Cephalonia from Colonel Duffie of the Eighth Regiment of Foot, entered a small boat, and was rowed across the lagoon to the town. He was greeted with salvos of artillery, the firing of muskets, and a burst of barbaric music. Soldiers and townsfolk thronged the square when he stepped ashore, and Colonel Stanhope and Prince Mavrocordato welcomed him at the door of his house. Gamba, who had miraculously escaped from the Turks at Patras, was already there, and could hardly contain his tears at this affecting scene.

Missolonghi was a fishing-town, built just above the level of the sea. Marshy meadowland surrounded it, and in the rainy season even the streets became swamps. No drainage was practicable, and the water lay in stagnant pools right up to the houses. Yet Missolonghi had a curious, inhuman charm; half-swallowed by the sea, this Atlantis seemed like a place cut off from the world. Shepherds clad in goatskins lived in huts among the reeds, beneath the purple mountains. Everything was redolent of salt and fish and sludge. Lord Byron's house was a slightly raised building, in which Colonel Stanhope had already been living. There was a fine view from the windows, and beyond the silvery mirror of the lagoon one saw the dark streak formed by the string of islands, surmounted by their small lake-dwellings, the wooden piles of which stood out sharply against the sky. In clear weather Cephalonia was visible in the distance, the spot where Byron had been happy. Fletcher, Tita, and Lega Zambelli did their best to improve the appearance of Lord Byron's dismal apartment. He set some books and some weapons against its bare walls, and in the large hall on the ground floor he stationed a Suliote guard. Outside, in the Missolonghi cafés, fugitives and soldiers in broidered tunics were bandying taunts. It seemed a far cry to the Greece of Leonidas.

Byron summed up the whole situation very coolly. His ally, Alexander Mavrocordato, was an honest man, but he had no will of his own and no authority over his troops. The town was packed with these everlasting Suliotes, starving, underpaid by the Greek Government, and forming a more immediate danger than the Turks. The war of independence had little interest for them; they had always been mercenaries. The very name of Suli made them sigh and turn their gaze northward, where their native rocks were sometimes visible jutting through the clouds. Mavrocordato was afraid of them, and begged Byron to take them into his pay.

They were still waiting for the said Argo, on board which the London committee were supposed to be sending artillery and mechanics. It was a matter of urgency to recruit a unit of specially trained men who could serve these guns when they did arrive; and for this unit, subscribing a preliminary sum of £100, Byron tried to enroll certain Germans and Swedes. He himself showed most soldierly qualities, and daily attended the drilling of his brigade on the marshy flats. "Nothing is so insupportable to me, but patience is indispensable. . . . I have not much hope of success; but something may be done, if it be only to employ ourselves and these troops, and keep them at least from being idle and creating disturbances."

The most tempting enterprise on the horizon was to storm the town of Lepanto, situated a little farther up the Gulf of Corinth and still occupied by the Turks. Byron dispatched two of his officers, an Englishman and a German, to examine the fortifications of Lepanto. Its Albanian garrison, it appeared, had not been paid by the Turks for sixteen months, and they informed Byron's emissaries that they would gladly surrender if they were promised a decent compensation and whole skins. So the siege would be easy; but at the same time, the renowned name of Lepanto in the news of the success would make an effect in Europe, and help the completion of the loan which the Greeks were then negotiating in London.

The weather was frightful, and the rain streamed down unceasingly; and as riding was impossible on the sodden roads, Byron and Gamba went out rowing on the lagoon, discussing their war against Lepanto. Byron confessed that he had no confidence in his troops, but said that in order to improve them he would make a show of admiring them. He wanted to lead them to the attack in person. "Above all, these semi-barbarians should never entertain the least suspicion of your personal courage." Mavrocordato offered him the title of *archistrategos,* or commander-in-chief. He had a laugh over this with Gamba, as he always did when afraid of the laughter of others.

On the other side of the balance, he was exasperated by the entirely political activities of Colonel Stanhope, his committee colleague. The "typographical colonel," as Byron called him, held it of greater importance to provide the Greeks with a Press of advanced views than with an army. He strove to set up schools, believing that a country's liberty is assured by its instruction in the theory of Liberty; but Byron would hear of no school but a gunnery school. Stanhope had also a plan for organising a post-office, a plan for building model prisons, a plan for making Mr. Bentham the apostle of the Greeks. Perhaps a saint—but no soldier, thought Byron, consenting to give £100 for the newspaper, but telling Prince Mavrocordato that, if he were in his place, he would set up a censorship. Stanhope flared up: "If your Lordship was serious, I shall consider it my duty to communicate this affair to the Committee in England, in order to show them how difficult a task I have to fulfil in promoting the liberties of Greece, if your Lordship is to throw the weight of your vast talents into the opposite scale."

To which Byron replied, that he was a partisan of the liberty of the Press, but not in a primitive and inflammable society; that the liberty of the Press might be an excellent thing in Great Britain, where one journal was counterbalanced by another; but that a Press consisting of one single journal could not, by very definition, be free. The first number of the *Cronica Greca* showed that he was right. Its motto was Bentham's axiom—"the greatest happiness of the greatest number." One article revealed to the Suliotes that Jeremy Bentham was the greatest man of his time, perhaps of all time. The Colonel's foreign policy was dangerous; taking up arms against the Holy Alliance, he adjured the Hungarians to imitate the Greek insurrection. Now Byron detested the Holy Alliance as much as any man alive, but he thought it absurd to compromise the Greek revolt in European revolutionary currents.

The practical poet and the chimerical soldier stood face to face: "It is odd enough," said Byron, "that Stanhope, the soldier, is all for writing down the Turks; and I, the writer, am all for fighting them down." Yet Stanhope could not but recognise Byron's kindness and good faith; he could detect neither pedantry nor affectation in this man who was as natural and straightforward as a child. He was a patient listener too, in general most attentive, and chivalrous to the verge of quixotry. All who lived with Byron at this time found in him what Lady Blessington had caught glimpses of, and what Trelawny denied—greatness of character. He had realised ever since he set foot in this realm of Mud and Discord that the adventure would be neither dazzling nor picturesque. "I am come here not in search of adventures," he said, "but to assist the regeneration of a nation whose very debasement makes it more honourable to become their friend."

To set an example, he imposed on himself the duty of subsisting on rations as simple as those issued to the Greek troops. His generosity had made him as popular amongst the peasantry round Missolonghi as it had at Ravenna. Although constantly in danger in the midst of violent creatures who forced their way into his house, dragged him into their quarrels, and threatened him, he still remained both cool and energetic. Once his room was invaded by some Greek sailors from the islands, insolently demanding the handing over of a prisoner to themselves. Byron, who had personally had the man put in safe keeping, refused. The sailors declared they would not leave the room without their Turk. Byron pointed a loaded pistol at them, and with such a resolute look that they filed out. On several occasions he sent prisoners over to Patras in order to save them. In every plan of operations he asked for the most dangerous post. "As for personal safety," he said, "besides that it ought not to be a consideration, I take it that a man is on the whole as safe in one place as another; and, after all, he had better end with a bullet than bark in his body."

There were moments when he regretted having come. One day, having received a long-overdue letter from Hobhouse, who advised him not to leave Cephalonia without plenty of precautions, he exclaimed: "Ah! it comes too late; it is like telling a man to beware of his wife after he has married her." But he soon recovered self-control, declaring that he far preferred a wretched existence in Missolonghi to doing as Tom Moore did, singing and drinking all night in a London drawing-room after he was forty. "Poverty is wretchedness; but it is perhaps to be preferred to the heartless unmeaning dissipation of the higher orders. I am thankful I am now clear of that, and my resolution to remain clear of it for the rest of my life is immutable."

Poet and soldier had triumphed over the dandy and the man of the world. Would it be so, as he believed, for the rest of his life? Would he resist temptation if he once more found himself afloat on that "sea of silk and jewellery?" In this austere Missolonghi adventure the Puritan and Cavalier, so long trifled with, were at last finding their stern enjoyment.

On his birthday, January 22, 1824, he came into a room where Stanhope, Gamba, and a few friends were sitting together. "You were complaining, the other day," he said with a smile, "that I never write any poetry now. This is my birthday, and I have just finished something which I think is better than what I usually write." And he then read them the verses which he had headed "On this Day I complete my Thirty-sixth Year"—

'Tis time this heart should be unmoved,
Since others it hath ceased to move:
Yet, though I cannot be beloved,
Still let me love!

My days are in the yellow leaf;
The flowers and fruits of love are gone;
The worm, the canker, and the grief
Are mine alone!

The fire that on my bosom preys
Is lone as some volcanic isle;
No torch is kindled at its blaze—
A funeral pile.

The hope, the fear, the jealous care,
The exalted portion of the pain
And power of love, I cannot share,
But wear the chain.

But 'tis not *thus*—and 'tis not *here*—
Such thoughts should shake my soul, nor *now*,
Where glory decks the hero's bier,
Or binds his brow.

The sword, the banner, and the field,
Glory and Greece, around me see!
The Spartan, borne upon his shield,
Was not more free.

Awake! (not Greece—she *is* awake!)
Thy life-blood tracks its parent lake,
Awake, my spirit! think through *whom*
And then strike home.

Tread those reviving passions down,
Unworthy manhood!—unto thee
Indifferent should the smile or frown
Of beauty be.

If thou regrett'st thy youth, *why live?*
The land of honourable death
Is here:—up to the field, and give
Away thy breath!

Seek out—less often sought than found—
A soldier's grave, for thee the best;
Then look around, and choose thy ground,
And take thy rest.

On that day he was entering upon that thirty-seventh year which, according to prophecy, would be fatal to him. He enquired of Tita whether he had any desire to return to Italy.—"Yes, if your lordship goes, I go." Lord Byron smiled.—"No, Tita," he said, "I shall never go back from Greece. Either the Turks, or the Greeks, or the climate, will prevent that."

His military hopes brightened with the news of the arrival of Mr. William Parry, thc artilleryman and mechanic sent out by the London Committee. Mr. Parry brought cannon, and English engineers as well; it was said that he knew how to make these famous Congreve fuses. With Mr. Parry he could doubtless capture Lepanto. Parry turned out to be no more than a naval petty-officer and an official in an arsenal; but he was not displeasing to Byron, who was always fond of specialists. His vulgarity was diverting. He was fond of a drink, and a certain quantity of brandy always brought forth amusing stories. In his eyes, as in Byron's, the London committee was the most comical band of theorists that was ever gathered together. He shared his new chief's horror of enthusiasm, declared that Blaquiere and Hobhouse were humbugs, and made Byron laugh till he cried with the story of his first interview with Mr. Jeremy Bentham, who, breaking off a conversation, even leaving a sentence unfinished, broke into a trot down a London street to the great amazement of the passers-by, because this was beneficial to his health. Byron then undertook the task of explaining to Parry the difficulties of the Greek situation, and the strife in Missolonghi itself. Parry's impression was unfavourable; he felt that Byron was anxious, almost despairing of success, but that he would still go through with the adventure. "There was then a pallidness in his face, and knitting of his brows, that indicated both weakness and vexation."

The arrival of Parry and his men was a confounding of confusion. For the construction of an arsenal they had been allotted the small building of the Seraglio. It had to be cleaned out, and the material had to be transported thither; but almost every day was a saint's day, and the Greek soldiers did not like fatigue-parties. Byron was so annoyed that in the end he hobbled about at the work himself. The English workmen, sent out by the committee were shocked by the filth of the site and the gloominess of the town. The lading-list of the cargo was disappointing. The famous Congreve fuses were missing. The German officers of the artillery brigade were offended when Byron wished to place Parry as major in command of them; he was not even an officer, and was, they declared, incompetent, appearing on parade in an apron and carrying a hammer.

Byron saw well enough that Parry was no great soldier, but at least he was a man of common sense. And Byron felt so much alone: all his entourage were at daggers drawn, and quarrelling for his money. Apart from Gamba and his personal servants, there was nobody he could count upon. Stanhope was a worthy fellow, but mad. In Mavrocordato's eyes, victory seemed to depend not on any preparatory work, but on brute courage. The foreigners of the artillery brigade bickered over questions of precedence. Parry and Byron were the two modern soldiers of the expedition.

Byron had come upon the scene as an observer, resolved to obey the professionals and to keep his place; but little by little, he found himself being pushed willy-nilly into the supreme command by the sheer incompetence of the rest. Yet he too was weak, and knew it; the hateful régime which he imposed on himself in the name of military rigour was enfeebling him; one day his nerves betrayed him. These were the hard facts—but he was "a man," and the only one. "Well, it seems that I am to be Commander-in-Chief," he commented, "and the post is by no means a sinecure. . . . Whether we shall have a boxing bout between the Captain and the Colonel, I cannot tell; but, between Suliote chiefs, German barons, English volunteers, and adventurers of all nations, we are likely to form as goodly an army as ever quarrelled beneath the same banner."

Up till the middle of February he continued to keep a good face on things. He could not ride through the town, for its streets were a quagmire, but he got Gamba to row him over daily in a small boat to the house of a fisherman named Ghazis, where horses awaited him and he could gallop in an olive-grove. Then the boat brought him back across the lagoon. The sunsets were superb. He talked to Gamba of the past, of Aberdeen and Newstead and Cambridge, and of the boat at Brighton in which he used to take out his first mistress. He still found the same pleasure in unrolling the vividly coloured panorama of his youth, and Gamba and Parry were both touched by the childlike simplicity of his character. Opposite his own house at Missolonghi there stood a Turkish house, its turrets studded with ornaments; and every time he came out-of-doors he used to demolish one of these ornaments with a pistol-shot. The report brought the women on to the balcony, whence they hurled a picturesque gibberish of insults at Byron's head. How he enjoyed that! In his own quarters, he liked going down into the paved hall which served as the Suliotes' guard-room, and would play there with his dog. For an hour on end he would keep saying, "Lyon, thou art more faithful than men. . . . Lyon, thou art an honest fellow. . . ." And Lyon sat on the floor wagging his tail contentedly, and Byron seemed happy.

The appointed date for the assault on Lepanto drew near. Gamba, entrusted with a reorganisation of the Suliote corps, found on the rolls numerous names of soldiers who had never existed. The fraud was a time-worn custom of the mercenaries, which provided the leaders with some useful additional pay. Gamba tightened up the control, but the Suliotes grumbled. They could not abide these finical Westerners. Colocotronis, in the Morea, had learned of the strategical plans of the Greeks at Missolonghi, and was afraid lest their success might strengthen the power of his rival, Mavrocordato. He sent emissaries to beguile Byron's Suliotes away from him. Imbecile rumours went the rounds—that Mavrocodato would certainly sell the country to the English

. . . that Lord Byron was no Englishman, but a Turk under an assumed name. Just when the last details of the attacks were being arranged, the Suliotes, under pressure from the Colocotronis agents, suddenly demanded that appointments should be made from their number of two generals, two colonels, two captains, and a large number of other officers. Out of three or four hundred of these Suliotes, one hundred and fifty would thus have received officers' pay. Byron lost his temper, and vowed he would have no more to do with the Suliotes. On February 15 he called the chiefs together and announced that he was dismissing them. But he was sick at heart. This meant the end of the plan of campaign to which he had pinned his hopes through the whole of that long winter.

During the late afternoon of this difficult day he was joking with Colonel Stanhope, when he complained of feeling thirsty, and called for cider. He drank some, stood up, staggered, and fell into the arms of Parry. His features were distorted, his mouth was twisted, and his frame violently convulsed. After a couple of minutes he came round, and his first words were: "Is not this Sunday?" It was, they told him. "I should have thought it most strange if it were not," he replied. Sunday was one of his unlucky days.

Dr. Bruno wanted to bleed him, but the idea of letting anyone take his blood filled Byron with that invincible horror which it has for certain primitive beings. Bruno was distraught, wrung his hands, applied leeches to Byron's temples, and was unable to check the subsequent hæmorrhage. The terrified Tita and Fletcher dashed to the dispensary to fetch Dr. Julius Millingen, a German in the Greek Government service, who contrived to stop the vein with caustic, though not without causing pain. Byron's mind was still confused. "In this world," he murmured, "there is nothing but pain."

Round him, Gamba, Fletcher, Tita and Bruno were in a state of distraction, all wondering what this seizure had been. Epilepsy? Or apoplexy? The doctors inclined to recognise epileptic symptoms. But the evening's anxieties were not yet over. Byron had hardly recovered consciousness when word came that the Suliotes had mutinied and were marching on the Seraglio. Gamba, Parry and Stanhope had to run through darkness and rain, along those muddy streets where one had to jump from one paving-stone to another. The artillery brigade was ordered to stand to. A couple of drunken troopers pushed right into Byron's room, where he lay resting, weak and still only half-conscious. "He did not understand what they were saying. He was helpless and alone. The noise around him was pierced by the falsetto protests of Bruno. Bruno was already in tears. To Byron's fuddled consciousness the scene in the damp and ill-lit room adjusted itself gradually to a vague turmoil of confusion, helplessness, and terror. And above and behind it all came the sound of rain pouring relentlessly upon the roof, and splashing from the gutters upon the mire of the yard below."

It was a gloomy week that followed. Ever since Byron heard the word "epilepsy" spoken before him, he feared for his reason. He continued to feel bouts of dizziness, and unpleasant nervous sensations which, he said, resembled fear, although he knew he had no cause for alarm. "Do you suppose that I wish for life?" he said to Dr. Millingen. "I have grown heartily sick of it, and shall welcome the hour I depart from it. Why should I regret it? Can it afford me any pleasure? . . . Few men can live faster than I did. I am, literally speaking, a young old man. Hardly arrived at manhood, I had attained the zenith of fame. Pleasure I have known under every form it can present itself to mortals. I have travelled, satisfied my curiosity, lost every illusion. . . . But the apprehension of two things now haunts my mind. I picture myself slowly expiring on a bed of torture, or terminating my days like Swift—a grinning idiot! Would to Heaven the day were arrived in which, rushing, sword in hand, on a body of Turks, and fighting like one weary of existence, I shall meet immediate, painless death."

A letter from Lady Byron, forwarded by Augusta and giving him all the details he had asked about, arrived immediately after the crisis. It gave him pleasure. Annabella mentioned him without horror, and answered all his questions about little Ada. "Is she social or solitary?" he had written, "taciturn or talkative, fond of reading or otherwise? . . . Is she passionate? I hope that the Gods have made her anything save poetical—it is enough to have one such fool in a family." The replies were reassuring; Ada was big and strong, preferred prose to poetry, had a taste for mechanics, and her favourite occupation was building little boats. . . . Would he ever see these three women again?—"My dearest Augusta,—I received a few days ago yours and Lady Byron's report of Ada's health, for which I ought to be and am sufficiently thankful, as they were of great comfort and I wanted some, having been recently unwell. . . ."

Four days after Byron's mishap, Lieutenant Sass, a good Swedish officer who had arrived with Parry, was killed by one of the Suliotes. He had been trying to prevent the man from gaining access to the arsenal; it was no more than a misunderstanding between two men speaking different tongues; but blood lay upon this tower of Babel.

The murder of Sass added the last touch of discouragement to the English mechanics, who had already been affected by the mud and misery of the town, by a slight earthquake shock, and by the barbarian soldiery. They were seized with panic, and demanded to be shipped home to England. Byron tried to reassure them, but Colonel Stanhope told them that he could not positively say their lives were safe.—"I should like to know," muttered Byron, "*where* our life *is* safe, either here or anywhere else?" One of these mechanics, a Wesleyan missioner, had arrived laden with Bibles in modern Greek. These he left with Byron, for him to continue their distribution. Byron conscientiously did so. He found a certain grim humour in the way in which all responsibilities, military, political and religious, came one after another to be thrust upon his feeble carcase.

Even the townspeople of Missolonghi were alarmed by the murder of Sass, and demanded the dismissal of the Suliotes. To procure their departure, they would have to be given their back-pay, three thousand Spanish dollars in all; and Byron, of course, would have to foot the bill. In the course of three months he had spent fifty-nine thousand dollars at Missolonghi—and with what result? "No guard to stand sentry at the depot of munitions; no artisans to make munitions; no munitions with which to arm the soldiers; no soldiers to use munitions, could they have been made. . . ." And walking with Gamba one day, Byron was forced to admit: "I begin to fear that I have done nothing but lose time, money, patience, and health; but I was prepared for it; I knew that ours was not a path of roses, and that I ought to make up my mind to meet with deception, calumny, and ingratitude."

Colonel Stanhope might be insufferable, but he was a just man, and recognised that Byron was behaving with admirable fortitude. He wrote as much to the committee, and Hobhouse indulgently told them: "Stanhope says Byron behaved with great firmness. He always does on emergencies." Byron even retained his taste for undergraduate practical joking, and on learning that Parry had been alarmed by the earthquake, stage-managed an artificial cataclysm a few days later; he instructed fifty men to hide in the cellars and make the house shake. It duly rocked, not being very solid, while cannon-balls were rolled over the upper floors to complete the illusion. Parry fled—and Byron was hugely amused.

But notwithstanding his humour, he was often disheartened. His life had always been subject to a definite rhythm: a bold attack upon the universe—and discouragement when he provoked the irresistible counter-blows of the universe. How could he work usefully with men who hated each other? The situation of the town was precarious. The ramparts were in bad repair and ought to have been rebuilt. In the moats there were old Turkish cannon to be seen, which ought to have been extricated and put into use. The islet which commanded the entrance to the lagoon was barely protected. What would have happened if a Turkish vessel had seized it and sent a few gunboats into the lagoon? That in itself would have made short work of Missolonghi. Byron and Parry were alive to these dangers and eager to take action, but Mavrocordato wavered and lingered and could not succeed in getting his men to work. One day it was shortness of money, the next it was a saint's day, the next a disagreement amongst the leaders. Sometimes when the Greeks told him that they really needed a King, Byron thought they were not far wrong. But Colonel Stanhope was most indignant; he wanted to provide them with the constitution of the Swiss Cantons.

In fact, the sole favourable event of these bad days was the departure of the typographical colonel. He left for Athens, not without having founded a new weekly journal, the *Greek Telegraph,* published in three languages. At Athens he ran across Trelawny once more, now on the staff of Odysseus, and more piratical than ever. He had adopted Suliote costume and provided himself with a harem of about ten women; Odysseus had personally presented him with one of his sisters. Since this marriage Trelawny had had a passionate admiration for the former brigand chief; "a glorious being," he declared, "brave, clever and noble." Odysseus knew that a man should always be lured through his outstanding weakness, and with Stanhope he was no less adroit: he accordingly held the Swiss constitution in reverence, declared himself a thorough democrat, scoffed at the princely title of Mavrocordato, and gave every appearance of a lively interest in the doctrines of Mr. Jeremy Bentham. Stanhope wrote back to Byron: "I have been constantly with Odysseus. He has a very strong mind, a good heart, and is brave as his sword. . . . He puts complete confidence in the people. He is for a strong government, for constitutional rights. . . . He has established two schools here, and has allowed me to set the press at work." Trelawny and Stanhope were keenly anxious for a meeting which should bring Mavrocordato and Odysseus together at Salona. Possibly a reconciliation could be arranged, and then they would doubtless offer Byron the title of Governor-General of Greece.

Byron was tempted. The distrustful Mavrocordato was afraid that the sole aim of Odysseus was to drag him, the prince, into an ambush and make certain of securing the person of Byron. He was quite right. Trelawny had formed a scheme of installing Byron on the Acropolis, a plan of campaign which looked remarkably like an abduction. But Byron was anxious to proceed to this interview. He felt an urgent need of extricating himself for a few days from this Missolonghi nightmare—endless demands for cash, claims for rations, bread so bad that, as he said, they must really find a baker to replace the brickmaker who had made it hitherto, a threatened plague, an attack on the town by neighbouring tribes. Up to the present he had kept his courage in this inferno; but his nerves were on edge.

On April 9 he received letters from England with good news of the Greek loan. Almost two and a half million pounds had been subscribed; he would be able to organise a new artillery brigade and an infantry corps of two thousand men. Given fresh heart by the news, he decided to go out riding with Gamba that day, in spite of threatening weather. Three miles out from the town he was caught by the rain. On his way home, when they reached the fisherman's hut, Gamba remarked that it was rash to sit still in a boat with soaking clothes, and that for once he would be wiser to return on horseback. "I should make a pretty soldier, indeed," said Byron, "if I were to care for such a trifle!" So they left their horses and came back to Missolonghi by boat across the lagoon.

A couple of hours after his return Byron was seized with shivering, and complained of fever and rheumatic pains. In the evening Gamba found him lying stretched out. "I suffer a great deal of pain," he said. "I do not care for death, but these agonies I cannot bear." Next day he sent for Parry and told him of the success of the loan, and together they prepared a plan of subventions for the summer campaign. Byron intended to pay out of his own pocket for the artillery corps, the equipment of two vessels, and the purchase of mountain artillery. That night, although feverish, he talked gaily with Dr. Millingen. Then he turned thoughtful, remembering the story of Mrs. Williams. To his visitors' reproaches of his superstition, he answered: "To say truth, I find it equally difficult to know what to believe in this world and what not to believe." During the night he sent for Bruno and told him he was shivering. First Bruno and then Millingen proposed to bleed him, but he refused. "Have you no other remedy than bleeding?" he asked. "There are many more die of the lancet than the lance."

Millingen pointed out to him that bleeding was dangerous in nervous afflictions, but not in inflammatory cases. "Who is nervous if I am not?" he replied irritably. "Drawing blood from a nervous patient is like loosening the chords of a musical instrument, the tones of which are already defective for want of sufficient tension. Before I became ill, you know yourself how weak and irritable I had become. Bleeding, by increasing this state, will inevitably kill me."

A violent hurricane, with a howling sirocco, was sweeping over Missolonghi. Rain was falling in torrents.

Parry had seen that Byron was very ill, and wanted to send him to Zante, where he could have better attention; but he had to drop the plan, as no ship could put to sea. For several days the doctors obstinately declared that Byron's illness was merely a chill and in no way grave. Fletcher's view was different. "I am sure, my lord," said he, "that you never had a cold of so serious a nature."—"I think I never had," said Byron.

On the 15th he had a long talk with Parry. "I have had most strange feelings," he told him, "but my head is now better; I have no gloomy thoughts, and no idea but that I shall recover. I am perfectly collected, I am sure I am in my senses, but a melancholy will creep over me at times. . . ." Then he remarked: "I am convinced of the happiness of domestic life. No man on earth respects a virtuous woman more than I do, and the prospect of retirement in England with my wife and Ada, gives me an idea of happiness I have never experienced before. Retirement will be everything to me, for heretofore my life has been like the ocean in a storm." He then spoke of Tita, who had been admirable and had never left his room for several days, and of Bruno, whom he liked but felt to be too excitable. He also spoke about religion: "You have no conception of the unaccountable thoughts which come into my mind when the fever attacks me. I fancy myself a Jew, a Mahomedan, and a Christian of every profession of faith. Eternity and space are before me; but on this subject, thank God, I am happy and at ease."

During the night the fever and restlessness grew worse. He was delirious. Millingen and Bruno threatened him with brain troubles if he did not allow himself to be bled, and obtained his consent. He gave them one of those "under-looks" which, in the Childe Harold days, had sent tremors through the women in the London drawing-rooms, and held out his arm, saying: "Come, you are, I see, a damned set of butchers. Take away as much blood as you will; but have done with it."

On the 17th he was twice bled. He begged the doctors not to plague him with their continual demands for blood. Cold compresses were put on his forehead. One of the doctors proposed mustard plasters. Tita, alarmed by Lord Byron's delirium, took away the pistol and daggers which always lay at the bedside. Gamba, who had been unable to come on the previous evening, was horrified by the change he found, and such tears flooded his eyes that he had to leave the room. Round the bed was a Babel. Bruno and Tita spoke only Italian, Fletcher and Parry only English, and the Greek domestics were unintelligible to everybody. Byron drank large quantities of lemonade, and got up every now and then with the help of Fletcher and Tita. He was chiefly obsessed with his lack of sleep, and said: "I know that without sleep a man must die or go mad. I would sooner die a thousand times. . . . I am not afraid of dying. I am more fit to die than people think."

On the 18th a consultation took place between four doctors—Millingen, Bruno, Treiber (Millingen's assistant), and Lucca Vaya, Mavrocordato's physician. It was Easter Sunday. The townspeople had been requested not to make a noise, and instead of the traditional Easter greeting, "Christ is risen!" the Missolonghians were asking each other, "How is Lord Byron?" As they were accustomed to celebrate the day by firing off guns, it was decided that Parry should take the artillery brigade some way out from the town and carry out manœuvres, so as to divert the inhabitants over to that side. The streets were patrolled in order to ensure silence in the neighbourhood of the house. The doctors were divided, Bruno and Lucca Vaya proposing remedies employed for typhoid cases, while Treiber and Millingen wanted to go on with leeches and plasters, opposing the further blood-letting which Bruno wished to carry out. "Your efforts to preserve my life will be in vain," said Byron to Millingen. "Die I must: I feel it. Its loss I do not lament, for to terminate my wearisome existence I came to Greece. My wealth, my abilities, I devoted to her cause. Well: there is my life to her. . . ."

During this Easter day he was still able to read a few letters, and even to translate one written in Greek by the deputy Luriottis. In the late afternoon all who were at his bedside realised that the end was drawing near. Fletcher and Gamba had to go out; they were in tears. Tita remained, because Byron was holding his hand, but he turned away his head to hide his tears. Byron gazed at him fixedly and said in Italian, half-smiling: *"Oh questa è una bella scena!"* Immediately after that he fell into delirium, and began calling out, now in Italian, now in English, as if he were advancing to the attack: "Forward! Courage! Follow my example! Don't be afraid!"

In his lucid moments he realised that he was dying, and said to Fletcher: "It is now nearly over, I must tell you all without losing a moment."—"Shall I go, my lord, and fetch pen, ink and paper?"—"Oh, my God! no, you will lose too much time, and I have it not to spare, for my time is now short. Now, pay attention! You will be provided for." Fletcher begged him to turn to things of more consequence, and Byron went on: "Oh!

my poor dear child! My dear Ada! My God! Could I but have seen her! Give her my blessing! And my dear sister Augusta, and her children—and you will go to Lady Byron, and say,—tell her everything—you are friends with her."

At that moment he seemed to be deeply affected. His voice failed, and Fletcher could now only catch a word here and there. Byron went on very seriously, mumbling unintelligible sentences for some time. Then he raised his voice. "Fletcher," he said, "now if you do not execute every order which I have given you, I will torment you hereafter if possible."

He knew well how timorous and superstitious Fletcher was, and this threat was certainly the last flickering gleam of his humour. In consternation, his servant replied that he had not grasped a single word of what his lordship had said.

"Oh, my God!" said Byron, "then all is lost, for it is now too late! Can it be possible you have not understood me? . . ."

"No, my lord, but I pray you to try and inform me once more."

"How can I? It is now too late, and all is over!"

"Not our will, but God's be done!" said Fletcher.

And Byron, with a fresh effort went on: "Yes, not mine be done—but I will try. . . ."

Several times he struggled to speak, but could only keep on repeating: "My wife! My child! My sister!—You know all—You must say all—You know my wishes. . . ."

After that it became difficult to understand him. He uttered names and figures, speaking one moment in English and the next in Italian. Sometimes he said: "Poor

Greece,—poor town—my poor servants!"—and then: "Why was I not aware of this sooner?" and another time: "My hour is come! I do not care for death—but why did I not go home before I came here?" And later he said: *"Io lascio qualche cosa di caro nel mundo"* —"I am leaving something dear in the world. . . ."

About six in the evening he said: "I want to go to sleep now," and turning over, he fell into a sleep from which he never awoke. He seemed powerless to move a limb, but the onlookers observed symptoms of suffocation, and a rattle in his throat. Every now and then Fletcher and Tita raised his head, but he seemed to feel nothing. The doctors applied leeches to dispel this lethargy. Blood trickled down his face. For twenty-four hours he remained in this condition. On the evening of the 19th, in the twilight, Fletcher was keeping watch beside his master and saw him open his eyes, then shut them instantly. "My God!" he said, "I fear his lordship is gone. . . . " The doctors felt the pulse. "You are right," they said. "He is gone."

A few moments before, a terrible storm had broken over Missolonghi. Night was falling; lightning and thunderclaps came one on top of another in the gloom. Far off, across the lagoon, the fleeting gleam of flashes lit up the dark outlines of the islands. A scudding rain lashed the windows of the houses. The fatal tidings had not yet reached the Greek soldiers and shepherds who had taken refuge indoors; but like their ancestors they believed that the death of a hero came heralded by portents, and as they listened to the prodigious fury of this thunder, they murmured to each other: "Byron is dead."

EPILOGUE

1824–1900

> "There is a strange coincidence sometimes in the little things of this world," says Sterne, and so I have often found it.
>
> BYRON

A FEW hours before Byron's death a packet of letters had arrived from England. Stanhope's words of praise, and the tributes of the Greek deputies who came to London for the loan, had at last convinced Hobhouse of his friend's seriousness. One of the Greeks had declared that only Providence could have sent this man to their help; and Hobhouse was now writing respectfully to the "dear fellow."—"Your name and character," he said, "will stand far above those of any contemporary. . . . I can assure you that all the world here thinks what I say. . . . Your present endeavour is certainly the most glorious ever undertaken by man. Campbell said to me yesterday that he envied what you are now doing (and you may believe him, for he is a very envious man) even more than all your laurels, blooming as they are."

So England had forgiven. But by now Lord Byron lay in his agony in Fletcher's arms, and the letters lay unopened beside his bed.

That evening Mavrocordato issued a proclamation; at dawn next day, a salute of thirty-seven guns was to be fired from the great battery, "the number representing the age of the illustrious departed." The Greeks would gladly have dug Byron a grave in the Parthenon, or in the temple of Theseus, and Dr. Millingen declared that the dying man had charged him to let his bones moulder in some corner of Grecian soil. But Parry and Fletcher, closer intimates, swore that they had received orders to the contrary, and it was settled that the body should be embalmed and sent back to England.

The timid, mediocre quartet of doctors who had attended Byron assembled round his bed. Before beginning their autopsy, they gazed for a moment in admiration at the extraordinary beauty of this body. The hair (its curls were natural) was grey; the features retained a look of lofty sarcasm. Opening the skull, they were amazed to find that the brain was that of a very old man; the *dura mater* was adhering to the bony structure of the skull, and was inflamed; the *pia mater*, injected with blood, had the inflamed appearance of a diseased eye. Heart and liver were in bad condition. The doctors declared that, even had he escaped this illness, Lord Byron would not have lived very long.

Next day an uncanny silence lay over the whole town. So violent was the rain that the funeral ceremonies were postponed until the next day. On April 22 the coffin (the rough wooden coffin of a soldier) was borne over to the church, with a black cloak flung over it, and on the cloak a sword and a wreath of laurel. The poverty of the scene, the misery of the savage-looking soldiery who filled the church, were all part of a scene which was more affecting, said Gamba, than any that had ever been seen round the tomb of a great man.

On May 14 Hobhouse was roused by a violent knocking at his door. He rose. It was a note from Kinnaird announcing Byron's death. A bundle of letters was with it, one from Gamba, the rest from Fletcher, addressed to Lady Byron, to Mrs. Leigh, and to Captain George Anson, now the seventh Lord Byron. Hobhouse was overwhelmed, but he went to see Augusta, and handed her Fletcher's letter. Listening to that artless account of his, he could master his grief no longer and broke down. But he had presence of mind enough to counsel Mrs. Leigh not to make public that part of the letter which told how, every morning since his epileptic seizure, Byron had had a Bible laid on his table. "This circumstance," said Hobhouse, "which pleased his valet, I was afraid might be mistaken for cowardice or hypocrisy. I daresay that the Bible was on his table. I have long recollected his having one near him; it was a volume given to him by his sister, and I remember well seeing it on his table, but unless his mind was shaken by disease I am confident he made no superstitious use of it. . . . He often said to me: 'It may be true. It is, as d'Alembert said, a *grand peut-être*'; but I own that I think he was rather inclined to take the opposite line of thinking when I saw him at Pisa."

Augusta promised. Augusta always promised. But she entrusted the news of Byron's conversion to her confidant, the Rev. Francis Hodgson. Her chief consolation, she said, was in the thought that her "poor dear Byron was now snatched from us to spare him future trials and temptations. . . . Fletcher says that for the last year his mind and feelings appeared to be changed much for the better. He expressed concern at having written *Don Juan* and other objectionable things. . . . I think it is impossible that Fletcher, who had lived with him twenty-three years, and must have known his habits so intimately, could have been struck with such an idea without there had been grounds for it. . . . You see, dear Mr. Hodgson, that Mr. Hobhouse and a certain set imagine that it might be said by his enemies, and those who have no religion at all, that he had turned Methodist, if it was affirmed that he paid more attention to his religious duties than formerly. But let them say what they will, it must be the first of consolations to us that he did so." Thus did the living make tools of the dead to satisfy their passions.

Captain George Byron was sent to Lady Byron's to break the news. He returned with word that she was deeply afflicted, and anxious to see the accounts of his last moments. Hobhouse and Kinnaird spent the evening together talking of their friend, recalling that magical influence of his, the spell that was felt by all who came near him, that well-hidden sensibility, that refusal to let his feelings sweep him away.

All England, that evening, had thoughts of Byron, and only of Byron. "Among the youth of that day a growing diversion from Byron to Shelley and Wordsworth had just commenced—but the moment in which we heard he was no more, united him to us at once, without a rival. . . . So much of us died with him, that the notion of his death had something of the unnatural, of the impossible. . . ." Thus wrote Edward Bulwer. And Jane Welsh wrote to Thomas Carlyle: "If they had said the sun or the moon was gone out of the heavens, it could not have struck me with the idea of a more awful and dreary blank in the creation than the words: Byron is dead." Alfred Tennyson, a lad of fifteen, ran and hid himself in a wooded dell, and there on a stone amongst the moss and bracken he wrote the three words —"Byron is dead."

In France many young men wore bands of crape round their hats. A picture was exhibited in the Passage Feydeau representing Byron on his death-bed, and crowds of people filed past the painting. It was remarked in many newspapers that the two greatest men of the century, Napoleon and Byron, had disappeared almost at the same time. In the schools the senior boys gathered together and spent a day of melancholy pleasure in re-reading *Childe Harold* and *Manfred.*

Almost immediately Caroline Lamb claimed back her letters. But Hobhouse had other cares on his shoulders. During his visit to Augusta to tell her of her brother's death, he had said to her: "Now the first thing that we have to think of is to protect Lord Byron's fame; there are those Memoirs. . . ." John Murray the publisher had bought them from Moore for two thousand guineas, and Hobhouse feared that Byron's terrible sincerity might make their publication dangerous. Kinnaird offered to buy them back for the family. Murray called on Hobhouse and told him, very disinterestedly, that he would accept whatever decision was reached by Byron's friends, even if they could not reimburse him. The ever-prudent Augusta was anxious that these memoirs should be not only suppressed but destroyed; and Hobhouse approved. Moore continued to protest for some time, urging that destruction would be contrary to Byron's desires, and insisting that they should be preserved, sealed if need be, in the safe-keeping of Mrs. Leigh's attorney. But in the end, bowing before the opposition of the others, he yielded. Murray wanted the manuscript to be read before it was destroyed, but Augusta made an impassioned protest, and the memoirs were duly burnt. The newspapers accused Lady Byron of demanding this destruction—but she had not even been consulted.

On July 1 Hobhouse learned that the brig *Florida,* which was bringing Byron's body home from Greece, had arrived. Going on board, he was met by Stanhope and Bruno, and by Fletcher, who burst into tears as he recounted the illness and agony of his master. Slowly the vessel sailed up the Thames. Three dogs which had belonged to the dead man were playing on deck. Hobhouse thought of the day when Byron had waved his cap as the vessel that bore him into exile was pitching out of Dover harbour into a rough sea. Fletcher and Stanhope described Missolonghi and the lagoon, the mutinous soldiery and the rain.

The vessel moored in London Docks, and Mr. Woodeson, an undertaker, came on board and emptied the large cask filled with spirits in which the encased body had been transported. He asked Hobhouse whether he would care to take a last look at his friend. "I believe I should have dropped down dead if I had ventured to look at it," he said. "I felt an inclination to take a last look at my friend, just as one wishes to jump down a precipice, but I could not, and I walked away, and then I came back again, and rested on the coffin. Lord Byron's large Newfoundland dog was lying at my feet. . . ." Fletcher continued talking of his master, and told Hobhouse that Byron had loved him (Hobhouse) better than any man on earth, and yet had never passed twenty-four hours without quarrelling with him.

A crowd of onlookers invaded the quayside when the coffin was brought ashore. General Lafayette, who was just then sailing for America, asked to be allowed to see the body, but his request was refused. Augusta had the courage to view it. His face had altered, she said; for she remembered the Byron of 1816, his features convulsed with suffering, and was now confronted by an icy mask expressive simply of a mocking serenity. Hanson likewise confessed that he would not have recognised it. When Kinnaird in his turn arrived, Hobhouse felt moved by an irresistible attraction and followed him on tip-toe until the face was visible.

Lady Byron was approached for her instructions regarding the burial, and replied that Hobhouse could do as he pleased. Burial in Westminster Abbey was refused by the Dean, so Byron's friends decided that he should rest in the little church at Hucknall Torkard, the village close to Newstead where all his ancestors lay buried.

The funeral procession set out for Nottingham. From the window of a small house in the outskirts, Clare Clairmont and Mary Shelley watched it go by. Farther on, a carriage was emerging from the gates of a park, and had to pull up. An invalid lady was reclining in it, and her husband, riding on horseback in front of the carriage, asked whose funeral this might be. The drivers of the procession told him—"Lord Byron's." But he refrained from telling his wife. She was Caroline Lamb.

At Nottingham the cortège was joined by the mayor and councillors, a few old friends such as Hodgson and Wildman, and a crowd of townspeople. It moved slowly on towards Newstead, passing across those level fields where Byron and Mary Chaworth had galloped in their childhood. A year before, to the very day, Byron had been climbing for the last time to the Casa Saluzzo above Genoa, and gloomily asking Gamba—"Where shall we be in a year's time?" As they passed the foot of the Diadem Hill, Hobhouse was thinking of that dinner at Annesley when he had witnessed Byron's first meeting with the married Mary Ann.

A few days later Lady Byron received a visit from Fletcher. She listened to his story walking up and down the room, sobbing so violently that her whole body was shaken. For nearly twenty minutes she besought Fletcher to recall the message which the dying Byron had murmured for her. A few words . . . at least a few words. . . . But Fletcher could not add a single one.

By his will Byron had left all his fortune to Augusta and her children. It amounted to over £100,000, besides the £60,000 reverting by settlement to Lady Byron. The new Lord, Captain George Anson Byron, was in financial difficulties, and Annabella, with her usual generosity, offered to cede her dowry to him, in view of the fact that she herself and her daughter were to inherit the Noels' fortune; and, unable to maintain his new position by any other means, he accepted.

In two years Augusta had scattered this great inheritance. She had had to pay off countless creditors, settle her husband's gaming debts, as also those of her sons, who were showing themselves worthy of their sire. She was, moreover, a victim of blackmail, subjected to threats of the publication of Caroline Lamb's private journal, containing Lord Byron's confessions regarding Mrs. Leigh. In all her troubles she was helped by Lady Byron, who was almost incredibly indulgent towards her. Yet in 1829 Augusta at last wore out the patience of her sister-in-law, and they ceased to meet.

The rest of Lady Byron's life was given over to works

of charity. She set up in her own house a school on a "co-operative plan of education," in which children of all classes were to be taught together: "castes," she said, "are as much the disgrace of England as of Hindustan." Later she busied herself with agricultural and industrial schools, remaining generous to the end, and remarkable for her methodistical exaltation of spirit. Towards the end of her life she developed a passionate friendship for the Rev. F. W. Robertson of Brighton. He became her trusted intimate, and to him she confided all that hitherto she had noted only for herself in her diary: "Byron was no sceptic. . . . God was a God of Vengeance. . . . The fancied contrast between himself and me rendered me habitually an object of the greatest irritation. . . . Conscious as he was of the weakness of his own character, the aspiration after its opposite (or what appeared to him such) was the more natural. . . .

"Can I not be believed when, after all I have disclosed, I say that there was a higher, better being in that breast throughout . . . one which he was always defying, but never could destroy. . . . Let it be supposed to have been the illusion of Love on my part, *then*—but the conviction remains unaltered *now*.

"Towards the close of his life, his feelings towards me were softening. . . . He must have come, had he lived, to the belief that from first to last I had been his only truly devoted friend. It was not permitted!" So she also, like Byron, had dreamed of peace in old age.

Regarding Augusta, she wrote to Robertson: "I thought Mrs. Leigh my friend—I loved her—I love her still!—I cannot help it. I shall see her once more in this world before we both die. People have called that in me a want of strength, of moral principle, the inability to detach affection from one whom I have found unworthy. It may be, but it is my nature. Can it be wrong?"

They saw each other "once more in this world." In 1851—when Lady Byron was fifty-nine and Augusta sixty-seven—Emily Leigh, Annabella's god-daughter, laid before her godmother the wretched plight of Mrs. Leigh, who was crippled with debts and ill. Annabella offered an interview at the White Hart Hotel in Reigate. Mrs. Leigh went. Lady Byron arrived with a memorandum: "How . . . Where . . . My line of conduct. . . ." But Augusta proved to be as confused and equivocal as ever, and the two women parted without being reconciled. Six months later, when Augusta was dying—and so poor that she was actually selling certain letters from Byron—Annabella wrote to enquire for her, and offered money: "I wrote to Emily, alone by the death-bed, bidding her whisper two words of affection long disused. . . . *'Dearest Augusta . . .'* I was told, in answer, that tears long dry had flowed again, and that her words were 'Joy . . . her greatest consolation . . . ' with a message unintelligible to the hearer. . . . A second message lost!"

The last years of Lady Byron's life were heavy with sorrows. In 1852 she lost her only daughter, Lady Lovelace, and in the following year her confidant, the preacher Robertson. She wore a transparent widow's cap on her silver-white hair—the hair that her grandchildren loved to brush, so long that it touched the ground when she was seated. She died in 1860. By her own wish she was buried, not at Hucknall Torkard where

Byron and her daughter lay, nor even amongst her own ancestors at Kirkby, but alone, in a London cemetery.

When Ada, Byron's daughter, reached her fifteenth birthday, her Aunt Augusta sent her a prettily bound prayer-book; and in the following year, for the first time, Lady Byron read her some of her father's poems—*The Giaour,* which she liked, and *Fare Thee Well,* which she thought exaggerated and artificial. Her genius, however, inclined to the metaphysical and mathematical rather than to poetry; she translated and annotated Menabrea's tract on Mr. Babbage's calculating machine. She was a pretty woman, a little eccentric, with her father's musical voice, and at the age of twenty married Lord King, who later became the second Earl of Lovelace.

Babbage was her undoing. In the course of studying him, she conceived the idea of an infallible system for betting on horse-races. Infallibility was an inherited illusion. She failed, obstinately persisted, and in the end lost so heavily that she did not dare to tell her husband. Her mother saved her, but she died, despairing and in shattered health, in 1852. Her age then was the same as her father's, thirty-six and a few months; and at her own request she was buried beside him in the church of Hucknall Torkard.

Medora's life was sadder still. In 1826 her eldest sister, Georgiana Leigh, married—as her mother had done, as all the Byrons did—one of her cousins, Mr. Henry Trevanion. Three years later he seduced his young sister-in-law, Medora, and left her with a child who died out at nurse. Augusta, to whom Trevanion had made full confession, wrote to Medora telling her that she realised "the weakness of the human nature and the strength of its temptation," but that an end must be put to this liaison.

Trevanion and Medora went off to France together, and lived for some time in Normandy, under the name of Mr. and Mrs. Aubin. Then Medora fell ill, grew disheartened, and broke with her brother-in-law. She was anxious to retire to a convent in Brittany, the Abbey of Relecq; but a month after her admission to this house she discovered that she was again pregnant. She then rejoined Trevanion at the château of Penhoat, in Finistère, and was there delivered of a daughter, Marie, whom she had baptised by a Catholic priest. Like her father, Lord Byron, Medora felt the attraction of the firmness of the Roman Church.

Life with Trevanion became impossible. He had brought a new mistress to the house, and forced Medora to wait upon her. She implored help from her mother, and obtained a capital of £3,000 (the sum given by Byron to Augusta at the time of Medora's birth); but this money was inalienable, and being in need of ready-money she conceived the idea of writing to Lady Byron. "I received a most kind answer," she noted, "with money, and offers of protection for me and Marie." Lady Byron was at that time travelling in France, and sent for Medora and Marie to meet her at Tours, where she took them both under her wing.

On Lady Byron, Medora exerted a strange and potent fascination. For the third time the helpless Annabella was falling under the Byron spell. She was not long in confessing to Medora the reason for the profound interest she had in her. "Her husband had been my father," Medora was told one day at Fontainebleau. Lady Byron hated the name Medora, and called her niece Elizabeth, but asked the girl to call her "Pip"—as a man with the same face had called her long ago. Medora was very like Byron. In a room, she would turn and lower her head uneasily, as she watched people going in or out,—just as her father did. Even the style of her letters recalled Byron's: they began with "Dearest Pip. . . ." "Dearest Pip," she wrote, "I suppose I shall quit London Saturday, for I cannot begin a journey Friday." A strange obsession. . . .

But to a daughter of Byron the wind of good fortune was uncongenial. "Adversity is her best friend," Annabella was forced to admit, "and she can not bear kindness." Very soon her rages recalled the Halnaby days. She fled to Paris, and there, incapable of holding her tongue, she handed over the secret of her birth to several persons. "Her mother's carelessness and lack of foresight had put into her hands a mass of letters, scraps of paper, and copies of letters, from which it emerged that she was the fruit of sin." The French lawyer, Berryer, who acted for her, wrote to Lady Byron that the allowance of £150 a year made by the family was insufficient. Byron himself, that connoisseur of coincidence, would have noted that it was exactly the sum on which his own mother had had to live in Aberdeen.

The allowance was raised, on condition that the casket containing the papers should be entrusted to Sir John Hughes, the solicitor. But Medora was incapable of behaving with moderation; obtaining advances on her income for several years, she was again reduced to penury, and then lived at Saint-Germain. Her daughter Marie she entrusted to the Sisters of the Nativity, and herself entered the service of Commandant de Grammont, of the Eighth Hussars. The commandant's orderly, Jean Louis Taillefer, became enamoured of her. He could not marry her, for at that date a serving private soldier was not allowed to marry, but as she was expecting a child by him he sent her to his own home, at Saint-Affrique, in Aveyron, to await her confinement.

Down there she gave birth to Jean Marie Élie Taillefer, grandson of Byron, recognised by his soldier-father, and legitimatised in 1848 by the marriage of Medora and Taillefer, who was by then out of the army. It is curious, and not without pathos, to observe how Medora's life followed the same curve as Byron's, a period of passion and defiance being followed by a period of redemption. As a farmer's wife in the village of Lapeyre, in Aveyron, Medora Taillefer was faithful to her husband, brought up her children well, and showed herself generous and charitable. She had become converted to Catholicism. From her early education she retained a taste for music, and in that farm at Lapeyre there was a piano.

But this happiness lasted only one year. In 1849, on the eve of her thirty-sixth birthday, Medora died; and the whole village came mourning to her funeral. She left a will in the following terms: "I, Elizabeth Medora Leigh, give and bequeath all my worldly goods and chattels, the Deed of Appointment under the will of the late Lord Byron, to Jean Louis Taillefer and to my children, Marie and Élie. . . . I hereby declare my forgiveness of my mother and all those who have so cruelly persecuted me, as I hope for forgiveness for myself. I request Sir John Hughes to hand over to the said Jean

Louis Taillefer the casket containing my papers which is in his hands."

The casket, however, was never delivered to Medora's husband. Taillefer later became the valet of M. Arthur de Waroquier, of Toulouse, whose father approached the French Embassy in London with a view to obtaining the return of the casket. But the Embassy's legal adviser replied that it was the usage in England to burn all such papers as tended to show immorality, and that this was the case with these documents. The contents of the casket were accordingly burnt in Sir John Hughes' chambers, in the presence of the Chancellor of the French Embassy, on May 19, 1863.

Marie, the daughter of Medora and her brother-in-law Trevanion, and the grand-daughter of Byron and Augusta, was a handsome girl, with a fine yet firm gentleness about her. It was her desire to become a nun, but she hesitated for a long time because her dying mother had begged her to look after her brother Élie. But after M. de Waroquier had taken charge of the boy, she took her vows at the Convent of the Nativity at Saint-Germain-en-Laye, and became Sister Saint-Hilaire. She was familiar with her origins, and it was said of her that she felt that she had more to expiate than others, and that she sometimes insisted on tightening for herself the strictness of the rule she had embraced, reproaching it for being, more often than not, too gentle towards her. In her Book of Hours she drew a kind of tombstone memorial to her mother, on which she styled her "Elizabeth Medora Byron"; and underneath the design she wrote (changing *il* into *elle*) Lamartine's lines:

Étends sur elle la main de ta clémence;
Elle a péché, mais le ciel est un don;
Elle a souffert, c'est une autre innocence;
Elle a aimé, c'est le sceau du pardon. . . .[1]

And she recorded her reflections: "My life," she wrote, "is like the autumnal leaf that trembles in the pale moonbeam. Frail is its hold, brief its anxious span." Occasionally she would speak of Lord Byron to her companions: "Poor Byron," she used to say, "I am very fond of him." She died in 1873, making the responses to the Litany of Our Lady which the community was reciting beside her bed.

Her brother Élie, last descendant of the illegitimate branch, was a handsome autumn-haired youth, with a strong-willed chin. He was by turns a clerk, a commercial traveller, and then a wine-broker, and died in the hospital of Sète on January 22, 1900. That day was the anniversary of Byron's birth.

Byron had often exclaimed on the fact that those to whom he felt attached came to tragic ends; and the curse extended to almost every woman whom he had loved. Mary Ann Chaworth had long been unhappy. About 1830 she was to be seen in the village church on Sundays, bent low by cares and hopelessness. When Tom Moore after the destruction of the memoirs decided to write his own life of Byron, he went to see her in search of material. Her husband, Mr. Musters, was away. Moore sang her one of the Irish songs which Byron had been fond of, and Mrs. Musters wept. Her end was

[1] Stretch over her thy pardoning hand.
She sinned—but Heaven is a gift;
She suffered—'tis but innocence;
She loved—'tis the seal of forgiveness. . . .

hastened by a riot amongst the Nottingham weavers, who attacked her house at the time of the Reform Bill agitation in October, 1832. She had to take refuge in a shed during the night, and caught a chill of which she soon died at the age of forty-seven. Her statue stands in the church at Colwick.

Teresa Macri, the "Maid of Athens," married an Englishman, John Black by name, who came to fight for the Greeks after Byron's death. Black became an English consul and settled in Greece. The poem had made Teresa Black a celebrity, and no English traveller missed seeing her. She used to talk about Byron with many sighs, and when circumstances obliged her husband to live at Missolonghi, she really suffered; the conversations about Byron, and the endless questions about the way in which she had known him, had produced in the end a genuine grief in her. At night she would see Byron in her dreams, often threatening her angrily. "What torture!" she said to Mr. Black. "Why shouldn't you dream about him, since you do nothing but think of him?" he answered peevishly.

But Byron was never forgiven by Clare, and when Mary Shelley wrote in praise of the poet in her novel *Lodore,* she wrote to her: "Good God! To think a person of your genius should think it a task befitting its powers, to gild and embellish and pass off as beautiful what was the merest compound of vanity, folly, and every miserable weakness that ever met together in one human being."

Caroline Lamb remained for the rest of her life a dazzling and pitiful mixture of brilliance, despair, and futility. In April 1824 she had undergone a crisis of hallucination: "In the middle of the night, I fancied I saw Lord Byron—I screamed, jumped out of bed and desired them to save me from him. He looked horrible, and ground his teeth at me; he did not speak; his hair was straight; he was fatter than when I knew him, and not near so handsome."

A month later a letter from her husband informed her of Lord Byron's death. He wrote to her, bidding her behave with propriety, warning her that the news would be a blow to her—Lord Byron was dead. She was just beginning to recover when the meeting with the funeral, and then the appearance of Medwin's recollections, revived her madness. Medwin's book was very cruel to her; it was there that she first knew of that terrible poem:

> Remember thee! remember thee!
> Till Lethe quench life's burning stream
> Remorse and shame shall cling to thee,
> And haunt thee like a feverish dream! . . .

She wrote to Medwin, saying: "Byron never could say I had no heart. He never could say, either, that I had not loved my husband. In his letters to me, he is perpetually telling me I love him the best of the two; and my only charm, believe me, in his eyes was, that I was innocent, affectionate, and enthusiastic. . . ."

Distance had given her clearer understanding. Yes, what Byron was capable of loving in another was a certain kind of innocence and youthfulness—whence Mary Duff and Margaret Parker, whence Edleston and Nicolo Giraud, or later, Teresa Guiccioli and the page Loukas. Caroline herself, for a few days during 1812, must have pleased him with a sort of pureness. But how quickly she had tired him. After reading Medwin, a crisis of mental bewilderment overwhelmed her; but her poor sick head was light, and she forgot. The scandal caused by the book had made her married life difficult, and she spent the winter at Brocket Hall without her husband. A young neighbour of hers, Edward Bulwer, had been fascinated by the extraordinary originality of her conversation, and was frequently her guest. Life at Brocket Hall remained "Carolinish." She sent one of her pages at three in the morning to rouse her guests and fetch them to hear her playing the organ—then talked to them about Byron until sunrise. She wore a ring which he had given her, and entrusted it to Bulwer, telling him that she made the men whom she loved wear it. Shortly afterwards she took it back from him, and he found it on another young man's finger. He was most indignant.

Lady Caroline returned one evening to London to witness *Faust*. The setting she found superb; it reminded her of Byron, that angel, that unhappy, dangerous Byron whom she adored for all the terrible heritage—"Remember thee, remember thee!"—which he had left her. She died in her husband's arms at the age of forty-two; and her husband, William, later Lord Melbourne, was to write that her ways might have been a little eccentric, this was apparent rather than real; their fascination, in any case, was such that those who never came within its range could scarcely conceive its strength.

The Countess Guiccioli had no vocation for woe. She was able to fashion a life for herself in which Byron's phantom was simply a pleasing and honourable companion. In 1829 Lord Malmesbury met her in Rome, at a ball at the Austrian Embassy. "Her face was handsome," he noted, "with a brilliant complexion and blue eyes, and full of animation, showing splendid teeth when she laughed, which she was doing heartily at the time I remarked her. . . . Byron had been dead only five years, and she was then twenty-six. We became great friends, and I found her a charming companion, with a cultivated mind, yet with all the natural *bonhomie* of her race, and fond of fun. She had got over her grief (which I heard was very violent at first) for the loss of her poet, and she liked to talk of him and his eccentricities, but was very proud of her conquest." The Countess told Lord Malmesbury that Byron wrote "all the last cantos on playbills (some of which I saw myself) or on any odd piece of paper at hand, and with repeated glasses of gin-punch by his side. He then used to rush out of his room to read to her what he had written, making many alterations and laughing immoderately." She was extremely proud of him, and no less fond, describing him as having "a very capricious temper, and with nothing of the passion which pervades his poetry . . . in fact with a cold temperament." Teresa had never enjoyed cynicism.

In 1832 she came over to London, made a pilgrimage to Harrow, dined with the Drurys, went to pray before Byron's tomb at Hucknall Torkard, and paid a visit to Augusta, with whom she spent three hours of continuous talk about Byron. About the age of fifty she married the Marquis de Boissy, an eccentric and very wealthy Frenchman, and was mistress of a very fine house in Paris. But "the *bonhomie* of the Italian altered for the artificial manner of a *grande dame,* and not to its advantage." Her drawing-room contained a large portrait of Byron, before which she liked to stand when she had visitors, saying: "How beautiful he was! Heavens, how beautiful!" Her husband used to introduce her as "My wife, Madame la Marquise de Boissy . . . formerly mistress of Lord Byron." After the Marquis's death she published her recollections of Byron, in which she turned him into the fond, romantic hero which in his life-time he had always refused to be. She survived until 1879.

If Countess Guiccioli had been safeguarded against the Byron curse by an impermeable sentimentalism, John Cam Hobhouse was preserved by a self-centred naïveté. In the Reform of 1832 he reaped the harvest of his advanced political opinions, entered the cabinet, and remained in office for a long time. Later he became Lord Broughton, one of the most conservative members of his party, and died at the age of eighty-three. He earned enduring fame as the inventor of the political formula—"His Majesty's Opposition."

Tita, the gondolier, as is well known, became a servant of the Disraeli family at Bradenham. And as for Fletcher, he established a macaroni factory and ruined himself in the process, was helped, like everybody, by Lady Byron, and in his last years became the beadle of Golden Square, in Soho, where he could be seen, wearing a tall hat with gold bands, and staff in hand, chasing the children of the French Protestant School.

In Brompton Cemetery is the tomb of Jackson, the boxer, a flat slab upheld at each corner by a classical athlete. This monument was erected to his memory by the British peerage, in token of the high esteem in which they held him.

During the last weeks of his life, Byron might well have thought that his death would be vain and that Greece would never be set free. In 1826 Missolonghi was besieged for a second time, and almost all its houses were destroyed by bombardment. In the end the Greeks were forced by famine to abandon the town. Men, women and children sallied forth in an attempt to cross the enemy lines. Large numbers were killed, and the town was given over to pillage. Bishop Joseph and the Primate Capsalis had barricaded themselves in the cartridge factory, the last relic of Parry's sojourn in charge of the ordnance, and were blown up with it.

If Europe at that moment had deserted the Greek cause, it would have foundered. Austria let things take their course, from fear of Russia; France did not dare to take action; everything depended on England. By the sacred axioms of the Foreign Office and the Duke of Wellington, Greece stood condemned. "But the British public, moved by Byron's self-sacrifice and death, and at that time profoundly classical in its culture, idealised the Greek Klephts as heroes of Thermopylæ." The Canning ministry fell back for support on this sentimental movement, and reversed the whole of British policy. At the battle of Navarino in 1827 the fleets of England, Russia and France assured the independence of Greece. The day of the Holy Alliance was over.

It is not too much to say that without the support lent to the Greek cause by Byron's name and Byron's death, Canning would certainly not have been upheld by English public opinion. At Missolonghi, which nowadays is a little town grown both prosperous and healthy, the Greeks have laid out a Garden of Heroes, where a column stands bearing the name of Byron, together with those of Marco Botzaris, Capsalis and Tsavellas. The fisher-folk in this strange realm of water and brine still live in their huts of platted reeds; but they are no strangers to the name of Byron. They do not know that he was a poet; but if asked about him, they will answer—"He was a very brave man—and he came to die for Greece because he loved freedom."

CHRONOLOGICAL TABLE

1643 Sir John Byron created 1st Baron Byron by Charles the First.

1747 JULY 28: Birth of Sir Ralph Milbanke.

1751 NOVEMBER 14: Birth of Hon. Judith Noel (later Lady Milbanke).

1752 Birth of Elizabeth Milbanke (later Lady Melbourne).

1755 Birth of John Byron ("Mad Jack").

1765 Birth of Catherine Gordon of Gight.
JANUARY 26: The Chaworth-Byron duel.

1769 APRIL 13: Elizabeth Milbanke marries Sir Peniston Lamb.

1770 JULY 8: Sir Peniston Lamb created Lord Melbourne.

1777 JANUARY 9: Sir Ralph Milbanke marries Hon. Judith Noel.

1779 Birth of William Lamb.
The Marquis of Carmarthen divorces Amelia D'Arcy, Baroness Conyers.

1779 Lady Conyers marries Capt. John Byron.

1784 JANUARY 26: Birth of Hon. Augusta Mary Byron (later Mrs. Leigh).

1785 MAY 13: Capt. John Byron marries Miss Gordon of Gight.
NOVEMBER 13: Birth of Hon. Caroline Ponsonby (later Lady Caroline Lamb).

1786 JUNE 27: Birth of John Cam Hobhouse.

1788 JANUARY 22: Birth of GEORGE GORDON BYRON, later 6th Lord Byron.

1789 MARCH 8: Birth of George Anson Byron, later 7th Lord Byron.

BYRON

1790 SEPTEMBER 1: Birth of Margaret Power, later Countess of Blessington.

1791 Death of Capt. John Byron at the age, fatal to the Byrons, of thirty-six.

1792 MAY 17: Birth of Anne Isabella Milbanke (later Lady Byron).
AUGUST 4: Birth of Percy Bysshe Shelley.

1797 The Mary Duff episode.
AUGUST 30: Birth of Mary Godwin, later Mrs. Shelley.

1798 APRIL 27: Birth of Clare Clairmont.
MAY 19: Byron succeeds to the barony.

1800 Birth of Teresa Gamba, later Countess Guiccioli.

1801 Byron enters Harrow.

1803 Byron at Nottingham and Annesley.

1804 Stay at Southwell with Mrs. Byron.

1805 JUNE 3: Lady Caroline Ponsonby marries Hon. William Lamb.
AUGUST: Mary Chaworth marries John Musters.
OCTOBER: Byron enters Trinity College, Cambridge.

1806 Byron prepares a collection of his poems.

1807 MARCH: Byron publishes *Hours of Idleness.*
AUGUST 17: Hon. Augusta Byron marries Lt.-Col. George Leigh, Tenth Dragoons.

1808 JANUARY-AUGUST: Byron at Cambridge and in London.
SEPTEMBER: Byron settles at Newstead.
NOVEMBER 18: Death of the dog Boatswain.

1809 JANUARY 22: Byron's majority celebrated at Newstead.
MARCH 13: Byron takes his seat in the House of Lords.
MARCH 16: Publication of *English Bards and Scotch Reviewers.*
JUNE 11: He leaves London with Hobhouse.
SEPTEMBER 1-21: Visit to Malta.
DECEMBER 25: Arrival at Athens.

1810 JANUARY-FEBRUARY: Byron in Athens.
MAY 3: He swims the Hellespont.
MAY 14: Arrival in Constantinople.

CHRONOLOGICAL TABLE

1811 JANUARY: Byron settles at the Capucin monastery in Athens.
JULY 17: He returns to England.
AUGUST 1: Death of Mrs. Byron.

1812 FEBRUARY 27: Byron's maiden speech in the House of Lords.
FEBRUARY 29: Publication of Cantos I and II of *Childe Harold*.
MARCH 10: "I awoke one morning and found myself famous."
MARCH 25: Waltzing-party given at Melbourne House by Lady Caroline Lamb. Among the guests were Lord Byron, Miss Milbanke, Rev. Sidney Smith, Lady Jersey, Lord and Lady Kinnaird, Miss Mercer Elphinstone, Mrs. Lamb, Lord Palmerston, etc.
MARCH 27: Lady Caroline Lamb's first love-letter to Byron.
Between OCTOBER 1 and 10 Byron asks for the hand of Miss Milbanke. She refuses.
NOVEMBER 13: He leaves Eywood after his stay there with Lady Oxford.
NOVEMBER: Byron writes "Thou art not false but thou art fickle. . . ."
NOVEMBER 9: Byron writes to Lady Caroline Lamb the final letter which she was later to reproduce in her novel, *Glenarvon*.

1813 JANUARY: Second stay at Eywood.
Byron publishes *The Giaour*.
JUNE 28: Lady Oxford's departure for the Continent closes her liaison with Byron. Mrs. Leigh comes to live in London, in rooms at St. James's Palace.
JULY-AUGUST: Byron and Mrs. Leigh in London, which they only leave for two short visits to Six Mile Bottom.
JULY 6: Ball at Lady Heathcote's, and scene with Lady Caroline Lamb.
SEPTEMBER 21: Byron at Aston Hall, where he makes love to Lady Frances Webster. In OCTOBER he returns there, and the Websters visit Newstead.
NOVEMBER-JANUARY (1814): Byron in London.
DECEMBER: He publishes *The Bride of Abydos*, and is writing *The Corsair*.

BYRON

1814 January 17: Byron at Newstead with Augusta. They spend three weeks there.

March 28: Byron takes rooms in Albany, Piccadilly.

April 10: He writes the *Ode to Napoleon Bonaparte*.

April 15: Birth of Elizabeth Medora Leigh.

Byron writes "I speak not, I trace not, I breathe not thy name. . . ." He begins *Lara*.

September 15: Byron makes a second request for the hand of Miss Milbanke. They are betrothed.

November: Byron's stay as prospective bridegroom at Seaham.

December: He writes the *Hebrew Melodies*.

December 24: Byron and Hobhouse leave London.

December 30: They arrive together at Seaham.

December 31: Signature of the marriage contract.

1815 January 2: Lord Byron marries Miss Milbanke.

January 21: Lord and Lady Byron return from Halnaby to Seaham.

March 12: Lord and Lady Byron arrive at Six Mile Bottom.

March 28: Lord and Lady Byron take up their home at No. 13 Piccadilly Terrace, London.

April: Mrs. Leigh comes to stay at 13 Piccadilly Terrace.

April 17: Death of Lord Wentworth, Lady Byron's uncle.

May 20: Sir Ralph Milbanke obtains authorisation from the Prince-Regent to take the name and arms of Noel.

Late in June: Mrs. Leigh leaves Piccadilly Terrace and returns to Six Mile Bottom.

July 29: Byron makes his will in Mrs. Leigh's favour.

August: He writes "Star of the Brave . . ." and *Napoleon's Farewell*.

November 15: Mrs. Leigh comes to live at 13 Piccadilly Terrace.

December 10: Birth of Augusta Ada Byron.

1816 January 6: Byron writes to his wife asking her to leave the house.

January 8: Lady Byron consults Dr. Baillie as to Byron's possible insanity.

January 15: Lady Byron leaves London with Ada.

January 16: She arrives at Kirkby Mallory.

CHRONOLOGICAL TABLE

1816 FEBRUARY 2: Byron is informed by a letter from Sir Ralph that Lady Byron desires to be separated from him.

During FEBRUARY Byron publishes *Parisina.*

MARCH 16: Mrs. Leigh leaves Piccadilly Terrace after four months there, and goes to her rooms in St. James's Palace.

MARCH 17: Byron accepts the principle of a mutual separation, and on the same day writes "Fare thee well. . . ."

MARCH 29: He writes *The Sketch.*

APRIL 8: Reception at Lady Jersey's. Among the guests were Byron and Mrs. Leigh, Miss Mercer Elphinstone, the Comte de Flahault, Benjamin Constant and his wife, Mrs. George Lamb, Lord Brougham, etc.

APRIL 14, EASTER SUNDAY: Mrs. Leigh pays a farewell visit to Byron.

APRIL 21: Byron signs the deed of separation.

APRIL 23: Byron goes to Dover with Hobhouse and Scrope Davies.

APRIL 25: Byron sails for Ostend.

MAY 3: Shelley, Mary Godwin and Clare Clairmont leave Dover for Geneva.

During MAY Byron begins Canto III of *Childe Harold.*

MAY 25. Byron arrives at Geneva and lodges at the Hôtel d'Angleterre, Sécheron.

During MAY Lady Caroline Lamb publishes *Glenarvon.*

JUNE: Byron is living at the Villa Diodati, near Geneva.

JUNE 23: Byron and Shelley start on their tour of the Lake.

JUNE 27: They visit Ouchy, where Byron writes *The Prisoner of Chillon.*

During JULY Byron finishes Canto III of *Childe Harold,* and writes *The Dream,* the *Stanzas to Augusta,* and other poems.

AUGUST 29: Shelley, Mary and Clare leave Geneva to return to England.

SEPTEMBER 17-29: Byron makes a tour of the Alps with Hobhouse, and begins *Manfred.*

NOVEMBER 1: Ada Byron's christening. Mrs. Leigh, who was to be godmother, excluded from the ceremony. The godfather was Capt. George Anson Byron, and the godmothers, Lady Noel and Viscountess Tamworth.

1816 NOVEMBER 11: Byron settles in Venice.
DECEMBER 30: Shelley marries Mary Godwin.

1817 JANUARY 12: Birth of Allegra, natural daughter of Byron and Clare Clairmont.
FEBRUARY: Byron concludes *Manfred*.
APRIL 29-MAY 26: Journey to Rome.
JUNE: Byron, in Venice, begins Canto IV of *Childe Harold*.
OCTOBER: Byron writes *Beppo*.
NOVEMBER: Byron sells Newstead to Col. Wildman.

1818 FEBRUARY 16: Lord Blessington marries Margaret Power, widow of Mr. St. Leger Farmer.
APRIL 6: Death of Lady Melbourne.
SEPTEMBER: Byron finishes Canto I of *Don Juan*.

1819 JANUARY 20: Byron finishes Canto II of *Don Juan*.
APRIL: Byron meets Teresa Guiccioli at the Countess Benzoni's in Venice.
Late in MAY he joins Countess Guiccioli at Ravenna.
AUGUST 10: He leaves for Bologna.
SEPTEMBER 18: Byron and Countess Guiccioli leave together for La Mira, near Venice.
NOVEMBER: Byron finishes Canto III, and is writing Canto IV, of *Don Juan*.
DECEMBER 24: Byron settles at Ravenna.

1820 MARCH: Byron writes *The Prophecy of Dante*.
APRIL: Byron takes part in the insurgent movement against Papal and Austrian domination.
JULY 12: The Pope pronounces the separation of the Count and Countess Guiccioli. Teresa goes to live with her father, Count Gamba; Byron stays on in the Palazzo Guiccioli for fifteen months.
NOVEMBER: Byron finishes Canto V of *Don Juan*.

1821 FEBRUARY 24: Failure of the Carbonari plan.
MARCH: Allegra is sent to the convent of Bagnacavallo.
MAY: Byron finishes *Sardanapalus*.
JULY: Byron writes *Cain*. Banishment of the Gamba family.
OCTOBER 29: Byron leaves Ravenna to rejoin Countess Guiccioli at Pisa.

CHRONOLOGICAL TABLE

1821 November: Byron, at Pisa, begins *The Deformed Transformed.*

1822 January 28: Death of Lady Noel. Lord and Lady Byron take the additional name of Noel.
February: Byron writes Cantos VI, VII, and VIII of *Don Juan.*
April 20: Death of Allegra.
July 8: Death of Shelley.
August 16: Byron, Trelawny and Leigh Hunt burn the corpse of Shelley.
August: Byron is writing Cantos IX, X, and XI of *Don Juan.*
September: He settles at Genoa.

1823 March 31: Lady Blessington arrives at Genoa, with her husband and Count D'Orsay.
May: Byron receives a message from the Greek Committee in London.
June 3: The Blessingtons leave Genoa.
July 13 (Friday): Byron embarks on the *Hercules.*
August 3: Arrival at Cephalonia.
September 22: Stanhope arrives at Argostoli.
December 28: Byron leaves for Missolonghi.

1824 January 5: Byron arrives at Missolonghi.
January 22: He writes his *Lines on Completing my Thirty-sixth Year.*
February 15: Byron has an epileptic seizure.
April 9: Byron catches a chill after riding.
April 19: Death of Lord Byron.
May 14: News of Byron's death reaches London.
May 17: Destruction of Byron's *Memoirs.*
May 25: Byron's coffin embarked on the *Florida* at Zante.
June 29: His body arrives at London.
July 12: Byron's funeral.
July 16: Burial at Hucknall Torkard.
November 20: Death of Lady Oxford.

1825 March 19: Death of Sir Ralph Noel.

1826 February 4: Georgiana Leigh, eldest daughter of Augusta, marries her cousin, Henry Trevanion.

1828 January 23: Death of Lady Caroline Lamb.

1831 AUGUST 15: Hobhouse becomes Sir John Hobhouse, Bart.

1832 FEBRUARY: Death of Mary Chaworth-Musters.

1834 MAY 19: Birth of Marie, natural daughter of Medora Leigh and her brother-in-law, Henry Trevanion.

1835 JULY: Ada Byron marries William, 8th Lord King.

1837 Death of Lady Frances Webster.

1838 JUNE 30: Lord King becomes Earl of Lovelace.

1846 JANUARY 27: Birth of Élie, natural son of Medora Leigh and Jean-Louis Taillefer.

AUGUST 23: Medora Leigh marries J.-L. Taillefer, the latter legitimatising his son Élie, and also the girl Marie, daughter of Medora by Henry Trevanion.

1849 JUNE 4: Death of Lady Blessington.
AUGUST 28: Death of Elizabeth Medora Leigh, Madame Taillefer.

1850 MARCH 3: Death of Col. George Leigh.

1851 FEBRUARY 1: Death of Mary Shelley.
FEBRUARY 26: Sir J. C. Hobhouse created Lord Broughton of Giffard.
APRIL 8: Lady Byron's last interview with Mrs. Leigh, at Reigate.
OCTOBER 12: Death of Mrs. Leigh.

1852 NOVEMBER 27: Death of Ada, Countess of Lovelace.

1854 Death of Henry Trevanion.

1856 Marie, daughter of Trevanion and Medora Leigh, takes her religious vows.

1860 MAY 16: Death of Lady Byron.

1863 MAY 19: Destruction of Medora's papers.

1868 Death of Admiral Lord Byron.

1869 Death of Lord Broughton (Hobhouse).

1873 Death of Sister Saint-Hilaire (Marie Taillefer).
Death of the Marquise de Boissy (Teresa Guiccioli).

CHRONOLOGICAL TABLE

1879 Death of Clare Clairmont.

1893 Death of William, 1st Earl of Lovelace.

1900 JANUARY 22: Death of Élie Taillefer.

1906 Death of Ralph, 2nd Earl of Lovelace, grandson of Lord Byron.

SOURCES

It was my first intention to give references for the passages quoted, at the foot of each page in this book. But two objections were raised which led me rather to group these references by separate chapters: first, because the bracketed numerals, cutting into sentences, are an annoyance to readers who are seeking in a book an emotion or a subject for reflection; and second, because, although a particular book may have given the author most valuable suggestions, yet if he has not actually quoted one of its sentences, it will not figure in his footnotes.

The method here adopted, I think, not only permits the author to indicate the general sources of each chapter, but also enables the reader desirous of consulting the original text of an important quotation, to find it promptly.

The most frequently cited works are indicated by initial letters, as follows:

L.J. *Letters and Journals of Lord Byron.* 6 vols. Edited by R. E. Prothero (Lord Ernle). (John Murray, 1898-1901). Page numbers here given are from the re-issue of 1922.

C. *Lord Byron's Correspondence.* 2 vols. Edited by John Murray (John Murray, 1922).

P. *The Poetical Works of Lord Byron.* Edited by E. H. Coleridge (John Murray, 1905).

H. *Recollections of a Long Life,* by Lord Broughton (John Cam Hobhouse). 6 vols. Edited by his daughter, Lady Dorchester (1909).

B.M. The Manuscript Department of the British Museum.

M. *Byron's Life,* by Thomas Moore (John Murray). Page numbers here given are from the 1847 edition in one volume.

E.C.M. *Byron,* by Ethel Colburn Mayne. 2 vols. (Methuen, 1912.)

SOURCES

L.B. *The Life of Lady Byron,* by Ethel Colburn Mayne (Constable, 1929).

H.N. *Byron, the Last Journey,* by Harold Nicolson (Constable, 1924). Page numbers here given are from the re-issue of 1929.

Other works frequently cited are as follows:

Astarte, by Ralph Milbanke, Earl of Lovelace. Revised and expanded edition by the Countess of Lovelace (Christophers, 1921).

In Whig Society, by Mabell, Countess of Airlie (Hodder and Stoughton, 1921).

Recollections of the Life of Lord Byron, by R. C. Dallas (Charles Knight, 1824).

Journal of the Conversations of Lord Byron, by Thomas Medwin (Baudry, 1824).

A Journal of the Conversations of Lord Byron, by the Countess of Blessington (Bentley, 1834). Page numbers here given are from the re-issue of 1894.

Lord Byron and Some of His Contemporaries, by Leigh Hunt (Colburn, 1828).

A Narrative of Lord Byron's Last Journey to Greece, by Count Pietro Gamba (John Murray, 1825).

The Last Days of Lord Byron, by William Parry (Knight and Lacey, 1825).

The Real Lord Byron, by John Cordy Jeaffreson (Hurst and Blackett, 1883).

Le Secret de Byron, by Roger de Vivie de Régie (Émile-Paul, 1927).

PART I

I

The foundation charter of Newstead is in B.M.

The details on the spoliation of the monasteries come from Cardinal Gasquet's *Henry VIII and the English Monasteries* (1888-99).

BYRON

The details on the trial of the "Wicked Lord" come from a contemporary pamphlet, *The Trial of William, Lord Byron* (B.M.6485.h.2). See also *State Trials,* XIX, 1177.

The shipwreck of Byron's grandfather is told in his *Narrative,* etc. (1768).

For the depredations of the "Wicked Lord" at Newstead, see Albert Brecknock's *Byron* (1926).

II

The chief authority on Byron's Scottish ancestry is J. M. Bulloch. See his articles on *Tragic Adventures of the Gordons of Gight* (1898: cf. B.M. Catalogue).

See also J. D. Symon's *Byron in Perspective* (1924), and J. W. Duff's *Byron and Aberdeen* (1902).

Captain Byron's letters are unpublished. They have been communicated to me by Lady Lovelace.

Mrs. Byron's letters to Mrs. Leigh are in the British Museum (Add.MSS.31037).

The most detailed facts regarding Byron's lameness are to be found in J. D. Symon.

Mrs. Byron's letter to Augusta: L.J.,I,19.

III

On the Aberdeen schools: L.J.,V., 406-407; Symon, 49-67.

On May Gray: L.J.,I,10; J.,36; E.C.M.,I,25; Karl Elze's *Life of Lord Byron,* 16-17.

On *Zeluco:* Elze, 20-21.

Regarding the Mary Duff episode, a hitherto unpublished note of Hobhouse's reads: "With respect to the early development of these propensities in Byron, I am acquainted with a regular fact scarcely fit for narration, but much less romantic and more satisfactory than the amour with Mary Duff."

It is also following a note by Hobhouse that I describe how Byron learned that he had become Lord Byron. Hobhouse says that Byron told him how the schoolmaster sent for him, gave him some cake and wine, telling him that his great-uncle was dead and he was now a lord. Byron added that this little treat, and the respectful manner of the master had instantly given him high notions of his new dignity.

SOURCES

IV

M. *passim*.

Hanson's letter: L.J.,I,10.

On Lord Carlisle: L.J.,I,36.

On Margaret Parker: L.J.,V,449.

V

On Dr. Drury: see Percy W. Thornton's *Harrow School* (1885).

Anecdote of the basin of water: J.,60.

Anecdote of Napoleon's bust: L.J.,II,324.

Lines on the death of Margaret Parker: P.,2.

VI

Epigraph: P.,33.

On Mary Chaworth and John Musters, see Grantley Berkeley's *Reminiscences of a Huntsman* (1854). From this author, who was intimately acquainted with John Musters, are derived all the details given regarding this couple.

Anecdote of the ghost: M.,27.

Mary Chaworth's remark to the maid: M.,28.

Byron's letters: L.J.,I,16,17.

Quarrel with Lord Grey: L.J.,I,53. Regarding Lord Grey, Hobhouse writes on the margin of a letter of Moore's: "And a circumstance occurred during [this] intimacy which certainly had much effect on his future morals."

Lines on leaving Newstead: P.,2.

VII

On Byron's friendships at Harrow, Hobhouse notes: "M. knows nothing or will tell nothing of the principal cause of all these boyish friendships."

Poem quoted: P.,25.

Letters exchanged with Clare: M.,24.

Anecdote "one, two, three . . .": L.J.,I,130.

Meeting with Elizabeth Pigot: M.,32.

Mrs. Byron's letter to Augusta: L.J.,I,19.

Byron's letters to Augusta: L.J.,I,20,42,49,29,35,30,46,47,40, 49,62.

Marriage of Mary Duff: L.J.,II,347.

VIII

Farewell to Mary Chaworth: P.,386.

Poems quoted: P.,3,37.

Regarding Dr. Drury's departure, I have adopted the version given me by Mr. Du Pontet, the Harrow librarian, according to which it was not Byron who stopped his comrades from scattering the powder.

On Byron's work at Harrow, Hobhouse notes: "but Lord Byron did not leave Harrow, at least did not come to Cambridge with any reputation for superior attainments or extraordinary talents."

Hobhouse also notes, regarding the list of books read by Byron, which is given by Moore and presumes extensive reading, as follows: "Lord Byron says he read these books. I am inclined to believe the fact but it is certain that he never gave any sign of this knowledge afterwards."

Letter from Byron to Augusta: L.J.,I,68.

On Byron's oratorical gifts: L.J.,V,453.

On Byron's cricket: L.J.,I,71.

On the note in his *Scriptores Græci:* M.,30.

Poem quoted: P.,6.

IX

Byron's letters: L.J.,I,81,76.

On the morals of the time and their influence on Byron's development, see H. J. C. Grierson's *The Background of English Literature,* 167-199.

On Byron's life with Long: L.J.,V,445,446, and M.,32.

On Edleston: L.J.,I,130,132,133; P.,19; E.C.M.,I,90.

Byron's letter to Augusta: L.J.,I,93.

Mrs. Byron's letter to Hanson: L.J.,I,95.

Byron's letter on Cambridge: L.J.,I,83.

X

Epigraph: Byron's remark quoted by Thomas Medwin, I,70.

Byron's letters on his mother: L.J.,I,100,101,105.

Stay at Harrogate: M.,37,38.

Lines to John Pigot: P.,16.

"Hills of Annesley": P.,62.

Conversation between Byron and Becher: M.,45.

Poem to Becher: P.,31.

Physical transformation in Byron: L.J.,I,126.

Anecdote of the agate: M.,45.

Regarding Southwell, Hobhouse notes: "It was at this place that he learnt not only his first lessons in sensuality, but had an opportunity of seeing to what base expedient self-interest will resort—one of the families he mentioned winked at an intercourse between him and one of the daughters in hopes of entangling him in an unequal marriage."

Letter to Elizabeth Pigot: L.J.,I,131.

Letter of Mrs. Byron: L.J.,I,128

Letters of Byron to Elizabeth Pigot: L.J.,I,142,137,141,144, 147.

Letter of Dallas to Byron: Dallas's *Recollections,* 3,4.

Byron's reply: L.J.,I,169,170,173.

Anecdote of Byron swimming in the Thames: Leigh Hunt's *Lord Byron and Some of His Contemporaries,* I,1.

XI

Edleston: L.J.,I,134,135.

On Matthews: L.J.,I,150-160.

On Hobhouse, Davies, and their relations with Byron, numerous recollections are to be found in Byron's journals (L.J.,V), and likewise in H.

Letter to Hanson: L.J.,I,150.

On Byron's debts: L.J.,I,187.

Letter to Becher: L.J.,I,184.

The *Edinburgh Review* article is reprinted *in extenso* in L.J.,I, appendix, 344. Moore says (69) that Byron's sense of humiliation was only momentary. Hobhouse comments in a marginal note that this was not the case, and that he was "very near destroying himself."

Letter quoted: L.J.,I,186.

XII

Letters of Mrs. Byron: B.M., Egerton MSS.,2611. M. Emmanuel Rodocanachi has already published some of these documents in his *Byron* (Hachette, 1924).

Byron's letter to his mother: L.J.,I,192.

Letter on Mrs. Musters: L.J.,I,198.

Poems to Mrs. Musters: P.,81,82.

The monument to Boatswain still stands at Newstead.

Quarrel with Lord Carlisle: L.J.,I,217.
Byron taking his seat in the House of Lords: Dallas, 50-54.
Letters on debts and Newstead: L.J.,I,174,200,216,217.
Mrs. Byron's letter to Hanson: L.J.,I,205,206.
Loan from Scrope Davies: L.J.,II,11.
Poem on the skull: P.,80.
On life at Newstead: L.J.,I,153-156.
Letter to Augusta: L.J.,I,203.
Lord Delawarr's indifference: Dallas, 62-64.
Stanzas to Mary Ann Chaworth: P.,83.

XIII

On the departure: L.J.,I,230. See also P.,1016.
Letter to Mrs. Byron: L.J.,I,225.
On Lisbon and Portugal: L.J.,I,233, and H.,I,6-10.
On Spain: L.J.,I,238.
Robert Rushton sent home: L.J.,I,283.
The crossing from Gibraltar to Malta: John Galt's *Life of Lord Byron,* 65-74 (1830).
Lines on Mrs. Spencer Smith: *Childe Harold,* II,32.
On Mrs. Spencer Smith: see the Duchesse d'Abrantès' *Mémoires,* XV,4,5 (1831-35).
On Albania and Ali Pacha: L.J.,I,248,250,251.
On the storm at sea: L.J.,I,253.
On the Albanians: L.J.,I,254.
Byron's letters on Fletcher: L.J.,I,256,308.
On the stay in Greece: H.,I,25-27; see also Harold Spender's *Byron and Greece* (1924), which gives both the poems and the letters.
Quotation: *Childe Harold,* II,73.
On the Macri family: L.J.,I,269. For further details see the article by M. Camborouglou in the *Messager d'Athènes* (1924). See also M.,101,102,105.
"Maid of Athens . . .": P.,246.
Hobhouse on despotism: H.,I,26.
Swimming the Hellespont: L.J.,I,285.
On Constantinople: L.J.,I,282, and H.,I,30.
Byron to his mother on Hobhouse's departure: L.J.,I,295.
Hobhouse on his departure: H.,I,32.
Hobhouse to Byron, and Byron's reply: L.J.,I,305.
On the Capucin convent: C.,I,29,30.
On Nicolo Giraud: C.,I,15.

On Theodora Macri: C.,I,16.
Lady Hester Stanhope on Byron: L.J.,I,190.
Byron's illness: L.J.,II,21.
On Delawarr's ingratitude: *Childe Harold*, II, note B.
Byron's letters to his mother: L.J.,I,291,292,311,312.
Letter to Dallas: L.J.,I,313.

PART II

XIV

Account of the return: Dallas, 103, etc.
Quotations from *Childe Harold,* I,2,3,4,5,10,7; II,2.
Dallas's letter to Byron: Dallas, 114.
Letter from Byron to his mother: L.J.,I,319.
Mrs. Byron's letters and accounts: B.M., Egerton MSS.
Mrs. Byron's death: M.,121.
Byron's letter to Pigot: L.J.,I,320,321.
Letter from Byron to Hobhouse: C.,I,44.
Other letters quoted from: L.J.,I,338,324,325; C.,I,44; L.J., II,7,5,46.
Comments of Dallas on *Childe Harold:* Dallas, 124,125.
Letters from Byron to Augusta: L.J.,I,332; L.J.,II,18.
Letters from Augusta to Byron: L.J.,II,10,11.
Letters from Byron to Augusta: L.J.,II,17,31.
Byron's Will: M.,130,131.
Letters from Byron to Hodgson: L.J.,II,21,22,36,100,90.
Epistle to Hodgson: P.,250.
Letter quoted: L.J.,II,55.

XV

On John Murray: see Samuel Smiles, *A Publisher and his Friends* (1891).

On Rogers: see P. W. Clayden, *Rogers and his Contemporaries* (1889), and *Table Talk of Samuel Rogers.*

On Byron's political début: see Dallas, 188-218, and Dora N. Raymond, *The Political Career of Lord Byron,* 34-61 (1925).

On the success of *Childe Harold:* see H. J. C. Grierson, *The Background of English Literature.*

The Duchess of Devonshire's opinion of *Childe Harold:* L.J., II,106.

XVI

On the history of the Melbournes: see Torrens, *Melbourne Papers,* and Mabell, Countess of Airlie, *In Whig Society.*

On Lady Caroline Lamb, see: L.J.,II,114,115.

The letters of Caroline Lamb are quoted in the *Memoirs* of Lady Morgan.

Extracts from the journal of William Lamb and the letters of Lady Caroline to her husband are in Torrens.

The phrase in quotation marks on Lady Melbourne and her daughter-in-law is from *In Whig Society,* 117.

Byron on Lady Melbourne: *Conversations of Lord Byron with the Countess of Blessington,* 200.

Letters from Caroline Lamb to Byron: L.J.,II,446.

The meeting with Miss Milbanke is described in the unpublished Journal of Miss Milbanke (Lovelace Papers). On this first interview see also Medwin, I,37.

Letter from Byron to Caroline Lamb: L.J.,II,116,117.

The Duchess of Devonshire on Caroline Lamb: L.J.,II,136.

On the liaison of Byron with Lady Caroline: see Medwin, II,64-67, and Medwin, I,81.

Letter of Byron to Caroline Lamb: L.J.,II,121.

The Duchess of Devonshire on Miss Milbanke: L.J., II,120.

On the eccentricities of Lady Caroline and the intervention of the Prince-Regent: see *In Whig Society,* 127-131.

Letter from Caroline Lamb to Byron: L.J.,II,448.

Lady H. Leveson-Gower on Lady Caroline Lamb: L.J.,II,187.

Letter from Byron to Lady Melbourne: C.,I,71-72.

Letters from Lady Melbourne to Byron: *In Whig Society,* 145,147.

Letters from Byron to Lady Melbourne: C.,I,79,87,88.

Letters from Lady Melbourne to Byron: *In Whig Society,* 146.

On Miss Milbanke at home I follow her unpublished Journal (Lovelace Papers).

Letters from Miss Milbanke to Lady Melbourne: *In Whig Society,* 141.

XVII

Epigraph: *Don Juan,* III,3; P.,829.

On the sale of Newstead: L.J.,II,251.

On Lady Oxford, see Lady Blessington, 233; and Medwin, I,76,77.

Lady Caroline Lamb to Lady Oxford: *In Whig Society,* 151.

Byron to Lady Melbourne: C.,I,104,145.

Lady Melbourne to Byron: *In Whig Society,* 147.

Byron to Lady Caroline Lamb: L.J.,II,136.

Verses of Lady Caroline Lamb, recited at Brockert Hall: L.J.,II,447.

Appreciation by Byron on the *auto-da-fé:* C.,I,123.

Byron on Lady Bessborough: C.,I,137.

Ball at Lady Heathcote's: *In Whig Society,* 152-157.

Article from *The Satirist:* L.J.,II,242,243.

"Remember thee . . .": P.,258, and Medwin, II,68,69.

Verses of Lady Oxford: P.,259.

Byron to Lady Melbourne: C.,I,161.

XVIII

Epigraph: C.,I,196.

For a very acute psychological interpretation of this period, see Charles Du Bos' *Byron* (1929). The precise fact which enables one to declare that the liaison between Byron and Mrs. Leigh began at this moment, is the birth of Medora on April 15, 1814. The correspondence between Byron and Lady Melbourne offers confirmation.

Letters from Byron to Augusta: L.J.,II,226,227.

The phrase between quotation marks, "They had not been brought up together—" is from Lord Ernle, "Lady Byron and her Separation," an article in the *Quarterly Review,* of January 1930.

Letters from Lady Byron: C.,I,254,255.

Letters from Byron to Moore: L.J.,II,251.

On Lady Melbourne's intervention: see *Astarte,* 33,34.

Letters from Byron to Lady Melbourne: C.,I,177,173.

Quotation from *The Giaour:* lines 1181-1191; P.,277.

XIX

Epigraph: C.,I,255.

Letters from Byron to Lady Melbourne: C.,I,183,181,186,191, 192,193,194,198,200,199,200,203,204,209.

XX

Byron's Journal: L.J.,II,321.

Letter from Byron to John Galt: L.J.,II,305.

Letter from Byron to Lady Melbourne: C.,I,219.

Byron's Journal: L.J.,II,323,346,319,348,345.

Letter from Byron to Lady Melbourne: C.,I,226,232,233.

Letters from Mary Chaworth-Musters to Byron: C.,I,223,240, 225,228.

Letter from Lady Melbourne to Byron: *In Whig Society,* 165.

Letter from Augusta Leigh to Byron: *Astarte,* 263.

On the Byronic hero: see Edmond Estève's *Byron et le Romantisme Français* (1907).

On *The Corsair:* L.J.,II,382.

Quotation from *The Corsair:* I,11; P.,300.

Byron's Journal: L.J.,II,377.

Letters from Byron to Lady Melbourne: C.,I,241,276,256,257.

Quotation concerning Mrs. Leigh: *Astarte,* 34,35.

Lines to the Princess Charlotte: P.,254.

Regarding the success of *The Corsair,* see Mark Rutherford's *The Revolution in Tanner's Lane* (1881), 27.

Byron's Journal: L.J.,II,384,385,389,390,408,409.

Letter from Byron to Lady Melbourne: C.,I,251.

Poem to Augusta: P.,349; *Astarte,* 328.

Quotation from *Lara,* I,17-18; P.,328.

The phrase "the ex-future Byron" is in a letter of Sr. Miguel da Unamuno.

XXI

The betrothal letters of Byron and Miss Milbanke were published in L.B. A few extracts from Byron's letters to his betrothed had already appeared in L.J.,III.

Letter from Byron to Moore: L.J.,III,126.

Letter from Byron to Lady Melbourne: C.,I,137.

Byron's Journal: L.J.,II,380.

Letters from Miss Milbanke to Byron: L.B.,58.

Letters from Byron to Miss Milbanke: L.J.,III,398,399,402, 403,408.

Letters from Byron to Lady Melbourne: C.,I,178,253,254.

Letters from Byron to Miss Milbanke: L.B.,103,111.

Anecdote of the ring: M.,264.

Letters from Miss Milbanke to Byron: L.B.,111,112.

Letters from Byron to Miss Milbanke: L.B.,112,113,444.

Letter from Byron to Lady Melbourne: C.,I,270.

Letter from Byron to Moore: L.J.,III,138,139.

Letters from Byron to Miss Milbanke: L.J.,III,146,160.

Letter from Miss Milbanke to Miss Emily Milner: L.J.,III, 148.

Letters from Byron to Miss Milbanke: L.B.,447,448,449.

Letter from Miss Milbanke to Byron: L.B.,451.

XXII

Epigraph, *Don Juan:* III,8; P.,829.

On Byron's marriage contract, see E.C.M.,I,306,307.

Letter from Byron to Lady Melbourne: C.,I,272.

Tom Moore's song: *The English Poets,* edited by Thomas Humphry Ward, IV,320 (1881).

For the visit to Seaham in Nov., 1814, I follow the unpublished journal of Miss Milbanke and Byron's letters to Lady Melbourne.

Letters from Byron to Lady Melbourne: C.,I,287,290,288.

Letters from Miss Milbanke to Byron: L.B.,127,128,129,134, 140,149.

Letters from Byron to Miss Milbanke: L.B.,150,151,153,154.

Of the second stay at Seaham and the marriage ceremony, Hobhouse gives an excellent account: H.,I,191-197.

Byron's thoughts during the religious service are derived from his poem *The Dream:* P.,387.

XXIII

This chapter is entirely written with the help of Lady Byron's Journal. It is a remarkable document, very well written and very precise. It is to be hoped that it may one day be published *in extenso.* Miss Mayne has quoted numerous passages from it in her *Life of Lady Byron.* I add a certain number of extracts, particularly those concerning Byron's religious attitude. I cannot, however, indicate these references more exactly as the manuscript is unpublished.

L.B.,194.

Letters from Byron to Lady Melbourne: C.,I,295,300.

Letters from Lady Melbourne to Byron: C.,I,297,303.

Letter from Byron to Hobhouse: C.,I,306.

Letters from Byron to Moore: L.J.,III,176,182,175.

XXIV

General sources: Lady Byron's Journal; H.; Leigh Hunt; and E.C.M.

Letters from Lady Byron to Mrs. Leigh: L.J.,III,210.

L.B.,181.

The interviews with Scott are described in M.,280.

Letter from Byron on the fall of Napoleon: L.J.,III,208,209.

Don Juan, III, 5 and 8; P.,829.

L.B.,166.

Letters from Lady Byron to Mrs. Leigh: L.J.,III,210.

Hobhouse's journal: H.,I,324,325.

Letter from Byron to Lady Byron: *Astarte,* 39.

Lady Byron's reply: *Astarte,* 40.

Letters from Lady Byron to Byron: Sir John Fox's, *The Byron Mystery,* 98,99(1924); and H.,II,203.

XXV

Regarding the separation: see L.B.,199-232; *Astarte;* and the very carefully worked-out book of Sir John Fox (*vid.sup.*). The sources of all these books, and of my own, are the archives at Ockham Park—the Lovelace Papers. Hobhouse, who devoted 164 pages of his *Memoirs* to this single episode (H.,II,191-355), seems at first to have been totally ignorant of the relations between Byron and Mrs. Leigh. A little later one can detect a shade of annoyance with Byron for having concealed part of the facts from him. In his own copy of Moore's *Life,* against the passage where Moore says that Byron's affection for his sister was due to the fact of their having lived so much apart and so kept his feelings for her "fresh and untried," Hobhouse made this marginal note: "My dear M., you know nothing of this matter."

Letter from Mrs. Leigh to Lady Byron: Fox,105.

Letters from Lady Byron to Mrs. Leigh: L.J.,III,299,295.

Letter from Dr. Le Mann: Fox,104.

Letter from Lady Noel to Lady Byron: Fox,106.

Letters from Byron to Lady Byron: H.,II,239,240; and L.B., 212,403.

Letter from Lady Byron to Mrs. Leigh: L.J.,III,311.

Letter from Byron to Lady Byron: L.B.,134.

Letter from Lady Melbourne to Byron: C.,I,307.

Letter from Lady Caroline Lamb to Byron: L.J.,II,449.

Letter from Mrs. Leigh to Rev. F. Hodgson: L.J.,III,317.

Letter from Byron to Moore: L.J.,III,272.

On Hobhouse's intervention, see H.,II,225; Fox,111,112.

Poem, "Fare Thee Well . . .": P.,377.

Lines on Mrs. Clermont, *The Sketch:* P.,377.

Byron's despair on the occasion of his last interview with Mrs. Leigh was described by Mrs. Leigh herself to Lady Byron, who records it in her Memoir. See *Astarte,* 65.

The quoted sentence, "He had posed as a rebel . . .," etc., is from Sir Leslie Stephen's article on Byron in the *Dictionary of National Biography*.

On Lady Jersey's reception, see M.,302,303; *Astarte,* 30.

Clare Clairmont's letters to Byron: L.J.,III,435,436,437.

Byron's farewell letter to Lady Byron: *Astarte,* 51; L.J.,III, 280.

Quatrain, "A year ago you swore . . .'" etc.: P.,1027.

Letter of Isaac Nathan to Byron: L.J.,III,283.

John William Polidori's journal was edited by W. M. Rossetti (Elkin Mathews, 1901).

Byron's visit to Churchill's tomb: H.,I,335.

Lines to Tom Moore: P.,1028.

The anecdote of the packet addressed to Miss Elphinstone is told in the Countess Guiccioli's *My Recollections of Lord Byron,* translated by Hubert Jerningham, 184 (1869). To Lord Lansdowne I am indebted for the knowledge of what the packet contained: it was a Virgil, still preserved at Bowood.

Byron's departure: H.,I,336.

PART III

XXVI

Childe Harold, III,2: P.,185.

Childe Harold, III,6: P.,186.

Childe Harold, III,16: P.,187.

Childe Harold, III,21;III,40,42:P.,188,191.

Conversation between Byron and Polidori: M.,319.

Childe Harold, III,55: P.,193.

Childe Harold, III,86,99,72:P.,197,199,195.

The Dream: P.,385.

Stanzas to Augusta: P.,391.

Letters from Byron to Mrs. Leigh: *Astarte,* 265,273,272.

Lines on hearing that Lady Byron was ill: P.,393,394.

On Byron at Madame de Staël's: see Dora N. Raymond, *The Political Career of Lord Byron,* 104 (1925).

Epigraph of *Glenarvon: The Corsair,* III,24: P.,321.

Lines on *Glenarvon,* etc.: L.J.IV,79.

Letter from Byron on *Glenarvon:* L.J.,IV,12.

Letter from Byron on Shelley: L.J.,V,496.
Letter from Byron to Mrs. Leigh: *Astarte,* 267.

XXVII

Letter from Hobhouse to Mrs. Leigh: L.J.,III,347.
On Byron and Hobhouse at Coppet, see H.,II,26.
Hobhouse's parody of the *Stanzas to Augusta:* L.J.,IV,74.
Byron and Hobhouse in the Alps: H.,II,19.
Byron's Journal: L.J.,III,349,355,356,360,362,364,365.
Manfred, I,1: P.,399.
Manfred, II,2: P.,404.
Manfred, II,2: P.,408.
The quoted sentence "If Augusta . . .," etc. is from *Astarte,* 63.
Letters from Lady Byron to Mrs. Villiers: *Astarte,* 220,212.
Letter from Lady Byron to Mrs. Leigh: *Astarte,* 210.
Letter from Mrs. Leigh to Lady Byron: *Astarte,* 214.
Letter from Mrs. Villiers to Lady Byron: *Astarte,* 238.
Letter from Mrs. Leigh to Lady Byron: *Astarte,* 242.
Lady Byron's Memoir: *Astarte,* 253.
Letter from Lady Byron to Mrs. Leigh: *Astarte,* 275.
Hobhouse's journal: H.,II,53.

The letter from Luigi de Brême is unpublished, and is in the archives of the Château of Coppet.

See also, regarding this period, Stendhal's *Racine et Shakespeare* (1823-25).

XXVIII

Letter from Byron to Murray: L.J.,IV,14.
Letter from Byron to Moore: L.J.,IV,7.
Letters of Byron: L.J.,IV,18,19.
Childe Harold, IV,8: P.,212.
Letter of Byron: C.,II,23.
Lines to Moore: L.J.,IV,29.
Lines to Marianna Segati: L.J.,IV,60.
Letters of Byron to Mrs. Leigh: *Astarte,* 285,286.
Letter from Mrs. Leigh to Lady Byron: *Astarte,* 70.
Manfred, III,1: P.,410,411.
Manfred, III,4: P.,414.
Letter from Mrs. Villiers to Lady Byron: *Astarte,* 69.
Letter from Lady Byron to Mrs. Leigh: L.B.,271.
On Byron in Rome: see M.,356; and L.J.,IV,122,123.

SOURCES

On Byron and Thorwaldsen's bust: see Elze's *Life of Lord Byron,* 220,221.

Childe Harold, IV,132: P.,233.
Hobhouse's journal: H.,II,78,84.
Dedication of *Childe Harold,* IV: P.,208.
Childe Harold, IV,121,137,184,185: P.,231,234,241.
Beppo, 47,48: P.,424.
The Margarita Cogni episode: L.J.,IV,328,330.
Hobhouse's journal: H.,II,90.
Letter from Byron to Moore: L.J.,IV,262.
Letter from Byron to Rogers: L.J.,IV,208.
Letter from Byron on the death of Lady Melbourne: C.,II,1.
Lady Byron at Newstead: L.B.,277,278.
Letter from Shelley to Byron: C.,II,52.
Letter from Byron to Kinnaird: C.,II,65.
Letter from Byron to Hobhouse: C.,II,71.
Letter from Byron to Mrs. Leigh, on Allegra: L.J.,IV,250.

XXIX

Byron's letter jokingly signed "Fletcher": L.J.,IV,234.
Don Juan, I,120: P.,802.
Don Juan, I,12,17: P.,781,782.
Don Juan, I,214,215,220: P.,803,804.
Julian and Maddalo: Shelley's *Poems,* 185 (Oxford).
On the Hansons' visit to Venice, see C.,II,93.

XXX

Countess Guiccioli's account of her second meeting with Byron is given in M.,393.

Byron on love in Italy: Medwin,26.
Letter from Byron to Hobhouse: C.,II,107.
Letters of Byron: L.J.,IV,307,308,325,326.
Conversations of the Countess Guiccioli are quoted in M.,400.
"Ave Maria . . .," etc.: *Don Juan,* III,102: P.,842.

Pilgrimage to tomb of Dante, see Nazzareno Meneghetti's *Lord Byron a Venezia* (Fableris, n.d.).

Letter from Byron to Mrs. Leigh: *Astarte,* 291.
Letter from Byron to Murray: L.J.,IV,349.
Letter from Byron on Bologna: C.,II,121.
Byron on his projected voyages: L.J.,IV,357.
Police reports on Byron: L.J.,IV,460,462,463.

Letter from Byron to Countess Guiccioli on her copy of *Corinne:* L.J.,IV,350.

Letters of Byron: L.J.,IV,371, and C.,II,128.

Letters of Byron to Countess Guiccioli: L.J.,IV,379,391.

Letter of Byron to Mrs. Leigh: *Astarte,* 85.

XXXI

Letters of Byron: L.J.,IV,409,400.

Conversations of Countess Guiccioli: L.J.,V,32.

Letter from Byron to Mrs. Leigh: *Astarte,* 307.

Byron's Journal: L.J.,V,152,147,149,152,153,154,155,198,199.

Lady Byron's Journal: L.B.,292.

Letter from Byron: C.,II,135.

Lady Byron's Journal: L.J.,V,181.

Sardanapalus, I,2: P.,557.

Cain, I,1: P.,627,632.

Cain, III,1: P.,651.

Letter from Scott to Murray regarding *Cain:* P.,625.

Byron's Journal: L.J.,V,159.

Letter from Byron to Hoppner: L.J.,V,74.

Letters from Shelley to Mary Shelley: *Letters of P. B. Shelley,* edited by R. Ingpen, II,887,893,894.

Letter from Countess Guiccioli to Shelley: Ingpen,II,902.

Letter from Shelley to Byron: C.,II,292.

Byron on Lord Clare: L.J.,V,463.

XXXII

Epigraph: L.J.,VI,99.

Letter from Shelley: Ingpen,II,931.

Byron's confidences to Medwin: Medwin,I,65; II,65; I,76,36, 38,119,120,121,131.

Mary Shelley's letter on Trelawny is in Edward Dowden's *Life of P. B. Shelley,* II,462 (1886).

Letter from Clare Clairmont to Byron: L.J.,V,498.

Countess Guiccioli on Byron's behaviour after Allegra's death: L.J.,VI,52,53.

Letter from Shelley to Byron: C.,II,223.

Letter from Byron on Allegra's burial: L.J.,VI,69.

Letter from Byron on *Don Juan:* L.J.,VI,95.

Letter from Byron to Mary Shelley: L.J.,VI,119.

SOURCES

XXXIII

The crossing to Genoa: Leigh Hunt, I,102.

Letter from Mary Shelley to Byron: C.,II,143.

Letter from Byron to Mary Shelley: L.J.,VI,174.

Letter from Leigh Hunt to Byron: H.N.,29.

On the Blessingtons at Genoa: see "A Byron Mystery Resolved," by John Gore, in *Cornhill Magazine,* 39-53, January 1928.

Don Juan, X,65; X,82: P.,936,938.

Letter from Byron to Lady Byron: L.J.,V,479.

Quotations from Lady Blessington's *Conversations:* 95,91,125, 112,149.

Don Juan, XIV,3; IX,24,25; XIII,9,10; XVI,99: P.,974,921, 961,997.

XXXIV

Byron's Journal: L.J.,II,340. See also M.,585.

Poem quoted: L.J.,VI,238.

Letter from Byron: C.,II,255.

Letter from John Browning to Byron: William Parry's *The Last Days of Lord Byron,* 188.

Letters from Byron on Countess Guiccioli: C.,II,258,260.

On Pietro Gamba, see H.N.,81.

On the homeric helmets, see H.N.,83

Byron to Lady Blessington: see her *Conversations,* 288.

Byron on board the *Hercules:* H.N.,109.

Conversation between Fletcher and Capt. Scott: H.N.,111,112.

On Byron's sensibility: H.N.,122.

Letter from Byron on his income: L.J.,VI,252.

Letter from Byron to Mrs. Leigh: L.J.,VI,260.

On Byron's relations with Dr. Kennedy, see James Kennedy's *Conversations on Religion with Lord Byron,* 46,47,56,66,136,154, 172 (1831).

Letters from Mavrocordato to Byron: Pietro Gamba's *A Narrative of Lord Byron's Last Journey into Greece,* 295.

Conversation of Byron with Pietro Gamba: Gamba, 48.

Letters from Byron: L.J.,VI,291,293,295,294.

XXXV

Letter from Byron to Col. Stanhope: L.J.,VI,297.

Conversations of Byron with Gamba: Gamba,122,123,121,115.

BYRON

Quarrel between Byron and Stanhope: Gamba,138; H.N.,206.

On Byron's nobility of spirit at this time, see Grierson, *The Background of English Literature,* 199, and H.N.,206.

Arrival of Hobhouse's letter: H.,III,62.

Quotation from Grierson, 199.

Byron's birthday, poem quoted: Gamba,127.

Byron's physical appearance: Parry,21.

Letter from Byron: L.J.,VI,318.

Byron and his dog: Parry,75.

On Byron's epileptic seizure, see H.N.,224, and Julius Millingen's *Memoirs of the Affairs of Greece, with various anecdotes relating to Lord Byron* (1831).

Letters from Byron to Mrs. Leigh: *Astarte,* 313; L.J.,VI,330.

On the situation at Missolonghi, see Raymond,265.

Byron's discouragement: Gamba,192.

Hobhouse's opinion: H.,III,35.

Trelawny's letter: H.N.,233.

Byron's last ride: Gamba,249.

On Byron's illness, see Millingen,129,131; Gamba,249.

Conversation of Byron with Fletcher: H.N.,253.

Conversation of Byron with Parry: Parry,121,122.

On Byron's death: Millingen,132; H.N.,260; Parry,126; Millingen,141;H.N.,265,266; Galt, *Life of Lord Byron,* 300,301; Gamba,265.

EPILOGUE

Epigraph: L.J.,V,462.

Letter from Hobhouse to Byron: C.,II,292,299.

Hobhouse learns of Byron's death, H.,III,38,39.

Letter from Mrs. Leigh to Hodgson: Hodgson,II,148,149.

Effect of news in England: S. Chew, *Byron in England,* 194 (1924).

Arrival of body: H.,III,65.

The destruction of the *Memoirs* is described in detail in H.

On the end of Lady Byron's life, see L.B.,323,400,401,403,404, 405,413,414,393.

On Mrs. Leigh's death, see *Astarte,* 31,32.

On Ada Byron: see *Ralph, Earl of Lovelace: a Memoir,* by Mary, Countess of Lovelace (1921). See also *The Next Generation,* an appendix by the same writer to L.B.

On Medora Leigh, see *Medora Leigh, a History and an Auto-*

biography, by C. Mackay (1869). Also Fox 48-53; L.B.,340-369; E.C.M.,II,327-334. On Medora Leigh's life in France and on her children, see De Régie, *Le Secret de Byron,* from which I quote some extracts: 100,45,48,49,197,200,204.

On Teresa Macri, see the study by M. Camboroglou (*vid.* Preface).

On the end of Mrs. Chaworth-Musters: see Grantley Berkeley's *Reminiscences of a Huntsman* (1854).

The letter from Clare Clairmont to Mary Shelley is quoted by Chew,151.

On the later life of Countess Guiccioli, see Lord Malmesbury's *Memoirs of an ex-Minister.*

The sentence commenting on the Greek insurgents is quoted from G. M. Trevelyan's *History of England,* 629.

INDEX

INDEX

INDEX

INDEX

INDEX

INDEX

3-29

4-7

4-26

5-17